KU-574-819

ingapore
BURMA
LAOS
NDIA
THAILAND
VIETNAM
CAMBODIA
Bay of
Bengal
South China Sea
SRI
LANKA
MALAYA
SUMATRA
SINGAPORE
BORNEO
Johor Strait
Sembawang
Woodlands
Yishun
Kranji
Lim Chu
Kang
Murai
Reservoir
Selatar
Reservoir
Jalan
Kayu
Pungoll
PULAU
UBIN
Changi Point
Bukit
Timah
Poyan
Reservoir
Choa Chu
Kang
Pierce
Reservoir
Sernagoon
Pasir
Ris
Changi
Tengah
Reservoir
MacRitchie
Reservoir
Tampines
Jurong
Toa Payoh
Paya
Lebar
Changi
International
Airport
Tuas
Clementi
Bedok
Geylang
Katong
Queenstown
Fort Canning
Pasir
Panjang
Telok
Blangah
Mt Faber
SENTOSA
N
Main Roads
(National Highways)
Restricted Zone
km
5
miles
3
Built Up Areas

Singapore Handbook

Published by Footprint Handbooks
6 Riverside Court
Lower Bristol Road
Bath BA2 3DZ. England
T +44 (0)1225 469141
F +44 (0)1225 469461
Email handbooks@footprint.cix.co.uk
Web www.footprint-handbooks.co.uk

ISBN 1 900949 19 9
CIP DATA: A catalogue record for this book is available from the British Library

In North America, published by
Passport Books, a division of NTC/Contemporary Publishing Group
4255 West Touhy Avenue, Lincolnwood (Chicago), Illinois 60646-1975, USA
T 847 679 5500 F 847 679 24941
E NTCPUB2@AOL.COM

ISBN 08442-4945-9
Library of Congress Catalog Card Number: 98-66128

© Footprint Handbooks Ltd 1999

Footprint Handbooks and the Footprint mark are a registered trademark of Footprint Handbooks Ltd.

All rights reserved. No part of this publication may be reproduced, stored in a retrieval system, or transmitted, in any form or by any means, electronic, mechanical, photocopying, recording, or ortherwise, without the prior permission of Footprint Handbooks Ltd.

Credits

Series editor: Patrick Dawson
Editorial
Senior editor: Sarah Thorowgood
Maps: Alex Nott
Production
Typesetting: Jo Morgan, Richard Ponsford and Ann Griffiths
Maps: Kevin Feeney and Rob Lunn
Proof reading: Rod Gray

Marketing
MBargo, Singapore

Designed
Mytton Williams

Photography
Front cover: Robert Harding Picture Library
Back cover: La Belle Aurore
Colour section: John Wright, Singapore Tourist Board, Emma Lee (Life File), Steve Davey (La Belle Aurore).

Printed and bound
in Italy by LEGOPRINT

Every effort has been made to ensure that the facts in this Handbook are accurate. However, travellers should still obtain advice from consulates, airlines etc about current travel and visa requirements before travelling. The authors and publishers cannot accept responsibility for any loss, injury or inconvenience however caused.

Neither the black and white nor coloured maps are intended to have any political significance.

Footprint Singapore Handbook

Joshua Eliot and Jane Bickersteth

Hail, Mother! East and West must seek thy aid
Ere the spent hull may dare the ports afar,
The second doorway of the wide world's trade
Is mine to loose or bar.

Rudyard Kipling *The Song of the Cities* 1893

Contents

A foot in the door

Highlights

Most visitors to Singapore are pushed for time: the average length of a traveller's stay is just three and a half days. While the industrious tourist can cover a lot of ground in this time, it is far more worthwhile to decide upon a few special areas to explore rather than attempting the near impossible. The undoubted highlights of this tiny city-state are the Colonial core, Chinatown, Little India and Arab Street and even the most fleeting of visits to Singapore should allow time to take in their unique atmospheres. This convenient cultural coding is one of Raffles' many legacies and each is small enough - just - to explore on foot. Then there is Orchard Road - Singapore's hedonistic streak.

The Colonial core Covering the area to the north of the Singapore River is the Colonial core, where Sir Stamford Raffles landed in January 1819 and where he decided to found his 'Emporium of the East'. There is a strong fragrance of colonial days here: the tree-ringed Padang with the Cricket Club, City Hall, Supreme Court and Victoria Memorial Hall; the Raffles Hotel, where Coward, Maugham and Kipling all stayed; and St Andrew's Cathedral and the Armenian Church. Several of Singapore's best museums are here too: the Singapore Art Museum, the Asian Civilisations Museum and the Singapore History Museum.

Chinatown The Singapore River divides the Colonial core from Chinatown. This area was the commercial and trading heart of the island during colonial days and, to a significant extent, remains so. The skyscrapers of the financial district loom over what is left of the godowns that used to line a boat-choked river. Fortunately, the core of Chinatown was not entirely torn down in the frenzy of redevelopment that followed Independence. Most old buildings are now protected by law and while the opium dens and rickshaws may have gone, the essential fabric of Old Singapore remains. It is a fascinating area to explore, with its temples and shophouses and there are plenty of chic coffee bars and restaurants to provide places for rest and reflection.

Little India The architecture of Little India appears very similar to that of Chinatown at first glance but it doesn't take long to realize that this is not a piece of China but a slice of India. The aromas of cardamom, turmeric and cumin infuse the air, dark Tamil faces line the streets, and Indian music blares out from open doors. Shops sell saris, bidis, Bollywood videos and sweetmeats, while Hindu worshippers still visit the temples. This is, of course, the best place to sample Singapore's fine array of Indian cuisines.

Arab Street Also known as *Kampong Glam*, Arab Street is Singapore's Malay quarter and at its heart is the Sultan Mosque. This area of the city may not be as obviously atmospheric as Chinatown and Little India but it offers an insight into another important facet of Singapore's cultural life, with its Koranic schools and Indonesian and Malay restaurants serving halal food.

Orchard Road and Outer Singapore While Chinatown, Little India and Arab Street are redolent of the histories and cultures of Singapore's three main cultural groups, Orchard Road is the symbol of New Singapore. With a higher density of shops than anywhere else in the world, this is consumerism gone berserk. Most places of interest are concentrated in the city but Outer Singapore also has its attractions. The Jurong Bird Park, Singapore Zoo and Night Safari are first class; the Haw Par Villas and Tang Dynasty City are worthwhile if you like that kind of thing; the Science Centre and Singapore Discovery Centre are fun for children; while Sentosa offers a Disney-esque escape.

***Left**: Lau Pa Sat Festival Market, the last remaining Victorian cast-iron structure in Southeast Asia, is a national monument and now a thriving food centre too. **Below**: Singapore skyline from the harbour at dusk.*

***Below**: National day at the Padang, site of most Singaporean sporting events. Originally known as The Plain, this was where English and Indian troops were quartered.*

***Above**: Raffles Place, the heart of Singapore's financial machine. **Right**: Chinatown is one of the most attractive areas of Singapore. It is a great place to explore and has an abundance of cafés, bistros and bars.*

FATMAN SATAY
STALL NO 1

The epicurean experience

Gastronomic wonderland

Because Singapore is multi-cultural and multi-ethnic it is also multi-gastronomic. And it's not just a case of Chinese, Indian or Malay. Take 'Chinese' food. There are restaurants serving delicately flavoured Cantonese dishes; fiery Szechuan foods infused with chilli and garlic; imperial recipes like Peking duck with the skin glazed and roasted to a crisp; the heart-warming and stomach-filling peasant dishes of Hainan Island including chicken rice – the closest thing Singapore has to a national dish; and the plump spring rolls of Singapore's large Hokkien community, stuffed with pork, beansprouts and vegetables, then deep fried.

Taste of India and Malaysia

The Indian population of the country has also left a rich array of cuisines. There are the succulent tandoor-baked meats of north India served with puffy breads like nan, the vegetarian curries of the south, and Singaporean specialities like fish-head curry – far more delicious than the name might imply. Closer at hand are the curries of Singapore's Malay community, cooked in coconut milk and served with pungent shrimp paste. And, of course, there is satay – sticks of barbecued meat served with compressed rice, cucumber sticks and a spicy peanut sauce.

Fusion

As if this array of cuisines were not enough to tempt the visitor, the intermingling of cultures has produced its own unique repertoire of dishes. The Straits Chinese community, the first Chinese to make their home on the Malay Peninsula, long ago appropriated the spices of their adopted land to produce what is known as Nonya or Peranakan cuisine. This is Chinese in style but Malay in inspiration. More recently, trendy young chefs have taken this further with *Fusion* or *New Asia* cuisine. Like the Straits Chinese, they have tried – often with startling results – to blend East and West.

Eating out

Singapore's reputation as one of the world's gastronomic wonderlands does not end with the range of foods on offer. There are so many excellent restaurants in Singapore that everyone has their own recommendations. New restaurants open every other day and in this gourmet paradise, chefs are eminently poachable. In recent years, however, there has been a gluttonous trend towards value-for-money, where quantity rules and patrons are encouraged to cram their plates. Hotel buffets compete to offer the biggest and cheapest spread and advertisements in *The Straits Times* announce the latest offers.

A local favourite

Banned from public transport and hotels because of its pungent smell, the Durian fruit, with its alluring custard-yellow flesh and prickly skin, is beloved by most Singaporeans. During the Malaysian and South Thai montong durian seasons (June/July and November/December), fleets of trucks ferry durians over the causeway. The roadside market on the junction of Albert and Waterloo streets is probably the best durian centre, but Smith Street (Chinatown), Lavender Street and Geylang Serai market are also well known by durian-lovers. An average-sized durian costs around S$10, but big Thai ones command more than S$100. Alfred Russel Wallace wrote that to eat durian is "worth a voyage to the East to experience". And he was writing in 1869 when it took months to get there and death from disease was rather more than a distant niggle at the back of the mind.

***Left**: Satay man. Sticks of barbecued meat are served with compressed rice, cucumber sticks and a spicy peanut sauce. Singapore's culinary diversity is perhaps best experienced through the ubiquitous hawker centre or food court. They offer a fantastic way to browse through the country's cuisines for just a few dollars. There are also scores of cheap restaurants where a banana leaf curry or a palate-burning Padang meal from West Sumatra can be obtained for less than a taxi fare.*

Previous page: *a local speciality, the Singapore Sling, is the island's best-known cocktail. It was invented in the Raffles Hotel in 1915 and contains a blend of gin, cherry brandy, sugar, lemon juice and angostura bitters. For some strange reason armies of visitors feel that they cannot leave Singapore without parting their lips for this concoction - and then parting with the contents of their wallets.*

Clockwise from top left: *a man celebrating the Hindu festival of Thaipusam impales himself in honour of the deity Lord Subramian; wayang singer performing a traditional Chinese opera; colourful shophouses in the Joo Chiat area; the dragon at the entrance to Sentosa Island welcomes visitors to Singapore's dream factory (see page 16).*

Cultural Singapore

Singapore does not naturally conjure up images of untold cultural riches. In *Figures of Speech*, D.J. Enright's novel, the English-educated Singaporean Mattie Neo remarks that "In my country we have a Ministry of Culture but not very much culture...." She continues, "Our Indians find Chinese music incomprehensible, our Chinese find Indian music boring...[and] to be bored is a perfectly legitimate reaction...." However, Singapore is far from a cultural wasteland.

Festival city

Singapore's multi-ethnic society means that it is almost over-endowed with festivals. The Chinese have their Chinese New Year and Festival of the Hungry Ghosts, both marked with parades, puppet shows, Chinese street operas – and, appropriately, the giving or burning of money. The Hindu Indian community celebrate Thaipusam with a masochistic orgy of self-impalement. Muslim Malays mark the end of Ramadan with rather less frenetic celebrations and Singapore's Christian community traditionally celebrate Easter and Christmas.

Arts and music

Singapore is manoeuvring to become the artistic heart of the Southeast Asian region. This means Western as much as it means Eastern art. A new arts centre is under construction near the Padang and there is already a biennial month-long Festival of Arts and an International Film Festival. When it is completed in 2001, the Esplanade: Theatres on the Bay project will house a concert hall, lyric theatre, three smaller studios, and an outdoor performing space. The Singapore Symphony Orchestra is well respected and there are mainstream and avant-garde theatre and dance companies. Singapore's wealth also attracts a fair number of visiting performers from rock stars to mime artists. In terms of the Eastern arts, there are regular Chinese classical and folk music concerts and Chinese street opera or wayang performances are held twice weekly at Clarke Quay as well as at festival time.

Museums

Singapore's museums stand out in regional terms as well-run and amply-funded. They are also building up impressive collections and attract prestigious travelling exhibitions. Between them, the Singapore Art Museum, the Singapore History Museum and the Asian Civilisations Museum offer an absorbing escape from the heat.

Singapore: the dream factory

Singapore is an unlikely place. It has been engineered to unexpected economic success and *imagineered* into an entertainment playground for the historically and ecologically impaired citizens of Singapore, whose government once implored them to 'have spontaneous fun'.

Made-to-measure attractions

Singapore is not the place to unearth centuries of Chinese history but Tang Dynasty City offers the ancient Chinese capital of Chang An, a 600 metre-long slice of the Great Wall, and 1,500 terracotta warriors from Xian - all cut down in scale and conveniently assembled on a 12-hectare site. The Clarke Quay Adventure Ride takes the brave visitor drifting in a bumboat along the Singapore River and through generations of history in a handful of minutes. For those who perhaps like a little more veracity in their history, there is Canning Hill and the Malaya Command HQ where General Percival and his senior commanders re-enact that final, fateful, tragic day of 15th February 1942, when Singapore fell to the Japanese - over and over again.

Fantasy island Imagined or recreated history is one thing. Fantasy is another – but again, Singapore scores. Sentosa is Singapore's Fantasy Island. Volcanoland, for example – just one of many attractions – takes the visitor on a subterranean journey into the earth and to the beginnings of life. Or at least life *à la Sentosa*. Not far away is the grotesque Haw Par Villa – Singapore's most revolting theme park, a gaudy adventureland of Chinese folklore where tacky plaster figures show what life could be like should you mess with the Gods.

Urban jungle Singapore may be an over-civilised city state but there is packaged, expertly-managed wilderness on tap. The Night Safari runs through 40 hectares of 'jungle' and offers the intrepid explorer a 40-minute, geographically-compressed, cavalcade of animals, habitats and zoological experiences. There is also Sentosa's Underwater World, the Jurong Bird Park, the Singapore Zoo – even a handful of National Parks where lucky visitors may see more than a lizard or two.

Some of the products of Singapore's dream factory have educational value. In the Science Centre a Germanic-sounding Einstein welcomes visitors to an extravaganza of hands-on exhibits while Archie the Archaeopteryx enthuses about the wonders of flight. The Singapore Discovery Centre is, in effect, a S$70 million PR exercise for Singapore Inc concocted by the Singapore Defence Forces – and a lot of fun.

Essentials

Essentials

Before you travel

Best time to visit

There is no best season to visit Singapore and it is hot right through the year. It gets even stickier before the monsoon breaks in November, while the hottest months are July and August. The wettest months are November, December and January, during the period of the north-east monsoon, when it is also coolest. As one would expect, the hottest time of day is early afternoon when the mean temperature is around 30°C but even during the coolest time of the day, just before dawn, the mean temperature is still nearly 24°C. For daily weather reports after you have arrived, T5427788.

Finding out more

The Singapore Tourist Board is a useful place to contact. They produce a good free official guide called *New Asia-Singapore*, as well as pamphlets detailing hotels, restaurants and so on. Their web site has regularly updated information on hotels, festivals and other tourist-related information - *http://www.newasia-singapore.com*. Another good site is *http://www.technofind.com.sg*, the largest search engine for Singapore websites, updated daily. It covers just about every topic including tourism and is a good place to start hunting.

Singapore Tourist Boards

Australia *Level 11, AWA Building, 47 York St, Sydney, T(612) 9290 2888*
Canada *Standard Life Centre, 121 King St West, Suite 1000, Toronto, T(416) 36357552*
UK 1st Fl. Carrington House, 126-130 Regent St, London, W1R 5FE, T(0171) 4370033
USA *Two Prudential Plaza, 180 North Stetson Av, Suite 1450, Chicago, T(312) 9381888. 8484 Wilshire Boulevard, Suite 510, Beverley Hills, CA90211, T(213) 8520129. 590 Fifth Av, 12th Fl, New York, NY 10036, T(212) 3024861.*

For further listings of Singapore Tourist Boards world-wide, see page 63

Other useful web sites include:

http://www.sg the Singapore Infomap site which has website directories covering everything from leisure and entertainment to the economy, and from the National Heritage Board to Singapore's limitless choice of cuisine.

http://asiatravel.com/singapore.html Asia Travel's website. This is a useful site for hotel reservations, weather reports, the very latest travel information and exchange rates and also has a map detailing some places of interest.

http://asnic.utexas.edu/asnic.html the website for the Asian Studies Network Information Center at the University of Texas. This site will give you background information on the history and politics of Singapore. See also the Footnotes section at the end of this book for more background information.

For further listings of websites, see Further Reading at the end of this section on page 61

Getting in

Visas Visitors must possess a passport valid for at least 6 months, have a confirmed onward/return ticket, sufficient funds to support themselves in Singapore and, where applicable, a visa.

No visa is required for citizens of the Commonwealth, USA or Western Europe. On arrival in Singapore by air, citizens of these countries are granted a one month visitor's permit. Tourists entering Singapore via the causeway from Johor Bahru in Malaysia or by sea, are allowed to stay for 14 days. Nationals of most other countries (except India, China and the Commonwealth of Independent States) with confirmed onward reservations may stop over in Singapore for up to 14 days without a visa. It is necessary to keep the stub of your immigration card until you leave.

Nationals of the following countries require visas before entering Singapore: Afghanistan, Algeria, Armenia, Azerbaijan, Bangladesh, Belarus, Cambodia, China,

For Embassy listings see page 62

Estonia, Georgia, Hong Kong, India, Iraq, Jordan, Kazakhstan, Kyrgyzstan, Lao PDR, Latvia, Lebanon, Libya, Lithuania, Myanmar, Russia, Syria, Tajikistan, Tunisia, Tukmenistan, Ukraine, Uzbekistan, Vietnam and Yemen.

Visas can be extended for up to 3 months at the Singapore Immigration Head Office, Singapore Immigration Building, 10 Kallang Road, Singapore 208718, T(toll free information line) 1800-3916400. Applicants need to supply: 1. A completed Form 14, Form V3a and Data Amendment Card, all obtainable from the Visit and Visa Section of the Immigration Head Office. 2. A completed form V75 if the application is being made on medical grounds. 3. An onward/return ticket. Processing the application takes a minimum of one day. Alternatively, it can be just as easy to nip across the causeway to Johor Bahru (in Malaysia) and then re-enter Singapore on a 2 week permit.

Immigration Dept Singapore Immigration Head Office, Singapore Immigration Building, 10 Kallang Road, Singapore 208718, T 1800-3916400 (toll free information line).

Customs

Singapore is a free port.

Currency There is no limit to the amount of Singapore and foreign currency or TCs you can bring in or take out.

Duty free allowance 1 litre of liquor, 1 litre of wine or port, 1 litre of beer or stout. Note that because of the government's strict anti-smoking policy there is no duty free allowance for tobacco.

Export restrictions There is no export duty but export permits are required for arms, ammunition, explosives, animals, gold, platinum, precious stones and jewellery, poisons and drugs. No permit is needed for the export of antiques.

Prohibited items

Narcotics are strictly forbidden in Singapore and, as in neighbouring Malaysia, trafficking is a capital offence which is rigorously enforced. Dawn hangings at Changi prison are regularly reported. Trafficking in more than 30g of morphine or cocaine, 15g of heroin, 500g of cannabis or 200g of cannabis resin and 1.2kg of opium is punishable by death. In 1998 ecstasy was also added to the list of drugs that carry the mandatory death penalty. Those convicted of lesser drug-related offences face 20-30 years in Changi prison and 15 strokes of the rotan, a punishment devised by the British colonial administration. Passengers arriving from Malaysia by rail may have to march, single-file past sniffer dogs.

In 1992, the Singapore government banned the importation and sale of chewing gum, after the MRT Corporation claimed the substance threatened the efficient running of its underground trains. Chewing tobacco, toy currency, pornographic material and seditious literature are also prohibited items.

Health

Vaccinations Certificates of vaccination against cholera and yellow fever are necessary for those coming from endemic areas within the previous 6 days. Otherwise, no certificates are required for Singapore. There is no longer any malarial risk on the island, although sometimes there are outbreaks of dengue fever. Vaccination services are available at the Tan Tock Seng Hospital, Moulmein Road, T3595958 or 3595929 (telephone beforehand).

Water The water in Singapore, most of which is pumped across the causeway from Johor, but is treated in Singapore, is clean and safe to drink straight from the tap.

Medical facilities Singapore's medical facilities are amongst the best in the world. See the *Yellow Pages* for listing of public and private hospitals. Medical insurance is recommended. Hospitals are experienced in dealing with obscure tropical diseases and serious cases are flown here from all over the region. Most big hotels have their own doctor on 24 hours call. Other doctors are listed under 'Medical Practitioners' in the *Yellow Pages*. Pharmaceuticals are readily available over the counter. The Singapore Medical Centre (6th Floor, Tanglin Shopping Centre), houses a large community of specialist doctors. Local Chinese cures can be found in traditional clinics in Chinatown where there are medical halls and acupuncture centres. Acupuncturists and herbalists are listed in the *Yellow Pages*.

Ambulance: *T995*
Hospitals:
Alexandra, T4755222
East Shore, T3447588
Gleneagles, T4737222
Mount Elizabeth, T7372666
National Univerisity, T7795555
Singapore General, T2223322

Money

Currency Local currency is dollars and cents. Bank notes are available in denominations of S$2, 5, 10, 20, 50, 100, 500, 1,000 and 10,000. Coins are in 1, 5, 10, 20 and 50 cent and 1 dollar denominations. In December 1998, the Singapore dollar was valued at S$1.65 to US$1 or S$2.73 to £1. Brunei currency is interchangeable with Singapore currency; the Malaysian Ringgit is not.

It is possible to change money at banks, licensed money changers and hotels - although a service charge may be added. Licensed money-changers often give better rates than banks. It is also possible to withdraw money from cashpoint machines if you have a credit card with a PIN. Singapore is one of the major banking centres of Southeast Asia, so it is relatively easy to get money wired from home. Bank opening hours: 0930-1500 Mon-Fri, 0930-1130 Sat. There is no black market. (See listing of Banks & money changers, page 62.)

Credit cards Most of Singapore's hotels, shops, restaurants and banks accept the major international credit cards, and many cash machines allow you to draw cash on Visa or MasterCard. After bargaining, expect to pay at least 3% for credit card transactions; most shops insist on this surcharge although you do not have to pay it. **Notification of credit card loss** American Express, T2998133; Diners Card, T2944222; MasterCard, T5332888; Visa Card, T1-800-3451345.

Goods and Services Tax refund scheme Visitors can claim back their 3% Goods & Services Tax from shops displaying the 'Tax Free for Tourists' sign when they spend S$300 or more. A claim form is issued and this is then presented at customs on leaving the country, when visitors are reimbursed. It is also possible to claim by post; the refund is paid either by bank cheque or to a credit card account. The Singapore Tourist Board publishes a brochure, *Tax refund for visitors to Singapore*.

Getting there

Air

For Airport Information see page 25

As an international crossroads, Singapore is within easy reach of all key points in the region and there are flights from Changi (Singapore's airport) to destinations throughout Southeast Asia. Over 70 airlines service Singapore, flying to 131 cities in 56 countries. Long-haul prices are not as competitive as London bucket shops, although they undercut some other Asian capitals. Tickets to Southeast Asian destinations are subject to minimum selling price restrictions imposed by a cartel of regional airlines. It is still possible to get special deals to selected destinations from the discount travel agents (see page 27 and Singapore *Yellow Pages*) but tickets bought in Bangkok and Penang are now marginally cheaper.

The Singapore-Kuala Lumpur air shuttle (operated jointly by SIA and MAS) runs every 50 minutes from Changi Terminal 1. Singapore-KL shuttle tickets can be bought on a first-come-first-served basis at Changi Airport. For timetables, call SIA on T2238888 or MAS on T3366777. For return flights to Kuala Lumpur, just buy a single ticket as it is cheaper to purchase tickets in Malaysia.

Long haul flights from Kuala Lumpur, particularly on MAS, can be considerably cheaper than outbound flights from Singapore. It is also much cheaper when flying between Singapore and other points in Malaysia to use Johor Bahru's airport across the causeway. Johor Bahru is well connected to the Malaysian domestic network. Chartered express coaches ply between Singapore and JB airport; they leave Singapore from the *Novotel Orchid Inn* on Dunearn Road but are reserved for MAS passengers only, S$12 (adult), S$10 (children). The courier ensures express clearance of Malaysian customs and immigration. Details from MAS office in Singapore: 190 Clemenceau Avenue, T3366777. For those wishing to fly to destinations in Indonesia, it is cheaper to take the ferry to the Indonesian island of Batam (see page 34) and then catch a domestic flight from there.

Train

The railway station is on Keppel Road, T2225165, to the south of the city centre. Singapore is the last port of call for the Malaysian railway system (Keretapi Tanah Melayu - KTM). The domed station - apparently inspired by Helsinki's - opened in 1932 and was renovated in 1990. The design, with its rubber-covered walls and their images of rubber tappers, tin miners and other Malay scenes, was heralded when it opened. Also notable are the four fine Art Deco images on the front of the station depicting commerce, agriculture, industry and shipping - suitably industrious for the new, as well as the old, Singapore. Malaysian immigration and customs clearance for inbound and outbound passengers is taken care of in the Singapore station (sometimes with the help of sniffer dogs).

There are two main lines connecting Singapore and Malaysia: one up the west coast to KL and Butterworth and on to Thailand and another line which goes through the centre of Peninsular Malaysia and on to Kota Bahru on the northeast coast. Some travellers use the train to go to Johor Bahru to avoid the long wait going through customs at the border (S$2.90). There are departures daily at 0845, 1120 and 1805, journey time 30-40 minutes. Three fully air-conditioned express trains make the trip daily between Singapore and Kuala Lumpur, 5-7 hours (S$19-60) departing at 0815, 1425 and 2230. The overnight sleeper arrives in Kuala Lumpur at 0655. There is a cheaper, but slower, mail train which leaves at 2015 each evening and stops at every station en route taking 10 hours to reach Kuala Lumpur at the bargain fare of S$14.80. There are also daily trains from Singapore to Butterworth, opposite Penang, 13 hours and an express train 3 times a week to/from Bangkok (Thailand) crossing the Malaysian/Thai border at Padang Besar. Trains are clean and efficient and overnight trains have cabins in first class, sleeping berths in second class and restaurants.

Airline offices in Singapore

Aeroflot Soviet Airlines, 01-02 Tan Chong Tower, 15 Queen St, T3361757.
Air Canada, UOB Travel, 101 Thomson Rd, No 01-10, T2561198; Tan Chong Tower, 15 Queen St, T3361757
Air France, 400 Orchard Rd 14-05, Orchard Towers, T7376355
Air India, 17-01 UIC Building, 5 Shenton Way, T2205277
Air Lanka, 02-00 PIL Building, 140 Cecil St, T2257233
Air Mauritius, 01-00 LKN Building, 135 Cecil St, T2223033
Air New Zealand, 24-08 Ocean Building, 10 Collyer Quay, T5358266
Alitalia, 20-01 Wisma Atria, 435 Orchard Rd, T7373166
All Nippon Airways, 01-01 Cecil House, 139 Cecil St, T3234333
American Airlines, 108 Middle Rd, No 04-01, T3390001
Bangladesh Biman, 01-02 Natwest Centre, 15 McCallum St, T2217155
British Airways, 56 United Square, 101 Thomson Rd, T8397788
Cathay Pacific, 16-01 Ocean Building, 10 Collyer Quay, T5331333
China Airlines, 08-02 Orchard Towers, 400 Orchard Rd, T7372211
Czechoslovak Airlines, 1 Scotts Rd, 18-02, T7379844
El Al Israel Airlines, 03-33 Golden Landmark Hotel, 390 Victoria St, T2933622
Emirates, 19-06 Wisma Atria, 435 Orchard Rd, T7353535
Finnair, 18-01 Liat Towers, 541 Orchard Rd, T7333377
Garuda, 13-03 United Sq, 101 Thompson Rd, T2502888
Indian Airlines, 01-03 Marina House, 70 Shenton Way, T2254949
Japan Airlines, 01-01 Hong Leong Building, 16 Raffles Quay, T2210522
Korean Air, 07-08 Ocean Building, 10 Collyer Quay, T5342111
KLM, 391A Orchard Rd, 12-06/07, 108 Ngee Ann City, Tower A, T7377622
Kuwait Airways, 391A Orchard Rd, 12-05, T7359989
Lufthansa, 05-01/02 Palais Renaissance, 390 Orchard Rd, T7379222
MAS (Malaysian Airline System), 02-09 Singapore Shopping Centre, 190 Clemenceau Ave, T3366777
Northwest Airlines, 08-06 Odeon Towers, 331 North Bridge Rd, T3363371
Olympic Airways, 10-05 Parkmall, 9 Penang Rd, T3366061
Pakistan International, 01-01 United Sq, 101 Thomson Rd, T2512322
Philippine Airlines, 01-022 Parklane Shopping Mall, 35 Selegie Rd, T3361611
Qantas, 04-02 The Promenade, 300 Orchard Rd, T8397788
Royal Brunei, 01-4a Royal Holiday Inn Shopping Centre, 25 Scotts Rd, T2354672
Royal Jordanian, 01-05 Beach Centre, 15 Beach Rd, T3388188
Royal Nepal, 03-07, 3 Coleman St, T3395535
SAS, 23-01 Gateway East, 152 Beach Rd, T2941611
Saudi, 035-24 Changi Airport, Passenger Terminal 1, T5452041
Silk Air, 6 Shenton Way, 07-10 DBS Building, Tower 2, T3226859
Singapore Airlines, SIA Building, 77 Robinson Rd, T2238888; Mandarin Hotel, Orchard Rd, T2297293; Raffles City Shopping Centre, T2297274
Swissair, 18-01 Wisma Atria, 435 Orchard Rd, T7378133
Thai, 01-00 and 02-00 The Globe, 100 Cecil St, T2249977
Trans World Airlines (TWA), 08-01, 391A Orchard Rd, T7354718
Turkish Airlines, 06-11, 300 Orchard Rd, T7324556
United Airlines, 44-02 Hong Leong Building, 16 Raffles Quay, T2200711.

The first number in the address refers to the floor level within the building.

Transport to town From the station, bus 10 travels up Robinson Road, past Collyer Quay to Empress Place and the Nicoll Highway; bus 100 goes up Robinson, Fullerton and Beach roads; bus 30 travels west; bus 84 goes to the World Trade Centre; and buses 97 and 131 travel through the centre of town and then up Serangoon Road and through Little India.

Orient-Express Hotels, which operates the Venice Simplon Orient-Express also runs the luxury *Eastern & Oriental Express* between Singapore, Kuala Lumpur and Bangkok. From Bangkok the train continues north to the ancient Thai capital of Sukhothai and onward to Chiang Mai. This locomotive extravaganza departs from Singapore station every Sunday and returns from Bangkok on Wednesday. The journey takes 41 hours (two nights, one day) to cover the 2,000 km one-way trip. Passengers can disembark at Kuala Lumpur, Butterworth (Penang), and Hua Hin (Thailand). A single fare from Singapore to Bangkok starts from S$2,140pp in a shared cabin and rises to S$5,510 for the presidential suite. Reservations can be made at Orient-Express Hotels, Sea Containers House, 20 Upper Ground, London SE1 9PF, UK T(0171) 928 6000; *Orient-Express Hotels* also has agents in Singapore, Kuala Lumpur and Bangkok to handle reservations - in Singapore contact: 90 Cecil St 14-03, Carlton Building, T3923500 or 3234390; in Kuala Lumpur T2329615; and in Bangkok T2514862.

Bus The new Express Highway into Malaysia makes for a more efficient bus service and faster travel. Bus 170 goes to Woodlands immigration point and across the causeway to Johor Bahru's (JB) Larkin bus terminal as well as the train station. Note that boarding in JB is only permitted at these two stops. Buses leave every 6-10 minutes or so (more frequently during peak hours) from the Ban San Terminal at the northern end of Queen Street (at the junction with Arab Street) and then runs along Rochor Road and Bukit Timah Road to Woodlands Road. The journey to JB takes about an hour, including customs and immigration formalities at the border. There is also the rather more luxurious Singapore-JB Express which departs from the Ban San Terminal every 10 minutes.

Most long distance buses to and from Malaysia operate out of the Lavender Street Terminal at the junction of Lavender Street and Kallang Bahru. Destinations include KL (S$17), Melaka (S$11), Butterworth (S$30), Mersing (S$11), Kota Bahru (S$30), Kuantan (S$17), Ipoh (S$27), and Penang (S$30). Buses to the more distant destinations like Butterworth, Kota Bahru and Ipoh tend to leave in the late afternoon. It is best to book tickets a few days ahead of departure, especially if intending to travel over a holiday period. As well as the Lavender Street services, there is also the Singapore-KL Express which departs from the Ban San Terminal on Lavender Street with buses leaving at 0900, 1300 and 2200 (S$17.30 normal coach, S$25 deluxe). Again, it is best to book a couple of days ahead.

Long distance bus companies: *Singapore-Johor Bahru Express*, T2928149; *Kuala Lumpur-Singapore Express*, T2928254; *Malacca-Singapore Express*, T2935915; *A&S Bus Services*, T2816161; *WTS*, T3370337.

Buses to Thailand leave from the Golden Mile Complex on Beach Road: Hat Yai (S$35, S$45 for VIP coach), Bangkok (S$70). There are several agents selling tickets close to the station. Note that it is cheaper to book a ticket to Hat Yai, and then pay for the rest of the journey in Thai baht; or even cheaper still to catch a bus to JB, one from JB to Hat Yai, and then a third from Hat Yai to Bangkok.

Taxis Long distance taxis to Malaysia leave from the Rochor Road terminus. Taxis go as far as Johor Bahru (S$7); from here there are Malaysian taxis on to Melaka (M$80), Kuantan (M$120-150), KL (M$100) and Butterworth (M$180-200).

Boat A small fraction of Singapore's visitors arrive in the world's busiest port by ship, although cruising has become fashionable again and sea arrivals are growing by nearly 50% a year. Passenger lines serve Singapore from Australia, Europe, USA, India and Hong Kong. Ships either dock at the World Trade Centre or anchor in the main harbour with a launch service to shore. Entry formalities as above. *Star Cruises*, T7336988, F7333622 are one of the biggest companies operating in the region. Orient Lines, Pearl Cruises, Seabourn Cruise Lines, Silversea Cruises and Seven Seas Cruise Lines also dock at Singapore.

There are regular high speed ferry connections between **Singapore and Indonesia's Riau islands** of Batam (Sekupang and Batu Ampar) and Bintan (Tanjung Pinang and Loban). Return fares vary from S$27 to Sekupang (40 minutes journey time) to S$58 to Tanjung Pinang (1½ hours journey time). Most leave from the World Trade Centre not far from the city centre, although there are also services from Tanah Merah ferry terminal, east of the city. From the Riau islands it is possible to travel by boat to Sumatra or by air to many other destinations in Indonesia (cheaper than flying direct from Singapore). See page 34 for a table of ferry departures. It is also possible to take a high-speed catamaran from Tanah Merah to Pulau Tioman, off the east coast of Peninsular Malaysia, 4½ hours (S$148-168 return). Ferry operators have their offices at the World Trade Centre and include Auto Batam, 1 Maritime Square #02-40/42, World Trade Centre, T2714866, F2733573, autobatam@sembcorp.com.sg, http://www.sembcorp.com.sg/autobatam/; Sri Sinjori Ferries Pte Ltd, T2727540; Dino Shipping, 1 Maritime Square, #03-32 World Trade Centre, T2700311, F2700322.

For domestic and international ferry services see page 34

There is also a ferry from Changi Ferry Terminal to Tanjung Belungkor, east of Johor Bahru in Malaysia. Most people use this service to get to the beach resort of Desaru. Passengers S$19 (S$26 return); cars S$20; journey time 45 minutes. **NB** If travelling from Tanjung Belungkur to Singapore fares are considerably cheaper (payable in ringgit). Ferry times 0815, 1115, 1415 and 1715, Singapore to Tanjung Belungkur; 0945, 1245, 1545 and 1845, Tanjung Belungkor to Singapore. Contact Ferrylink Pte, T5453600/7336744. To get to the terminal take bus 2 to Changi Village and then a taxi.

It is possible to enter Singapore from Malaysia by bumboat from Johor Bahru (S$5), Tanjung Pengileh or Tanjung Surat (S$6) in southern Johor to Changi Point, on the northeast tip of Singapore - a good way of beating the bottleneck at the causeway. First boat 0700, last at 1600. Boats depart as soon as they have a full complement of 12 passengers.

A timetable of all shipping arrivals and departures is published daily in the *Shipping Times* (a section of the *Business Times*). According to some travellers freighter operators are reasonably amenable to marine hitchers who want lifts to Vietnam (although it is difficult to enter Vietnam by sea), the Philippines or Indonesia.

Touching down

Airport information

Almost all visitors arrive at Singapore's Changi Airport - regularly voted the world's leading or favourite airport. The old British military base at Seletar is used for small plane arrivals and departures, notably flights from/to Pulau Tioman, off the east coast of Malaysia (see below for details).

Changi airport is at the extreme eastern tip of the island, about 20 km from town. Changi gets its name from *changi ular*, a climbing shrub. But Changi is mainly associated with the World War Two POW camp based here, where 12,000 American, Australian and British servicemen were interned. The name Changi, which for one generation meant misery and squalor, now stands for comfort and efficiency. The spacious, uncluttered terminals are adorned with cool fountains, luxuriant plants and tropical fish tanks and boast an array of executive leisure facilities, including saunas

Emergencies: Police: T999. Ambulance/Fire brigade: T995.
***Hours of business**: Normal banking hours are 0930 -1500 Monday-Friday, 0930-1130 Saturday. Some do not offer foreign exchange dealings on Saturday although money changers operate throughout the week and for longer hours. Most shops in the tourist belt open around 0930 and close at 2100. Around Orchard and Scotts roads, Sunday is a normal working day.*
***Official time**: 8 hours ahead of GMT.*
***Voltage**: 220-240 volts, 50 cycle AC; most hotels can supply adapters.*
***Weights and measures**: Metric.*

and squash courts, to help jet-lagged executives unwind. The airport's stress-free terminals belie its status as one of the world's most hectic transit hubs. In 1995 the airport processed 23,196,242 passengers - eight times more than the population of Singapore. About 80% of Singapore's tourists arrive by air and it takes only 20 minutes from touch down to baggage claim - characteristically called "accelerated passenger through flow". True to form, Singapore's far-sighted government planners have already got a third terminal on the drawing board, which will cater for a further 10 million.

Changi's facilities are excellent and include banks, hotel reservation and Singapore Tourist Board desks, a medical centre, business centre, children's discovery corner, internet centre (open 24 hours), day rooms, restaurants, left-luggage facilities, mail and telecommunications desks, shopping arcades, supermarkets, sports facilities and accommodation, all open from 0700-2300. Everything is clearly signposted in English and the two terminals are connected by a monorail. Flight information is available by calling: T5424422 (give flight number). There is an excellent canteen/food centre in Terminal 2, reached via the multi-deck car park. A tourist information pack is available just after Immigration, near the Customs Hall.

Airport tax Payable on departure - S$15 for all flights to all countries. A PSC (Passenger Service Charge) coupon can be purchased at most hotels, travel agencies and airline offices in town before departure, which saves time at the airport.

Free city tours for transit passengers For those who are here in transit and want a snifter of what Singapore has to offer, the Singapore Tourist Board offers free tours of the city. They are run on a first come, first served basis, and for those with time on their hands who do not want to bankrupt themselves wandering the shops of Changi, they offer an excellent interlude. Passengers must show their boarding pass and are then ushered through immigration to a waiting bus. Passports are kept by the officials until they return and no airport departure tax is charged. The tours themselves are rather banal but it is a great idea and works without a hitch, as one might expect. For more details and to book a tour visit one of the Free City Tour desks on arrival.

Sleeping at Changi

A+ ***Le Meridien Changi***, 1 Netheravon Rd, T5427700, F5425295. Very well run, first class hotel, situated on Changi Beach, just north of the airport. Recommended for efficiency. **A** ***Transit Hotel 1***, level 3 Changi Airport Terminal 1, T5430911, F5458365. Short term rate quoted (6 hours). A good place to take a break if you are stuck at Changi for an extended period. **B** ***Transit Hotel 2***, departure/transit lounge south, Terminal 2 T5428122, F5426122, airport@pacific.net.sg, excellent hotel on the airport property, with short stay facility (price quoted is for 6 hours). Booking is recommended as it is so popular. They also provide a 'freshen up' service including use of showers, sauna and gym from S$5.

Transport to town

Public transport to and from town Hotels will only meet guests with a previous arrangement; some charge but others offer the service free. The car pick up area is outside the arrivals halls of both terminals.

The most convenient **bus** is the *Airbus*. There are two services which connect Changi with most of the major hotels. Buses run every 20 minutes from 0820-2210 to the airport and from 0900-2300 from the airport to the city, S$5, S$3 for children. Tickets available from the driver (exact change in S$ only) or in the arrivals area of terminals 1 and 2; an efficient, comfortable service, T5421721 for information.

A number of buses run between the airport and nearby bus interchanges. **Bus 16** runs to Raffles City and then down Orchard Road, takes less than 1 hour and costs S$1.20 (non-a/c) or S$1.50 (a/c). It is easy to catch from Orchard Road. **Bus no. 36**, which also runs along Orchard Road to Raffles City, is faster but only operates in the morning between 0600 and 0900 when the service operates from the city to airport and from 1700 and 2000 in the evening when it plys between the airport and city. Exact fare needed.

A **MRT** line is currently under construction from the city out to Changi. It is scheduled for completion in 2001 and will provide quick and easy access by train.

Car rental Avis and Hertz desks are in the arrivals hall (close 1800). See page 32 for listings.

Taxis queue up outside the arrival halls. They are metered plus there is an airport surcharge of S$3. In 1998 the airport introduced a limousine service (London cab or Mercedes) with a flat rate of S$35. Available from the booking counter in terminal 2 and soon to be extended to terminal 1, 0730-2330.

Seletar Airport is a military airport but is also used for connections with Pulau Tioman off Malaysia's east coast and for some charter flights. Although the authorities do not allow photographs on the tarmac, checking-in is all very relaxed and informal - very different from the rather brusque efficiency of Changi. There are no public buses to Seletar, most people take taxis, and as at Changi there is a S$3 surcharge. When a scheduled flight is arriving from Tioman the airline usually calls so that the required number of taxis are waiting.

Tourist information

Singapore Tourist Board Singapore Tourist Board, Tourism Court, 1 Orchard Spring Lane, Singapore 247729, T7366622; Raffles Hotel Shopping Centre, 02-34 Raffles Hotel Arcade, T3341335/3341336 (open 0830-2000). These are both very helpful, supplying brochures and maps. Complaints can also be registered at these offices. There is a 24 hour Touristline which gives automated information in English, Mandarin, Japanese and German, T1800 8313311 (tollfree). **Indonesian Tourist Board**, Ocean Building, 11 Collyer Quay, T5342837. **Malaysian Tourist Board**, Ocean Building, 11 Collyer Quay, T5326351.

Student/Young Person STA Travel in the *Orchard Parade Hotel* on Tanglin Road, T7345681, or at the Singapore Polytechnic (next to Canteen 5), Dover Road, T7742270, is Singapore's top student and youth (under 26) travel centre, offering student fares, discounted tours and budget accommodation.

Maps *American Express/Singapore Tourist Board Map of Singapore* and *The Map of Singapore* endorsed by the Singapore Hotel Association are both available gratis from STB offices and many hotels.

Guides *The Singapore Official Guide* and the STB's *Singapore Tour it Yourself* are available from STB offices. The STB are also producing a series of more detailed 'Yours to Explore' guides to selected areas of the city. By mid-1998 they had produced guides

Temple manners: a guide to avoiding giving offence

General advice
all temples, mosques and churches are places of worship and visitors should dress appropriately

Hindu temples
remove shoes on entry and leave them outside the gates
walk clockwise around the temple hall and circumambulate an odd number of times for good luck
menstruating women are considered 'unclean' and should not enter

Mahayana Buddhist (Taoist) temples
no need to remove shoes here - but don't step on the wooden door sills

Theravada Buddhist temples
remove shoes on entry and leave them outside the gates
women should avoid personal contact with monks

Mosques
remove shoes on entry and leave them outside the gates
ensure legs and shoulders are covered
note that only worshippers are allowed to enter the prayer hall
it is best not to visit during Friday prayers and in the evenings

to *Chinatown*, *Little India* and the *Singapore River* and have *Kampong Glam* and the *Civic District* in the pipeline. Well worth picking up.

Disabled visitors The Singapore Council of Social Services publishes *Access Singapore*, a guidebook especially for physically disabled visitors, which gives information on easily accessible tourist attractions and facilities for the disabled. Copies can be picked up from the SCSS offices at 11 Penang Lane, T3361544 or by post from National Council for Social Service, Disabled Service Department, 11 Penang Lane, Singapore 238485. Their offices are open: 0900-1300, 1400-1800 Monday-Friday.

Rules, customs and etiquette

Clothing Singapore dress is smart but casual. It is rare to find places insisting on jacket and tie, although jeans and T-shirts are taboo at some nightclubs. Flip-flops, singlets and denim cut-offs look out of place in Singapore.

Conduct in private homes Most Singaporeans remove their shoes at the door - more out of a keen sense of cleanliness than any deep religious conviction. No host would insist on his visitors doing so, but it is the polite way to enter a home.

Eating Chinese meals are eaten with chopsticks and Malays and Indians traditionally eat with their right hands. It is just as acceptable, however, to eat with spoons and forks. In Malay and Indian company, do not use the left hand for eating.

Prohibited within Singapore There are several rules and regulations visitors should note: smoking is discouraged and prohibited by law in many public places, such as buses, taxis, lifts, government offices, cinemas, theatres, libraries and department stores and shopping centres - and all air-conditioned restaurants. First offenders can be fined up to S$1,000 for lighting up in prohibited places. Many hotels now provide non-smoking floors. Littering may incur a fine of up to S$1,000 for first time offenders and up to S$2,000 for repeat offenders with the added prospect of corrective work of some kind. Although jaywalking is less rigorously enforced than it used to be, crossing the road within 50 metres of a pedestrian crossing, bridge or underpass could cost you S$500.

The old joke is that Singapore is a 'fine' place to live; you get a fine for smoking, spitting, breeding mosquitoes, not flushing the toilet and road hogging. From time to time Singapore, which is totally dependent for its water supplies from Malaysia, tries to 'conserve water'. At such times, stickers appear in toilets saying 'conserve water'. These are plastered next to the stickers reading, 'Penalty for not flushing $500'. During a campaign in the late 1980s, a much worse fate awaited people who urinated in lifts and were caught doing so: they had their pictures printed on the front of the next day's *Straits Times*. People could rat on the forgetful by calling the *Straits Times* 'Toilets of Shame Hotline'. In January 1991 chewing gum was prohibited. The *Economist* noted: "The nanny of Southeast Asia has swooped again". Chewing gum was said to be a "perennial nuisance", jamming doors in the MRT and glueing pedestrians to the pavement. Wrigley's traffickers now face a year's jail or a fine of up to S$6,200. The fact that you can now buy T-shirts ridiculing all this might suggest that things have eased up a bit.

Safety Singapore is probably the safest big city in Southeast Asia. Women travelling alone need have few worries. It is wise, however, to take the normal precautions and not wander into lonely places after dark.

Tipping Tipping is unusual in Singapore. In cheaper restaurants it is not expected, although in more upmarket places when a service charge is not automatically added to the bill, a tip is usual. Most international hotels and restaurants, however, add 10% service charge and 4% government tax to bills. In general, only tip for special personal services.

Where to stay

In December 1997 Singapore had 94 gazetted hotels (approved by STB) with 29,583 rooms and there are scores more that are not gazetted. Many of the excellent international class hotels are concentrated in the main shopping and business areas, including Orchard and Scotts roads, and near Raffles City and the Marina complexes. They are all run to a very high standard and room rates range between S$250 and S$650, although discounts are almost always on offer and few people pay the full rack rate. Enquire at the airport hotel desk on arrival whether there are any special offers. After a room glut in the early 1980s. Singapore's hotel industry is now suffering a room shortage and when a large convention or two hits town, rooms can be hard to find.

Singapore offers an excellent choice of hotels in our upper categories, from luxury to tourist class. Though rooms may be more expensive than equivalent classes of hotels elsewhere in the region, they try to make up for this in terms of service. It is rare to stay in a hotel that does not offer attentive and professional care. Budget hotels are thin on the ground and expensive, and budget travellers find that money which may last a week in neighbouring Indonesia or Malaysia disappears in a day or two. However, there are a few cheaper places to stay for hotel listings and comments.

Taxes of 10% (government) plus 3% (goods) plus 1% (services) are added to bills in all but the cheapest of hotels. See **Sleeping** at the end of each district section for hotel listings and comments.

Hotel prices and facilities

L+ (S$400+) and **L** (S$300-400) Singapore has some of the very best hotels in the world. These offer unrivalled personal service, sumptuous extras, luxury rooms and bathrooms, and just about every amenity that you can think of. Most of the top hotels now provide two in-room phone lines (for modems and calls), 24-hour business facilities, several pools, jacuzzis, health spas, tennis courts, numerous restaurants, and much else besides.

A+ (S$200-300) Most of the middle to upper range hotels in this category will

Dorm beds

Singapore is not the cheapest of places to stay but there are a number of budget hotels and guesthouses which offer dorm beds, usually with lockers for safe-keeping, for around S$8-15 per night for fan-cooled dorm rooms and S$25 for more salubrious a/c dorms. For the full entry on each hotel or guesthouse listed below see the respective accommodation sections in the main text.

Colonial core

***Willy's Homestay**, 494 North Bridge Rd, T3370916, E willys@mbox2.singnet.com.sg.*
***Travellers' Nest**, 28C Seah St, T3399095.*

Orchard Road

***YWCA**, Fort Canning Rd, T3384222, F3374222, a/c dorms.*
***YMCA International House**, 1 Orchard Rd, T3366000, F3373140, a/c dorms.*

Little India

***Hawaii Hostel**, 2nd Flr, 171B Bencoolen St, T3384187.*
***Lee Boarding House**, 7th Flr, 52 Peony Mansion, 46-52 Bencoolen St, T3383149, F3365409.*

Arab Street

***Lee Travellers' Club**, 6th Flr of the Fu Yuen apartment block (and next to the* Park View Hotel*), 75 Beach Rd, T3395490.*
***Season Homestay**, 26A Liang Seah St, T3372400, W http://www.sgweb.com.sg/homestay.*
***Cozy Corner Lodge** (formerly the* Backpackers' Cozy Corner*), 2a Liang Seah St, T3348761.*

Essentials

provide a business centre (although it is worth checking whether these operate around the clock). Coupled with this, there will be an executive floor or two, with a lounge for private breakfast and evening cocktails, or for entertaining clients. Most of these hotels will also provide a personal safe in each room. There will be a fitness centre and swimming pool and they may have a health centre as well as several restaurants.

A (S$150-200) and **B** (S$100-150) Hotels in this category will range from very comfortable to functional. Rooms in the 'A' category will have most extras – like a minibar, television, and tea and coffee making facilities. They may also have a swimming pool but it is likely to be small. They will have a coffee shop and perhaps a restaurant. Rooms in the 'B' category may be lacking some, or most, of these amenities but should still be clean, comfortable and serviceable.

C (S$50-100) There are not many hotels in this category in Singapore. Rooms may be air-conditioned with a hot water shower attached; there might also be a coffee shop. These are no-frills, functional affairs. There are some bargains to be had, but there are also hotels in this category which are pretty sordid.

D (S$25-50) and **E** (less than S$25) Hotels and guesthouses in these two categories (and there aren't many) are basic places, with shared bathroom facilities and box-like rooms. There are a few that are clean and perfectly adequate, and these are the registered establishments; others are squalid. The places on third or fourth floors of apartment buildings usually have no licence and they are often the dirtiest and least well run. Most of these places provide a basic breakfast.

Essentials

Getting around

In an attempt to discourage Singaporeans from clogging the roads with private cars, the island's public transport system was designed to be cheap and painless. Buses go almost everywhere, and the Mass Rapid Transit (MRT) underground railway provides an extremely efficient subterranean back-up. Smoking is strictly banned on all public transport - transgression is punishable by a large fine. (Big Macs and durians are also not allowed on the MRT.)

Mass Rapid Transit (MRT)

Since November 1987 Singapore has had one of the most technologically advanced, user-friendly light railway systems in the world – about a third of the system is underground. The designer-stations of marble, glass and chrome are cool, spotless and suicide-free, thanks to the sealed-in, air-conditioned platforms. Nine of the underground stations serve as self-sufficient, blast-proof emergency bunkers for Singaporeans, should they ever need them.

The US$5bn MRT is indeed a rapid way of transiting - it is electrically driven and trains reach 80 km/hour. Within minutes of leaving the bustle of Orchard Road passengers hear the honey-toned welcome to the Raffles City interchange. The MRT's 66 fully automated trains operate every 3-8 minutes, depending on the time of day, between 0600 and 2400. There is a north-south loop and an east-west line with interchanges at Raffles City/City Hall and Jurong East. The lines cover the main tourist belt. A new line is currently under construction from the city out to Changi Airport and is scheduled for completion in 2001. Fare stages are posted in station concourses, and tickets dispensed, with change, from the vending machines. Fares range from 60¢ to S$1.60. Stored value tickets, in various denominations, can be bought at all stations from ticket dispensing machines. (There are note changing machines which will change S$2 notes into coins.) **NB** Children pay the same price as adults.

It is also possible to buy Transitlink cards for the MRT and buses, prices from S$10 to S$50 (including a S$2 refundable deposit) from the Transitlink ticket booths at MRT stations. Buses have 'validator machines'.

MRT System

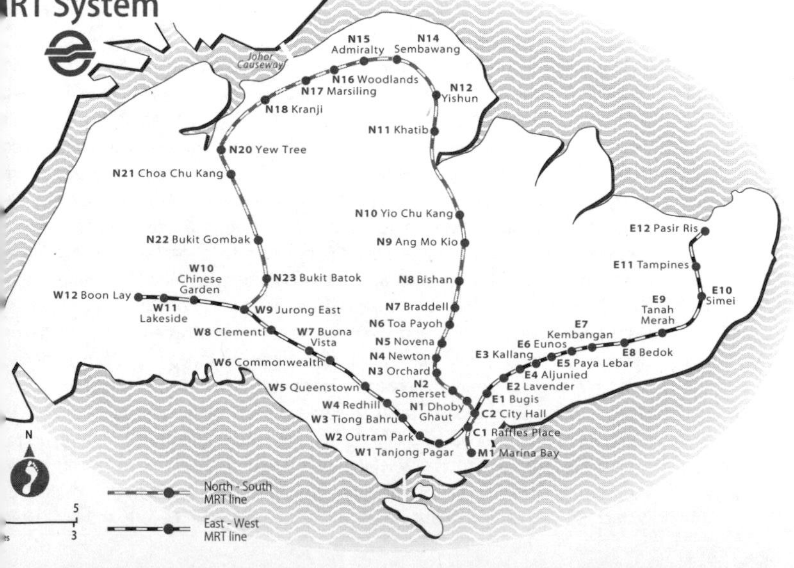

Bus

For anyone visiting Singapore for more than a couple of days, the bus must be the best way of getting around. SBS (Singapore Bus Service) and TIBS (Trans-Island Bus Services) are efficient, convenient and cheap. Routes for all the buses are listed (with a special section on buses to tourist spots) in the pocket-sized and pocket-priced (S$1.40) TransitLink Guide available at news outlets, bookshops and MRT stations, as well as at many hotels. If you intend to do much bus travel, then this guide is well worth buying. The Singapore Tourist Board's *Official Guide* (free-of-charge from STB offices) also carries a tourist-friendly synopsis of the service. All buses are operated by a driver only, so it is necessary to have the exact fare to hand. Fares range from 60¢ (non a/c) to S$1. 50 and buses run from 0630 to 2330 Monday to Sunday. For those intending to use the bus system extensively then it is well worth considering purchasing a Singapore Explorer ticket - S$5 for one day, S$12 for three days unlimited travel on both SBS and TIBS services. Tickets are available from TransitLink offices at Raffles Place, City Hall, Bugis, Dhoby Ghaut, Somerset, Orchard and Newton MRT stations and at many hotels. The sight-seeing Singapore Trolley travels between Orchard Road, the River, Chinatown, Raffles Hotel, Boat Quay, Clarke Quay, Suntec City all day. S$9 for adults, S$7 for children, provides you with unlimited rides throughout the day. For more information call Singapore Explorer Pte T3389205/3396833.

Car hire

One of the most expensive ways to get around. It is not worth it unless travelling to Malaysia, as parking is expensive in Singapore (parking coupons can be bought in shops and daily licence booths). If travelling to Malaysia, it is cheaper, in any case, to hire a car in Johor Bahru. Rental agencies require a licence, passport and for the driver to be over 20. Car rental cost is anything from S$60 to S$350/day, depending on size and comfort, plus mileage. Vans and pickups are much cheaper as they are classified as commercial vehicles and are taxed at a lower rate.

Driving is on the left, the speed limit 50 km/hour (80 km/hour on expressways) and wearing a seat-belt is compulsory. Avoid bus lanes (unbroken yellow line) during rush-hours. Remember that to drive into the restricted zone a licence must be purchased (S$3). In addition to car hire counters at the airport and booking offices in some top hotels, the *Yellow Pages* lists scores of local firms under 'Motorcar Renting and Leasing'.

Avis, Cuscaden Road, Suntec City and Changi Terminals 1 and 2, T1800-7379477; ***Hertz***, Ngee Ann City Tower B and Changi Airport, T1800-8393388; ***Budget***, 24 Raffles Place, Clifford Centre, T5324442.

Other local transport

Taxis are the fastest and easiest way to get around in comfort. More than 15,000 taxis, all of them metered and air-conditioned, ply the island's roads. Taxis cannot be hailed anywhere; it's best to go to a taxi stand or about 50m from traffic lights. The taxis' bells are an alarm warning cabbies once they're over the 80 km/hour expressway speed limit. Fares start at S$2.40, for the first 1 km, and rise 10¢ for every subsequent 240m up to 10 km, after which they rise by 10¢ every 225m. 10¢ is also added for every 30 seconds waiting time. There is a peak period surcharge of S$1 for trips commencing between 0730 and 0930 Monday-Saturday, between 1630 and 1900 Monday-Friday, and from 1130 to 1400 on Saturday. These surcharges do not apply on public holidays. A surcharge of S$1.50 is levied on all trips beginning from the Central Business District (CBD) between 1630 and 1900 on weekdays and between 1130 and 1400 on Saturday (except on public holidays). If this surcharge is levied then the peak period surcharge does not apply. If there are more than two passengers there is a 50¢ surcharge; luggage costs S$1 extra and there's a 50% 'midnight charge' from 2400 to 0600. There is also a S$3 surcharge for journeys starting from (but not going to) Changi International Airport or Seletar Airport, and a S$3.20 flat fee for calling a radio taxi which rises to S$5.20 if booked more than 30 minutes in advance. Trips paid for with credit cards enjoy a ten per cent surcharge on top of the fare, and taxis hired between 1800 on the evening before a public holiday up to 2400 on the day of the public holiday also get hit with a S$1 surcharge. TIBS taxis now has a fleet of London cabs which may be hired by the hour, and have the advantage of accommodating five passengers. There's a surcharge here too though, of S$1. Even with this veritable extravaganza of surcharges, Singapore's taxis are still excellent value for money and are certainly worth considering if in a group of three or four. Not only do they provide a view of Singapore which is absent from the MRT (at least in the city centre), but taxi drivers, like their brothers (and a few sisters) in most cities, are a great source of information, from political opinion to tourist practicalities. Unlike most of the rest of Asia, language is not a barrier to communication.

The CBD area scheme restricts all cars and taxis from entering the area between 0730-1900 Monday-Friday, 0730-1015 Saturday, unless they purchase an area licence (S$3 cars, $1 for motorbikes). Passengers entering the restricted zone are liable unless the taxi is already displaying a licence. Taxis displaying red destination labels on their dashboards are going home and are only required to take passengers in the direction they are going. Taxis are usually plentiful; there are stands outside most main shopping centres and hotels. Smoking is illegal in taxis. For taxi services ring: ***Comfort CabLink*** T5521111, ***Premier Cabs*** T5522828, ***City Cab*** T5522222, ***TIBS*** T4811211.

Trishaw, descendants of the rickshaw, they have all but left the Singapore street-scene. A few genuine articles can still be found in the depths of Geylang or Chinatown, Serangoon Road, by Bugis Village, off Victoria Street, or outside Raffles City, but most now cater for tourists and charge accordingly, making trishaws the most expensive form of public transport in town. As ever, agree a price before climbing in and expect to pay about S$20 for a moderate length journey. Top hotels offer top dollar trishaw tours. Off-duty trishaw drivers hang out in a large pack at the bottom of Bras Basah Road, near the Singapore Art Museum. The eponymous Trishaw Tours Pte, T5456311/8283133 also offer trishaw tours.

Hitchhiking The idea is anathema to most Singaporeans and those trying are unlikely to have much success.

Boat Ferries to the southern islands - Sentosa, Kusu, St John's etc - leave from the World Trade Centre or it is possible to hire a sampan from Jardine Steps on Keppel Road or Clifford Pier. Boats for the northern islands go from Changi Point or Ponggol Point. For table of ferry services, see page 34.

Tours of the island

For those constrained by time, there is a wide choice of organized tours which cover everything from cultural heritage to island-hopping, eating and shopping. Most city and island tours take about 3½ hours, and depending on admission fees to various sights, cost between S$25 and S$50. For a full day tour expect to pay around S$60-70. Children usually go for slightly more than half-price.

City tours Most popular are the city tours which involve coach rides along Orchard Road, past the Istana, through Little India and visit Shenton Way, Raffles Place, Chinatown, Mount Faber and the Botanic Gardens, 3½ hours (S$23-29, children S$14-15) 0900/0930 and 1400/1430 Monday-Sunday. ***Singapore Explorers***,T3396833, run a trolley/tram service for S$9, S$7 for children, providing all day, unlimited travel tickets.

Attractions tours There are tours to Singapore's main attractions from the zoo and bird park to the Haw Par Villas and Tang Dynasty City. Prices vary according to tour length, whether meals are included, and the entrance fee for the attraction but range from a low of S$27 (Haw Par Villas, 3½ hours, no guide) to S$56 (Haw Par Villas and Jurong Bird Park, 7 hours, lunch included).

Domestic and international ferry servic

Destination	Departing from	Journey time & fa (S$, return)
Domestic ferry services		
Sentosa (see page133)	World Trade Centre	15 minutes
Pulau Ubin (see page 157)	Changi Point	
Pulau Kusu (see page 156)	World Trade Centre	30 minutes
St John's (see page 156)	World Trade Centre	1 hour
Sisters Island (see page 157)	Jardine Steps or Clifford Pier	
Cruises		
Singapore River (see page 36)	Clarke Quay, Raffles Landing	30 minutes
Southern Islands cruises (page 157)	Clifford Pier, World Trade Centre	1-2½ hours
Dinner cruises (see page 36)	Clifford Pier, World Trade Centre	2-2½ hours
International ferry services		
Sekupang, Batam (Indonesia)	World Trade Centre	40 minutes, S$27
Batu Ampar, Batam (Indonesia)	World Trade Centre	40 minutes
Tanjung Balai, Karimun (Indonesia)	World Trade Centre	
Tanjung Pinang, Bintan (Indonesia)	Tanah Merah	1½ hours, S$63
Lobam, Bintan (Indonesia)	Tanah Merah	45 minutes, S$54
Tioman (Malaysia)	Tanah Merah	4 hours, S$160
Tanjong Belungkor (Johor, Malaysia)	Changi Ferry Terminal	45 minutes, S$24

Eco-tours *Eureka Travel*, 277A Holland Avenue, Holland Village, T4625077, F4622853, organizes local and regional tours with an environmental bias. From ornithological tours of Singapore to trips to national parks in East and West Malaysia.

Guides For private guided tours, call the Registered Guides Association, T3383441; S$50 for a minimum of four hours. Licenced tourist guides wear official badges and should produce ID on request.

Round-island tours There are quite a few to choose from, ranging from history tours of the colonial buildings, to west coast and Sentosa tours, to Singapore by night. See Tour Operators listing below and expect to pay upwards of S$40.

Keeping in touch

Language

No English-speaking visitor to Singapore need fear that they will not be able to make themselves understood. The official languages are Malay, Chinese (Mandarin), Tamil and English. Interestingly, Malay is the national language and English, the language of administration. Because of the Republic's importance as an international trade centre, there is a high standard of English in business. Many dialects of Chinese are also spoken although the government's 'Speak Mandarin' campaign has begun to change this. Most Singaporeans speak their own lilting and musical version of English, which is dubbed 'Singlish', and is an English patois full of curious Chinese (largely Hokkien and Cantonese) and Malay-inspired idiosyncracies and phonetic peculiarities.

As in neighbouring Malaysia, *'lah'* is a favourite suffix to just about any sentence. The words *'izzit'* and *'izzinit'* also figure prominently at the end of sentences. *'Wah!'* is a typical Singlish expression of surprise, horror, delight and disappointment. Singlish is generally spoken at high speed and incorporates numerous syntactical contortions, designed to make the language virtually unintelligible to the first-time visitor. Some Singaporeans object to Singlish, regarding it as a crude perversion of the English language. They fear that it may undermine Singapore's reputation and should be stamped out. Singlish has been banned, for example, from TV and radio commercials and the *Straits Times* occasionally opines that Singlish may be bad for business. For most, though, it is a badge of national identity to be relished. A few examples: "You makan (eaten) already or not?"; "Why you Kaypoh (busybody) lah!"; "Why you so acksi borak (show-off) like that, man?"

The most commonly used words and phrases of Singapore's lingua-franca are linguistically related to 'Manglish', the mangled English dialect spoken across the causeway. Malaysian satirist Kit Leee has unravelled its complex vocabulary and phraseology in his book *Adoi*.

Postal services

The main **Post Office** is in Crosby House, Robinson Road and offers a basic service round the clock. **Local postal charges**: start at 22¢, aerograms, 35¢. **International postal charges**: 50¢ (postcard), S$1 (letter, 10g). **Post Office opening hours**: 0830-1700 Monday-Friday, 0830-1300 Saturday. Changi Airport, 0800-2000 Monday-Sunday. **Fax and telex services**: all post offices and almost all hotels have facilities for outgoing messages. The Singapore Post Office provides four sizes of sturdy carton, called Postpacs, for sending parcels abroad. These can be bought cheaply at all post offices. **Poste Restante**: Poste Restante Service, Crosby House, Robinson Road, Singapore. Correspondents should write the family name in capital letters and underline it to avoid confusion.

Telephone services

Local In public phones the minimum charge is 10¢ for 3 minutes. Card phones are quite widespread - cards can be bought in all post offices as well as in supermarkets and newsagents and come in units of S$2, S$5, S$10, S$20 and S$50.

Directory enquiries: ***T103***
Local call assistance: ***T100***
Operator-assisted and international calls: ***T104***
Operator-assisted calls to Malaysia: ***T109***

International Singapore's IDD code is 65. For details on country codes dial 162. International calls can be made from public phones with the red 'Worldphone' sign; these phones take 50¢ and S$1 coins or phonecards. International Phone Home Cards are available at all post offices and come in units of S$10 and S$20. Credit card phones are also available. IDD calls made from hotels are free of any surcharge.

Media

Newspapers/Magazines The press is privately owned and legally free but is carefully monitored and strictly controlled. It runs on Confucianist principles - respect for one's elders - which translates as unwavering support of the government. In the past, papers that were judged to have overstepped their mark, such as the former *Singapore Herald*,

Short wave radio (Khz)

British Broadcasting Corporation *(BBC, London) Southeast Asian service 3915, 6195, 9570, 9740, 11750, 11955, 15360; Singapore service 88.9MHz; East Asian service 5995, 6195, 7180, 9740, 11715, 11750, 11945, 11955, 15140, 15280, 15360, 17830, 21715.*

Voice of America (VoA, Washington) *Southeast Asian service 1143, 1575, 7120, 9760, 9770, 15185, 15425; Indonesian service 6110, 11760, 15425.*

Radio Beijing *Southeast Asian service (English) 11600, 11660.*

Radio Japan (Tokyo) *Southeast Asian service (English) 11815, 17810, 21610.*

have been shut down. The *Straits Times* has been likened to Beijing's *People's Daily* for the degree to which it is a mouthpiece of the government.

The English language dailies are: the *Straits Times* (and the *Sunday Times*) which runs better foreign news pages than any other regional newspaper (available on the Web at http://www. asial.com.sg/straitstimes); the *Business Times* and the *New Paper* Singapore's very own tabloid. A more recent addition is the *Asian Times* printed in Singapore, Bangkok and Hong Kong. It is an independently run and owned newspaper with high standards of reporting and photography. So far it has escaped the censors In 1989 The *Straits Times* banned the use of pseudonyms on its letters page, and all would-be correspondents are vetted for authenticity before their letters are published. This has proved an effective form of censorship although, since the early 1990s as Singaporeans have got braver with the emergence of a more relaxed government, so more letters critical of the government have appeared. Walter Woon, an outspoken law lecturer at the National University of Singapore, believes the Singapore media is now entering a new period of glasnost, although it is extremely unlikely that the government will allow a truly free press.

The international press is rigorously monitored and, due to its aversion to criticism, the government has traditionally kept foreign journalists on a short leash. Having watched correspondents being unceremoniously expelled and a number of legal battles go the government's way, some foreign publications have given up caring about their Singapore circulation. A rift between the government and the New York-based Dow Jones meant that the *Asian Wall Street Journal*'s circulation was heavily restricted until 1991, and the *Far Eastern Economic Review* also had its circulation cut after a spat with the government. *Asiaweek* and *Time* have both had their circulation curtailed in the past, although the former kowtowed sufficiently to the government and was allowed unrestricted circulation of its English and Chinese-language editions.

International editions of most leading foreign newspapers are available however. Most international news and business magazines can be found in bookshops and on news stands. Many other US, Australian and European general interest glossies are also on sale. Pornographic publications are strictly prohibited under Singapore's Obscene Publications Act. Sometimes this extends to weekly glossies like *Cosmopolitan*. In 1998 the Ministry of Information and the Arts revoked the publishing permit of the British men's magazine *FHM* because it persisted in publishing 'illustrations normally associated with risqué soft porn' magazines.

Radio Daily services in English and Chinese from 0600-2400, in Malay from 0445-2400 and Tamil from 0500-2100. There are five local radio stations and two on nearby Batam Island which blast rock music across the Straits of Singapore. The BBC World Service broadcasts 24 hours a day on FM 88.9 thanks to an old British forces transmitter. The "London Calling" programme guide is available from bookshops.

Television Channels 5, 8 and 12 show English, Chinese, Malay and Tamil programmes; most sets also receive Malaysian channels. Many large hotel TV sets eceive satellite channels and are also linked with the teletext system, which has information on entertainment, sports, finance, aircraft arrivals and departures and special events from 0700-2400. Programmes for all channels are listed in the daily newspapers.

nternet Cafés *T2* Changi International Airport, 036-120/121 (Level 3), PO Box 1046 Changi Airport, 918156, T5461968, F5461969. ***Cybernet Café***, 57 Tanjong Pagar Road, 088478, T3244361, F3244362. ***Internet Centre***, Transit North, Changi International Airport, 026-110-01, T5461968, F5461969. ***Café@Boat Quay***, 82 Boat Quay, T230014. ***Cyberheart Café***, Orchard Road, T7343877.

Food and drink

Restaurant prices
5 over S$40
4 S$20-40
3 S$10-20
2 S$5-10
1 below S$5

Eating is the national pastime in Singapore and has acquired the status of a refined art. The island is a tropical paradise for epicureans of every persuasion and budget. While every country in the region boasts national dishes, none offers such a delectably wide variety as Singapore. Fish-head curry must surely qualify as the national dish but you can sample 10 Chinese cuisines, North and South Indian, Malay and Nonya (Straits Chinese) food, plus Indonesian, Vietnamese, Thai, Japanese, Korean, French, Italian (and other European), Russian, Mexican, Polynesian, and Scottish. There's a very respectable selection of western food at the top end of the market, a few good places in the middle bracket and swelling ranks of cheaper fastfood restaurants like *Kentucky Fried Chicken* and *McDonald's* and an explosion of pizza outlets. For young, trendy Singaporeans, coffee culture has replaced food court fare and the favoured spots are places like *Delifrance*, *Spinelli's* and *Starbuck's* which are giving a buzz to thousands.

Do not be put off by characterless, brightly lit restaurants in Singapore: the food can be superb. Eating spots range from high-rise revolving restaurants to neon-lit pavement seafood extravaganzas. A delicious dinner can cost as little as S$3 or more than S$100 and the two may be just yards away from each other. For example, it is possible to have a small beer in one of the bars of the Raffles Hotel for S$8 or more and then stagger 10m across the road and indulge in a huge plate of curry and rice for S$2. For a listing of over 100 more pricey restaurants, *Singapore's Best Restaurants* is worth purchasing; it gives a description of the food and a price guideline and is available from most bookstores for $10.30. It is updated annually. *The Secret Food Map* (available at most bookstores - S$5) is also a good buy.

Hawker centres and food courts

The government might have cleared hawkers off the streets, but there are plenty of hawker centres in modern Singapore. Food courts are the modern, air-conditioned, sanitized version of hawker centres. They provide the local equivalent of café culture and the human equivalent of grazing. Large numbers of stalls are packed together under one roof. Hawker centres are found beneath HDB blocks and in some specially allocated areas in the city; while food courts are usually in the basement of shopping plazas. The seats and tableware may be basic, but the food is always fresh and diners are spoilt for choice. Customers claim themselves a table, then graze their way down the rows of Chinese, Malay and Indian stalls. It is not necessary to eat from the stall you are sitting next to. Vendors will deliver to your table when the food is ready and payment is on receipt. The food is cheap and prices are non-negotiable.

Coffee shops

Mainly family concerns, traditional Singaporean coffee shops or *kopi tiam* are located in the older part of the city, usually in old Chinese shophouses. They serve breakfast, lunch and dinner, as well as beer, at prices only marginally higher than those at hawker centres.

Fast-food cafés Despite Singapore's gourmet delights, fast-food outlets do a roaring trade in Singapore. As well as the standard names in fastfood fare, there are now chains of more sophisticated 'cafés', selling a wider range of European food. In particular, there is *Spinelli's*, who provide a very good range of fresh coffees (ground or beans) and *Delifrance*, known for its freshly-baked croissants, danish pastries and filled baguettes. Ask whether the pastries are freshly baked, as they weren't on an occasion we sampled their food. Check the *Yellow Pages* for branch addresses of the various fastfood restaurants. They include: ***A&W*** (which in 1968 became the first fast-feeder in town), ***Burger King***, ***Denny's***, ***KFC***, ***McDonald's***, ***Milano Pizza***, ***Orange Julius***, ***Pizza Hut***, ***Shakey's Pizza*** and one called ***Fat Mama***. ***Delifrance*** has probably expanded fastest with restaurants at Clifford Centre, Marina Square, The Dynasty, Wisma Atria, The Promenade, Holland Village and Changi Airport. They also run several bistros at Holland Village and Tanglin Mall.

Singapore's cuisine

Chinese

Each province of China has its own distinct cuisine. A balanced meal should contain the five basic taste sensations: sweet, bitter, salty, spicy and acidic to balance the *yin* and *yang*.

Cantonese Light and delicately-flavoured dishes are often steamed with ginger and are not very spicy. Shark's fin and birds' nest soups, and *dim sum* (mostly steamed delicacies trolleyed to your table, but only served until early afternoon) are Cantonese classics. Other typical dishes include fish steamed with soya sauce, ginger, chicken stock and wine; wan ton soup; blanched green vegetables in oyster sauce; and suckling pig.

Hainanese Simple cuisine from the southern island of Hainan; chicken rice with sesame oil, soy and a chilli and garlic sauce is their tastiest contribution.

Hakka Uses plenty of sweet potato and dried shrimp and specializes in stewed pigs trotters, *yong tau foo* (deep fried bean curd), and chillis and other vegetables stuffed with fish paste.

Hokkien Being one of Singapore's biggest dialect groups means Hokkien cuisine is prominent, particularly in hawker centres, although there are very few Hokkien restaurants. Hokkien Chinese invented the spring roll and their cooking uses lots of noodles and in one or two places you can still see them being made by hand. Hokkien cuisine is also characterized by clear soups and steamed seafood, eaten with soya sauce. Fried Hokkien *mee* (yellow wheat noodles stir-fried with seafood and pork), *hay cho* (deep fried balls of prawn) and *bee hoon* (rice vermicelli cooked with prawns, squid and beansprouts with lime and chillies) are specialities.

Hunanese Known for its glutinous rice, honeyed ham and pigeon soup.

Peking (Beijing) Chefs at the imperial court in Peking had a repertoire of over 8,000 recipes. Dumplings, noodles and steamed buns predominate, since wheat is the staple diet, but in Singapore, rice may accompany the meal. Peking duck, *shi choy* (deep fried bamboo shoots), and hot and sour soup are among the best Peking dishes. Peking duck (with the skin basted with syrup and cooked until crisp) it is usually eaten rolled into a pancake and accompanied by hoisin sauce and spring onions. Fish dishes are usually deep-fried and served with sweet and sour sauce.

Shanghainese Seafood dominates this cuisine and many dishes are cooked in soya sauce. Braised fish-heads, braised abalone (a large shellfish) in sesame sauce, and crab and sweetcorn soup are typical dishes. Wine is often used in the preparation of meat dishes, hence drunken prawn and drunken crab.

Steamboat The Chinese answer to fondue is a popular dish in Singapore and can be found in numerous restaurants and at some hawker centres. Thinly sliced pieces of raw meat, fish, prawns, cuttlefish, fishballs and vegetables are gradually tossed into a bubbling cauldron in the centre of the table. They are then dunked into hot chilli and soya sauces and the resulting soup provides a flavoursome broth to wash it all down at the end.

Szechuan Very spicy (garlic and chilli are dominant), Szechuan is widely considered the tastiest Chinese cuisine. Szechuan food includes heaps of hot red peppers, traditionally considered to be protection against cold and disease. Among the best Szechuan dishes are smoked duck in tea leaves and camphor sawdust; minced pork with bean curd; steamed chicken in lotus leaves; and fried eels in garlic sauce.
Teochew Famous for its *muay* porridges. This is a light, clear broth consumed with side dishes of crayfish, salted eggs and vegetables.

Indian

There is probably as wide a selection of Indian edibles in Singapore as there is on the entire Indian sub-continent, from scorching-hot Madrasi curries to the mild, creamy kormas of the north. There is also the Indian Muslim food that is special to Singapore and Malaysia *prata kosong* (*roti prata*, the skilfully stretched Indian dough-bread, fried and served with a thin curry sauce) and fish-head curry are both delicious local specialities. Other typical Indian dishes include *murtabak* (*paratha* filled with meat, onion and egg), southern Indian vegetarian food such as *masala dosa* (Indian pancake) and *thali* (several curries eaten with rice and served on a banana leaf).

Malay

In Singapore Malay cooking is overshadowed by the Chinese gastronomic array, and because Malay curries take much longer to prepare, they do not lend themselves so easily to instant hawker food. But the Malay hawker's trump card is *satay*. Islam bans the use of pork (Chinese hawkers have a monopoly in pork satay) and Malay stalls and restaurants rarely serve alcohol. Coconut milk and flesh, *belacan* (pungent dried shrimp paste) and fresh chillies are vital ingredients in Malay cooking. *Roti John* (a French loaf, sliced open and fried with mutton, egg and onion) is the Malay interpretation of the European breakfast.

New Asia (Fusion)

This is a blending of cuisines and ingredients from East and West. So far, the foodies have not agreed on a single name. It is sometimes termed 'Fusion' cuisine, sometimes Trans-ethnic, and sometimes New Asia. Perhaps this confusion over what to call the food is because people don't seem to be able to agree what constitutes the cuisine(s) in the first place. Some chefs and food critics maintain that it involves cooking Eastern ingredients using Western cooking techniques. Others see it as a combination of two styles of cooking and two sets of ingredients. One chef believes you should be able to drink wine with New Asia cuisine, something that you cannot do with Chinese food, as soya sauce kills the taste of wine. But like most things, you'll know it when you see it.

Nonya (Peranakan)

The cuisine of the Straits Chinese blends tastes from China and Malaya. Coconut, candlenut, turmeric and lemon grass are essential ingredients. *Poh piah* (savoury spring rolls filled with shredded turnip and bamboo shoots, beancurd, prawns and pork), and *otak-otak* (coconut milk with spices, prawns and fish, wrapped in a banana leaf) are typical Nonya dishes. Nonya desserts and snacks, many based on rice and coconut, are if anything more popular than the rest of the cuisine.

Seafood

Singapore offers a vast array of seafood. There are specialist seafood centres where fish dishes from all cuisines are prepared. Chilli or pepper crabs, 'drunken' prawns (cooked in rice wine) and deep-fried squid (*sotong*) dishes are Singaporean favourites.

Drink

Every hawker centre has at least a couple of stalls selling fresh fruit juice, a more wholesome alternative to the ubiquitous bottles of fizzy drink. A big pineapple or papaya juice costs S$2. You can choose any combination of fruits to go in your fruit punch. Freshly squeezed fruit juices are widely available at stalls and in restaurants. Fresh lime juice is served in most restaurants, and is a perfect complement to the banana-leaf curry, tandoori and dosai. Carbonated soft drinks, cartons of fruit juice and air-flown fresh milk can be found in supermarkets. For local flavour, the Malay favourite is *bandung* (a sickly-sweet, bright pink concoction of rose essence and condensed milk), found in most hawker centres, as well as the Chinese thirst quenchers, soya bean milk or chrysanthemum tea. *Red Bull* (*Krating Daeng*), the Thai energy tonic is also widely available and is the toast of Singapore's army of Thai building site labourers.

Tiger and Anchor beers are the local brews and Tsingtao, the Chinese nectar, is also available. Tiger Beer was first brewed at the Malayan Breweries with imported Dutch hops and yeast on Alexandra Road in 1932 and was the product of a joint venture between Singapore's Fraser & Neave and Heineken. Recently, Tiger Beer has produced two new brews: Tiger Classic is a strong bottled beer and Tiger Light, which is now available on draught in some bars. Anchor was the result of German brewers Beck's setting up the rival Archipelago Brewery. Because of its German roots, Archipelago was bought out by Malayan Breweries in 1941 and is today part of the same empire. Some bars (such as *Charlie's* at Changi) specialize in imported beers but even local beer is expensive (around S$6 a bottle in hawker centres and S$8 a glass in bars and pubs). There is an international selection of drinks at top bars but they're often pricey. Coffee houses, hawker centres and small bars or coffee shops around Serangoon Road, Jalan Besar and Chinatown have the cheapest beer. Expect to pay around S$8-10 for a half pint of beer in most smart bars. Most bars do have a Happy Hour (or Hours) though, where bargains can be had.

There is no shortage of wine available in Singapore, but it is expensive; Australian wines are generally a better deal than imported European ones. Supermarkets all have good wines and spirits sections.

The Singapore Sling is the island's best known cocktail. It was invented in the Raffles Hotel in 1915 and contains a blend of gin, cherry brandy, sugar, lemon juice and angostura bitters.

Shopping

Singapore is a shopper's paradise. There is an endless variety of consumer goods and gimmicks, with no import duty or sales tax on most items. The choice seems almost unlimited. But don't be deluded that there are bargains galore with rock bottom prices to match the variety. Prices are, in fact, much the same as, say, those in Europe or the US. High wages, soaring rents and a strong dollar have all eaten into the country's price advantage. Singapore's retailers have had to weather several years of stagnant demand. Local shoppers seem to be spending their disposable income in other ways (or themselves go shopping abroad) and tourists no longer come with empty suitcases to stuff full of goodies. Even the people who used to come here from places like Manila, Bangkok and Jakarta can buy just about everything at home. That said, there are some good buys and sales can throw up the odd bargain.

Probably the best area for window shopping is the Scotts and Orchard Road areas, where many of the big complexes and department stores are located (see page 46). This area comes alive after dark and most shops stay open late. The towering Raffles City complex, Parco at Bugis Junction and Marina Square, are the other main shopping centres. The East Coast shopping centres are not frequented by tourists. Serangoon Road (or Little India), Arab Street and Chinatown offer a more exotic shopping experience with a range of 'ethnic' merchandise.

Tips on buying

It does not take long to get the feel of where you can bargain and where you cannot. Department stores are fixed-price, but most smaller outfits – even those in smart shopping complexes – can be talked into discounts. As ever, it is best not to buy at the first shop; compare prices; get an idea of what you should be paying from big department stores – Tang's Department Store on Orchard Road is a good measuring rod – which you can nearly always undercut. In ordinary shops, 20-30 per cent can be knocked off the original asking price, sometimes more. Keep smiling, joking and teasing when bargaining and never believe a shopkeeper who tells you he is giving you something at cost or is not making a profit. The golden rule is to keep a sense of humour. If you lose face, they've won.

For big purchases, ask for an international guarantee (they are often extra), although sometimes you will have to be content with Singapore-only guarantees.

Once goods are sold they are not returnable, unless faulty; make sure you keep your receipt.

Deposits, not usually more than 50% of the value of the goods, are generally required when orders are placed for custom-made goods.

Make sure electrical goods are compatible with the voltage back home.

Complaints about retailers (who from time to time exhibit aggressive tendencies when selling merchandise to tourists) can be registered at the Consumers' Association of Singapore, T2224165.

Best buys

Singapore has all the latest electronic gadgetry and probably as wide a choice as you will find anywhere. It also has a big selection of antiques (although they tend to be over-priced), arts and crafts, jewellery, silks and batiks. For branded goods, Singapore is still marginally cheaper than most other places, but for Asian produced products it is no longer the cheapest place in the region.

The Good Retailers Scheme

The Good Retailers Scheme has been set up by the Singapore Tourist Board and has 500 shops on its books. Retailers who belong to this scheme are expected to abide by a code of conduct. The mark of a 'good retailer' is the red and white merlion emblem, and it is valid for the year it displays. The STB produce a booklet listing all their members.

GST (Goods and Service Tax) Tourist Refund Scheme See page 21.

Small Claims Tribunal

Feel you've been unfairly ripped off? Then contact the Small Claims Tribunal on the 5th Floor of the Apollo Centre, T4355937, F4355994. There's a fast track claims mechanism where visitors, after paying a S$10 fee, can have their cases against errant retailers heard, often within 24 hours.

Touts

Although the government has come down hard on copy-watch touts, tourists can still occasionally be accosted (and ripped off), particularly along Orchard Road.

Shopping guide

Antiques

Singapore's antique shops stock everything from opium beds, planters' chairs, gramophones, brass fans, porcelain, jade, Peranakan marble-top tables and 17th century maps to smuggled Burmese Buddhas, Sulawesian spirit statues and Dayak masks. There are few restrictions on bringing antiques into Singapore or exporting them. Many of the top antique shops are in the **Tanglin Shopping Centre**. They include the old map shop, ***Antiques of the Orient***, on the first floor, T7349351. This is probably the best place to buy antique maps and prints in Southeast Asia and is a wonderful place to browse. They also have a library. ***Apsara*** for lacquerware chests; ***Tiepolo***,

T7327924, was established over 20 years ago and David Mun has a fabulous range of Chinese and Indonesian porcelain, wooden pieces and bronze. This is well worth a visit and Mr Mun is a mine of information and fascinating to talk with. ***Kensoon*** has exclusive Asiatic pieces. ***Tatiana*** is a long established treasure trove of mostly 'primitive' art. A considerable proportion is from Indonesia: antiques, great wooden sculptures and textiles, baskets, Vietnamese drums and jewellery. ***Mata-Hari***, sells Indo-Chinese lacquerware and a range of silver jewellery and silver pieces and textiles (as well as some good books for reference).

Another excellent place for Asian arts and crafts is the **Holland Village Shopping Centre** on Holland Avenue, west of the city (take the MRT to Buona Vista and then walk up Commonwealth Avenue to Holland Avenue - about 15 minutes - or take buses 106 or 200). There are a number of good shops here and on the surrounding streets. ***Tong Mern Sern Antiques***, at 51 Craig Road, Chinatown and at Block D, on the waterfront at Clarke Quay (also called ***Keng's***, after its inimitable owner), is a treasure trove. Keng's adage: "We buy junk and sell antiques; some fool buy and some fool sell". ***Eng Tiang Huat***, is at 282 River Valley Road, west of Clarke Quay, as is ***Hua Shi Oriental Arts***, at number 278 and ***Vivaldi Collection*** at number 296.

For general antiques, there are shops dotted around **Cuppage Terrace** behind Centrepoint (upstairs, above *Saxophone*, there are several good shops, selling antique Melaka furniture, porcelain, and Peranakan pieces); ***Abanico***, 5th Floor, Centrepoint Shopping Centre, antique and modern Asian pieces. **Dempsey Road**, off Holland Road, is a great place to browse amongst the furniture warehouses in some of the old army barracks there. Furniture from Indonesia, plantation chairs, opium couches, Burmese Buddhas and so on, are all available. Warehouse shops include: ***Asian Passion***, Block 13, T4731339, good for tables and cabinets; ***Renaissance***, Block 15, T4740338, range of restored Chinese furniture; ***Pasardina***, Block 13, T4720228, good range of new and old cabinets, planters chairs, beds and some small scale Indonesian pieces (spice boxes and baskets); ***Journey East***, Block 13 T4731693 for chests, planters chairs - old and new; ***Eastern Discoveries***, Block 26, T4751814, for wooden sculptures, amongst other things.

There are also some good shops (selling antiques and restored/imitation items) at **Binjai Park**, off Bukit Timah Road, which is rather off the beaten track to the north of Orchard Road. **Pagoda Street** in Chinatown has a number of antique shops, but these are very much geared to the tourist market. One of the best shops in Singapore is the oxymoronic ***Young Antique Co***. and **Geylang** (East coast area) has a number of good antique junk shops where occasional treasures can be found. ***Peter Wee's Katong Antique House*** (aka *Katong Antiques House* at 208 East Coast Road (half museum, half shop) has one of the best selections of Peranakan antiques. The shop has been established for 20 years and has become a focal point for Peranakan culture. He has established a Peranakan Association and publishes a newsletter. Groups from the National Museum visit him. He has a considerable collection of beaded shoes and holds classes on how to make them every Wednesday. ***A Guide to Buying Antiques, Arts and Crafts in Singapore*** by Anne Jones is recommended, available in most bookshops.

Art Galleries

With the arrival of both ***Christie's*** and ***Sotheby's*** and the increased interest in home decorating, art has taken on a new meaning for Singaporeans. For information on contemporary art shows contact the ***Art Galleries Association*** which represents the interests of 15 commercial galleries. There are a good number of galleries scattered around the city. ***Andres Contemporary Art***, 442 Orchard Road, T7352173 and 9 Raffles Place, T5331723 specializes in Spanish/Catalonian contemporary art. ***Eagle's Eye***, Stamford House, 39 Stamford Road (Colonial core), T3398297, is a little gallery packed with Asian contemporary artwork (70% Singaporean). ***Gauguin Gallery***, Orchard Hotel Shopping Arcade, 442 Orchard Road, T7334268, mounts changing exhibitions of international artists. ***Tzen Gallery***, Tanglin Shopping Centre, 19 Tanglin Road (Orchard Road), T7344339, shows mainland Chinese watercolours and pen and ink drawings and has a wide selection of scrolls, reasonable prices. ***Art-2***, The Substation, 45 Armenian St (Colonial core), T3388713, is a tiny gallery, but they work more as consultants than as an exhibiting gallery - http://www. planetwork.com/art2. ***Asian contemporary Art***, The Substation, 45 Armenian Street (Colonial core) has a good exhibition space, where they display changing exhibitions of local artists' work. ***Art Focus***, Top floor, Centrepoint, Orchard Road, T7338337, F7320448, exhibits a good range of work in an attractive gallery. The top floor of **Orchard Point**, Orchard Road, is dedicated to art galleries. ***Wetterling Teo Gallery***, 11 Kim Yam Road, off River Valley Road, T7382872, specializes in contemporary American art.

Batik and silk

Malaysian and Indonesian batiks are sold by the metre or in sarong lengths. **Arab Street** and **Serangoon Road** are the best areas for reasonably priced batik and silk lengths, but you should bargain; big department stores usually have batik ready-mades. Ready-made Chinese silk garments can be found all over Singapore in Chinese emporia. If you want silk without the hassle, at reasonable prices, big department stores (such as ***Tang's***, on Orchard Road) have good selections. The best known of the silk boutiques, with fine silks at high prices, is ***China Silk House***, which has shops in Tanglin, Scotts, Centrepoint (all on Orchard Road) and Marina Square shopping centres. ***China Silk House*** designers come up with new collections every month. There is also a ***Jim Thompson Thai Silk*** shop on Tanglin Road next to Tanglin Shopping Centre.

Books

There is a good selection of English language literature available in Singapore, including specialist books on the region. Either ***Times***, ***Kinokuniya*** or ***MPH bookshops*** can be found in most shopping complexes. In late 1997 the US-based company ***Borders Books & Music*** opened its first store in Singapore in Whealock Place on Orchard Road - and it was a raging success from the start. This is the best place to browse; there are 140,000 titles, the books are not sealed in polythene, and visitors are encouraged to linger (there's a café and seats to peruse books). ***MPH*** in Stamford Road was the largest bookshop in Singapore before *Borders* opened and was built in 1908 to house the Methodist Publishing House; ***Sogo Department Store*** (Raffles City and Wisma Atria) also has a books section. ***Select Books***, Tanglin Shopping Centre, Orchard Road, sell a good range of coffee table glossies of the region. ***FP Bookstore***, 56 Amoy Street, Chinatown, T2254763, is good for financial books. The ***Christian Bookshop***, next to MPH on Stamford Road, Colonial core is good for religious publications and tapes.

There are plenty of **second-hand bookshops**: ***New Bookstore***, west side of North Bridge Road, just south of the *Intercontinental Hotel* buy and sell second-hand books. ***Books Paradiz***, Paradiz Centre, 1 Selegie Road, south of Little India, have second-hand books for sale or rent. ***Sultana Bookstore***, Paradiz Centre, 1 Selegie Road, south of Little India, have an extensive range of second-hand books including a good assortment of Penguin fiction. ***Bookmark***, Marina Square, sells second-hand books while in the atrium of ***The Cannery***, Clarke Quay, there is a second-hand book mart every Saturday 1600-2100.

Cameras

There are several shopping centres which are dedicated to electronic equipment and they usually also house camera shops. ***Cathay Photo***, Marina Square, 3rd floor of Centrepoint (Orchard Road) or Peninsula Plaza (Colonial core) provide a good range and good advice.

Camping gear

Campers' Corner, 1, Selegie Road, 01-11 Paradiz Centre, south of Little India, T3374743. Stocks a good range of camping and trekking equipment for sale and hire. Also organizes trekking expeditions around Singapore and Malaysia.

Essentials

Shopping centres on Orchard Road

Centrepoint (1)*, dominated by* Robinsons *department store,* Mothercare, Lacoste, *large* Times Bookshop *and an* MPH Bookshop, *Art Gallery on top floor:* Art Focus.

Far East Plaza (3)*, 14 Scotts Road: good for leather goods, camera and watch shops. Money-changers, tailors and several reasonable restaurants and a small food court; also some good electronics shops. Local department store,* Metro, *in the basement, sells clothes, household goods, shoes and accessories. Probably stays open the longest.*

Forum (5)*, predominantly children's clothes and a* Toys 'R' Us *is here.*

Hilton Shopping Plaza (6) *– connects* Hilton *and* Four Seasons Hotel *– top haute couture designers. Escalators state "Ladies watch your gowns".*

HPL House (9) - Emporio Armani *and a good choice of younger designer ware.*

Lucky Plaza (8)*, one of Singapore's first big complexes, now rather down-market. Reasonably good for electronics and cameras, jewellery and watches, scores of tailors; at ground level, along the front there are a number of opticians offering good deals on Raybans and designer sunglasses. Copy-watch touts at the bottom. Bargaining is possible in most of the stores here.*

Meridien (7)*, by* Meridien Hotel, DFS Collections *in basement for duty free goods, large very good quality furniture store – old and new wooden products.*

Ngee Ann City (9)*, this massive complex houses the* Takashimaya *department store, and over 100 speciality stores, mainly fashion boutiques –* Burberrys, Louis Vuitton, Tiffanys, Chanel, Charles Jourdain *and several restaurants.* Sparks, *a disco, is on the top floor. Popular with the rich and famous and a hang out for the young and trendy.*

Orchard Emerald (10)*, Quirky little individual shops – jewellery, unusual boutiques, etc.*

Orchard Road: Shopping Centres

1. Centrepoint
2. Delphi Orchard
3. Far East Centre
4. Far East Plaza
5. Forum
6. HPL House
7. Hilton Shopping Plaza
8. Lucky Plaza
9. Meridien
10. Ngee Ann C
11. Orchard Em
12. Orchard Pla

Related maps:
Orchard Road hotels, page 94
Fort Canning, *page 78*
Colour maps, *inside back cover*

Orchard Point (12), *large Australian cut price textiles,* B&N Factory Outlet. *Whole of top floor has art galleries and jade shops.*

Palais Renaissance (14),*hideously trendy design, the best in designer-boutiques and branded goods* (Versace, DKNY, *etc.).*

Plaza Singapura (16), Yaohan *department store and several music shops – both for CDs and for instruments.*

Paragon (23), *one of the best places for boutique browsers, particularly mens fashions; branded names, but not that exclusive.*

Park Mall (15), *Penang Road one of the newer piazzas, full of interior design items: furniture, textiles, lamps. Food in basement.*

Scotts (17), *6 Scotts Road: department store, 'Picnic' food court in basement, smart female boutiques with contemporary designers. Good electronics shops.*

Shaw Centre (18), *corner of Scotts Road and Orchard Road: Massive hi-tech block, with a large* Isetan *department store with all the concessions (including* Laura Ashley*), big bookshop –* Kinokuniya, *with a good range of English books and Lido Cineplex on top floors.*

Specialists' Centre (19), *just across from Centrepoint; downmarket department store.*

Tanglin (20), *top end of Orchard Road: a treasure trove of Asian antiques and curios, Persian rugs, closes between 1800 and 1900.*

Tangs (22), *next to* Marriott Hotel. *Very smart department store; the* Harrods *of Singapore.*

Wisma Atria (25), Isetan *department store, smart fashion boutiques, an* MPH *bookshop, and small food court.*

Wheelock Place (24), *new store, so far it only has a big* Marks & Spencer *in it.*

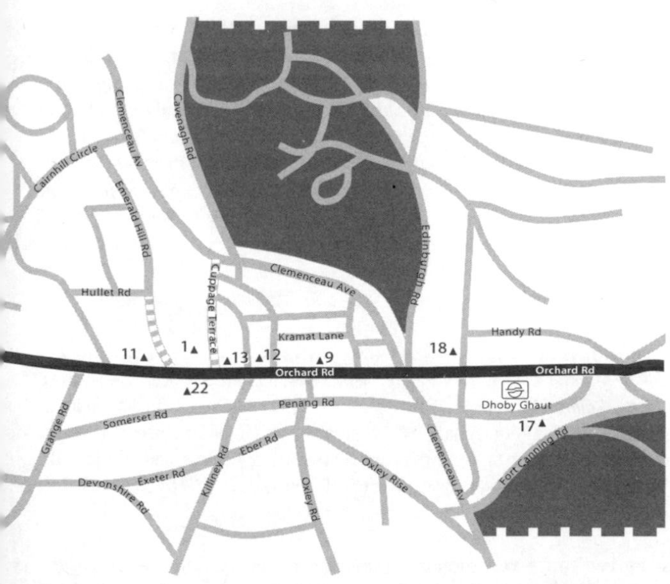

Orchard Point
Orchard Towers
Palais Renaissance
Paragon
17. Park Mall
18. Plaza Singapura
19. Scotts
20. Shaw Centre
21. Shaw House
22. Specialists' Centre
23. Tanglin
24. Tanglin Mall
25. Tang's
26. Wheelock Place
27. Wisma Atria

Shopping centres and plazas

Chinatown Point *Eu Tong Sen Street, Chinatown, specializes in small handicrafts.*
Funan Centre *Squeezed in between the Excelsior and Peninsula hotels in the colonial core, with five floors of shops. A good place for electrical equipment - in particular notebooks and software. One of the best and biggest food courts in the area in the basement. Huge screen in central atrium shows cartoons, opera, and pop concerts; makes a good stopping off spot if the children are tired.*
Liang Court *Opposite Riverside Point, and dominated by a large* Diamaru *department store, although there is also a big toy shop here -* The Toy Place *- as well as a good diving equipment shop. The Quayside Food Court in the basement is recommended (with a children's play area). There is also a* Swensen's *on the ground floor.*
Marina Square and Millenia Walk *A huge area of shops with a wide range of exclusive designer labels. There is also an Asian furniture and furnishings area and quite a few carpet shops.* ***Suntec City*** *close by has more shops of the same, a wide choice of restaurants and a big food court.*
Parco Bugis Junction *This very trendy a/c shophouse mall is on Victoria Street, north of the colonial core. It is packed with international names, as well as some quirky little shops and cafés, and is more fun to visit than most shopping centres. Mesmerizing fountain in the centre.*
Peninsula Plaza *Next to the Peninsula Hotel this is an old style shopping centre, mostly dedicated to electrical goods - cameras, videos and mobile phones.*
Pidemco Centre *South Bridge Road, Chinatown, good for traditional jewellery.*
Raffles City Complex *Opposite the Raffles Hotel, this huge glitzy, noisy and trendy shopping complex holds all the international (but not designer) labels - including* M&S, Max Mara, Body Shop *and* Knickerbox. *There are upmarket foodstalls on the lower level, with another mesmerizing fountain.*
Riverside Point *On the south side of the river, overlooking Clarke Quay. This new dockside development is reminiscent of London's Docklands or San Francisco's Canary Wharf. Totally un-Asian in design, and quite attractive. Cinema on the top floor, restaurants along the riverfront.*
Sim Lim Tower and Sim Lim Square *Both these shopping centres are on the edge of Little India on Jalan Besar and both sell the same range of electrical equipment - cameras, hi-fi and desktop computers.*
Stamford House *On the corner of Stamford Road and Hill Street this is a renovated and ornate colonial building with a range of upmarket shops. These include the* Eagle's Art Gallery, *an exclusive lighting shop, and the* Pennsylvania Country Oven Restaurant *and* Pennsylvania House *on the first floor for all your New England needs, nutritional and otherwise.*
For details of shopping plazas on Orchard Road, see previous page.

Children *Paw Marks*, 1st Floor, The Cannery, Clarke Quay, sells every conceivable type of teddy bear. ***Rainforest Shops***, 1st Floor, The Cannery, Clarke Quay, is an emporium of children's goodies from teddies to clocks, mobiles and furniture. There is a good model train shop in Liang Court. ***The Forum***, corner of Orchard Road and Cuscaden Road, is an entire shopping plaza given over to children, with ***Toys 'R' Us*** on the top floor and lots of other individual shops on the other 3 floors.

Children's clothes The best choice is to be found at ***The Forum***, corner of Cuscaden and Orchard roads, where there are at least 20 shops selling children's clothes. ***Papermoon***, Millenia Walk, Marina Square, T3378403, for pretty children's clothing.

Chinese porcelain

Ju-I Antiques and *Moon Gate*, both at Tanglin Shopping Centre (Orchard Road) and *Toh Foong* and *Soon Thye Cheang*, both on Temple Street in Chinatown are all good shops for porcelain. At the ***Ming Village***, 32 Pandan Road, visitors can watch reproduction Ming bases being made (see page 144). ***Holland Village***, west of the Botanic Gardens, has quite a number of porcelain shops.

Computers

The **Funan Centre** on North Bridge Road is computer city; even the Japanese buy here. **Sim Lim Tower** (upper floors) and the nearby **Albert Complex**, both just off Bukit Timah on Rochor Canal Road (see Little India map), are also good.

Fashion

Singapore boasts all the international designer labels - many of the shops are strung out along **Orchard Road**, although there are now quite a few shops in Marina Square. Designer fashion comes a bit cheaper in Singapore than other Southeast Asian capitals, as no duty is levied. *Emporio Armani*, with a big choice of younger designer wear is in HPL House, behind The Forum on Cuscaden Road (Orchard Road). Locally-designed clothes keep up with the trends and are very reasonably priced; look out for work by Benny Ony, Celia Lo and Tan Yoong. For exceptional value, slightly damaged clothes and factory seconds can be purchased from the *B&N Factory Outlet*, which has branches in several shopping centres and at The Cannery, Clarke Quay.

Electronic goods

Singapore has all the latest electronic equipment hot from Japan at duty free prices. Prices are still cheaper than in Europe, but can vary enormously. Check that items come with an international guarantee. The centres for electronic goods are **Sim Lim Tower** (corner of Jl Besar, Little India), and **Sim Lim Square** (corner of Rochor Canal Road, south of Little India). Of these two, Sim Lim Tower does not have a very good reputation. **Funan Centre** (between North Bridge Road and Hill Street, Colonial core) and **Peninsular Plaza**, next to Grand Plaza Hotel, Coleman Street (colonial core) have dozens of shops dedicated to cameras, phones, walkmans, video cameras, etc. **Lucky Plaza** (Orchard Road) and **Far East Plaza** (Scotts Road) both also have many electronics shops. The **Changi Airport duty free** is very competitive.

Fabrics

Mountain Looms, Block 16 Dempsey Road, west of Orchard Road, T4767629, very fine pieces of cloth from all over the region. See also Batik and silks, above.

Furniture

Singapore now has a plentiful range of old (or distressed) and new furniture, thanks to the boom in interest in interior design. **Dempsey Road** (west of Orchard Road) is a good place to start, as there are half a dozen warehouses there, with a good range of products (see the Antique section above for a listing). *Rustic Charm*, 1st Floor, The Cannery, Clarke Quay, T3343713, is a treasure trove of Asian reproduction furniture (both large and small) ranging from spice chests to Javanese benches to planters, chairs - well worth a browse and it's not too expensive. *Renee Hoy Fine Arts*, 1st Floor, Tanglin Shopping Centre, 19 Tanglin Road (western end of Orchard Road), T2351596, for a wide choice of Korean chests and some Thai furniture. *Babazar*, 31-35A Cuppage Terrace, off Orchard Road, T2357866, F7348665, has an excellent selection of beautiful Indian furniture. *A2 Atelier*, Le Meridien Shopping Centre, 100 Orchard Road, T7375081, F7359912, sells an extensive choice of reproduction furniture including 4-poster beds and some attractive chairs and chests. **Pacific Link Shopping Centre**, Marina Square, for shops selling a range of contemporary furniture and furnishings. Antique furniture in varying states of decay can be found at **Upper Paya Lebar Road**, just north of Macpherson Road; *Chin Yi Antique House, Mansion Antique House*, and *Tech Huat Antique House* can all be found here. *Just Anthony* is also on this road, south of Upper Serangoon Road; it sells antique and reproduction furniture. **River Valley Road**, just up from Tank Road, has several antique and second-hand furniture dealers (see the Antiques section). Reproduction antique furniture can also be found on Kelantan Lane.

Handicrafts Assorted Chinese knick-knacks including kites, lanterns, silk dressing gowns, opera masks, incense sticks, candle holders, lucky money and all the paraphernalia required for visiting a Chinese temple and attending a funeral can be found in several shops in **Chinatown**, notably on Smith and Sago streets. It is cheap and prices are not negotiable. The biggest Chinese emporia are in the **People's Park Complex**, Eu Tong Sen St and **Katong Shopping Centre**, East Coast Road. ***Singapore Handicraft Centre***, at Chinatown Point Shopping Centre on New Bridge Road specializes in small handicrafts, all a bit naff, but a good place to browse for small Asian gifts. ***Kuna's*** on Buffalo Road at the southern end of Little India sells Indian handicrafts. There are other shops around hère where Indian knick-knacks can be found. ***The Substation***, 45 Armenian St, Colonial core, runs a market on the last Sunday of every month where some arts and crafts are on sale; there is also a flea market every Sunday at Clarke Quay, where anyone can hire a pitch for S$25 for the day; there might be some bargains to be found.

Indian/Southeast Asian goods For Indian silks, sarees, gold jewellery and trinkets try Serangoon Road, otherwise known as Little India, but by far the best shop for Indian exotica is ***Natraj's Arts & Crafts***, 03-202 Marina Square shopping centre, which is in a row of Far Eastern handicraft shops. Natraj's specialities are the papier maché, Bharata Natayam dancing girl dolls which wobble and shake just like the real thing. For Malay handicrafts there's a handicraft centre in a reconstruction of a Malay kampung at Malay Village on Geylang Serai (east of the city) (see page 146).

Interior Decorating ***Rustic Charm***, 1st Floor, The Cannery, Clarke Quay for a good range of small, quirky pieces; ***Pennsylvania House***, Stamford House, Stamford Road (Colonial core) for New England knick knacks; ***Peter Hoe***, CHIJMES, 30 Victoria Street, T/F3396880, for an interesting assortment of small scale pieces, some Indonesian.

Jade ***Kwok Gallery***, Far East Shopping Centre (Orchard Road) and in The Cannery, Clarke Quay.

Jewellery Gold (mostly Asian, 18, 22 or 24 carat), precious stones and pearls (freshwater and cultured) are all easily found in Singapore and good value. **NB** Styles and designs are quite different from the west. Gold is a good buy but it too looks different. The Singapore Assay Office uses a merlion head as a hallmark. Most of the jewellery shops are in **South Bridge Road**; **Pidemco Centre** on South Bridge Road, Chinatown, is known as Jewellery Mart. **North Bridge Road** and **People's Park**, both in Chinatown, have reputable goldsmiths selling items by the weight set for the day's prices. For Indian goldsmiths, go to **Serangoon Road**. *Zero Gravity*, Ground Floor, Merchant Court, Clarke Quay. For unusual contemporary jewellery try an un-named shop in the basement of Raffles City Complex (Colonial core) has some perspex jewellery and strange puzzles, quirky key rings and mobiles. ***Peter Hoe***, CHIJMES, 30 Victoria Street (Colonial core) offers a good range of Indonesian jewellery. Don't be taken in by shops along Orchard Road advertising 'incredible reductions' - usually they're not. Bargaining is de rigeur, and it requires much shopping-around to gain an appreciation of what the true price should be. ***Singapore Gems & Metals Co***, 7 Kung Chong Road, T4759733, organize tours around their processing workroom to see gems cut, polished and set.

Markets The most accessible market of interest is the **Zhujiao (formerly KK) Market** on the corner of Bukit Timah and Serangoon roads, at the southern end of Little India. It is a hive of activity and sells everything from flowers to fish and meat to spices, and every

Almanacs) The Hindu festival of lights commemorates the victory of Lord Krishna over the demon king Narakasura, symbolizing the victory of light over darkness and good over evil. Every Hindu home is brightly lit and decorated for the occasion. Shrines are swamped with offerings and altars piled high with flowers. Row upon row of little earthen oil lamps are lit to guide the souls of departed relatives in their journey back to the next world, after their brief annual visit to earth during Deepavali.

Guru Nanak's Birthday (movable) The first of the ten gurus of the Sikh faith. The domed Gurdwara in Katong (Wilkinson Road) is buzzing on the Sikh holy day.

Thimithi Festival (movable, in the Hindu month of Aipasi) This Hindu festival in honour of the goddess Draupadi, often draws a big crowd to watch devotees fulfil their vows by walking over a 3m long pit of burning coals in the courtyard of the Sri Mariamman Temple on South Bridge Road. Fire walking starts at around 1600 on the arrival of the procession from Perumal Temple on Serangoon Road.

Essentials

December

Christmas Day (25th: public holiday) Christmas in Singapore is a spectacle of dazzling lights, the best along Orchard Road, where the roadside trees are bejewelled with strings of fairy lights. Shopping centres and hotels compete to have the year's most extravagant or creative display. These seasonal exhibitions are often conveniently designed to last through to Chinese New Year. It would not be untypical, for example, to find Santa riding on a man-eater in the year of the tiger. In shopping arcades, sweating tropical Santa Clauses dash through the fake snow. Choirs from Singapore's many churches line the sidewalks and Singaporeans go shopping.

Entertainment

For hotels, restaurants, bars, clubs and theatre see listings by areas in Section 3.

Cabaret/Music

Neptune Theatre Restaurant, Collyer Quay. *Studebakers*, Penthouse of Pacific Plaza, Orchard Road. Live performances and dancing. *Boom Boom Room*, 3 New Bugis Street. Cabaret.

Chinese Street Opera (Wayang)

Dramatizations of Chinese legends (the heroes wear red or green, the emperor, yellow and the villains, black). Clarke Quay now has a permanent (though it looks deliberately temporary) stage, where there are short performances every Wednesday and Friday at 1945-2030 (see page 88). The audience is encouraged to watch the artists apply their make-up backstage from 1815 and the performance starts at 1930. Subtitles are projected onto a screen.

Cinema

With more than 50 cinemas, Singapore gets most of the blockbusters soon after their release in the States. These will be more entertaining now that the censors are easing up; there's a new RA category for those over 21 years of age, which means a little more sex and violence hits the screens. The *Straits Times* Life section publishes listings daily. When the *Cathay*, at the southeastern end of Orchard Road, opened in 1939 and became the first air-conditioned public building in Singapore, local celebrities turned up in fur coats. It is still screening films 60 years on - Dhoby Ghaut is the closest MRT stop. There are several new cinemas, showing three or four films at any one time. These include the complex at *Riverside Point* opposite Clarke Quay, *Parco Bugis Junction* on Victoria Street, opposite Bugis MRT, the *Lido Cineplex* at the Shaw Centre, Orchard Road and another new complex at *Suntec City*, Marina Square. For arthouse films, *The Picturehouse* next to the *Cathay* on Orchard Road is your best bet.

Live music in town

Most of the larger hotels have live music, usually house bands - often Filipino - playing covers, along with the statutory pianist tinkling in the lobby. Below are just some of the better known venues. See the detailed listings in each area for more information.

Colonial core

Somerset's, Westin Stamford Hotel,. *Raffles City: jazz.*

Singapore River and the City

***Crazy Elephant**, Clarke Quay. House band, mostly covers.*

***Harry's Quayside**, 28 Boat Quay: jazz Wednesday-Saturday, buses on Sunday.*

Orchard Road

***Brannigan's**, Basement,* Hyatt Regency, *10/12 Scotts Road: funk and soul covers by regional combos.*

***Fabrice's World Music Bar**, Basement,* Singapore Marriott Hotel, *320 Orchard Road: good bands from around the world*

***Five Disco**, Orchard Plaza, Orchard Road: good house covers band.*

***Hard Rock Café**, Cuscaden Road: AOR covers, forget conversation.*

***Jack's Place**, Yen San Building (opposite* Mandarin Hotel), *Orchard Road: regional bands play covers.*

Kaspia Bar, Hilton Hotel, *Orchard Road: jazz.*

***Saxophone**, 23 Cuppage Terrace: good jazz, also R&B.*

***Top Ten Club**, Orchard Towers, 400 Orchard Road: good black American or Philippine disco funk bands, some soul as well.*

Sport

Spectator sports See *Straits Times* for current listings. Most games of any significance take place on the Padang or at the National Stadium which seats up to 60,000 and regularly stages Malaysia Cup football matches and the occasional exhibition match with touring league sides from abroad (buses 14 and 16 go direct from Orchard Road).

Bicycling This is not a bicycle-friendly city. Bicycles are available for hire at a number of public parks and other quieter spots on the island including East Coast Parkway, Sentosa, Pasar Ris, Bishan and Pulau Ubin. Expect to pay S$3-8/hour or around S$20/day; some outfits also ask for a deposit. ***East Coast Bicycle Centre***, East Coast Parkway, bikes for rent, including tandems, (S$3/hour), open 0800-1830. ***Sentosa Island Bicycle Station***, near Ferry Terminal S$3/hour, Monday-Friday 0900-1800, Saturday and Sunday 0900-1900.

Bowling Most alleys charge from S$3.00-$4.00 a game; bowling after 1800 and on weekends is more expensive. Shoe hire, S$0.50. Some recommendations out of the 16 alleys in Singapore: ***Jackie's Bowl***, 542B East Coast Road; ***Kallang Bowl***, 5 Stadium Walk; ***ODS Bowl***, 269 Pasir Panjang Road; ***Orchard Bowl***, 8 Grange Road; ***Plaza Bowl***, Textile Centre, Jl Sultan; ***Super Bowl***, 15 Marina Grove. Contact the Singapore Tenpin Bowling Congress, T3550136, for more information.

Canoeing ***Canoe Centre***, 1390 East Coast Parkway (just along the beach from the Lagoon Food Centre). Monday, Tuesday, Friday 1000-1800, Sunday 0930-1830. Closed on public holidays, S$15 for 2 hours. Also possible to hire canoes at the swimming lagoon on Sentosa Island and at Changi Point.

Cricket ***Singapore Cricket Club***, Connaught Drive, matches played most weekend afternoons.

Flying

Republic of Singapore Flying Club, T4810502, book 1 month in advance; S$300/hour. Open 0900-1800 Monday-Sunday.

Golf

There is no shortage of courses; they are beautifully kept and non-members can play at most of the private club courses on weekdays. Green fees are expensive and increase significantly at weekends. Many also have driving ranges. ***Changi Golf Club***, Nethavon Road, 9-hole, par 68, green fees S$50 weekdays, caddy S$14-19, T5455133; ***Keppel Club***, Bukit Chermin. 18-hole, par 72, green fees S$90 weekdays, S$150 weekends, caddy S$18-25, T2735522; ***Raffles Country Club***, Jl Ahmad Ibrahim, Tengah Reservoir, two 18-holers, par 71 and 69, green fees S$100 weekdays, S$160 weekends, T8617655; ***Seletar Country Club***, Seletar Airbase, 9-hole, par 70, green fees S$80 Tuesday-Friday only, caddy, S$15-20; ***Sembawang Country Club***, Sembawang Road, 18-hole, par 70, green fees S$60 weekdays, S$100 weekends, caddy S$18-24, T2570642; ***Sentosa Golf Club***, Sentosa Island, 18-hole, par 72, green fees S$60 weekdays, S$120 weekends, T2750022; ***Wondergolf*** on Sentosa provides a choice of courses for young and old, one 9-hole course and two 18-holes. Admission: S$8, S$4 for children, open 0900-2115 (last entry). Take monorail to station 4. ***Singapore Island Country Club***, Upper Thompson Road, two 18-holers, both par 72, green fees S$130 weekdays only, caddy S$18-21, T4592222; ***Warren Golf Club***, Folkstone Road, 9-hole, par 70, green fees S$50 weekdays only, caddies compulsory, S$18-25, T7776533.

Golf Driving ranges Many of the golf courses listed above also have driving ranges including ***Keppel Club***, ***Raffles Country Club***, ***Sembawang Country Club*** and ***Warren Golf Club***. The following are dedicated driving ranges: ***Green Fairways***, Fairways Drive, off Eng Neo Avenue, S$3 for 48 balls. Open 0700-2200 Monday-Sunday, T4688409; ***Marina Bay Golf and Country Club***, 6 Marina Greens, 150 bays, 230m fairway, S$9 for 100 balls, open 0700-2300 Monday-Sunday, T2212811; ***Parkland***, 920 East Coast Parkway, 60 bays, 200m fairway, S$6 for 95 balls (S$5 weekdays before 1530), open 0700-2200 Monday-Sunday, T4406726.

Horse racing

At the ***Singapore Turf Club***, Bukit Timah Road, T4603400. Race days are Saturday or Sunday with the first race at 1330 and the last at 1800. In 1998 there were 32 race days spread through the year. Malaysian racing is also broadcast on huge 18 x 16 metre screens. No jeans, T-shirts, flip-flops etc, weekend only. Admission S$5.15 or S$10.30 for the public stands. Foreign passport holders (excluding Malaysian) can gain access to the air-conditioned Members' enclosure for S$20.60. Dress code is smart casual.

Horse riding

Singapore Polo Club, 80 Mount Pleasant Road, T2564530 for details, courses Monday-Sunday 0700-1000 and 1630-1900. ***Green Dale Riding School***, 0830-2130 daily, S$145 for an introductory class, T4602209.

Polo

Singapore Polo Club on Thomson Road, every Tuesday, Thursday and Saturday.

Roller skating

Sentosa Roller Skating, Jelly Road, Sentosa Island.

Sailing and windsurfing

Changi Sailing Club, Changi Village, for those interested in crewing yachts, the club has a noticeboard listing possibilities; ***East Coast Sailing Centre***, East Coast Park Swimming Lagoon, 1210 East Coast Parkway, T4495118, two day courses in small craft: Lasers (S$270) and windsurfers (S$80), rental rates: lasers and windsurfers, S$20/hour, barbecue restaurant.

Scuba diving

PADI have now opened an office in Singapore where you can get all the latest information on the best dive spots in the region and can also acquire certification, 39 Tampines St 92, #05-00 Form Building, T7859896, F7858168. Most diving schools will run courses (PADI and/or NAUI) and many offer rental of equipment and dive guides.

Asia Aquatic, T5368116; ***Great Blue Dive Shop***, T4670767; ***Leeway Sub-Aquatic Paradise***, T7431208; ***Mako Sub-Aquatics***, T7741440; ***Marsden Bros***, T7788287; ***Pro Diving Services***, T2912261; ***Sentosa Sports Centre***, Eastern Lagoon, rents out diving gear and snorkels. Equipment hire and open water scuba diving instruction; ***Sentosa Water Sports Centre*** (Scuba Schools International), World Trade Centre; ***Sharkeys Scubanauts***, T5383733.

Snooker Singapore has several huge snooker halls, where dress code is casual-smart. Prices between S$5 and S$10/hour. ***Academy of Snooker***, Albert Complex, Albert Street, T2862879; ***King's Leisurium***, Marina Square, T3393811; ***King's Snookerium***, Amara Hotel Shopping Complex and Marina Square, S$6.60-9.80/hour, open 1000-1400 Monday-Friday, 1000-1500 Saturday-Sunday.

Squash ***200***, Yio Chu Kang Road, S$6/hour, 0700-2300 Monday-Sunday; ***National Stadium***, S$6/hour, 0700-2200.

Swimming Most of the big hotels have swimming pools, some of which are open to non-residents for a fee. ***River Valley Swimming Pool***, River Valley Road, opposite Clarke Quay. Open Monday-Sunday until 2200, admission $1 weekdays, $1.20 at the weekends, enormous lengths pool and a children's pool, recommended for the serious swimmer; ***Yan Kit Swimming Pool***, Yan Kit Road, southern end of Chinatown, open Monday-Sunday 0800-2130, admission $1 weekdays, $1.20 at the weekends, probably the oldest public pool in Singapore but still popular and a good place for lengths; ***Big Splash***, East Coast Parkway, wave pool, current pool and the longest water-slides in Southeast Asia, admission S$3, S$2 for children, open 1200-1800 Monday-Friday, 0900-1800 weekends; ***CN West Leisure Park***, 9 Japanese Garden Road, wave pool and 15 metre long water-slide, admission S$4, S$2 for children, open 1200-1800 Tuesday-Friday, 0930-1800 weekends. Singapore has 20 public swimming pools listed in the *Yellow Pages*.

Tennis All courts charge about S$6-10/hour and are open 0700-2300 Monday-Sunday. ***Burghley Squash and Tennis Centre***, 43 Burghley Drive; ***Clementi Recreation Centre***, 12 West Coast Walk; ***Dover Tennis Centre***, Dover Road; ***Farrer Park Tennis Courts***, Rutland Road; ***Kallang Tennis Centre***, Stadium Road; ***Singapore Tennis Centre***, 1020 East Coast Parkway; ***St Wilfrid Squash and Tennis Centre***, St Wilfrid Road.

Water skiing Water skiing off Sembawang, on the island's north coast or on the Kallang River. ***Bernatt Boating and Skiing***, T2575859, S$80/hour; ***William Water Sports***, Ponggol Point, T2826879, S$60-80/hour; ***Cowabunga Ski Centre***, T3448813.

Further reading

Libraries National Library, Stamford Road (next to the National Museum). Plenty of English books and travel guides and an array of computers providing information on just about anything - an excellent place to spend a rainy afternoon.

Singaporean novelists **Baratham, Gopal** (1991) *A candle or the sun*, Times Books: Singapore. A book which deals with some of the less savoury aspects of living in Singapore. The story is based on the experience of a novelist who is asked by the government to spy on his lover.

Dingwall, Alastair (1994) *Traveller's literary companion to South-east Asia*, In Print: Brighton. Experts on Southeast Asian language and literature select extracts from novels and other books by western and regional writers. The extracts are annoyingly brief, but it gives a good overview of what is available.

Jeyaretnam, Philip (1987) *First loves*, Times Books: Singapore. A collection of sharply observed short stories, with an emphasis on material accumulation in a society whose soul is lost in the quest for money.

Jeyaretnam, Philip (1994) *Abraham's promise*, Times Books: Singapore. An excellent novel about a teacher whose life is ruined when he falls foul of the ruling party. It is hard to believe that the fact that Philip Jeyaretnam's father is Joshua Jeyaretnam (JBJ), the opposition politician who was bankrupted by former prime minister Lee Kuan Yew and publicly disgraced, is a coincidence. The book, though, has been published by a Singaporean publisher possibly indicating a slight softening on the part of the authorities.

Lim, Catherine (1978) *Little ironies*, Heinemann Asia: Singapore. Lim is another of Singapore's younger breed of novelist, more introspective and critical of the Republic's progress, and more concerned with getting beneath the façade of unity and success. *Little ironies* is a collection of short stories. Her other books include *They do return*, a collection of ghost stories and *Or else, the lightning God* (1982), another set of short stories. Her work is very popular in Singapore.

Shelley, Rex (1991) *The shrimp people*, Times Books: Singapore. A novel about the experiences of the Eurasian community in Singapore during the 1950s, when the Communists were in the ascendancy.

Soh, Michael (1973) *Son of a mother*, Oriental Press: Singapore. Singaporean novelist Michael Soh recounts the story of a grocer threatened with eviction, in the process showing the emphasis on filial duty and respect.

Other Singaporean writers with a considerable local following, and whose books can be easily purchased in Singapore, include **Ho Min Fong** and **Lim Thean Soo**.

Essentials

Novels about Singapore

Anderson, Patrick (1955) *Snake wine: a Singapore episode*, Chatto and Windus: London. Anderson taught at the University of Malaya in Singapore during the 1950s and this novel is semi-autobiographical, tracing life on the campus during a particularly volatile period.

Clavell, James *King Rat*. Perhaps the single most widely read novel based in Singapore, it tells of life in the Japanese prisoner of war camp at Changi where Clavell was incarcerated.

Conrad, Joseph (1915) *Victory: an island tale*, Penguin: London. Arguably Conrad's finest novel, based in the Malay Archipelago.

Conrad, Joseph (1920) *The rescue*, Penguin: London. Set in the Malay Archipelago in the 1860s; the hero, Captain Lingard, is forced to choose between his Southeast Asian friend and his countrymen.

Conrad, Joseph (1988) *Lord Jim*, Everyman Classic: Dent. Conrad visited Singapore during his years as a seaman and the 'eastern port' in Lord Jim is unmistakably Singapore.

Farrell, JG (1979) *The Singapore grip*, Fontana: London. A best-selling thriller about Singapore during the months leading up to the Japanese invasion and occupation.

Theroux, Paul (1973) *Saint Jack*, Penguin. Paul Theroux taught in the English Department at the University of Singapore and this novel is set in Singapore. Its main character is Jack Flowers who sets up a boat-brothel to meet the demands of American GIs visiting the island.

Theroux, Paul (1977) *The consul's file*, Penguin. A collection of short stories, mainly based in Malaysia but also drawing on Singapore material.

History

Barber, Noel *Sinister twilight*, Arrow: London. A book about the fall of Singapore, a well-respected account.

Collis, Maurice *Raffles*, Century: London. An easy to read biography of Raffles, fascinating for those with an interest in the history, not just of Singapore, but of the Dutch East Indies too.

Elphick, Peter (1995) *Singapore: the pregnable fortress,*London: Coronet. Thick and highly-informed history of the Malaya campaign and the fall of Singapore, drawing on recently released British documents. Portrays the loss of the island as the result of a series of blunders from Churchill right down to officers on the ground.
Lee Kuan Yew (1998) *The Singapore story*, Prentice Hall. The first volume of the former Prime Minister's two-volume memoirs. It is typical Lee: forthright, opinionated and pulling no punches. A remarkable insight into the mind of a remarkable man. This first volume covers the years from childhood to 1965.
Osborne, Milton (1979) *Southeast Asia: an introductory history*, Allen & Unwin: Sydney. Good introductory history, clearly written, published in a portable paperback edition and recently revised and reprinted.
Pastel Portraits (1984) *Singapore's Architectural Heritage*. A coffee table book with good pictorial record of the variety of shophouses to be found around the city and descriptions of the evolution of the different sections of town.
Steinberg, DJ et al (1987) *In search of Southeast Asia: a modern history*, University of Hawaii Press: Honolulu. The best standard history of the region; it skilfully examines and assesses general processes of change and their impacts from the arrival of the Europeans in the region. Only a small proportion, though, deals with Singapore.
Tarling, Nicholas (1992) *Cambridge history of Southeast Asia*, CUP: Cambridge. Two volume edited study, long and expensive with contributions from most of the leading historians of the region. A thematic and regional approach is taken, not a country one, although the history is fairly conventional.
Turnbull, Mary C (1989) *A history of Malaysia, Singapore and Brunei*, Allen and Unwin. A very orthodox history of Malaysia, Singapore and Brunei, clearly written for a largely academic/student audience.
Wurtzburg, CE *Raffles of the Eastern Isles*, OUP (1954). Comprehensive account of Raffles' life in this dense volume.

Culture, politics and economics

Buruma, Ian (1989) *God's dust*, Jonathan Cape: London. Enjoyable journey through Burma, Thailand, Malaysia and Singapore along with the Philippines, Taiwan, South Korea and Japan; journalist Buruma questions how far culture in this region has survived the intrusion of the West.
Craig, Jo Ann *Culture Shock Singapore!*, Times Books: Singapore. This recounts the do's and don'ts of living in Singapore. Useful for those moving to Singapore for a longer stretch.
Minchin, James *No man is an island*, Allen and Unwin: Sydney. A biography of Lee Kuan Yew, and none too laudatory. Best to buy it before arrival, or in Malaysia - Singapore's bookshops do not stock it.
Selven, TS (1990) *Singapore: the ultimate island*. Another critical biography of Lee Kuan Yew and Singapore Inc. Again, it's not available in Singapore.
Sesser, Stan (1993) *The lands of charm and cruelty: travels in Southeast Asia*, Picador: Basingstoke. A series of collected narratives first published in the *New Yorker* including essays on Singapore, Laos, Cambodia, Burma and Borneo. Finely observed and thoughtful, the book is an excellent travel companion. The 66-page essay on Singapore is possibly the best available.

Travel and natural history

Young, Gavin (1991) *In search of Conrad*, Hutchinson: London. This well-known travel writer retraces the steps of Conrad; part travel-book, part fantasy, it is worth reading but not up to the standard of his other books.

Business

Leeson, Nick (1996) *Rogue trader*, London: Little Brown. The story from the horse's mouth, so to speak, and not surprisingly the author (Leeson) ends up being an apologist for the subject (Leeson).
Rawnsley, Judith (1995) *Going for broke: Nick Leeson and the collapse of Barings Bank*,

London: Harper Collins. This book is written by a former employee of Barings in Tokyo. It has perhaps the best feel for the company and its business ethos - an ethos which created the environment in which Leeson could have got away with so much for so long and at so great a cost. Rawnsley's book, though, was published before the London and Singapore authorities published their reports on the debacle.
Fay, Stephen (1996) *The collapse of Barings*, London: Richard Cohen Books. Fay's book is probably the most detailed of the three and although it may not have the 'insider' feel of Rawnsley's volume, does have the opportunity to pick over the bones of the Singapore and London reports.

Magazines

Asiaweek (weekly) Rather like a regional *Time* magazine in style. *The Far Eastern Economic Review* (weekly) Authoritative Hong Kong-based regional magazine; their correspondents based in each country provide knowledgeable, in-depth analysis particularly on economics and politics.

Government publications

The Singapore government's Ministry of Information and the Arts publishes a wide range of useful information on the country. They produce, for example, an annual volume called *Singapore facts and figures* as well as a more detailed yearbook.

Transport guides

Invaluable for making the most of Singapore's incomparable public transportation is the annual *TransitLink Guide* which lists all bus and MRT routes and stops. A snip at S$1.40 for 413 pocket-sized pages.

Maps

Regional maps Bartholomew *Southeast Asia* (1:5,800,000); Bartholomew *Singapore and Malaysia* (1:150,000); Nelles *Southeast Asia* (1:4,000,000); Hildebrand *Thailand, Burma, Malaysia and Singapore* (1:2,800,000); ITM (International Travel Map) *Southeast Asia*.
Country maps Nelles *Singapore* (1:22,500); Bartholomew *Singapore*.
Other maps *Secret Map of Singapore; Secret Food Map of Singapore; Singapore Street Directory*.
Free maps Various free maps are available and can be picked up from hotels and tourist offices. The best is *The map of Singapore* published by Miller Freeman Pte Ltd.

Singapore on the internet

Listed below are Internet addresses which access information on Asia generally, the Southeast Asian region, or Singapore. Web sites offer a whole range of information on a vast variety of topics. Below is only a selection. Note that Web sites on Asia are multiplying like rabbits and this makes searching a sometimes frustrating business.
http://www.singnet.com.sg/~leeahkee/
Good links to government, educational, travel, employment, leisure and food sites.
http://www.yahoo.com/Regional Countries/[name of country]
Insert country name to access information including material from other travel guides.
http://www.city.net/regions/asia
Pointer to information on Asian countries.
http://www.branch.com:80/silkroute/
Information on hotels, travel, news and business in Asia.
http://www.agora.stm.it/politic
Information on political parties and organizations, good links, by country or by region
http://www.aseansec.org
Homepage of the Asean Secretariat, the Southeast Asian regional organization of which Singapore is a founder member. Lots of government statistics, acronyms etc.
http://www.ste.com.sg
Provides a bulletin board for businesses to post notices and advertisements and to market their products; also a directory of licensed travel agents in Singapore.

Useful addresses

Banks and money changers in Singapore Singapore has 13 local banks but the big four are DBS Bank, United Overseas Bank, Overseas-Chinese Banking Corporation and Overseas Union Bank. Most leading foreign banks are well represented in Singapore, although some in the financial district are offshore branches only and may not provide services to the public. All local banks and the majority of big names have foreign exchange facilities and most have branches within easy access of the main tourist areas. Check *Yellow Pages* for lists of branches. There are also licenced money-changers in all main shopping centres; many give better rates than the banks for TCs, but it's worth shopping around.

Chase Manhattan Bank NA, Shell Tower, 50 Raffles Place. ***Citibank NA***, Robina House, 1 Shenton Way. ***DBS Bank***, DBS Building, 6 Shenton Way. ***Deutsche Bank AG***, 15-08 DBS Building Tower 2. ***Far Eastern Bank***, 156 Cecil St. ***Hong Kong and Shanghai Banking Corporation***, Ocean Building, 10 Collyer Quay. ***Keppel Bank***, 10 Hoe Chiang Road, 06-00. ***Overseas Chinese Banking Corporation***, OCBC Centre, 65 Chulia St. ***Overseas Union Bank***, OUB Centre, 1 Raffles Place. ***Standard Chartered Bank***, 0900/1100 Plaza by the Park. ***United Overseas Bank***, UOB Plaze 1.

Churches **Anglican** *St Andrew's Cathedral*, Coleman Street, T3376104, services at 0700, 0800, 0930 and 1100; *St George's*, Minden Road, opposite the entrance to Botanic Gardens, very popular evangelical church, services at 0800 and 1000.

Roman Catholic *Cathedral of the Good Shepherd*, Victoria Street, mass at 0800, 1000 and 1800 on Sunday, Monday-Friday at 0700 and 1315, Saturday at 0700 and 1830; *St Joseph's Church*, Victoria Street, mass on Sunday at 0830, 1000 and 1700, weekdays at 1745.

Others *Wesley Methodist*, 5 Fort Canning Road (Dhoby Ghaut MRT), T3361433; *Fairfield Methodist*, on corner of Tanjong Pagar and Maxwell roads. Services at 0830 and 1030 on Sunday, with communion on 1st Sunday of the month; *Orchard Road Presbyterian*, 3 Orchard Road, T3376681, services at 0900 and 1800; *Prinsep Street Presbyterian*, 144 Prinsep Street, T3384571; *Queenstown Baptist*, 495 Margaret Drive; *Calvary Charismatic Centre*, 179 River Valley Road (5th Floor, former SISIR Building), T3392955.

Singaporean embassies worldwide

Australia High Commission, 17 Forster Crescent, Yarralumla, Canberra ACT 2600, T(6) 273 3944

Austria c/o Embassy in Bonn; Consulate: Raiffeisen Zentral Bank, Osterreich AG, Am Stadtpark 9, 1030 Vienna, T(222) 71707 1229

Belgium 198 Ave Franklin Roosevelt, 1050 Brussels, T(2) 660-30908

Canada 1305-999 Hastings St, Vancouver, T(604) 669 5115

China 4 Liangmahe Nanlu, Sanlitun, Beijing 100600, T(1) 432 3926

CIS Per Voyevodina 5, Moscow, T(095) 241 3702

Denmark c/o High Commission in London

Finland c/o Embassy in Moscow

France, 12 Square de l'Ave Foch, 75116 Paris, T4500 3361

Germany Sudstrasse 133, 5300 Bonn 2, T(228) 31 2007

Greece 10-12 Kifissias Ave, 151 25 Maroussi, Athens, T(1) 683 4875

Hong Kong Units 901-2, Admiralty Centre Tower 1, 9th Flr, 18 Harcourt Rd, Hong Kong, T527 2212

India High Commission E-6 Chandragupta Marg, Chanakyapuri, New Delhi 110021, T(11) 60 4162. Consulates: Bombay T(2) 204 3205; Madras T(44) 47 6637

Indonesia Block X/4 KAV No 2, Jl HR Rasuna Said, Kuningan, Jakarta 12950, T(21) 520 1489. Consulate: Medan, North Sumatra, T(61) 51 3366

Japan 14th Flr, Osaka, Kokusai Building, 3-13 Azuchimachi 2-Chome, Chuo-Ku, Tokyo T(6) 261 5131
Malaysia 209 Jln Tun Razak, Kuala Lumpur 50400, T(03) 261 6277
Netherlands Rotterdam Plaza, Weena 670 3012 CN, Rotterdam, T(20) 404 2111
New Zealand 17 Kabul St, Khandallah, Wellington, T(4) 79 2076
Norway c/o High Commission in London. Consulate: Oslo, T(47) 2 485000
Portugal Lusograin, Rua dos Franqueiros 135-1, 1100 Lisbon, T(1) 87 8647
Spain, Huertas 13, Madrid 28012, T(1) 429 3193
Sri Lanka High Commission c/o High Commission in New Delhi
Sweden c/o Embassy in Bonn. Consulate: Stockholm T(8) 663 7488
Switzerland c/o Embassy in Bonn
Thailand 129 South Sathorn Rd, Bangkok, T(2) 286 2111
UK 9 Wilton Crescent, London, SW1X 8SA, T(0171) 235 8315
USA 1824 R St NW, Washington DC 20009-1691, T202 667 7555. Consulates: Los Angeles T714 760 9400; Minneapolis T612 332 8063.

Foreign embassies and consulates in Singapore

Australia 25 Napier Rd, T7379311
Austria Shaw Centre, 1 Scotts Rd, 24-05/06, T2354088
Belgium International Plaza, 10 Anson Rd, T2207677
Brunei 325 Tanglin Rd, T7339055
Canada 15th Storey IBM Towers, 80 Anson Rd, T3253200
China People's Republic of, 70-76 Dalvey Rd, T7343080
Denmark 13-01 United Sq, 101 Thomson Rd, T2503383
Finland 21-03 United Sq, 101 Thomson Rd, T2544042
France 5 Gallop Rd, T4664866
Germany 14-01 Far East Shopping Centre, 545 Orchard Rd, T7737135
Greece 11-25 Anson Centre, 51 Anson Rd, T2208622
India 31 Grange Rd, T7376777
Indonesia 7 Chatsworth Rd, T7377422
Ireland 08-06 Tiong Bahru Plaza, 298 Tiong Bahru Rd, T2768935
Israel 58 Dalvey Rd, T2350966
Italy 27-02 United Sq, 101 Thomson Rd, T2506022
Japan 34th Storey IBM Towers, 80 Anson Rd, T2358855
Malaysia 301 Jervois Rd, T2350111
Myanmar (Burma) 15 St Martin's Drive, T7350209
Netherlands 13-01 Liat Towers, 541 Orchard Rd, T7371155
New Zealand 15th Storey, Ngee Ann City, Tower A, 391A Orchard Rd, T2359966
Norway 44-01 Hong Leong Building, 16 Raffles Quay, T2207122
Philippines 20 Nassim Rd, T7373977
Poland 33-11 Shaw Towers, 100 Beach Rd, T2942513
South Africa 15-00 Odeon Towers, 331 North Bridge Rd, T3393319
Spain 05-08/09 Thong Teck Building, 15 Scotts Rd, T7329788
Sweden 05-08 PUB Building, 111 Somerset Rd, T7342771
Switzerland 1 Swiss Club Link, T4685788
Thailand 370 Orchard Rd, T7372644, open 0915-1215, 1500-1645, applications for visa am only
UK 100 Tanglin Rd, T4739333
USA 27 Napier Rd, T4769100
Vietnam 10 Leedon Park, T4625938

Singapore Tourist Boards

Australia Level 11, AWA Building, 47 York St, Sydney, T(61-2) 9290 2888, F(61-2) 9290 2555, and 8th Flr, St George's Court, 16 St George's Terrace, Perth, T(09) 3258578, F(09) 2213864
Canada Standard Life Centre, 121 King St West, Suite 1000, Toronto, Ontario, T(416)

Essentials

3638898, F(416) 3635752

France Centre d'Affaires Le Louvre, 2 Place du Palais-Royal, Paris, T(01) 42971616, F(01) 42971617

Germany Hochstrasse 35-37, Frankfurt, T(069) 920 7700, F(069) 297 8922

Italy c/o Theodore Trancu & Associates, Corso Plebisciti 15, 20129 Milano, Italy, T(39-2) 7000 3981, F(39-2) 738 1032

Japan 1st Flr, Yamato Seimei Building, 1 Chome, 1-7 Uchisaiwai-cho, Chiyoda-ku Tokyo 100, T(81-3) 3593 3388, F(81-3) 3591 1480; and Osaka City Air Terminal, 4F 1-4-1, Minato-Machi, Naniwa-ku, Osaka 556, T(81-6) 635 3087, F(81-6) 635 3089

Hong Kong Room 2003, Central Plaza, 18 Harbour Rd, Wanchai, T5989290, F5981040

New Zealand 3rd Flr, 43 High St, Auckland, PO Box 857, T(64-9) 3581191, F(64-9) 3581196

Switzerland Löwenstrasse 51, CH-8044, Zurich, T (01) 2117474, F(01) 2117422

South Africa 52 3rd Ave, Parktown North 2193, PO Box 81260, T(27-11) 788 0701, F(27-11) 442 7599

Thailand c/o MDK Consultants, Ruamrudi Building, 4th Flr, 566 Ploenchit Rd Lumpini, Bangkok 10330, T(66-2) 252 4117, F(66-2) 252 4118

UK 1st Flr Carrington House, 126-130 Regent St, London W1R 5FE, T(0171) 4370033 F(0171) 7342191

USA Two Prudential Plaza, 180 North Stetson Ave, Suite 1450, Chicago, T312 9381888, F 312 9380086; 8484 Wilshire Blvd, Suite 510, Beverley Hills, CA 90211 T(213) 8521901, F(213) 8520129; 590 Fifth Ave, 12th Flr, New York, NY 10036, T(212) 3024861, F (212) 3024801

The Singapore Tourist Promotion Board also has offices in Seoul, South Korea, in Bombay, India, and in Shanghai, China. There are representative offices in Buenos Aires, Argentina; Sao Paulo, Brazil; Santiago, Chile; and Mexico City, Mexico.

Singapore

Singapore

To some, it has all the ambience of a supermarket checkout lane. It has even been described as a Californian resort-town run by Mormons. It has frequently been dubbed sterile and dull - a report in The Economist *judged Singapore to be the most boring city in the world and for those who fail to venture beyond the plazas that line Orchard Road, or spend their three and a half days on coach-trips to the ersatz cultural extravaganzas, this is not surprising. But there is a cultural and architectural heritage in Singapore beyond the one which the government tries so hard to manufacture. Despite its brash consumerism and toytown mentality, Singapore is certainly not without its charm.*

For those stopping over in Singapore for just a few days - en route, as most of the island's tourists are, to somewhere else - there are several key sights that should not be missed. Many who visit, however, consider that it is far more important to enjoy the food. The island has an unparalleled variety of restaurants to suit every palate and wallet. Hawker centres in particular are a highly recommended part of the Singapore epicurean experience - they are inexpensive, and many are open into the early hours.

Colonial core

At the heart of the Colonial core is the Padang - an open, grassed area surrounded by languid rain trees. Many of the great events in Singapore's short history have been played out within sight or sound of the Padang. It was close to here that Stamford Raffles first set foot on the island on the morning of 28 January 1819, where the Japanese surrendered to Lord Louis Mountbatten on 12 September 1945, and where Lee Kuan Yew, the first prime minister of the city state, declared the country independent in 1959.

Ins and outs

Getting there If you are staying outside the immediate area, take the MRT to City Hall which is conveniently located between the Padang and Raffles City. If you are only interested in visiting the Singapore Art Museum, Singapore History Museum or Fort Canning Park, all situated in the north-west corner of this area, then Dhoby Ghaut MRT is marginally more convenient.

Getting around Small enough to walk around - just. To walk from the Singapore Art Museum in the far north-west corner of this area to the mouth of the Singapore River shouldn't take more than 30 minutes. You may want to grab a cab to get over to Fort Canning Park if it is a particularly hot and humid day. Several of the newer hotels are in the Marina Bay area at the eastern edge of the Colonial core.

The area

The Colonial core lies to the north of the Singapore River. It is bordered to the northeast by Rochor Road and Rochor Canal Road, to the northwest by Selegie Road and Canning Hill, and to the southeast by the sea. Compared with Chinatown or Little India, the Colonial core can seem rather cold. The buildings are grand rather than homely, and the roads more like boulevards than lanes. After all, this was where the business of adminstration was carried out - it was not where people lived.

The area to the north of the Padang has been gradually reclaimed over the years. Until the 1880s, Beach Road was just that - on the beach - while it is now some way inland. The Marina Bay area to the southeast of Nicoll Highway has only been reclaimed and developed since the 1980s and is now a confection of luxury hotels, air-conditioned shopping arcades and conference halls.

Rather more enticing is the area northwest of the Padang where there are several excellent museums, the grand *Raffles Hotel*, and the sights of Canning Hill. Many of the early buildings were designed by the Irish architect, George Coleman including the Armenian Church, Caldwell House and Maxwell House. Singapore's other main architect of the period was Alfred John Bidwell - responsible for the main wing of *Raffles Hotel*, the *Goodwood Park Hotel*, Stamford House, St Joseph's Church, the Singapore Cricket Club and the Victoria Memorial Hall.

Sights

The Padang The **Padang** ('playing field' in Malay), the site of most big sporting and other events in Singapore - including the National Day parades - is at the centre of the colonial area. It originally fronted on to the sea, but due to land reclamation now stands a kilometre inland. After the founding of Singapore in 1819, English and Indian troops were quartered here and the area was known as the Plain. The name was only later changed to Padang. In 1942, when Singapore fell to the invading Japanese, all the European population of the colony were massed on the Padang before the troops were marched away to prisoner-of-war camps, some to camps in Malaya and Siam (where they helped to build the infamous Bridge over the River Kwai), others to Changi (see page 148). The **Cricket Club**, at the end of the Padang, was the focus of British activity. A sports pavilion was first constructed in 1850 and a larger Victorian clubhouse was built in 1884 with two levels, the upper level being the ladies viewing gallery. The new **Singapore Recreation Club**(the SRC) building, at the northern end of the Padang, has been built on the site of a former club built in 1883 by the Eurasian community, who were excluded from the Cricket Club. The new building is a modern, green-glass, aquarium-esque affair with polished brown columns: a nouveau antidote to the venerable Cricket Club at the other end of the Padang. In 1963 the club lifted its membership restrictions and allowed anyone to join and today fewer than a fifth of the members are Eurasian.

Flanking the Padang are the houses of justice and government: the domed **Supreme Court** (formerly the *Hotel de l'Europe*) and the **City Hall**. The neo-classical **City Hall** was built with Indian convict labour for a trifling S$2 million and was finished in 1929. On 12 September 1945 the Japanese surrendered here to Lord Louis Mountbatten and on the same spot, former-Prime Minister Lee Kuan Yew declared Singapore's independence in 1959. Today it contains law courts - the overflow from the Supreme Court next door. To get in, enter via the lower entrance at the front. Hearings usually start at 1000 and the public are allowed to sit at the back and hear cases in session.

On the seaward side of the Padang from the City Hall is **Tan Kim Seng's Fountain**. Along the base the following words are inscribed: This fountain is erected by the municipal commissioners in commemoration of Mr Tan Kim Seng's donation towards the cost of the Singapore Water Works. This tells only part of the story for the fountain is a remnant of pristine Singapore's filthy past. Mr Tan, a prosperous Straits Chinese, made a gift of S$13,000 in 1857 to finance the island's first municipal water works on the condition that the water be available to all, free of charge. At the time it was just beginning to be recognised that Singapore's appallingly high mortality rate - which was higher than the island's birth rate (only immigration kept the population growing) - was linked to dirty water. Unfortunately the terms of Mr Tan's gift were not adhered to; indeed some people question whether the money ever went on improving Singapore's water supply at all and instead suggest that it was, so to speak, syphoned off for some other nefarious purpose. Certainly, it was not for another 60 years that mortality rates declined significantly, especially among Singapore's Chinese, Indian and Malay communities. Perhaps the city fathers erected this fountain when their guilt got the better of them.

Esplanade and the river

For a detailed map of the esplanade and river, see page 86

Under construction and stretching right along the seafront is the **Esplanade: theatres on the Bay**. This will become the centre of Singapore's performing arts when it is completed in 2001. There will be a concert hall, lyric theatre, three smaller studios, and an outdoor performing space. It will all contribute to Singapore's medium-term plan to become the arts centre of the region.

Walking south along the Esplanade another point of some historical interest is the Chinese pagoda-like **Lim Bo Seng Memorial**. The story is more interesting than the memorial: Major Lim Bo Seng was a member of Singapore's resistance movement and having escaped to India in 1943 after the fall of Singapore returned to Malaya as a member of the guerilla Force 136. He was captured by the Japanese in Perak and died after three months of brutal torture - during which he never revealed details about his comrades. The memorial was erected in 1954, on the tenth anniversary of his death.

Between the High Street and Singapore River there are other architectural legacies of the colonial period: the **clock tower, Parliament House, the Victoria Memorial Hall and Victoria Theatre**, and Empress Place. It was in this area that the Temenggongs, the former Malay rulers of Singapore, built their kampung - the royal family was later persuaded to move out to Telok Blangah. The **Victoria Theatre** was originally built as the

Colonial core

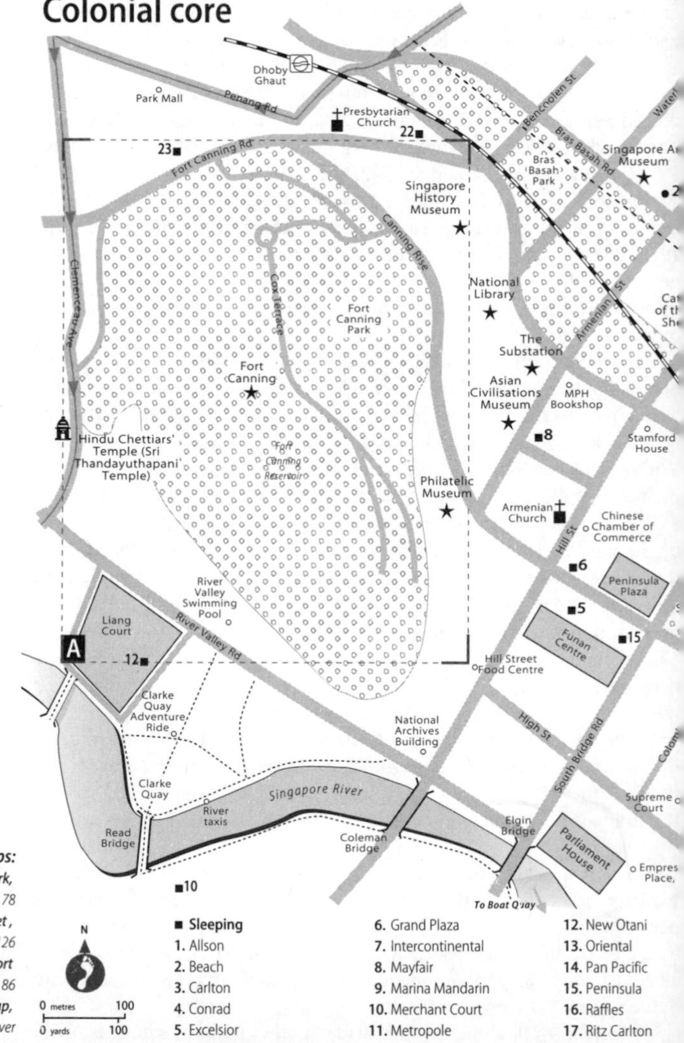

Related maps:
A. Fort Canning Park, page 78
B. Arab Street, page 126
River & Port (to the south), page 86
Coloured map, inside back cover

■ Sleeping
1. Allson
2. Beach
3. Carlton
4. Conrad
5. Excelsior
6. Grand Plaza
7. Intercontinental
8. Mayfair
9. Marina Mandarin
10. Merchant Court
11. Metropole
12. New Otani
13. Oriental
14. Pan Pacific
15. Peninsula
16. Raffles
17. Ritz Carlton

Town Hall in 1856 but was later adapted by Swan and Maclaren, to celebrate Queen Victoria's jubilee, integrating a new hall (the Memorial Hall) and linking the two with a central clock tower. (During the Japanese Occupation the clock, like those in other occupied counties, was set to Tokyo time which seems a strange thing to do even during the world war.) The buildings are still venues for Singapore's multi-cultural dance, drama and musical extravaganzas. The Victoria Concert Hall (the right hand section of the building) is the home base of the Singapore Symphony Orchestra.

In front of the theatre is the original **bronze statue of Sir Thomas Stamford Raffles**, sculpted in bronze by Thomas Woolner in 1887. There is a story that the statue was saved from destruction at the hands of the invading Japanese by a cunning curator who hid it away. It seems however, that the truth is rather more banal: the colonnade previously surrounding the statue was destroyed during the fall of Singapore and the statue was

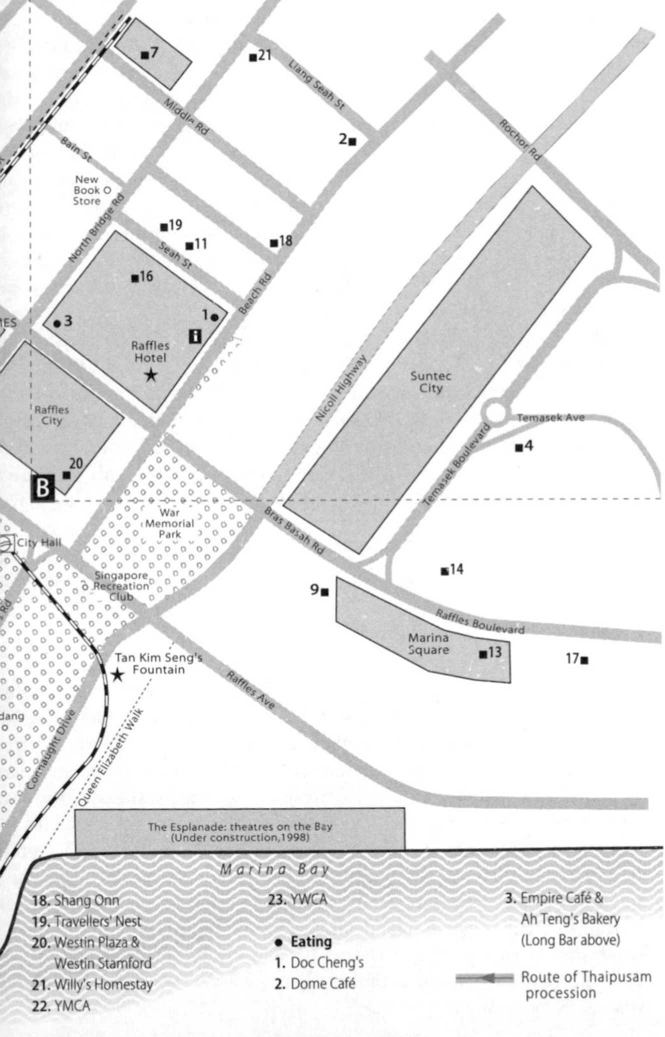

removed to the National Museum for the duration of the Occupation. When Lee Kuan Yew first came to power in 1965, his Dutch economic adviser Dr Albert Winsemius told him to get rid of the Communists but to "let Raffles stand where he is today. Say publicly that you accept the heavy ties with the West because you will very much need them in your economic programme".

Parliament House, built in 1827, is the oldest government building in Singapore. Designed by George Coleman, it was originally intended as a residence for the wealthy Javanese merchant John Maxwell, who was appointed by his friend Raffles as one of Singapore's first three magistrates. He never lived here however, because of a dispute over the legal rights to the land, and he later leased it out to the government as a Court House. With the construction of a Supreme Court in St Andrews Road in 1939, the building stood empty for a decade, before becoming the Assembly Rooms in the 1950s and later Parliament House. Just to the north of Parliament House is a bronze statue of an **elephant** - a gift from Siam's (Thailand's) King Chulalongkorn, Rama V, who visited Singapore in 1871.

Parliament House has become too small to accommodate the expanding body of MPs and a new S$80 million Parliament complex has been built next to the old building which is due to open for business in early 1999. Parliamentary debate in Singapore is modelled on the Westminster system and as in the old parliament there will be a Strangers Gallery where the public - and visitors - will be able to witness Singapore's democracy in action. In an attempt to educate Singapore's youth about their parliamentary system, there will be a sound-proofed gallery where a commentary will be provided, a Moot Parliament where school children will sharpen their debating skills and a History Corner with inter-active computer programmes.

Empress Place, on the river and near to the old parliament, was one of Singapore's first conservation projects. Built as the East India Company courthouse in 1865 and named after Queen Victoria, Empress of the Empire, it later housed the legislative assembly and then became in turn, part of the immigration department, the offices of other assorted government agencies, and a museum. Now this thoroughly confused building is undergoing yet another reincarnation as the second wing of the Asian Civilisations Museum, which is due to open in 2001 (see page). In its grounds stands the **Dalhousie Memorial**, an obelisk erected in honour of Lord James Dalhousie, Governor-General of India, who visited Singapore for three days in 1850. He is credited on the plaque as having emphatically recognized the wisdom of liberating commerce from all restraints.

Queen Elizabeth Walk: back to the Padang

Queen Elizabeth Walk, running from Raffles Avenue to the river-mouth, once ran along the waterfront but is now in danger of being swallowed up by the new opera house/theatre complex, which is under construction here. Further upstream, on the spot where he is believed to have first stepped on to the swampy shore in 1819, is a marble replica of the original **statue of Raffles**, founder of modern Singapore. The plaque on the base of the statue reads: "On this historic site Sir Thomas Stamford Raffles first landed in Singapore on 28 January 1819 and with genius and perception changed the destiny of Singapore from an obscure fishing village to a great seaport and modern metropole". The original, sculpted in bronze by Thomas Woolner in 1887, stands in front of the Victoria Theatre (see above). Within a betel spit of the statue is the wharf for cruises of the Singapore River (■*30 minutes, S$9 for adults, S$4 for children)*.

The Raffles Hotel– immortalized and sanitized

"Tiger shot in Raffles Hotel!" blazed a Straits Times headline in August 1902. The wild tiger was shot while cowering among the stilts under the Billiard Room. It was one more exotic claim to fame for an already legendary institution. The hotel's magnificent teak staircases, big verandahs, bars and palm courtyards had made it the haunt of the rich and famous. It had the first electric lights, lifts and ceiling fans on the island and a French chef. To use Somerset Maugham's oft-quoted cliché, the old hotel "stood for all the fables of the exotic East ... immortalized by writers and patronized by everyone".

The main building was completed in 1889, but the hotel began life as a bungalow on the beach front. An Englishman, Captain Dare, established a tiffin house there before he expanded it into a hotel. It was then bought by the Armenian hoteliers, the Sarkies brothers, in 1885 who had just set up the Eastern and Oriental (E&O) Hotel in Penang and went on to establish the Strand Hotel in Rangoon in 1892. Under the Sarkies' management, Raffles and its sister hotels were the epitome of British colonialism – even though the brothers were refused entry to the Singapore Cricket Club because they weren't 'white'.

Today Raffles boasts of its former guests like a public school would list its famous sons. They include celebrities, writers, kings, sultans, politicians, comedians and what one local journalist called "the flotsam and jetsam of a newly-mobile world". The hotel's literary tradition became its trump card: Somerset Maugham, Rudyard Kipling, Noel Coward and Herman Hesse all stayed here. Not all were particularly impressed: Kipling said the rooms were bad and recommended that travellers go to the Hôtel de l'Europe on the Padang instead. Even so, Raffles was the social epicentre of Singapore.

By the late 1920s, Arshak Sarkie – who had taken over the management of the Raffles and was known for his party-trick of waltzing around the Grand Ballroom with a whisky glass perched on his bald head – started gambling at the Turf Club. He fell into debt at the same time as he embarked on an expensive renovation programme. By the turn of the decade, the bottom had fallen out of the Malayan rubber industry and the local economy collapsed into the Great Depression, taking Raffles with it. Arshak Sarkies died in 1931, bankrupt and miserable. Its golden years died with the Sarkies'. During the war, the Japanese turned Palm Court into a drill ground. At the end of the war, patriotic British POWs gathered in the Ballroom to sing "There'll always be an England". The hotel served as a transit camp for them after the Japanese surrender.

By the mid-1980s the hotel had become a quaint, but crumbling colonial relic, which, like the back-packers who had taken to staying there, looked increasingly out of place in the brave new Singapore of glass and steel. The Raffles was rusting, peeling and mouldering. The Long Bar, the home of the Singapore Sling – first shaken by bar-tender Ngiam Tong Boon in 1915 – became a tourist gimmick. The record for Sing-Sling-slinging was set by five Australian visitors in 1985. They downed 131 inside two hours. Then suddenly the government woke up to the fact that it had unwittingly bulldozed over half of its cultural heritage. The hotel's neighbour, the Raffles Institution, had been demolished to make way for Raffles City. To save the old hotel from going the same way, it was declared a protected monument in 1987. Its recognition as an architectural treasure immediately put Raffles on the shortlist for a facelift. The developers spent S$160mn on consultants, white paint and fake Victorian trimmings. Shortly afterwards the group built the Raffles Hotel Arcade – from scratch – a pastiche with no history. Architect Richard Ho was appalled, writing in a letter to the Straits Times that it was "an atrocious and blatant falsification of our architectural heritage" adding the rebuke that it was "very much like tarting up your grandmother".

See also page 80.

Beyond the Padang is the world's tallest hotel, the *Westin Stamford*, part of the huge **Raffles City Complex** on Stamford Road. Designed by the Chinese-American architect, I M Pei (famous for the glass pyramid in front of the Louvre, and the Bank of China building in Hong Kong), it contains two hotels, offices and a shopping complex.

Just down the road are the four tapering white pillars of the **War Memorial** in Memorial Park on Beach Road - better known as the four chopsticks - symbolizing the four cultures of Singapore: the Chinese, Malays, Indians and 'others'. It was built in memory of the 50,000-odd civilians who died during the Japanese occupation. A memorial service is held at the monument on 15 February each year.

Raffles Hotel, watering hole or national monument?

The revamped Raffles Hotel , with its 875 designer-uniformed staff (there is a ratio of 2 staff to every guest) and 104 suites (each fitted with Persian carpets), eight restaurants (and a Culinary Academy) and five bars, playhouse and custom-built, leather-upholstered cabs, is the jewel in the crown of Singapore's tourist industry. In true Singapore-style it manages to boast a 5,000 sq m shopping arcade and theres even a museum of Rafflesian memorabilia on the 3rd Floor ■ *free 1000-2100 Monday-Sunday*. Next to the museum is the **Jubilee Hall Theatre** - named after the old Jubilee Theatre demolished to make way for the Raffles extension (see below).

Raffles Hotel's original (but restored) billiard table still stands in the Billiard Room. Palm Court is still there and so is the Tiffin Room, which still serves tiffin. Teams of restoration consultants undertook painstaking research into the original colours of paint, ornate plasterwork and fittings. A replica of the cast-iron portico, known as "cad's alley" was built to the original 19th century specifications of a Glasgow foundry.

Although just about anyone who's anyone visiting Singapore still makes a pilgrimage to the hotel, there has been a vigorous debate over whether or not in the process of its lavish restoration, Raffles has lost some of its atmosphere and appeal. (The same complaint has been levelled at the renovated *Railway Hotel* in Hua Hin, Thailand and the *Strand Hotel* in Rangoon, Burma.) There is no doubt that it has been done well - architecturally it can hardly be faulted and the lawns and courtyards are lush with foliage. There is also no doubt that it is an immensely comfortable and well-run hotel. But critics say they've tried a little too hard. The month after it reopened (on former Prime Minister Lee Kuan Yew's birthday, 16 September 1991), *Newsweek* said that in trying to roll a luxury hotel, a shopping mall and a national tourist attraction into one, "The result is synergy run amok ... great if you need a Hermes scarf, sad if you'd like to imagine a tiger beneath the billiard table." Other critics have asked whether the hotel should really be viewed as a national monument. While the hotel was undergoing expansion in 1990-91, the old Jubilee Theatre was torn down to make space for it. The Jubilee Theatre was not only genuinely old - and architecturally just as significant - but it had also played a considerably larger part in the lives of Singaporeans. As local writer Heng put it in 1991, "But it is Raffles and Coward *et al* which are being preserved as heritage and not [the] Jubilee where mothers, aunts and cousins cried their hearts out for actress Ng Kuan Lai and her misfortunes by the banks of the Li-Jiang [referring to one of the Hong Kong actress best known films, *Blood debt by the banks of Lijiang River*]."

Cathedrals and churches

South of Raffles lies **St Andrew's Cathedral**, designed by Colonel Ronald MacPherson and built in the 1850s by Indian (Tamil) convict labourers in early neo-gothic style. Its interior walls are coated with a plaster called *Madras chunam*, a decorative innovation devised by the Indian labourers to conceal the deficiencies of the building materials. The recipe for Madras chunam was egg white, egg shell, lime and a coarse sugar (called jaggery), mixed with coconut husks and water into a paste. Once the paste had hardened, it was polished to give a smooth surface, and moulded to give many of the buildings their ornate façades. Note the window commemorating Raffles as the founder of modern Singapore. The cathedral is often packed - 13 per cent of Singapore's population are Christian - and there are several services a day in different languages (see the notice board in the northwest corner of the plot for times of service).

Built in 1835 (the spire was added in 1850), the **Armenian Church of St Gregory the Illuminator** (the first monk of the Armenian church) on Hill Street is the island's oldest church and was designed by Irish architect George Coleman. This diminutive church seats 50 people at a squeeze. The design is said to have been influenced by London's St Martin-in-the-Fields and Cambridge's Round Church. The construction of the church was largely funded by Singapore's small Armenian community, although a number of non-Christian Asians also contributed. Agnes Joaquim is buried here - she discovered what is now the national flower of Singapore, the Vanda Miss Joaquim orchid (see page 175). On the other side of the road from the church is a strange pagoda-roofed block - the **Singapore Chinese Chamber of Commerce & Industry** building. This rather unhappy edifice was erected in 1964. Two stone lions imported from mainland China guard the entrance and the murals on either side of the gate are copies of similar murals in Beijing.

One of George Coleman's pupils, Denis McSwiney, designed the **Roman Catholic Cathedral of the Good Shepherd**, on the junction of Queen Street and Bras Basah Road. It was used as an emergency hospital during World War Two. The building has been gazetted as a national monument, but even so looks as though it could do with a lick of paint. **CHIJMES** or the **Convent of Holy Infant Jesus**, opposite the Cathedral on Victoria Street is a complex consisting of the convent, chapel and **Caldwell House** (designed by George Coleman). It has been redeveloped by a French architect into a sophisticated courtyard of shops, pubs and restaurants. Originally, the convent was run by four French Catholic nuns, opening its doors to 14 fee paying pupils, 9 boarders and 16 orphans in 1854. As well as being an orphanage and school for older girls, the convent became a home for discarded babies, who were often left at the gates of the convent at the point of death. The gothic-style church, designed by French Jesuit priest Father Beurel, was added at the turn of the century. The church is now used for concerts and wedding ceremonies (and photo opportunities). Even the stained glass was painstakingly dismantled and renovated to a high standard.

Asian Civilisations Museum

Also on Armenian Street, close to Stamford Road, is a newly restored school. Tao Nan School was built in 1910 and became one of the first Chinese schools in Singapore. It has been taken over by the Singapore Museums Department and in 1997 opened as the **Asian Civilisations Museum**. As its name suggests, the focus of the museum is Asian culture and civilization - 5,000 years of it. The emphasis is on East (especially China) and Southeast Asian civilizations although the museum's remit extends further west to include the countries of South Asia (India, Pakistan, Bangladesh, Nepal, Sri Lanka) and west Asia (the Middle East). It consists of 10 galleries on 3 storeys and most of the displays are arranged along thematic lines - for example, symbolism, architecture and city planning, the literati, and collecting and connoisseurship. While the museum's own permanent collection is modest (but expanding), the displays are first rate, with excellent background information and some good touch-screen interactive computer programmes. (These are being upgraded so that visitors can guide themselves through, for example, a virtual model of the ancient Chinese capital of Changan.) To distinguish itself from the Singapore History Museum the emphasis here is more on the pieces themselves than the context in which they were produced, although there is some overlap. Along with the permanent collection, the museum also accommodates travelling exhibitions, which are often excellent. The aim is for the museum to become a regional centre for Asian art history. The *Café Les Amis,* a French café, is attached to the museum. ■ *S$3 adults, S$1.50 children 0900-1730 Tuesday-Sunday. Free guided tours in English Tuesday-Friday 1100 and 1400, Saturday and Sunday 1100, 1400 and 1530. For information on fringe activities at the Asian Civilisations Museum contact suziwati_sarnan@nhb.gov.sg. web site: www.museum.org.sg/nhb. a second wing of the museum will be housed in Empress Place when major renovation works there are complete, see page 72.* Almost next door to the museum is **The Substation** at 45 Armenian Street which exhibits contemporary art and there is a rather alternative (for Singapore) coffee shop attached.

Nearby at 23B Coleman Street is the **Singapore Philatelic Museum** or **SPM** which opened to the public in 1995. It is a small but extremely well-run museum and is not just of interest to philatophiles. Children especially will find it a wonderful place to follow up on their stamp collections. Its aim is to educate the general public on the history of Singapore's - and, more widely, the world's - postal system. Children (or adults for that matter) can design their own stamps and print them out, use touch screen computers to test their knowledge of philately, tackle puzzles, or just admire the collection of stamps and envelopes. There is a good *History Thru Stamps* Gallery which uses stamps to recount aspects of Singapore's history. Children and adults can become members of the SPM and there is also a good resource centre where visitors can access the museum's book collection and data base. ■ *0900-1630 Tuesday-Sunday. S$2 (S$1 for children). 5 minutes walk from the City Hall MRT station.*

Singapore Art Museum

Bras Basah Road was so called because wet rice - *bras basah* in Malay - was dried here on the banks of the Sungai Bras Basah (now Stamford Canal). The former Catholic boys school, **St Joseph's Institution**, opposite the RC Cathedral at 71 Bras Basah Road, is another a good example of colonial religious architecture. Built in 1867, it is now home to the **Singapore Art Museum**, where there are several changing exhibitions every months or so. It can be a welcome break from the heat to wander through the wondrously cool galleries. The Singapore Art Museum's own collection is modest and, understandably, predominantly features Singaporean and Malaysian artists' work. There are always pieces from the collection on show and they are interesting for what they reveal about how Singaporean and Malaysian artists have selectively absorbed Western and Easten influences. The museum also entertains travelling shows, both modern and classical. While St Joseph's was being renovated, a feature wall was discovered behind a row of built-in cupboards. Two supporting columns bear an entablature emblazoned with the words *Santa Joseph Ora Pro Nobis* (Saint Joseph pray for us) and it is presumed that the school chapel was located here. ■ *S$3 adults, S$1.50 children and senior citizens. 0900-1730 Tuesday-Sunday. Guided tours at 1100 and 1400, Tuesday-Friday (1030 in Japanese) and 1100 and 1430 on Saturday and Sunday. For information on fringe activities at the museum contact suziwati_sarnan@nhb.gov.sg. Web site: www.museum.org.sg/nhb.*

Singapore History Museum

Across the green on Stamford Road is the **Singapore History Museum**. Until a few years ago this was the only national museum in Singapore. However, now that the contemporary fine art (paintings, sculpture) collection has been shifted across the square to the Singapore Art Museum (see above) and the collection of Asian art has moved to the Asian Civilisations Museum (see page) on Armenian Street, the gallery has been left with the task of exhibiting on and educating about Singapore's history. The idea of setting up a museum was first mooted by Stamford Raffles in 1823; it was finally built in 1887 and named the Raffles Museum. It was most recently renovated in 1991, after which it was renamed. As a whole, the museum is rather disappointing given the quality of Singapore's other attractions. There is little coherence between its varied exhibits and little sense of narrative. Nor are the pieces displayed terribly interesting or beautiful. Only the 20 dioramas on the left of the main entrance are a permanent exhibition. These scenes visually recount 20 important episodes in the history of Singapore from Raffles' first landing on a jungled island inhabited by fisherfolk through to Independence. They are interesting enough - especially for children - and provide an easy to digest, staccato view of Singapore over the last two centuries or so. All the other exhibits are temporary. For example, in 1998 the interior of a Peranakan home was reconstructed, with detailed information on the contents of each room, and there were exhibitions on Chinese secret societies and Singapore's transition from colony to nation. The attached **Children's Discovery Gallery** has changing exhibits every 6 months. During the week it is closed for 2 hours every morning and afternoon for school groups. Plenty of hands on activity for children. ■ *S$3, children S$1.50. 0900-1730, closed Monday. Conducted tours from the information counter at 1100 and 1400, Tuesday-Friday (1030 in Japanese). Slide shows through the day in the AV Theatre. For information on fringe activities at the museum contact suziwati_sarnan@nhb.gov.sg. Web site: www.museum.org.sg/nhb.*

Colonial core

National Library

The **National Library** is behind the museum, on the other side of Canning Rise. It is open daily until 1700 and is a good place to browse, either on one of the many computers or along the bookshelves. The library has recently installed a new computer retrieval system which goes by the acronym VEGAS - the Virtual Exhibition Gallery System. For this the library has digitized part of its archives and visitors can examine old photographs and documents.

Where Stamford Road meets Orchard Road, just up from the museum and next to the *YMCA*, is the **Presbyterian church**, built in 1878 and now a protected monument. While the church looks original it has in fact undergone considerable extension. In 1975 the wings were enlarged and the original columns replaced with steel ones. It was also airconditioned and insulated from traffic noise. The church's caretaker's house was the centre of the 1984 Curry Murder Horror. The Tamil caretaker was dismembered and his body disposed of by cooking it up with curry and rice. It was then discarded in rubbish bins around Singapore, masquerading as the remains of a hawker-stall takeaway. Six people, including a butcher and a mutto curry stall holder, were arrested in 1987, but later released for lack o evidence.

Fort Canning Park

Behind the museum is **Fort Canning Park**. The British called it Singapor Hill, but its history stretches back centuries earlier. It is known as Buki Larangan or Forbidden Hill by the Malays as this was the site of the ancien fortress of the Malay kings and reputedly contains the tomb of the las Malay ruler of the kingdom of Singapura, Sultan Iskandar Shah Archaeological excavations in the area have uncovered remains from th days of the Majapahit Empire. It is thought that the palace was built in th early 14th century and then abandoned in 1396 in the wake of Siames (Thai) and Majapahit (Javanese) attacks. Furthermore, when Raffles an his companions landed in 1819, it is said that Malay oral history still recalle the former 14th century palace and its sultans and would not accompan the British up the hill for fear of the spirits. In a letter written to Sir Willian Marsden at the time of his first landing on Singapore, Raffles mentions th ruins of the Malay fortress. The name Canning Hill was given to this sligh geological protuberance in the 1860s in honour of the first Viceroy of India Viscount George Canning.

The 20 hectare hill and its gardens come under the auspices of th National Parks Board and for a long time they were viewed only as a gree area where Singaporean's could picnic and wander. The gardens have bee alternatively billed as the lungs of the city, an oasis, and a green refuge. Th Amazon Basin this may not be, but it does make a welcome distraction fron the more urban delights of Singapore City. In addition, over the last fev years Canning Hill has evolved into something a little more ambitious thar just a park. (Although the authorities are apparently grappling with th problem of how to get people to climb the few metres up the hill to the sight and other attractions they have developed.) The **Battle Box** opened in 1997 It is a museum contained within the bunker where General Perciva directed the unsuccessful campaig against the invading Japanese Visitors are first shown a vide recounting, in 15 minutes or so, th events that led up to the capture o Singapore. They are then led into th Malaya Command HQ - the Battl Box - where the events of the fina historic day, the 15 February 1942 are re-enacted. Visitors are given ea phones and are then taken from th radio room, to the cipher rooms and on to the command roon before arriving at the bunker wher Percival gathered his senio commanders for their final, fateful meeting. It is very well done with good commentary, figures and film The bunker is also air-conditioned a big plus after the hot walk up During the War, though, it wa stiflingly hot - air was inefficientl re-circulated in case of gas attack

Fort Canning Park

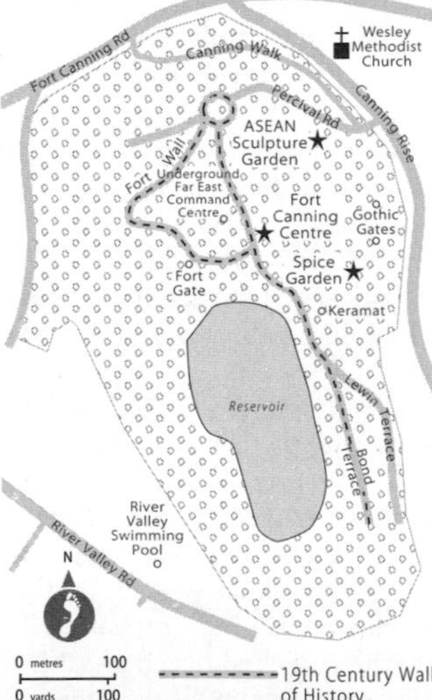

Related maps:
Colonial core, *page 70*
Orchard Road *(to the west), page 94*
Coloured map, *inside back cover*

There is also a small traditional museum and a souvenir shop. ■ *S$8 (S$5 children). Tuesday-Sunday 1000-1800, last admission 1700.*

Above the Battle Box are the **ruins of Fort Canning** - the Gothic gateway, derelict guardhouse and earthworks are all that remain of a fort which once covered 3 hectares. There are now some 40 modern sculptures here. Below the sculpture garden to the southeast is the renovated **Fort Canning Centre** (built 1926) which is the home venue of Theatre Works and the Singapore Dance Theatre. In front of Fort Canning Centre is an old Christian cemetery - **Fort Green** - where the first settlers, including the architect George Coleman, are buried. The graves of these early settlers have been exhumed but the gravestones remain, embedded in the boundary wall. Along with George Coleman, there is a Russian and, unusually, a Chinese - for this was a Christian burial ground - and it may indicate an early convert to Christianity. While Sir Stamford Raffles may have lived here, he did not die here. He suffered an ignominious death and funeral in North London and it was only later that he was reburied in Westminster Abbey (see box page 164). On one side of Fort Green is a **Spice Garden** which recreates, on a small scale, the garden that Raffles established in 1822. Various spices and aromatic plants, including nutmeg, lemon grass and chilli, are cultivated here. On the other side is the **Asean Sculpture Garden** to which each member of Asean has donated a piece of work (although Asean's most recent signatories - Vietnam, Laos and Myanmar - have yet to add their pieces). On the northwestern side of the Hill is the site of **Raffles' first house** which he had built in 1823, while the centre of the hill is given over to a reservoir and is out of bounds.

Colonial core

Chettiar Temple

Below Canning Hill, on Tank Road, is the Hindu **Chettiar Temple**, also known as the **Sri Thandayuthapani Temple**. The original temple on this site was built by wealthy Chettiar Indians (money lenders). It has been superseded by a modern version, finished in 1984, and is dedicated to Lord Subramaniam. The ceiling has 48 painted glass panels, angled to reflect sunset and sunrise. Its *gopuram*, the 5-tiered entrance, aisles, columns and hall all sport rich sculptures depicting Hindu deities carved by sculptors trained in Madras. This Hindu temple is the richest in Singapore - some argue, in all of Southeast Asia. It is here that the spectacular Kavadi procession of the Thaipusam festival culminates (see page 52). ■ *Many Hindu temples close in the heat of the day, so are best seen before 1100 and after 1500.*

Marina Square lies to the east of the colonial core on reclaimed land. This is home to Suntec City - Singapore's latest conference centre - bevvy of five star hotels, an entertainment centre, an exclusive shopping mall, a food court and an arcade of restaurants. The central feature of the square is the largest fountain in the world, known as the **Fountain of Wealth**, so-called because of its inward flow of water which, for the Chinese, symbolizes the retention of wealth. (It was, of course, built before the Asian economic crisis of 1997-98.) Its unbroken circular form represents harmony and the unity of humanity and nature. Though impressive, it can hardly (as the publicity blurb claims) be likened to viewing Ayers Rock or the Grand Canyon at sunset. ■ *A sound and light show takes place here every evening at 2000, 2045 and 2130.*

Essentials

Sleeping

■ *on maps*

Price codes: see inside front cover

Most accommodation in the Colonial core is well placed for exploring the sights o the colonial city on foot, as well as the restaurants and bars of Clarke and Boat quay The main shopping area (Orchard Rd) and the CBD are both a short taxi ride awa There is also a group of 5-star hotels in the Marina Bay area at the eastern edge c the Colonial core.

This whole zone was reclaimed from the sea a few years back. Three hotels wer constructed 10 years ago, but with the arrival of two 5-star hotels, the opening c Suntec City (a high-tech conference centre), 4 new office blocks, hundreds of ne shops and over 75 restaurants and an entertainment centre it has become almost self-contained district which, because of its proximity to the airport, is provin popular with business travellers.

L+ ***Conrad***, 2 Temasek Boulevard, Marina Bay, T3388830, F3388164. This is the late 5-star hotel to open in Singapore. It is the closest to Suntec City, and is good for th business traveller. 509 beautifully-designed contemporary-style rooms with lots c space, big windows and a large desk. Superb service, excellent meeting rooms, an an impressive mezzanine level for functions. US$1.3mn has been invested in almo 3,000 artworks throughout the hotel. Pool area is still a little bare but should improv the fitness centre is adequate. Recommended.

L+ ***Ritz Carlton***, 7 Raffles Ave, Marina Bay, T3378888, F3380001. Both this hotel and th *Conrad* were designed by Hirsch Bedner of the US. Very contemporary furnishing considerable investment in artworks (notably the Frank Stella and the Dele Chihu glass balls below the lobby area); rooms are very attractive, with wooden floors and bi bathrooms (providing stunning views of the harbour and river). Large pool area wit jacuzzi in well landscaped grounds, huge fitness centre. Good business facilitie Recommended.

L ***Marina Mandarin***, 6 Raffles Blvd, Marina Sq, T3383388, F3394977, mms888 singnet.com.sg, http://www.commerceasia.mandarin. A/c, restaurants, pool, we equipped fitness centre, good business facilities, large rooms. The hotel consists of giant blocks arranged in a triangle enclosing a vast atrium that rises to the very top c the building, filled with cascades of plants and caged birds giving the aur impression of a jungle.

L ***Oriental***, 5 Raffles Ave, Marina Bay, T3380066, F3399537. Another central atrium this time triangular, with exterior lifts. Its black marble interior and limited natur light makes it all a little sombre in feel. 522 bigger than average rooms with attractiv bathrooms. Harbour views are more expensive. It has a large lengths pool and separate children's pool and a fitness centre. Restaurants include the *Chinese Cher Garden*, Californian cuisine at *Liana's* and an outdoor Italian (*Pronto*) restaurant b the pool. All very efficient with, as one would expect, excellent service, however, th facilities here are not quite as abundant as elsewhere.

L-A+ ***Pan-Pacific***, 7 Raffles Blvd, Marina Square, T3368111, F3391861. Yet anothe open triangular 36-storey atrium with a rather claustrophobic feel. 800 rooms an about 70% of the guests are business travellers. The rooms are large and pleasantl laid out, with three views. Attractive fan-shaped pool, rather overlooked, two tenn courts and a *Clark Hatch* fitness centre. Famous Japanese restaurant *Keyaki*, with Japanese garden on the 4th Flr. Efficient service, yet lacking in atmosphere.

L+ ***Raffles***, 1 Beach Rd, T3371886, F3397650, raffles@pacific.net.sg. 9 restaurants an a Culinary Academy, 5 bars (see separate entries under Eating and Bars) an surrounded by 70 shops, much has been said about *Raffles* and, despite criticisms, it still a great place to stay - if you can afford it. The 104 suites have been immaculatel refurbished, with wooden floors, high ceilings, stylish colonial furniture and plenty c pace. Bathrooms are the ultimate in luxury and the other facilities are excellent - a peaceful rooftop pool with jacuzzis, state of the art fitness centre, both open 24 hours. About half Raffles' guests are business visitors; corporate rates available. Very exclusive and highly recommended.

. *Carlton*, 76 Bras Basah Rd, T3388333, F3396866. Pretty average 477-room hotel with business facilities, good-sized pool including a children's pool, fitness centre with sauna and jacuzzi. Most of the Carlton's guests are corporate visitors from Australia and Japan, good location.

Intercontinental, 80 Middle Rd, Bugis Junction, T3387600, F3387366. Attractive renovated and extended block of Art Deco shophouses, with a high rise block behind. Over 400 good sized rooms with spacious bathrooms and every luxury provided, attractive rooftop pool with jacuzzi and well-equipped fitness centre. Business centre with small meeting room. The only drawback of the more expensive rooms in the renovated shophouses is the distance of some rooms from the lifts. Beautifully designed to a high standard and one of the best hotels in Singapore. The *Shophouse Room* is the hotel's showpiece and costs an extra S$60 - for which you get original colonial furniture and parquet flooring.

. *Westin Stamford and Westin Plaza*, 2 Stamford Rd, T3396633, F3365117, westin1@singnet.com.sg, http://www.westin. com.sg. 13 restaurants, attractive triple circular pool (great for children), high-tech fitness centre, listed in the Guinness Book of Records as the tallest hotel in the world, this 2-tower complex was designed by Chinese architect IM Pei who also designed the futuristic Bank of China building in Hong Kong. The *Compass Rose Restaurant* on the top floor, provides stunning views over three countries - Singapore, Malaysia and Indonesia (haze permitting). With over 2,000 rooms and a vast echoing lobby it is all a little overwhelming - and too large for that personal touch. However, it has a good reputation in the business world. On our last visit they were too busy to let us see a room.

L-A+ *Grand Plaza*, 10 Coleman St, T3363456, F3399311. 2 restaurants, attractive but smallish pool and jacuzzi, gym and health spa all on 3rd floor. Large ballroom and 2 smaller meeting rooms, business centre with computers for guests use. Although the outside of this building is pretty hideous, with its marble cladding, the interior is not so ostentatious and despite its size (340 rooms), it feels quite intimate. Recommended.

A+ *Allson*, 101 Victoria St, T2260911, F3397019. Chinese in character with heavy furniture, rooms are adequate, average pool but fitness facilities are limited to a running machine. Live band in the bar, quite a friendly place, slightly off the beaten track.

A+ *Excelsior*, 5 Coleman St, T3387733, F3396236. Several restaurants but the hotel coffee shop is in the Excelsior Plaza next door, open 0600-2230. Small pool and no gym, limited business facilities. Guests may use all the facilities of the *Peninsula Hotel* next door, which is under the same management. Rooms are Art Deco in style and are of average size. Personal safe in every room. Cramped lobby and dreary corridors, definitely a tour group place.

A+ *Peninsula*, 3 Coleman St, T3372200, F3393580. Rooms are quite small and frayed at the edges, small pool, with adequate fitness centre, limited business facilities, 24-hour coffee shop, night club, cramped lobby area, friendly and in the heart of the colonial core.

B *Metropole*, 41 Seah St, T3363611, F3393610, metropole@metrohotel.com, http://www.metro-hotel.com. A smallish business hotel with 54 rooms and no frills.

C *Mayfair City*, 40-44 Armenian St, T3374542, F3371736, a/c. A hotel that has so far survived being renovated, it has both advantages and disadvantages. On the plus side it is quite cheap and has a quaint old lift and rooms with improbably tall doors, as if it were designed for a race of giants. On the down side, the rooms are a touch shabby and reveal no tell-tale signs of having come into contact with an interior decorator.

D *Willy's Homestay*, 494 North Bridge Rd, T3370916, willys@mbox2.singnet.com.sg.

Dorms available (**E**), breakfast included, central and clean.

D-E ***Travellers' Nest***, 28C Seah St, T3399095, (hard to spot - it is above the Thin Wa Tong Medical Hall and directly opposite the *Raffles*). This is the cheapest place to sta within spitting distance of the *Raffles Hotel* - here a bed can cost S$8; over the roa they start at S$650! But then you do get a little more for your money. Rooms at th *Travellers Nest* are small, they can be rather stuffy, and all have shared showers an toilets. Dorm bunk beds available. The price includes tea/coffee and a simpl breakfast. Roof garden for relaxing.

Eating: expensive

● *on maps*
Price codes: see inside front cover

4 ***Annalakshmi***, 02-10 *Excelsior Hotel* and Shopping Centre, 5 Coleman St, T3399993 (also at Terminal 2, Changi Airport, T5420407). **Indian** vegetarian cuisine, th *Annalakshmi* is run on the same basis as KL's *Annapoorna*, it is staffed by unpai housewives and profits go to the Kalamandhir Indian cultural group. The health drink are excellent - especially Mango Tharang (mango juice, honey and ginger) an Annalakshmi Special (fruit juices, yoghurt, honey and ginger) - the restaurant, whic sprawls out onto the verandah overlooking the tennis courts, serves North and Sout Indian vegetarian food. Samy's banana-leaf and fish-head curries are unrivallec closes at 2130. Recommended.

4 ***Bobby Rubinos***, Fountain Court, CHIJMES, 30 Victoria St, T3375477. **Internationa** good menu of ribs, burgers, chicken, booking recommended.

4 ***Doc Cheng's***, *Raffles Shopping Arcade*, Seah St. **New Asian**, unusual combinations c flavours but the rather irritating blurb on the menu may put some off. Even so, th food can be excellent.

4 ***Grappas***, CHIJMES, 30 Victoria St, T3349928, **Italian**. Large restaurant in this trend courtyard. Extensive menu, mostly pasta and risotto dishes with some meat entrees booking advisable, recommended.

5 ***Hai Tien Lo***, *Pan Pacific Hotel*, 37th Floor, Marina Square, T4348338. **Cantonese** restaurant in elegant surroundings with stunning views of the city. Sharks' fins steamed lobster and Kobe beef are specialities. Dim sum lunches on Sundays.

4 ***Imperial Herbal***, *Metropole Hotel*, 3rd Floor, 41 Seah St, T3370491, **Chinese**. Dr Li, a in-house herbalist, takes your pulse and recommends a meal with the appropriate rejuvenating ingredients to balance your *yin* and *yang*; unusual, delicately flavourec food, booking recommended for dinner.

5 ***Inagiku***, 3rd Floor, *Westin Stamford and Westin Plaza*, 2 Stamford Rd, T4315305 **Japanese**. The Raffles City corporate dinner brigade eat here and it is pricey, bookinc advisable. The restaurant is divided into sections, providing different food in each.

5 ***Lei Gardens***, Ground Floor, CHIJMES, 30 Victoria St, T3393822, F3342648. Outstandinc **Cantonese** food - silver codfish, emperor's chicken and such regulars as dim sum anc Peking duck - in fact a menu which is said to comprise 2,000 dishes. Dignatories, royalty and film stars dine here. Tasteful decor and a 2-tier aquarium displaying the day's offerings. Despite seating for 250 you need to book in advance. Worth every penny Recommended.

5 ***Maison de Fontaine***, Ground Floor, CHIJMES, 30 Victoria St. Excellent, sophisticated **French** restaurant in an attractive setting.

5 ***Migen***, Ground Floor, CHIJMES, 30 Victoria St, T3323003. Full choice of **Japanese** food in this attractive courtyard. Booking at weekends is recommended.

5 ***Raffles Grill***, *Raffles Hotel*, 1 Beach Rd (main building, first floor), T3311611. Elegant colonial surroundings, with silver plate settings, chandeliers and reproduction Chippendale furniture. Serves breakfast, lunch and dinner, excellent **French** cuisine, windows open onto Palm Court.

5 ***Ristorante Bologna,*** *Marina Mandarin Hotel*, 6 Raffles Blvd, Marina Square, T3318470. Award winning **Italian** restaurant, house specialities include spaghetti alla marinara and baked pigeon, diners lounge amidst sophisticated decor anc wandering minstrels strum.

Eating: cheaper

3 ***Empire Café***, Ground Floor, *Raffles Hotel*, 1 Beach Rd, **International**. Not bad for pork chops and oxtail stew, prepared by Chinese cooks and served on marble-topped tables, also serves chicken rice, burgers and ice-creams, open 24 hours. *Ah Teng's Bakery* adjoins, selling pricey pastries, pies and biscuits - mostly local favourites.
3 ***House of Sundanese Food***, several outlets spread around town eg Suntec City Marina Square, T5343775. Typical **Sundanese** dishes from West Java include spicy salad (*keredok*), charcoal-grilled seafood (*ikan Sunda*, *ikan mas*) and curries, simply decorated non-a/c restaurant, with a real home-cooked taste.
3 ***Han's***, 8 branches around the city including Raffles Link Marina Square. This chain of restaurants is Singapore's answer to the Greasy Spoon - cafes without the acute accent on the 'e', single dish **Chinese** meals, simple (largely fried) breakfasts, some **European** food including such things as steaks, burgers and fries all served in large helpings at very competitive prices.
2 ***Komala's Fast Food***, *Peninsula Plaza*, Coleman Street. One of Komala's fast food outlets - good **South Indian** delicacies including thalis, masala dosas and idlis served at competitive prices, air-conditioned (next door is the more upmarket *Ganges Restaurant* which lays on a good lunch time Indian vegetarian buffet spread).
3 ***Nomad's***, Fountain Court, CHIJMES, 30 Victoria St, T3346466, **Chinese/International**. Mongolian BBQ - choose your raw food (as much as you can eat) and your sauces and then it's cooked for you. Very trendy.
3 ***Pennsylvania Country Oven***, Stamford House, Stamford Rd. For Americans craving **New England** cooking, with kitsch interior to boot.
3 ***Ramayana***, 6 Raffles Boulevard, Marina Square, T3363317. **Indonesian** restaurant big on seafood and an extensive range of milk shakes.
3 ***Sanur***, 3rd Floor, 133 New Bridge Rd. Cramped **Malay/Indonesian** restaurant ideally placed for shoppers, specialities include fish-head curries and spicy grilled chicken or fish.
3 ***Stars***, Ground Floor, CHIJMES, 30 Victoria St, T3321033, **International**. Sandwiches, pizzas, burgers plus a very popular watering hole upstairs for Singapore's businesspeople.
3 ***Wayang Café***, Liang Seah St (North Bridge Rd end), trendy little open air café serving a limited **International** menu of sandwiches and salads along with coffee and beers.

Hawker centres & food courts

2 ***Fountain Terrace***, Suntec City, Marina Square. Trendy foodcourt situated under the enormous fountain. **2 *The Marketplace at Water Court***, basement of Raffles City. Sophisticated food court mostly frequented by businesspeople with a penchant for extravagant sandwiches and patisseries - no chicken rice or mutton biryani here. **1 *Funan Centre***, South Bridge Rd. This big shopping plaza contains one of the best food courts in Singapore in its basement, with a huge range of foods to choose from, in particular, an excellent Indian stall. **1 *Hill Street Food Centre,*** west side of Hill St. 3 floors of hawker stalls, lots of Muslim food and plenty of everything else, very popular and great value.

Tiffin

5 ***Tiffin Room,*** *Raffles Hotel*, 1 Beach Rd (main building, ground floor). Tiffin curry buffet (plus à la carte menu) in pristine white, over-lit ersatz Victorian grandeur. The food is good but at S$35 for the buffet, you're paying a lot more for the surroundings than for the curry, reservation recommended, no singlets or shorts.

Cafés

3 ***Café Les Amis***, Asian Civilisations Museum, Armenian St. New offshoot of *Les Amis*, Shaw Centre, exotic **international** menu. **3 *Dôme***, next door to the Singapore Art Museum on Bras Basah Rd. Delicious foccaccia sandwiches, patisseries and some of the best coffee in town, good café atmosphere and a pleasant stop for a midmorning break. **3 *Fat Frog***, The Substation, Armenian St. Attractive leafy courtyard, serving

wholefood snacks, sandwiches and soups. **3 *Café Aria***, Young Musicians' Society Art Centre, Waterloo St, popular for a coffee stop.

Tea, cakes & coffee **3 *Compass Rose Lounge***, *Westin Stamford Hotel*, 2 Stamford Rd. Best views i Singapore, strict dress code, expect to queue. **3 *Seah Street Deli***, Ground Floor, *Raffle Hotel*, North Bridge Rd. New York-style deli serving everything from corned beef an smoked-salmon to cheese cakes and Turkish pastries. **3 *Ah Teng's Bakery***, Raffle Arcade. Pricey but it has all the goodies you dream about at the end of a long tri away from home. Complimentary second cup of coffee.

Bars Bar and Billiard Room, *Raffles Hotel*, Beach Rd. Relocated from its original position, th bar is lavishly furnished with teak tables, oriental carpets and two original billiard table ***Father Flannagan's Irish Pub***, CHIJMES, 30 Victoria St. Ersatz Irish pub with Irish beer o tap and a high density of local businesspeople - some Irish food (stews etc) als available. Several other places within the CHIJMES redevelopment where it is possibl to drink al fresco or otherwise with Singapore's chuppies. ***Paulaner Brauhaus***, Milleni Walk, micro brewery serving pricey beer to businessfolk. German sausage and othe Teutonic delicacies also served. ***Somerset's***, *Westin Stamford*, Raffles City. Large an pleasant bar with frieze of the Padang in the days before Raffles City, live jazz music. ***Th Long Bar***, Raffles Hotel, 1-3 Beach Rd. The home of the Singapore Sling, originall concocted by bar-tender Ngiam Tong Boon in 1915 (see page 73), now on two level and extremely popular with tourists and locals alike, gratuitous tiny dancing mechanica punkawallahs sway out of sync to the cover band. ***Writers' Bar***, *Raffles Hotel*, 1 Beach R (just off the main lobby). In honour of the likes of Somerset Maugham, Rudyard Kipling Joseph Conrad, Noel Coward and Herman Hesse who were said either to have wined dined or stayed at the hotel. Bar research indicates that other literary luminaries fro James A Michener to Noel Barber and the great Arthur Hailey are said to have sippe Tigers at the bar - as the bookcases and momentoes suggest. ***Lock, Stock and Barre Pub***, 29 Seah St. Extended Happy Hour from 1600-2000, popular with expats on budget and backpackers - dark bar/pub with juke box.

Clubs & music Rascals, *Pan Pacific Hotel*, Marina Square, 6 Raffles Blvd. Open 1800-0300, extende Happy Hour, Sunday is gay night. ***Scandals***, *Westin Plaza Hotel*, Raffles City Complex popular hotel disco. ***The Reading Room***, *Marina Mandarin Hotel*, Marina Square, is smart, expensive and pretentious disco which attracts a younger crowd. Most classica music performances are held at The ***Singapore Cultural Theatre*** and the ***Victoria Hall*** the Singapore Symphony Orchestra gives regular performances and there are ofte visiting orchestras, quartets and choirs. Check the *Strait's Times* for details.

Theatre & dance Most theatrical and dance performances are held at the ***Victoria Hall*** and ar advertised in newspapers and tourist publications. The latest offering on the thespia and artistic scene is ***The Substation***, 45 Armenian St, set up in a former power station It has an intimate little theatre where it stages plays and shows avante garde films. I also holds drama workshops. Call T3377800 for details of what's on when. ***Raffles Jubilee Hall***, 328 North Bridge Rd holds occasional theatrical performances, fo information T3311732. ***The Esplanade: theatres on the Bay*** is under construction nex to the Padang (see page) and is due for completion in 2001. There will be a concer hall, lyric theatre, three smaller studios, and an outdoor performing space. ***Kal Mandhir*** is at the ***Temple of Fine Arts,*** 1st Floor, Excelsior Hotel Shopping Centre T3390492. Classes available in dance, instrumental music, percussion and singing Fabulous array of Indian instruments. It might be possible to take a one week cours here, although most are longer.

Singapore River and the City

The Singapore River separates the high-rise, hi-tech financial district from the colonial heart of town. During the colonial period the contrast between its two banks could hardly have been greater. To the north was the heartland of colonial Singapore, with its grand administrative buildings and promenading Europeans. And to the south, the godowns and shophouses of the Chinese merchant community.

Ins and outs

Getting there

The Raffles Place MRT station is in the heart of the financial district, just south of the Singapore River. Bus nos 124, 174 and 190 run direct from Orchard Road.

Getting around

It is best to explore this area on foot - especially the river. To walk from Cavenagh Bridge near the mouth of the Singapore River to Clarke Quay takes about 20 minutes. Bumboat tours of the river leave from Clarke Quay and Raffles Landing while a handful of boats offering an assortment of short cruises to the southern islands depart from Clifford Pier.

The area

When Major Farquhar landed here with Raffles in 1819 he deemed that the north bank of the river was the only place suitable for European settlement - the south being too marshy. The river itself was the place where Singapore's lifeblood - trade - was transacted and the river was jammed with tongkangs, sampans and twakows. Some of the shophouses have been preserved, most notably those of Boat Quay and Clarke Quay, although today they serve food and drink, not trading interests.

The heart of Singapore's new wealth lies concentrated just south of the Singapore River. From the north bank the godowns and shophouses of Boat Quay, emblematic of Singapore's past vitality, stand framed against the towering corporate headquarters of Singapore's new banks and finance houses. This is where Nick Leeson, the rogue trader who broke Britain's blue-blooded merchant bank Barings, lost hundreds of millions. It is also where Singapore Inc makes billions. The CBD doesn't offer much for most casual visitors, although some of the modern architecture is praiseworthy and there are one or two remnants of Old Singapore hidden away amidst the glass, steel and concrete. It is also worth coming here just to see how Modern Singapore ticks. There's only so much that a shophouse can tell you about the present, notwithstanding their evident aesthetic appeal.

Sights

Merlion

Standing guard at the mouth of the **Singapore River** - though rather dwarfed now by a new bridge - is the mythical **Merlion**, half-lion, half-fish, the grotesque saturnine symbol of Singapore. The statue was sculpted by local artist Lim Nang Seng in 1972 and stands in the miniscule **Merlion Park**, an unaccountably popular stop for tour groups, where there is a souvenir shop which is sometimes rather ambitiously billed a museum. The merlion is best viewed from the Padang side of the river. It is inspired by the two ancient (Sanskrit) names for the island: *Singa Pura* meaning 'lion city', and *Temasek*

'Ulysses by the Merlion'
...this lion of the sea
Salt-maned, scaly,
wondrous of tail,
Touched with power,
insistent
on this brief promontory...
Puzzles.
Edwin Thumboo

meaning 'sea-town'. The confused creature is emblazoned on many a trinket and T-shirt.

Cavenagh Bridge, erected in 1869 by convict labourers (the last big project undertaken by convicts here), was originally called Edinburgh Bridge to commemorate the visit of the Duke of Edinburgh. It was later renamed Cavenagh in honour of Governor W.O. Cavenagh, the last India-appointed governor of Singapore. The bridge was constructed from steel shipped out from Glasgow (supplied by the same company that furnished the Telok Ayer Market) and was built to provide a link between the government offices on the north side of the river and Commercial Square to the south. However, it was apparently built without a great deal of thought to the tides: *tongkangs*, the lighters that transferred cargo from ships to the godowns at Boat Quay, and vice versa, could not pass under the bridge at high tide and would have to wait for the water level to drop. It became a footbridge in 1909 when the Anderson Bridge superseded it, but it still bears its old sign that forbids bullock carts, horses and heavy vehicles from crossing.

Boat Quay

Along the south bank of the river, facing Empress Place, is **Boat Quay** – commercially-speaking, this is one of the Urban Redevelopment Authority's most successful restoration projects. At the beginning of the 19th century this part of the river was swampland and the original roomah [*rumah* = house] rakits were rickety, stilted affairs built over the mud. However, by the mid-1850s Boat Quay had emerged as the centre of Singapore River's commercial life with three-quarters of the colony's trade being transferred through the godowns here. The opening of the Suez Canal in 1869 increased trade still further but the development of the steamship around the same time threatened the commercial vitality of the area: vessels

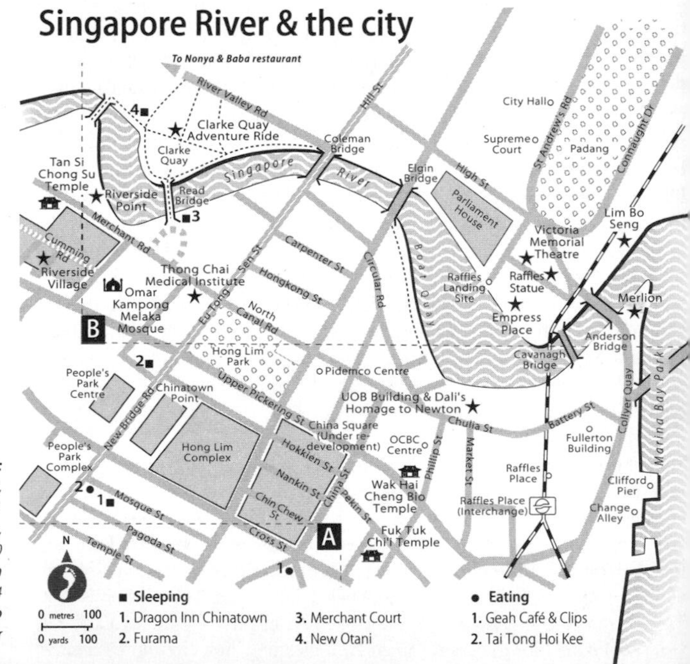

Related maps:
A. Chinatown detail, page 107
B. Colonial core, page 70
Chinatown (to the south), page 104
Coloured map inside back cover

became too large to dock here. Merchants, worried that shipping companies would move their business to the new port of Tanjong Pagar which opened in 1852, began to use lighters or *tongkangs* to load and unload ships moored outside the river; *tongkangs*, barges and sampans once littered the river, but they were cleared out to Marina Bay, or destroyed and scuttled, as part of the government's river-cleaning programme over a period of ten years. Singapore River is now said to be 'pollution-free' (although it only takes a quick glance to see that this is blatant rubbish) but what it gained in cleanliness, it has lost - some would argue (see page 177) - in aesthetics.

With technological advances threatening to undermine Boat Quay's vitality, it is perplexing that the area's merchants didn't sell up and move on. One popular explanation is that the curve of the river made it look like the belly of a carp - a sure indicator of commercial success. The wealthier the merchant the higher their godowns were constructed, giving the frontage an attractively uneven appearance. By the time the URA announced its conservation plans in 1986, Boat Quay had fallen on hard times. The original inhabitants were encouraged to leave, the shophouses and godowns were restored and renovated, and a new set of owners moved in. The strip now provides a great choice of drinking holes and restaurants for Singapore's upwardly mobile young, expats and tourists alike. They congregate here in the evening to eat and drink *al fresco*, overlooking the river. (In 1994, *al fresco* dining was banned by the authorities after four expats decided to swim across the river - the loser paid the bill. The restaurants and bars shrilly claimed that they depended on their pavement business and after a while the government relented.)

This is perhaps the most attractive place to eat or drink in Singapore: a sort of Fisherman's Wharf comes to Covent Garden, and consequently very popular with tourists. What is disturbing to the purist is that although 'conservation areas' such as Boat Quay, have been meticulously restored on the outside, they are now utterly divorced from their original purpose. Material fabric is painstakingly preserved or recreated; social fabric is torn down without an apparent second thought.

These sorts of concerns are unlikel to worry the visitor though. Boat Quay is lively and fun, attractive and atmospheric - and the bars and restaurants are generally excellent. The formerly famous *Harry's Bar* is yet more famous still: this is where Barings trader Nick Leeson would buy the rounds before he bankrupted his employer.

Elgin Bridge marks the up-river end of Boat Quay. The bridge was built in 1929 to link the community of Chinese merchants settled on the south side of the river with the Indian traders of the High Street on the north side and was named after Lord Elgin, Governor-General of India. It is, in fact, the fifth bridge to be built on this site. The first was constructed in 1819 and was the only bridge across the river at that time. Note the roundals depicting the Singapore lion under a palm tree on the base of each of the pair of cast iron lamps at either end of the bridge. They were designed by Cavalieri Rodolofo Nolli.

Clarke Quay

Clarke Quay, further up-river, has also been renovated and redeveloped too. This was once go-down country - in colonial days, the streets around the warehouses would have been bustling with coolies. It is now a pleasant pedestrian area with 150-odd shops, restaurants and bars. Clarke Quay has a slightly different feel to Boat Quay; while the latter consists of individual enterprises, the former is controlled by a single company which keeps close tabs on which shops and F&B outlets open. The atmosphere is more ersatz, more managed and controlled, and less vivacious. Unsurprisingly, this is more of a family place, while young, single people tend to congregate downriver at Boat Quay. In the pedestrian lanes, overpriced hawker stalls and touristy knick-knack carts set up from lunchtime onwards selling all manner of goods that people could do without. Despite this, it is still a lot of fun, especially at night, and unlike Boat Quay it is possible to snack from stalls while wandering the alleys of the area. On Sundays there is a flea market here.

The big family attraction at Clarke Quay is the **Clarke Quay Adventure Ride**, a Singaporean Pirates of the Caribbean in which visitors take bumboats along an underground river, floating past 80 animated figures, and the noises and sights of Old Singapore. The history begins when Singapore was little more than a jungled island infested with monster snakes, crocodiles and - zoogeographically improbably but historically appropriately - lions. It then passes through a series of vignettes including Singapore as a haven for pirates, its growth into one of the British Empire's most important entrepots, the ignominious fall of the city to the invading Japanese, and ending with its liberation in 1945 when Lord Louis Mountbatten took the surrender. ■ *S$5, S$3 for children, family tickets available. 1100-2230 Monday-Sunday.*

A good way of seeing the sights along Singapore River is on a bumboat cruise, which can be taken from Clarke Quay or Boat Quay. A rather banal recorded commentary points out the godowns, shophouses, government buildings and skyscrapers lining the riverbank. ■ *Bumboats operate 0900-2300, S$7 (S$3 for children). A river taxi also operates from here, S$1 (morning) and S$3 (afternoon).*

On the waterfront, a makeshift theatre provides **wayang performances**. Wayang was traditionally performed in tents by travelling artists who would move from town to town, performing for special occasions. The tongkangs moored alongside the quay are now used as floating restaurants. Traditionally they were used as lighters, to transport cargo from larger ships. The eyes were painted on them so that they could see where they were going. ■ *Every Wednesday and Friday at 1945-2030. The performers prepare themselves from 1800 onwards and onlookers are welcome to watch the making-up process.*

Riverside Point

Spanning the river at Clarke Quay is a pedestrian bridge, **Read Bridge**, erected in the 1880s and named after a famous businessman of the day. The antique lamps have been recently added to a structure which, when it was built, looked more modern than it does now. Read Bridge leads to **Riverside Point**, an arcade of upmarket shops and restaurants. Across Merchant Road via an aerial walkway is yet another shopping centre-cum-restaurant complex: **Riverside Village** with its component parts, **Merchant Square** and **Central Mall**. This was reputedly once a centre of prostitution and racketeering - which is hard to believe now that fornication and fraud have given way to fusion cuisine and fashion. At the north-west corner of the complex is the attractive **Tan Si Chong Su Temple** which has successfully resisted attempts at modernization. The temple was built in 1876 as an ancestral temple and assembly hall of the Hokkien Tan clan. The money was donated by Tan Kim Cheng (1829-1892) and Tan Beng Swee (1828-1884), sons of the wealthy philanthropist Tan Tock Seng. The temple faces the Singapore River - as *feng shui* (geomancy) dictates - and it is particularly rich in carvings and other decoration. The series of two courtyards and two altar halls symbolises *li*, the admired characteristic of humbling oneself in deference to others. The dragon-entwined columns, round windows and granite panels are comparatively unusual. Above the main altar table are four Chinese characters which translate as "Help the world and the people". Within the Central Mall is **HomeChef**, a culinary academy where visitors can enrol on a short *Flavours of Singapore* course and be introduced to the wonders of chilli crab, chicken rice and roasted fish in banana leaf. ■ *T5381238 for details or homechef@pacific.net.sg, 1000-1200, Tuesday-Saturday*. On the other side of Riverside Village is the **Omar Kampong Melaka Mosque** which was built in 1895 and then substantially re-modelled in 1981. There is no dome (with its pyramidal roofs it looks like a Javanese mosque) and the minaret was only added in 1985.

Collyer Quay runs south from Anderson Bridge, the last bridge across the Singapore River, past Singapore's national symbol the Merlion (see page 85), and the dour **Fullerton Building**, formerly the General Post Office. Until 1873 this site was occupied by Fullerton Fort, built to defend the Singapore River from seaborne attack. Fullerton Building was erected in 1925-1928 by a firm of Shanghai-based architects. Their heavy, almost Scottish design seems out of place in tropical Singapore and perhaps appropriately the firm left the colony in the early 1930s after they had been struck off the architect's register for professional misconduct. In 1998 the building was empty, but had been reputedly sold to a hotel chain which has plans to turn it into a six star hotel.

A little further south is **Clifford Pier**, built in the 1930s. It is possible to hire rather expensive boats here to cruise up and down the river and around Marina Bay. Bumboats and junks also take visitors on longer watery tours to Pulau Kusu and the islands of the south (see page 156). It is possible to hire a bumboat yourself - but expect to pay around S$60 per hour. Behind Clifford Pier (across the shopping arcade/footbridge) is **Change Alley** - once a crowded bazaar and the cheapest shopping spot in Singapore. Appropriately, Change Alley has changed more than anywhere else in Singapore - it has been knocked down and anything that remains has disappeared into the void between the two tower blocks that loom over it.

Singapore's financial centre

The financial centre is included on the map of Chinatown, page 104

From Change Alley it is a short walk to the heart of Singapores financial district. **Shenton Way** (Singapore's equivalent of Wall Street), **Raffles Place**, **Robinson Road** and **Cecil Street**, all packed-tight with skyscrapers, form the financial heart of modern Singapore. These streets contain most of the buildings that give the city its distinctive skyline and it is best seen from the Benjamin Sheares Bridge or from the boat coming back from Batam Island. The first foreign institutions to arrive on the island still occupy the prime sites - the Hong Kong and Shanghai Banking Corporation and Standard Chartered Bank. One of the more striking new buildings on the river is the headquarters of the **United Overseas Bank** (UOB) on Chulia Street, which towers to the maximum permissable height of 280 metres (to avoid collision with low-flying aircraft). The octagonal tower is said to represent a pile of coins, although this seems simply too crass to believe. Below, in the open under-court area, is a large bronze statue by Salvador Dali entitled *Homage to Newton*, cast in 1985. A short walk away down Philip Street is the small **Wak Hai Cheng Bio Temple** built in 1826, looking particularly diminutive against the buildings around it. The name means Guangdong [Canton] Province Calm Sea Temple and the purpose is pretty clear: to ensure that Chinese immigrants making the voyage through the dangerous South China Seas arrived safely. The two key gods depicted here

Bankers' rising aspirations

Singapore's big-four banks are obsessed with reaching for the sky. The city skyline is dominated by the banks' corporate pyramids. In the 1970s, the Oversea-Chinese Banking Corporation (OCBC) invited American-Chinese architect IM Pei to design its so-called 'vertical calculator' off Chulia Street. DBS Bank occupies a drab building on Shenton Way, but in the 1980s funded the construction of Raffles City, which boasts the tallest hotel in the world at 220m - again designed by Pei.

More recently, Overseas Union Bank (OUB) glossed its corporate image with a 280m-high aluminium triangle on Robinson Road designed by distinguished Japanese architect Kanzo Tange and became, for a while, the tallest building in the world, outside America. Not to be out-done, United Overseas Bank (UOB) also commissioned Kanzo Tange to dream up the S$500mn, 66-storey UOB Plaza which now presides over Boat Quay and Chinatown. UOB had long suffered a loss of face in the local financial community, thanks to its squat HQ on Bonham Street - a trifling 32 storeys. A picture of the new building appeared on a UOB Visa card as early as 1988, showing it towering over the nearby OUB building. But in fact, Singapore law states that 280m is the highest a building can go without becoming an aviation hazard and both buildings are exactly 280m high. A third building also reaches this magical height: the Republic Plaza.

UOB's move to its new premises may prove too much for Singapore's vertical marathon runners: the Singapore Adventurers' Club organizes an annual race to the top of the old UOB building and down again, the marathon consisting of six round trips - or 4,692 steps. The record is just under 27 minutes.

are Xuan Tien Shang Di (the Heavenly Father) in the right-hand hall and Tien Hou (the Heavenly Mother) in the left. Tien Hou is a particular favourite of sailors (see page 108). The figures on the roof are extremely vivid and so is some of the carving inside.

Another piece of old Singapore amidst the new is the **Lau Pa Sat Festival Market**, once known as Telok Ayer, between Robinson Road and Raffles Quay. This was the first municipal market in Singapore. The first market here was commissioned by Stamford Raffles in 1822 but the present structure was designed by James MacRitchie and built in cast-iron shipped out from a foundry in Glasgow in 1894. (A little piece of irrelevance: the same foundry cast the iron for Cavenagh Bridge.) It is said to be the last remaining Victorian cast-iron structure in Southeast Asia and was declared a national monument in 1973 but had to be dismantled in 1985 to make way for the MRT, and was then rebuilt. It is now a thriving Food Centre.

Essentials

Sleeping

■ *on maps*

Price codes: see inside front cover

A+ ***New Otani***, 177A River Valley Rd, T3383333, F3392854. Right next to Clarke Quay making it a lively place to stay. The rooms are average, there's a good sized pool for lengths and a fitness centre. Not surprisingly, it is popular with Japanese. Location is its strength.

A+ ***Merchant Court***, 20 Merchant Rd, T3372288, F3340606, mchotel@sing-net com.sg, http://www.raffles.com/ril. New, 500-room hotel, owned by the *Raffles* group. This is a welcome addition to the mid-range bracket of hotels, many of which are looking rather tired. Attractive freeform pool in rooftop garden setting with slides and a separate Jacuzzi overlooking the river. Excellent fitness centre managed by *Lifestyles*. Great location makes it an appealing choice.

Eating: expensive

● *on maps*
Price codes: see inside front cover

4 ***Bangkok Garden***, Keck Seng Tower, 133 Cecil St (financial district), T2207310. Almost anything **Thai** is available, even if it's not on the menu, speciality fruit juices and crab dishes are very popular.

3 ***Blaze Café***, Ground Floor, The Cannery, Clarke Quay, **international**. Pizza, pasta, hotdogs, fish and chips, burgers - a good place to bring the children.

3 ***Brewerkz***, Riverside Point, T4382311, a micro brewery with pricey beer and also serving **New Asia** cuisine.

3 ***Chilis***, 75 Boat Quay. **American** fare - burgers, grills, sandwiches - a good menu and reasonably priced for this prime location.

4 ***Diandin Leluk***, Riverside Point, 30 Merchant Rd, opposite Clarke Quay, T4382890, **Thai**. Newish restaurant, with special deals and plenty of seafood dishes, attractive location.

5 ***Hot Stones Steak and Seafood***, **International**, 53 Boat Quay, T5355188. Speciality: cooking slabs of meat or seafood on baking-hot Serpentine rock at the table.

4 ***Paladino di Firenze***, 7 Mohammed Sultan Rd, T7380917. Unusual **Italian** dishes in a restored shophouse setting - the broschetta is outstanding.

4 ***Pasta Fresca da Salvatore***, 30 Boat Quay, **Italian**. Fresh, tasty pizzas and a good range of pasta dishes, open 24 hours.

4 ***The Next Level***, Merchant Village, Merchant Road. New, trendy **fusion** restaurant just south of the river.

4 ***Riverside Indonesian Restaurant*** Riverside Point, 30 Merchant Rd, opposite Clarke Quay, T5350383. Bright functional interior, but some al fresco dining overlooking the river, baked pomfret, chilli crabs, grilled chicken - good menu and attractive location.

3 ***Pao Pao Cha Vegetarian Restaurant***, Riverside Point, 30 Merchant Rd, on river, opposite Clarke Quay. Camp little place with a range of teas and **vegetarian** small eats, strange decor.

3 ***Sushi Dokoro Yoshida***, 58 Boat Quay, T5341401. Another riverfront restaurant specializing in **Japanese** *izakaya* (barbecued fish) designed around a sushi bar, also a branch in Lucky Plaza, Orchard Rd.

4 ***Sukhothai***, 47 Boat Quay, T5382422. Extensive **Thai** menu but the food can be a little hit and miss, booking recommended.

3 ***Yu Kong Choon,*** Riverside Point, 30 Merchant Rd, opposite Clarke Quay, T4385880. Good location and good **seafood**, open until 0400.

Eating: cheaper

2 ***House of Sundanese Food***, 55 Boat Quay. Typical **Sundanese** dishes from West Java include spicy salad (*keredok*), charcoal-grilled seafood (*ikan Sunda*, *ikan mas*) and curries, simply decorated non-a/c restaurant, with a real home-cooked taste.

2 ***Nonya and Baba***, 262/264 River Valley Rd, T7341382. Simple place serving excellent **Peranakan** food which blends Chinese and Malay cuisine in a unique fusion. Lots of coconut milk and seafood with dishes such as *otak otak* (spicy pressed fish in coconut milk). The owner is an Elvis fan. The *Next Page Pub*, in a refurbished shophouse, is nearby (see Bars).

Hawker centres & food courts

2 ***Lau Pa Sat Festival Market*** (formerly the Telok Ayer Food Centre) at the Raffles Quay end of Shenton Way in the old Victorian market (see page 90). Good range of food on offer: Chinese, Indian, Nonya, Korean, Penang, icecreams, fruit drinks - it's well worth a browse. **2** ***Satay Club***, evening stalls in the pedestrian streets of Clarke Quay. The food is good but, being a tourist trap, it's almost double the price of other food courts. **1** ***Quayside Food Court***, Basement of Liang Court, next door to Clarke Quay. Good choice of Asian stalls and a *Burger King*, play area for children.

Cafés

Bar Gelateria Bellavista, Clarke Quay. Delicious Italian ice cream, indoor and outdoor seating. ***Polar Café***, B1-04 OUB Centre, Raffles Place (also branch in Lucky Plaza). The original home of the curry puff, first created at its former premises on Hill St in 1926 S$0.70 each. Recommended. ***Café Boat Quay***, 82 Boat Quay, T2300140. A refurbished shophouse. A dozen computers available for surfing the web, S$10 per hour. Built in NetNanny prevents any sleaze, if you let your children loose here. International 'snack food, live music some nights. **3 *Dôme***, in the heart of the business district on Cecil St Delicious foccaccia sandwiches, patisseries and some of the best coffee in town, good café atmosphere and a pleasant stop for a midmorning break.

Bars There are lots of bars on Boat and Clarke quays; those at the former are wilder and less packaged. It is best just to mosey along and take your fancy. ***Crazy Elephant***, Clarke Quay, T3371190, live music (house band), popular place for a drink following a meal ***Brewerkz***, Riverside Point, one of the micro breweries which are all the rage in Asia Good beer, but pricey. ***Escobar,*** 36 Boat Quay. A Latin American bar with salsa and cocktails to match. ***Espana,*** 45 Boat Quay. Marguerítas, daiquiris and jugs of Heineken, accompanied by Latin music. ***Harry's Quayside***, 28 Boat Quay. Large bar with seating outside overlooking the river, popular with City boys, serves food, pricey jazz band. ***Molly Malone's***, 42 Circular Rd, off Boat Quay, T5345100. Irish pub (complete with stout, Irish folk music etc) with a restaurant upstairs, usually packed ***Next Page Pub***, 15 Jl Mohamed Sultan (River Valley Rd), T2356967. A converted shophouse, great decor - salon style with opium beds, cubby holes and cushions - makes for a good evening if combined with a meal at the nearby *Nonya and Baba* restaurant on River Valley Rd. Recommended. ***Riverbank Bar***, 68 Boat Quay. Live music. ***The Yard,*** 294 River Valley Rd. The Singaporean version of a London pub complete with darts, dominos, fish 'n' chips and Newcastle Brown Ale. ***Trader Vics*** 5th Floor, *New Otani Hotel*, River Valley Rd. Hawaii 5-0 decor and Chin-Ho's favourite cocktails - try a few goblets of Tikki Puka Puka for something violently different. There is a strip of pubs on Jl Mohamed Sultan (River Valley Rd) - Peranakan-style - ***Wong San's*** at No 12 (T7383787) and ***Zens*** at No 10. The building site opposite detracts from the general ambience, but hopefully that is short-term.

Clubs ***The Warehouse***, 382 Havelock Rd, *River View Hotel*, large dance hall, mainly frequented by teenagers. ***Velvet Underground***, Jiak Kim St (off Kim Seng Rd) next door to *Zouk's* bar. Owned by Zouk's, small nightclub, open until 0300, cover S$25, free for women on Wednesday nights. Recommended. ***Zouk's***, 17-21 Jiak Kim St, T7382988, possibly the hippest club-bar in town with great music, a 2000-2100 Happy Hour and open Monday-Saturday 1800-0300.

Orchard Road

Before being cleared for the construction of colonial mansions in the mid 1800s, the Orchard Road area was one vast nutmeg plantation. Choon Keng Tang, a rags-to-riches immigrant from Swatow, bought a plot of land on Orchard Road in 1945 and built CK Tang's Oriental curio store, in Chinese imperial style. In 1982 the old shop was demolished and the new hotel and department store complex went up; the eye-catching pagoda-style Marriott Hotel *(once the* Dynasty*), with Tang's still next to it, is one of the last remaining remnants of Oriental style in an otherwise Occidental street.*

Ins and outs

Getting there

There are three MRT stations on, or close to, Orchard Road. Dhoby Ghaut MRT station lies at the eastern end of Orchard Road, close to the northwest corner of the Colonial core. The Somerset MRT stop is on Somerset Road, which runs parallel to Orchard Road. The Orchard MRT station is at the intersection of Orchard Road and Scotts Road, towards the western end of the strip and close to the main concentration of hotels. A profusion of bus services run along Orchard Road - at last count, some 20 in all.

Getting around

To walk Orchard Road from end to end is quite a slog - from Dhoby Ghaut to the north-western end of Orchard Road past Scotts Road is around 2.5 km. This is fine, though, if you're taking it slowly, stopping-off for brief respites in one of the many air-conditioned shopping arcades. Otherwise consider hopping on a bus or taking the MRT.

The area

Singapore's catwalk and a shoppers paradise

Orchard Road is Singapore's catwalk, where the young and beautiful strut and preen, showing off their latest purchases. It is a shopper's paradise and is said to have the highest density of shops in the world, as well as being one of the world's most expensive shopping streets. Most things that the human heart - if not the soul - could desire seem to be for sale here: camcorders and CDs, mules and micros, gold and garnet. CK Tang may have been a committed Christian - his Department store is dedicated with the inscription To God be the Glory - but Orchard Road is dedicated to Mammon.

Amidst this shopping extravaganza encased in grandiose high-rise blocks, there are some remnants of Old Singapore which have managed to escape the demolition ball. In particular, there are one or two buildings on Cuppage Road, as well as the pleasant and peaceful Emerald Hill, with its bars and street cafés (see bars and restaurants). The Peranakan (Straits Chinese) shophouses found here - which have been carefully restored to their original condition - were constructed at the beginning of this century and combine European and Chinese architectural elements.

Sights

Emerald Hill was laid out by 30 different owners between 1901 and 1925: conforming to the established theme was considered good manners, which has resulted in a charming street of shophouses. The **Peranakan Place Museum** on Emerald Hill gives some idea of what Straits Chinese townhouses were originally like inside, although this recreation is not the best example. For a detailed background on Peranakan culture, see page 186.

The museum is only open on request - contact George on T7326966, F7372411 - and usually only to groups. S$10 (S$5 for children).

About three-quarters of the way southeast down Orchard Road, towards Bras Basah Road, are the gates to an inviting shady avenue that leads to the **Istana Negara Singapura**, the residence of the former British governors of Singapore (from 1869-1959) and now home to the President of the Republic. The Istana was designed by the colonial architect Captain McNair, in Malay-cum-colonial style, with overhanging roofs blended with classical details. Like other colonial houses of this era (see page 181), it was raised off the ground to provide a cooling effect. It has been much altered over the years and is not open to the public.

Dhoby Ghaut, at the end of Orchard Road, got its name from the Bengali and Madrasi dhobies who used to wash the clothes of local residents in the stream which ran down the side of Orchard Road and dry them on the land now occupied by the *YMCA*. *Ghaut* is a Hindi word meaning landing place or path down to a river, while *dhoby* is from the Sanskrit word *dhona* meaning to wash. The dhobies would walk from house to house collecting their clients' washing, noting each piece down in a little book using a series of marks (they were illiterate). In 1998 a large chunk of Dhoby Ghaut was being redeveloped as part of the extension programme of the MRT. It will become an interchange linking the north-east with city hall. The plans are to make this an extensive entertainment and retail area - though it is not expected to be completed before 2002.

On Tank Road is **Tan Yeok Nee Mansion**, one of the very few remaining traditionally designed Chinese houses in Singapore. It was built in 1885 by a wealthy Teochew merchant who imported the granite columns from southern China. The building was badly damaged during the Japanese occupation but was later restored by the Salvation Army. It has been

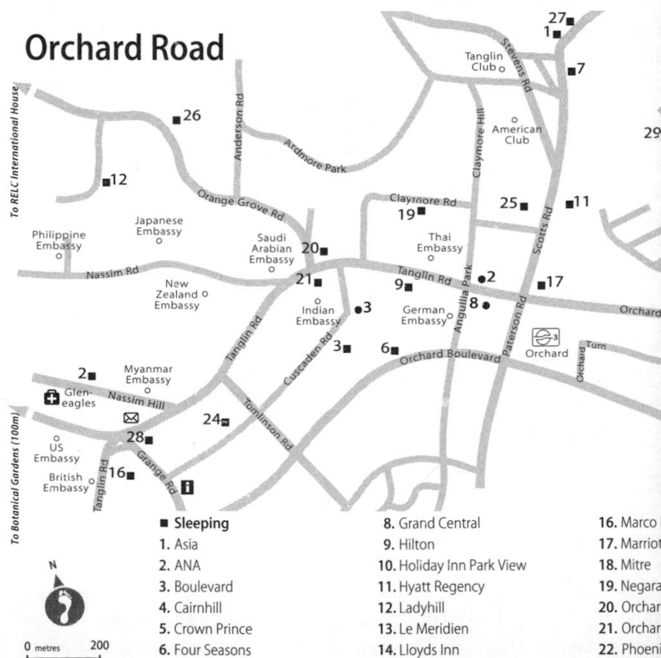

Related maps:
Orchard Road shopping centres, page 46
Fort Canning Park, page 78
Colonial core (to the east), page 70
Coloured map inside back cover

designated a national monument but remains boarded up and not open to the public.

Botanic Gardens

At the western end of Orchard Road are the **Botanic Gardens**, on Cluny Road, not far from Tanglin (T4709900). The gardens contain almost half a million species of plants and trees from around the world in its 47 hectares of landscaped parkland, primary jungle, lawns and lakes. The Botanic Gardens were founded by an agri-horticultural society in 1859. In the early years they played an important role in fostering agricultural development in Singapore and Malaya as successive directors collected, propagated and distributed plants with economic potential, the most famous of which was rubber. Henry Ridley, director of the gardens from 1888-1912, pioneered the planting of the Brazilian para rubber tree (*Hevea brasiliensis*). In 1877, 11 seedlings brought from Kew Gardens in London were planted in the Singapore gardens. An immediate descendant of one of the 11 originals is still alive in the Botanic Gardens today, near the main entrance. By the lake at the junction of Tyersall and Cluny roads there is a memorial to Ridley on the site where the original trees were planted. Ridley was known as 'Mad Ridley' because of the proselytizing zeal with which he lobbied Malaya's former coffee planters to take up rubber instead.

In 1963 former Prime Minister Lee Kuan Yew launched the successful Garden City campaign and most of the trees lining Singapore's highways were supplied by the Botanic Gardens. The gardens now cater for the recreational needs of modern Singapore. Every morning and evening the park fills with joggers and Tai Chi fanatics. During the day, wedding parties pose for pictures among the foliage. The gardens are beautifully laid out and are well worth a visit. A map can be acquired from the Ranger's office, 5 minutes walk into the garden. The bandstand in the centre of the gardens is

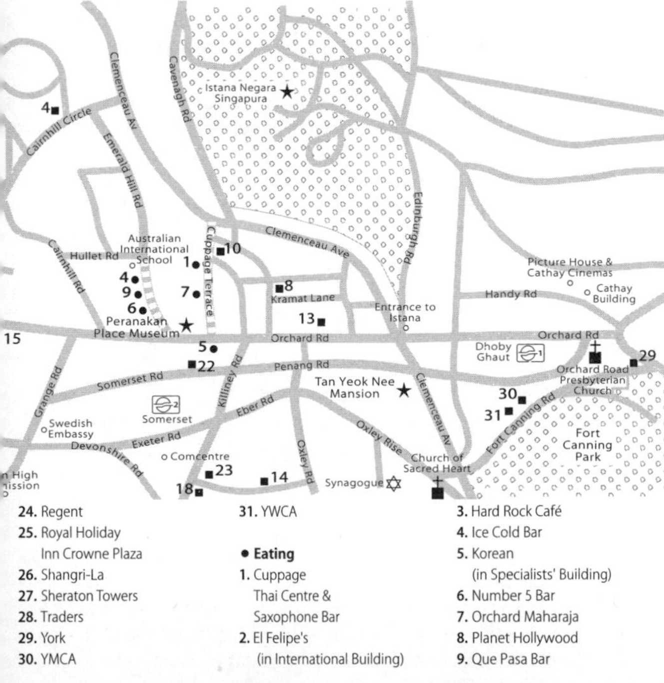

24. Regent
25. Royal Holiday Inn Crowne Plaza
26. Shangri-La
27. Sheraton Towers
28. Traders
29. York
30. YMCA
31. YWCA

• Eating

1. Cuppage Thai Centre & Saxophone Bar
2. El Felipe's (in International Building)
3. Hard Rock Café
4. Ice Cold Bar
5. Korean (in Specialists' Building)
6. Number 5 Bar
7. Orchard Maharaja
8. Planet Hollywood
9. Que Pasa Bar

used for live music performances at the weekends. ■ *0500-2400 Monday-Sunday*. The Botanic Gardens also houses the **National Orchid Garden** where 700 species and 2,000 hybrids of Singapore's favourite flower are lovingly cultivated. It is billed as the Largest Orchid Showcase in the World. The gardens began to breed orchids back in 1928 and those on show include Singapore's national flower, Miss Agnes Joaquim's orchid, discovered at the tail end of the 19th century (see page 175). The Mist House contains a collection of rare orchids. ■ *0830-1900, last ticket sales at 1800, admission S$2, S$1 children. The closest entrance to the Botanics for the Orchid Garden is on Tyersall Avenue. Lots of buses run past the Botanics including nos 7, 77, 105, 106, 123 and 174, alighting at the junction of Cluny and Napier roads, next to Gleneagles Hospital.*

Essentials

Sleeping

■ *on maps*

Price codes: see inside front cover

You could be forgiven for mistaking Orchard Rd for the US for it retains little that is Asian in character. There are numerous 4 and 5-star hotels strung out along the road, mostly concentrated towards the western end. There is often little to differentiate between them.

L+ ***Four Seasons***, 190 Orchard Boulevard, T7341110, F7330682. This intimate hotel of 250 rooms (and 400 staff) provides exceptional personal service; there's no check-in desk and all guests are greeted by name. Rooms are elegantly decorated in traditional European style, with feather pillows, writing desk, multi-disc player, modem/fax hook up and spacious bathrooms. The hotel has a unique Asian art collection, with attractive artwork in all the rooms. There are 2 pools - one is for lengths - and the hotel boasts the only air-conditioned tennis courts in Singapore, a golf simulator, and a well-equipped health and fitness centre, with attendants on hand all day. Restaurants include Cantonese and contemporary American cuisine, with lunch-time buffet. Although this is primarily a business hotel, children are well catered for and a special children's lunch is provided at the weekends. For service and general ambience, this hotel is hard to beat. Recommended.

L+ ***Hyatt Regency***, 10-12 Scotts Rd, T7381234, F7321696, sales@hyatt.com.sg, http://www.travelweb.com/hyatt.htm. Owned by the Sultan of Brunei, unusual lobby area with bird prints on the walls, bustling atmosphere, stunning flower arrangements, bigger than average rooms, all with an alcove sitting area (some with poolside view) and separate showers. Spectacular large 5th floor garden, with roaring waterfall and a very attractive pool area, poolside bar and restaurant. The executive class rooms have their own private Balinese garden (good for families) while those on the 5th Floor open out onto a large terrace area. Squash courts, 2 tennis courts, huge fitness centre with aerobics classes, fabulous jacuzzi and sauna. Very popular bar in the basement - *Brannigans*. Its selling point must be its garden and fitness facilities. 85% corporate clients and good discounts available. Recommended.

L+ ***Goodwood Park***, 22 Scotts Rd, T7377411, F7328558. Apart from *Raffles*, this is the only other colonial hotel in Singapore. It has had a chequered history, beginning life in 1856 as the German Recreation Club, the Teutonia. During World War One it was declared enemy property and was seized by the government. In 1929 it was converted into a hotel, but then during World War Two it was occupied by the Japanese. After the war it became a War Crimes Trial Court and did not resume functioning as a hotel until 1947. The exterior is looking a little scruffy and the lobby area isn't very encouraging, but the rooms are exceptional. Of the 235 rooms, there is a choice of colonial or modern style. The former have ceiling fans and windows that can be opened, with very stylish minimalist decor and lots of space. The modern rooms are slightly smaller, but they overlook the Mayfair pool and some rooms on the ground level lead straight out pool side. All rooms are fitted with the latest electronic equipment. Lovely pool area, set in a garden with pagodas, and another larger lengths pool. Several restaurants (see **Eating**). Recommended.

L+-A+ ***Melia at Scotts***, 45 Scotts Rd, T7325885, F7321332. This Spanish hotel has an unusual feel, with attractive contemporary art on the walls. The rooms are well appointed and bigger than average with high ceilings (unusual in modern hotels). There is a smallish pool and the only Spanish restaurant in Singapore. The hotel is popular with Japanese. Rather off the main drag but close to Newton MRT and near the huge hawker centre there, hospitable service. Recommended.

L ***Regent***, 1 Cuscaden Rd, T7338888, F7328838. Huge ostentatious lobby with bubble lifts and a rather sterile atmosphere reminiscent of tenement blocks. Gloomy corridors and 440 large but quite plain rooms. Excellent fitness centre but boring circular pool and barren sunbathing area. Quiet location at western end of Orchard Rd. Notable for its excellent service and attention to detail.

L ***Shangri-La***, 22 Orange Grove Rd, T7373644, F7373370. One of Singapore's finest hotels set in a beautifully maintained, spacious landscaped garden. 300 plus rooms, the standard ones are nothing exceptional but those in the refined and relaxed Valley Wing are superior and the service exceptional. Excellent leisure facilities: spacious pool area, surrounded by greenery and waterfalls, jacuzzi, indoor pool, good fitness centre, squash and tennis courts, and a three hole pitch and putt golf 'course'. Three restaurants - *Shang Palace* for dim sum, *Tanti Bacis* for poolside Italian and a Japanese restaurant. Winner of Singapore Tourism Board's award for best hotel year after year. Recommended.

L ***Hilton***, 581 Orchard Rd, T7372233, F7322917. The first international hotel in Singapore. Its 434 average-sized rooms were recently renovated and despite its age it maintains a good reputation. Particularly popular with business people (with its function rooms constantly in demand), and with Japanese tour groups. *Tradewinds* restaurant serves local and North Indian food in al fresco atmosphere at the poolside, the *Inn of Happiness* serves Chinese food, *Harbour Grill* for French cuisine (different French chefs visit every month), the *Checkers Deli* on the ground floor sells chocolates and desserts and has a reputation for its Philadelphia cheesecake. The *Kaspia Bar* has the largest range of vodkas in Singapore and live jazz. Small, rather dated pool, good facilities in the fitness centre.

L ***Holiday Inn Park View***, 11 Cavenagh/Orchard Rd, T7338333, F7324757. Grand entrance, attractive airy triangular layout of 300 plus rooms around an atrium. Good pool and fitness centre. Rooms provided for handicapped people. Quiet spot just off the main drag.

L ***Le Meridien***, 100 Orchard Rd, T7338855, F7327886. Open-plan lobby with 4 terraces of rooms and garlands of orchids. Good sized rooms (corner rooms are larger), queen sized beds, attractive decor, ask for a room overlooking the pool, as these have a balcony. Good pool for lengths, but barren seating area. Fitness centre with dance floor for classes.

L ***Mandarin***, 333 Orchard Rd, T7374411, F7322361, http://www.singnet.com.sg Rather disjointed lobby area, with nowhere comfortable to sit. Rooms (1,200) are large and well designed, uninviting pool area but large pool. Revolving *Top of the M* restaurant on the 39th Floor. No outstanding features to this hotel, but the service is reportedly good.

L ***Marco Polo***, 247 Tanglin Rd, T4747141, F4710521. 600 rooms and an attractive low-key lobby. Rooms are fairly standard but the pool area has very attractive gardens surrounding it. Excellent fitness centre. A short hop from Orchard Rd and a short jog from the Botanic Gardens. Corporate discounts of up to 50% may be possible. *La Brasserie*, French restaurant is very popular (booking recommended). Good bakery.

L ***Negara***, 10 Claymore Rd, T7370811, F8316617. This 200-room hotel prides itself on an intimate atmosphere. It pampers the businessman or woman away from home with personalized service (no reception counters here) and a very high standar throughout. There are no 'club' floors; but larger than average and unusual room Spacious bathrooms and separate showers, large pool but rather exposed sitting are Very sophisticated fitness centre and jacuzzi. Slightly off Orchard Rd, quieter and awa from the crowds. Recommended.

L ***Orchard***, 442 Orchard Rd, T7347766, F7335482. Rooms here have been recentl renovated - they are decent sized, all with personal safe and the bathrooms hav separate showers; a luxury in Singapore. Large pool but no shade, excellent fitnes centre and sauna. Its claim to fame is its magnificent ballroom which seats 1,000 fc dinner and 1,500 for conference. For the *Drake Restaurant*, see below.

L ***Sheraton Towers***, 39 Scotts Rd, T7376888, F7371072. Quietly sophisticated lobb with waterfalls and beautiful flowers everywhere. 400 rooms with bare corridors bu good rooms. The more expensive rooms provide an exceptional service, with lots o extras thrown in. The *Cabana* rooms on the rooftop overlook the pool. Attractive poc area with bar. 80 per cent business guests and popular with US visitors. Italia restaurant open evenings only and exclusive Chinese restaurant. The hotel has wo the Singapore Tourist Board service award for 6 years.

L-A+ ***ANA***, 16 Nassim Hill, T7321222, F732222, ANAhotel@singnet.com.sg Restaurants (including excellent Japanese, of course), pool, formerly the *Sheraton*, short walk from Orchard Rd.

A+ ***Royal Crowne Plaza***, 25 Scotts Rd, T7377966, F7376646. 500 rooms in an ugl block, built in 1974, renovations should be complete. Quite pleasant pool area, bi fitness centre. Owned by the Sultan of Brunei, for whom an entire floor of suites i permanently reserved, *surau* provided for Muslims to pray, popular with Japanes and US visitors.

A+ ***Marriott***, 320 Orchard Rd, T7355800, F7359800. Another 350-room monste which was once the *Dynasty*. Its distinguishing feature is its rather ridiculous pagod 'hat' at the top of the tower block. Unusual lobby with 10m-high palm trees and th usual array of facilities. Good fitness centre and large swimming pool with separat whirlpool and *Garden Terrace Café*. Extensive business services, efficient bu unwelcoming, very central.

A+ ***Novotel Orchid Singapore***, 214 Dunearn Rd, T2503322, F2509292. 44 unexceptional rooms in an unexceptional hotel. The pool is rather old fashioned an right next to a busy road. Added disadvantage of an inconvenient location.

A+ ***Orchard Parade***, 1 Tanglin Rd, T7371133, F7330242, htttp://www.singnet com.sg/~webworld/hotels/ orchardp/orchardp.html. Another featureless block bu the rooms have an unusual layout and the bathrooms are refreshingly different Otherwise quite bland. Decent sized pool with a large bare sitting area. Smallish gym under renovation. The hotel is planning an extensive 3-year expansion programm which will probably improve it.

A+ ***Traders***, 1A Cuscaden Rd, T7382222, F314314. Lavish pots of orchids at the entrance makes it feel special, but there isn't much to mark this hotel apart from the competition. It has 547 rooms and about three-quarters of its guests are business people. The rooms are average but there is an attractive pool area with a large pool. It has a fitness centre, a business centre and 3 restaurants. No frills.

A+-A ***Asia***, 37 Scotts Rd, T7378388, F7333563. Ugly block with basic rooms, discounts available.

A+-A ***Equatorial***, 429 Bukit Timah Rd, T7320431, F7379426. Very average establishment with a rather public pool and a small coffee house, not a good location either.

A+-A ***Grand Central***, 22 Orchard Rd, T7379944, F7333175. Restaurant and pool, nothing special but its name provides a clue to its key selling point - it's central.

A ***VIP***, 5 Balmoral Crescent, T2354277, F2352824, a/c. Restaurant, pool, situated in quiet area of the city close to *Garden Hotel* and west of the Newton MRT station, good rooms with TV, minibar etc.

B ***Lloyd's Inn***, 2 Lloyd Rd, T7377309, F7377847, a/c. Restaurant, scrupulously clean, well-appointed rooms - if a little cramped - quiet location in suburban road near River Valley Rd/Somerset MRT, off Killiney Rd.

B ***Regalis Court***, 64 Lloyd Rd, T7347117, F7361651. Attractive renovated colonial style boutique hotel, originally a school. It provides 43 beautifully appointed rooms, decked out with Indonesian furniture and decor and wooden floorboards. The standard rooms have no windows, but they are well lit. The price is so reasonable because there is no pool or fitness centre. *Peranakan* restaurant on the ground floor and self service breakfast. Set in a quiet street behind Orchard Rd, it's hard to beat at the price. Highly recommended.

B ***RELC International House***, 30 Orange Grove Rd, T7379044, F7339976. Basic no-nonsense hotel with no extras. An ugly featureless block but quite a good deal for businesswomen and men, conference rooms attached.

B ***YWCA***, Fort Canning Rd, T3384222, F3374222. Large new building with 200 plus rooms, pool, tennis courts, ballroom, exhibition hall. It is not clear why it's called a *YWCA* - it is not what you would expect from your average 'Youth Hostel'. Dorms **B**.

C ***Metropolitan YMCA***, 60 Stevens Rd, T7377755, F2355528. All rooms are a/c, a newly renovated no frills place providing efficient service and clean serviceable rooms. The added bonus is a large swimming pool. Very good value. Recommended.

C ***YMCA International House***, 1 Orchard Rd, T3366000, F3373140. The old *YMCA* which stood on Stamford Rd was used by the Japanese during the war as their dreaded interrogation and torture centre. Facilities are well above the usual *YMCA* standards, a/c, restaurant, rooftop pool, squash courts, badminton, billiards and fitness centre. Grotty from the outside, but it is very clean and efficient. Good value for this location, *McDonald's* on the ground floor, S$25 for 4 bed a/c dorm. Recommended.

D ***Mitre***, 145 Killiney Rd (up a side lane, parallel to Lloyd Rd), T7373811. On the verge of extinction, or ripe for redevelopment, the building is best described as 'crumbling colonial', so has heaps of character, but resembles a junk yard and the rooms are very run down. Nicer than the cheap places on Bencoolen St because of its character.

Eating: expensive

● *on maps*
Price codes:
see inside front cover

4 ***Bombay Woodlands***, 19 Tanglin Rd, Tanglin Shopping Centre, Orchard Rd, T2352712. Very reasonably priced for the area, **Indian vegetarian** food.

4 ***Bumbu***, Orchard Shopping Centre, Orchard Rd. Trendy new spot offering **Indonesian** cuisine.

5 ***Chico's N Charlie's***, 05-01 Liat Towers, 541 Orchard Rd, T7341753. An expat **Mexican** hang-out, good atmosphere, good choice of hacienda food, excellent margaritas and good value.

4 ***Esmirada***, No 01-01/02, Peranakan Place, 180 Orchard Rd, T7353476. **Mediterranean** food in Spanish style taverna, good salads, paella, couscous. Always packed, reservations recommended.

4 ***Dragon City***, *Novotel Hotel*, 214 Dunearn Rd, T2547070, popular **Szechuan** restaurant with classic ostentatious Chinese decor, renowned for its spicy seafood. The smoked Szechuan duck is a speciality (similar to Peking duck), booking advisable, recommended.

4 ***Drake Restaurant***, basement of *Negara Hotel*, 10 Claymore Rd, off Orchard Rd, T8316688, **international**. A theme restaurant taken to extremes, with duck decoys, duck noises, duck prints and an all-duck menu.

4 ***El Felipé's***, 360 Orchard Rd 02-09, International Building, T4681520, **Mexican**. *El Felipé's* frozen margaritas are even more delicious than the burittos. Recommended.

5 ***Gordon Grill***, Lobby, *Goodwood Park Hotel*, 22 Scotts Rd, T2358637. One of the last Grills in town, Singapore's only **Scottish** restaurant with haggis on the menu ... at 24 hours' advance notice. Plenty of choice cuts of meat to choose from. Superb desserts.

5 ***Harbour Grill***, *Hilton Hotel*, 581 Orchard Rd, T7303393, **International**. Contemporary surroundings, oysters are a speciality, but other delicacies include caviar and smoked salmon, impeccable service.

4 ***Kintamani***, *Apollo Hotel*, 405 Havelock Rd, T7332081. **Balinese**-style interior, extensive buffet spread available at lunch and dinner.

4 ***Korean Restaurant***, Specialists' Centre, Orchard Rd, T2350018. This imaginatively-named restaurant is well known for its *bulgogi* meat barbecues.

5 ***Latour***, *Shangri-La Hotel*, 22 Orange Grove Rd, T7373144. Sophisticated - and pricey - **French** restaurant serving classic cuisine, open for lunch and dinner.

5 ***Le Chalet***, *Ladyhill Hotel*, 1 Ladyhill Rd (off Orchard Rd), T7372111. Opened in 1968 this Swiss restaurant is still *the* place to eat fondue in Singapore.

3 ***Lei Gardens***, Ground Floor, CHIJMES, 30 Victoria St, T3393822, F3342648, also at Orchard Shopping Centre, 321 Orchard Rd, T7343988 and Orchard Plaza, 150 Orchard Rd. Outstanding **Cantonese** food - silver codfish, emperor's chicken and such regulars as dim sum and Peking duck - in fact a menu which is said to comprise 2,000 dishes. Dignatories, royalty and film stars dine here. Tasteful decor and a 2-tier aquarium displaying the days offerings. Book in advance. Worth every penny. Recommended.

5 ***Maxim's de Paris***, *The Regent*, 1 Cuscaden Rd, T7393091. **French** extravaganza in an art deco setting, booking recommended, excellent food and the most extensive wine list in Singapore, pay through the nose for this spot of sophistication.

4 ***Min Jiang***, *Goodwood Park Hotel*, 22 Scotts Rd, T7301704. Large, noisy room, expansive **Szechuan** menu, with excellent reputation - delicious hot and sour soup, and good choice of seafood, 7 private rooms as well, booking recommended.

5 ***Nutmegs***, *Hyatt Regency Hotel*, 10-12 Scotts Rd, off Orchard Rd, T7307112. A well established **New Asia** restaurant, guest chefs means that the menu changes regularly. Recommended.

4 ***Pasta Fresca da Salvatore***, Shaw Centre (convenient for movies upstairs at Shaw Lido Complex), **Italian**. Fresh, tasty pizzas and a good range of pasta, open 24 hours.

4 ***Paolo and Ping***, *Royal Crowne Plaza Hotel*, 25 Scotts Rd, T7317985. Popular **New Asian** restaurant.

4 ***Saigon***, Cairnhill Place, 15 Cairnhill Rd, off Orchard Rd, T2350626. Spacious and relaxed surroundings, superb **Vietnamese** food, with very helpful waiters to give advice, pan-fried beef recommended and innovative and tasty dishes such as crab in beer.

5 ***Seasons***, *Four Seasons Hotel*, 190 Orchard Blvd, T8317250, **International**. Sophisticated surroundings and unusual food combinations makes this a relaxed and pleasurable gastronomic experience, at weekends they cater for children.

5 ***Suntory***, 06-01 Delfi Orchard, 402 Orchard Rd, T7325111, **Japanese**. For sushi, tempura, teppanyaki and shabu-shabu-lovers with a serious yen (or two).

Eating: cheaper

2 ***Bintang Timur***, 02-08/13 Far East Plaza, 14 Scotts Rd, T2354539. Excellent **Malay** satays and curries, the ambience allows you to forget that you're in a shopping centre.

3 ***Chilli Buddy's***, 180 Orchard Rd, Peranakan Place, **International**. Outside dining under umbrellas, informal and relaxed.

3 ***Cuppage Thai Food***, 49 Cuppage Terrace, T7341116. Popular **Thai** restaurant with outside tables and photographs of the food to aid decision making, makes for a good evening if combined with a visit to *Saxophone bar*, just a few doors down. Recommended.

3-2 ***Han's***, 8 branches around the city including Park Mall (Dhoby Ghaut) and the Far East Plaza (Scotts Road). This chain of restaurants is Singapore's answer to the Greasy Spoon - cafés without the acute accent on the 'e', single dish **Chinese** meals, simple (largely fried) breakfasts, some **European** food including such things as steaks, burgers and fries all served in large helpings at very competitive prices.

3 ***Hard Rock Café***, 02-01 HPL House, 50 Cuscaden Rd, **International**. One of the best

bets for a decent steak, buffalo wings or a bacon cheeseburger, open until 0200.
2 ***Ivin's***, 19/21 Binjai Park, out of town, off Dunearn Rd (north of Orchard Rd). Very good, cheap food in hectic atmosphere, popular restaurant serving all main **Nonya** dishes.
3 ***Maharani***, 05-36 Far East Plaza, Scotts Rd, T2358840. Rated as one of the best for **North Indian** cuisine - tandoori chicken and kormas are specialities.
3 ***Next Level***, Merchant Village, Merchant Road. New, trendy **fusion** restaurant just south of the river.
3 ***Orchard Maharajah***, 25 Cuppage Terrace, T7326331. Excellent **North Indian** food - tandoori and Kashmiri, conveniently located next door to *Saxophone* in converted shophouse, 7 different types of bread to choose from.
3 ***Planet Hollywood***, 541 Orchard Rd, **International**. Opened to much showbiz fanfare in 1997, but it isn't up to much. There's a limited menu - pizza, pasta and burgers - young trendies come for the surroundings (leopard and zebra skin walls and carpets) and the merchandise, not for the food. No booking available.
3 ***Sanur***, 17/18, 4th Floor, Centrepoint, 176 Orchard Rd, T7342192. Cramped **Malay/Indonesian** restaurant ideally placed for shoppers, specialities including fish-head curries and spicy grilled chicken or fish.
3 ***Saxophone***, 23 Cuppage Terrace. Singapore's best live-music joint also has an excellent **French** restaurant: the menu is select, eat at the bar or on the terrace, escargots and chocolate mousse recommended.
3 ***Singapore Polo Club***, 80 Mount Pleasant Rd (just off Thomson Rd), **International**. If you're not put off by the polo set or visiting sultans, the Polo Club is a great place to dine (or drink Pimms) on the verandah - especially on match days (Tuesday, Thursday and Saturday) when there's plenty to look at. There is a snack menu (steak sandwich, fish and chips etc) for the verandah overlooking the turf and a smarter restaurant inside. Recommended.
3 ***Tambuah Mas***, 4th Floor, Tanglin Shopping Centre, T7332220 (another branch at Level 5, Shaw Centre), a/c restaurant. Very popular and cramped **Indonesian** restaurant. What it lacks in ambience, it more than makes up for with the food, specialities include *ayam goreng istimewa* (marinated fried chicken). Recommended.
3 ***Tony Romas'***, Orchard Rd Shopping Centre, Orchard Rd, **International**. Good ribjoint.
3 ***Papa Joes***, 01-01/02, 180 Orchard Rd, Peranakan Place, T7327012. Under the same ownership as *Chilli Buddy's* and *Esmirada*, serves **Caribbean** food at lunch and from 1800-2230 in the evenings, but is better known for its disco.
3 ***Yushiada Ya***, basement of Lucky Plaza, Orchard Rd, **Japanese**. Excellent sushi.

Hawker centres & food courts

Newton Circus, Scotts Rd, north of Orchard Rd. Despite threats of closure by the government, this huge food centre of over 100 stalls is still surviving and dishing up some of the best food of its kind. **1** ***Taman Serasi,*** Cluny Rd, opposite entrance to Botanic Gardens, small centre but well known for roti John and superb satay, mainly Malay stalls, excellent fruit juice. ***Cuppage Plaza*** and ***Orchard Point*** both have extensive foodcourts in their basements.

Cafés

Bar Gelateria Bellavista, Clarke Quay. Delicious Italian ice cream, indoor and outdoor seating. **2** ***Cyberheart Café***, basement of Orchard Shopping Centre, Orchard Rd. Pizzas, pasta and sandwiches and lots of fun with the net. **3** ***Dôme***, Lane Crawford House, Orchard Rd and The Promenade on Orchard Rd. Delicious foccaccia sandwiches, patisseries and some of the best coffee in town, good café atmosphere and a pleasant stop for a midmorning break. **3** ***Goodwood Park Hotel***, Scotts Rd. Sophisticated buffet tea, served on the lawn by the pool. **3** ***Shangri-La Hotel***, 22 Orange Grove Rd. Said to offer the best tea in town. Recommended.

Bars ***Brannigan's*** (basement of *Hyatt Regency*), 10/12 Scotts Rd. Open until 0100, 0200 on Friday and Saturday, American style, touristy bar with loud live music and video screens, haunt of the infamous SPG (Singapore Party Girl), very popular. ***Canopy Bar***, *Hyatt Regency*, 10/12 Scotts Rd. Singapore's only champagne bar for the more sophisticated *bon viveur*. ***Hard Rock Café***, Cuscaden Rd, west end of Orchard Rd. Complete with limo in suspended animation and queues to enter. ***Ice Cold***, 9 Emerald Hill. If you like a slightly anarchic feel to your bars, with loud music and darts, then this is a good place. In an old shophouse at the top of the pedestrianized section of Emerald Hill, good place for a drink away from Orchard Rd, popular with locals, Happy Hours 1700-2100. ***Jack's Place***, Yen San Building (opposite *Mandarin Hotel*), Orchard Rd. Cellar bar with live music, squashed and not very sophisticated. ***Kaspia Bar***, *Hilton Hotel*, Orchard Rd. For the widest selection of vodkas in Singapore and live jazz. ***Number 5***, 5 Emerald Hill. Happy hours 1200-2100 Monday-Saturday, 1700-2100 Sunday, at the top of the pedestrianized section of Emerald Hill, retro-chic restored shophouse bar and restaurant (upstairs), popular with young expats and Chuppies (Chinese yuppies), great music, recommended. ***Observation Lounge***, *Mandarin Hotel*, 333 Orchard Rd. Circular cocktail bar on 38th Floor. ***Que Pasa***, 7 Emerald Hill. This is a wine bar in a converted shophouse with a small snack menu of tapas, oysters and olives and an extensive wine menu. It is near the top of the pleasant pedestrianised section of Emerald Hill and next door to the slightly wilder ***Ice Cold Bar***. ***Saxophone***, 23 Cuppage Terrace, T2358385. One of Singapore's most popular bars - particularly with expats, offers good live music (usually rhythm and blues) and pleasant open-air terrace, opens at 1800, recommended. ***Woodstock***, Rooftop, 06-02 Far East Plaza, 14 Scotts Rd. Take the bullet lift up the outside of the building, expect to meet long-hairs and hear hard rock, open until 0200.

Clubs & discos Most big hotels have house discos - they all have a cover charge, usually S$25-30 (which normally includes a drink or two) - and dress is 'smart-casual'. Good hotel discos include: ***Boiler***, basement of *Mandarin Hotel*, Orchard Rd; ***Ridleys***, *ANA Hotel*, Nassim Hill. ***Chinoiserie***, *Hyatt Regency*, 10-12 Scotts Rd, off Orchard Rd. ***Xanadu***, *Shangri-La Hotel*, Orange Grove Rd, northwest end of Orchard Rd. ***Fabrice's World Music Bar***, Basement, *Singapore Marriott*, 320 Orchard Rd. Run by Fabrice De Barcy, the Belgian of *Saxophone* fame, Arabesque decor with low tables, candles and Persian rugs, live music and dance tracks, open 1700-0300 Monday-Sunday, no cover before 2200, S$25 thereafter. Recommended. ***Fire***, Orchard Plaza, T2350155. Two levels of music, very popular, admission charges vary. ***Rumours***, Level 3, Forum Gallaria, 583 Orchard Rd. Once it was the trendiest spot in town ... now it has gone off the boil. ***Sparks***, Ngee Ann City, Orchard Rd. The biggest disco in all of Asia, very glitzy with KTV rooms and jazz bar, packed at weekends, open 1700-0200 (to 0300 on Saturday and Sunday). Cover: S$15 Monday-Thursday, S$20 Friday-Sunday. Recommended. ***Top Ten Club***, Orchard Towers, 400 Orchard Rd. Huge converted cinema, often has live black-American or Filipino disco bands. Recommended. ***Club 392*** is also in Orchard Towers.

Music The ***Botanic Gardens*** at weekends. Chinese classical and folk music organized by the Nanyang Academy of Fine Arts (NAFA), T3376636 for performance details.

Chinatown

Chinatown is one of the most attractive areas of Singapore to explore. Not only is it visually appealing and comparatively compact; it also has an abundance of cafés, bars and restaurants to retreat to when hunger or the heat become overwhelming.

Ins and outs

Getting there

There is no MRT station within Chinatown proper, but there are two on the fringes. Raffles Place, within the financial district, is a short walk from the eastern edge of Chinatown while Outram Park is right at the western edge. Many bus services run through this area - nos 124, 143, 174 and 190 operate direct from Orchard Road. (A new MRT line currently under construction will run through Chinatown.)

Getting around

Chinatown is fairly compact: walking around it is no great sweat. Many of the most interesting streets and alleys are best explored on foot - they are too narrow for buses.

The area

While much of Old Chinatown has been consumed by Housing Development Board (HDB) blocks and high rise offices, the government recognised just in time that if the process of redevelopment continued unchecked, much of Singapore's urban history would be obliterated. To preserve some of the city's architectural history, the Urban Redevelopment Authority (URA) was established in the 1970s to list old buildings and provide a framework for restoration and conservation (see page 177).

After Raffles' initial foray to Singapore in 1819 he left the fledgling colony in the hands of Major Farquhar with instructions on how it should be developed. When Raffles returned for a shufti in October 1822 he was horrified to find his instructions being ignored and the city expanding in an alarmingly haphazard fashion. He promptly countermanded Farquhar's plans and orders and established a committee with even more explicit instructions. The committee allocated an area to each ethnic group and the Chinese were awarded this slice of land, southwest of the river. Chinatown is bordered by Havelock Road and Upper Pickering Street to the northeast, Cecil Street to the southeast, Cantonment Road and the Ayer Rajah Expressway to the south and southwest, and New Bridge Road to the northwest.

Immigrants from China settled in Singapore in the latter half of the 19th century, and recreated much of what they had left behind. Clan groups began migrating from the southern provinces of China to the *Nang Yang* or 'Southern Seas' in successive waves from the 17th century. By 1849 the Chinese population had reached 28,000, but the area they inhabited was largely confined to a settlement between Telok Ayer and Amoy streets. The greatest numbers migrated in the 40 years after 1870, mostly coming from the southeastern coastal provinces, with the Hokkiens forming the majority. Each dialect group established their own temple. The Hokkiens founded **Thian Hock Keng** in 1821, the Cantonese established **Fu Tak Chi** on Telok Ayer Street around the same time, as did the Teochews who built **Wak Hai Cheng Bio** on Philip Street. Streets, too, were occupied by different Chinese groups, with clubs and clan houses - or *kongsi* - aiding family or regional ties. The *kongsi* were often affiliated with secret societies, or *tongs* which controlled the gambling and prostitution industries and the drug trade.

Today, Chinatown is overshadowed by the 200m-high skyscrapers of the financial area and indoor markets have replaced the many street stalls and night markets that made the area a favoured tourist spot in days gone by. (These night markets - known by their Malay name, *pasar malam* - still reappear in the run-up to Chinese New Year). Expansion of the financial district meant that Chinatown was being demolished so rapidly that by the time the authorities realized that tourists actually wanted to see its crumbling buildings, many of the streets had already been destroyed. In any case, Chinatown had become a slum, with overcrowding and poor sanitation being very real problems. A clean up campaign was undertaken: its markets were cleared out; shops and stalls relocated; shophouses refurbished and the smells and noises of Chinatown banished to a world that only a few confused grandparents care to remember.

Many residents have moved out to new, modern flats in the Housing Development Board (HDB) estates scattered around the island. Despite all the refurbishment and 'urban renewal', Chinatown remains one of the most interesting parts of town. The rows of shophouses - once derelict -

Related maps:
A. Chinatown detail, page 107
B. River & port, page 86
Colonial core (to the north) page 70
Coloured map inside back cover

Secret Societies

Secret societies in Singapore evolved from support networks and quasi-political organizations for recently arrived immigrants - rather like Masons in the West - into triad gangs that posed a real threat to stability in the colony. Their menace increased, reaching a peak in the 1840s. The Ghee Hins, for example, waged a long-running war with the Ghee Hoks and the Hai Sans. In March 1846 the Ghee Hins and Ghee Hoks came to blows in truly spectacular style and for two weeks the city was effectively under seige. In May 1854 Singapore's secret societies overcame their differences and launched an attack on all Chinese Roman Catholic converts. Around 400 Chinese were killed in the mayhem and 800 or so were injured. Scores of houses were also burnt down. In the so-called Post Office Riots of 1876 the Teo Chews mounted a campaign against the colonial authorities who had set up a system to handle remittances. Previously Teo Chew merchants had monopolised the sending back of money to the homeland and, naturally enough, made a good profit from doing so. In the wake of these riots the British introduced policies to control secret societies. Every society had to be registered with the authorities and a new law was introduced which stipulated that any immigrant Chinese with a conviction would be automatically sent home to China. Needless to say, these policies were ineffective. Indeed, even today the government educates children not to get involved with gangs, and drug dealing and prostitution are still controlled by secret societies which have their roots in the tongs *of the past.*

have been bought up, redeveloped and rented out as office space for small design companies, publishing companies, art galleries and so on. (For more detailed information on the rights and wrongs of redevelopment, see page 177.)

Sights

The area known as **Kreta Ayer** encompasses **Smith**, **Temple**, **Pagoda**, **Trengganu** and **Sago streets**. This was the area that Raffles marked out for the Chinese kampong and it became the hub of the Chinese community, deriving its name from the ox-drawn carts that carried water to the area. Renovation by the Urban Redevelopment Authority (URA) has meant that these streets still retain their characteristic baroque-style shophouses with weathered shutters and ornamentation.

Chinatown architecture

The typical Straits Chinese house accommodated the family business on the ground floor leaving the second and third floors as family living quarters - sometimes accommodating two families (and in later years, as Chinatown became desperately overcrowded, up to five families). A few wealthy Chinese merchants - or *towkays* - built their houses according to traditional Chinese architectural conventions, but almost all of these have long since been demolished. One which has survived is **Tan Yeok Nee's mansion** on Tank Road, at the eastern end of Orchard Road (see page 94). Another is the **Thong Chai Medical Institute** on Eu Tong Sen Street, at the corner of Merchant Road. It was built in southern Chinese palace style with three halls, two inner courts and ornamental gables and was completed in 1892. By the end of the 19th century it had become a centre for traditional medicine, offering its services free to the poor - *thong chai* means 'benefit to all'. In 1911, during a malaria outbreak, it distributed free quinine. The building also became a focal point for the Chinese community, being the headquarters for the Chinese

Walking tour of Chinatown

Chinatown is sufficiently compact and interesting to explore on foot. Set out below are two suggested walking tours, which take in many of the more interesting streets and sights of interest in the area.

Walk 1 *Start at the* ***Jamae Mosque*** *on the corner of Mosque Street and South Bridge Road. Walk one block down South Bridge Road to Pagoda Street and the* ***Sri Mariamman Temple****. Turn into Pagoda Street and left down Trengganu Street to the* ***Chinaman Scholar's Gallery****, and then chicken foot through Temple, Smith and Sago Streets, to get a taste of the heart of Chinatown, to the* ***Jinricksha Station****, on the corner of Tanjong Pagar and Neil roads. From here, walk down* ***Neil Road*** *past* ***Tea Houses****, then turn left onto* ***Duxton Road*** *and right again into* ***Duxton Hill*** *- a quiet cul-de-sac of attractive restored shophouses. If you time this right, you could end up on Duxton Hill for an early evening drink in one of the bars here. Duxton Hill lies in the midst of the Tanjong Pagar conservation area, and is surrounded by streets of restored shophouses - Craig and Keong Saik roads display good examples of the Transitional Shophouse style (see page 180).*

Walk 2 *For a more modest stroll, start at Raffles Place (MRT station here) and wander through the high-rise blocks to the northern end of Telok Ayer Street. Walk the full length of Telok Ayer Street, taking in the various temples, mosques and churches along the way (see page 108 for details), ending up at the Amoy Food Centre to experience an original hawker centre. Walk north again up Amoy Street, which shows you how the shophouses look pre- and post-restoration and make your way back to Raffles Place or, if you have the energy, to Boat Quay for a drink or a bite to eat.*

First Traditional shophouse style No 120 Telok Ayer Street

guilds. The Chinese Chamber of Commerce began life here (its headquarters are now on Hill Street, see page 75). The building was made a national monument in 1973 and in 1998 was under renovation. What function it will fill when renovation is complete is not certain.

The streets of Chinatown

In Sago Street (or 'death house alley' as it was known in Cantonese, after its hospices for the dying), **Temple Street** and **Smith Street**, there are shops making paper houses and cars, designed to improve the quality of the after-life for dead relatives (by burning the models after the funeral, it is believed that one's worldly wealth hurries after you into the next world). Also on these streets, shops sell all the accoutrements needed for a visit to a Chinese temple. At Number 36 Smith Street there is a three storey building that was originally home to a famous Cantonese opera theatre - Lai Chun Yen - and formerly Smith Street was also known as 'Hei Yuen Kai', or Theatre Street. The English probably gave Sago Street its name in the early 19th century as Singapore became a centre of high quality sago production for export to India and Europe. By 1849, there were 15 Chinese and two European sago factories here.

Perhaps because death and health go hand-in-glove, there are also a number of **Chinese medicine shops** in this area - for example, *Kwang Onn Herbal* at 14 Trengganu Street and others on Sago Street. Chinese traditional medicine halls still do a roaring trade, despite the advantages of Medisave schemes and 21st century pharmaceuticals. On show are antlers and horns, dried frogs and flying lizards, trays of mushrooms and fungi, baskets of dried seahorses (S$10 each) and octopus, sharks' fins and ginseng. Presumably rarer, and perhaps because they are illegal, body parts like tiger penis and ground rhino horn are kept out of sight. Looking at this cornucopia of the dried and the pickled, it is easy to wonder how the Chinese ever discovered that flying lizard seeped in tea is good for athlete's foot. It shows enormous dedication. The **Hong Lim complex** on **Upper Cross Street** has several more such medicine halls. There are also a few skilled Chinese calligraphers still working from shops around Upper Cross Street.

Right next to *Kwang Onn Herbal* at 14b Trengganu Street, up a narrow staircase, is the **Chinaman Scholar's Gallery**, a mini-museum of life in the merchants' and scholars' houses in the 1920s. The gallery is run by Vincent Tan, an antique dealer. Visitors can sip Chinese tea as they wander around the kitchen, bedroom, dining and living areas, and flick through photographs. Mr Tan gives musical interludes with demonstrations of instruments from China, such as the lute, *pipa* (mandolin) and *yang chin* (harp). This is really a private home rather than a museum and there is a

Chinatown

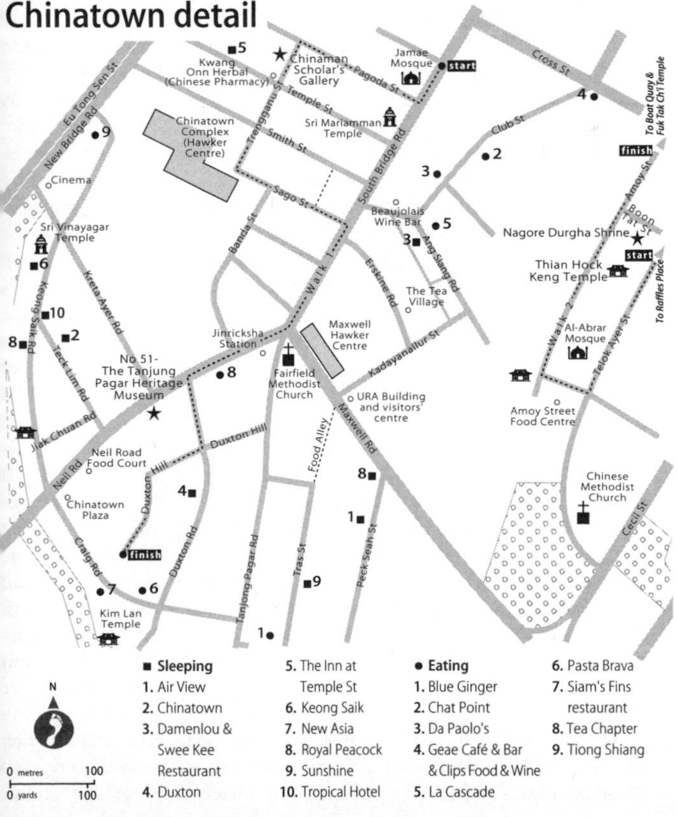

Related maps
Chinatown,
page 104
Coloured map
inside back cover

Tien Hou - Goddess of Seafarers

Tien Hou, or Thien Hau Thanh Mau (also Ma Tsu), is the goddess of the sea and protector of seafarers. She first appeared, so to speak, in Fukien province in China during the 11th century. Folklore has it that she was the daughter of a fisherman named Lin and that she died a virgin. She appears to seafarers in times of extreme peril and saves their lives. Tien Hou is usually represented seated, with a flattened crown. But the real giveaway are her two companions, who go by the great names of Thousand-mile Eye and Follow the Wind Ear. These are both tamed demons who the goddess uses to provide long range weather forecasts to fishermen. Thousand-mile Eye is red-skinned and peers towards the horizon, hand shading his eyes; Follow the Wind Ear is green-skinned and is usually depicted cupping his hand to his ear as he listens for minor climatic changes.

slightly odd notice at the entrance, in some ways disarming ('don't expect the V&A or the Metropolitan') and in some ways irritating ('if you want to leave the gallery without paying we suggest that you sign the cheques to pay the utilities and rental bills'). ■ *S$6 (S$4 for children) 0900-1700 Monday-Sunday, but sometimes it's inexplicably closed - knock on the door and hope that someone is in.*

Sri Mariamman Temple

As if to illustrate Singapore's reputation as a racial and religious melting-pot, the Hindu **Sri Mariamman Temple** is situated nearby at 244 South Bridge Road. There was a temple on this site as early as 1827, making it Singapore's oldest Hindu place of worship. Stamford Raffles is said to have granted the land to Narian Pillai, a Tamil who accompanied Raffles to Singapore during his second visit on board the *Indiana*, and set up Singapore's first brickworks. The basic layout of the present, gaudy Dravidian (South Indian) structure dates from 1843, although it has been much renovated and extended over the years. The temple shop is piled high with books on Hindu philosophy and cosmology and, unsurprisingly, is run by a Chinese family. The building is dedicated to Sri Mariamman, a manifestation of Siva's wife Parvati. (She is believed to be particularly good at curing epidemics and other major health scares - which at that time in Singapore were the norm rather than the exception.) The *gopuram* here is particularly exuberant and the sacred cows seated along the top of the boundary wall add a rather pleasing bucolic touch to the affair. The temple is the site of the annual Thimithi festival which takes place at the end of October or the beginning of November. Devotees cleanse their spirits by fasting beforehand and then show their purity of heart by walking over hot coals (see page 55). To the north of the temple, also on South Bridge Road, is the **Jamae Mosque**, built in 1826 by the Chulias from southern India. It harnesses an eclectic mix of Anglo-Indian, Chinese and Malay architecture.

Chinese temple-carvers still live on **Club Street** - which also has a number of *kongsi* along it. Many of the buildings along **Mosque Street** were originally stables. It was also home to Hakkas, who traded in second-hand paper and scrap metal - today it is better known for its Chinese restaurants. Number 37 Pagoda Street was one of the many coolie quarters in the area - home to Chinese immigrants, who lived in cramped conditions, sleeping in bunk spaces.

Thian Hock Keng Temple

Telok Ayer Street is another street full of shophouses and fascinating temples of different religions. This was once one of the most important streets in Singapore, packed with temples, businesses and clan associations.

The city's oldest Chinese temple, the Taoist **Thian Hock Keng Temple** or Temple of Heavenly Happiness is here, is a gem (notwithstanding the naff fibreglass wishing well in one corner). The temple is also very popular; the coaches lined up outside give the game away - but don't let this put you off. Telok Ayer Street was the perfect place for merchants and traders to establish themselves, as it was right on the seafront. (It also became notorious for its slave trade in the 1850s.) The temple was funded by a wealthy merchant of the same name and building commenced in 1839. Skilled craftsmen and materials were all imported from China, the cast-iron railings came from Glasgow and the decorative tiles from Holland. The building was modelled on 19th century southern Chinese architectural traditions, with a grouping of pavilions around open courtyards, designed to comply with the dictates of geomancy (*feng shui*) (see page 182).

The main deity of the temple is Tien Hou, the Goddess of Seafarers, and she is worshipped in the central hall (see box). The image here was imported from China in the 1840s and the temple soon became a focal point for newly arrived Hokkien immigrants who would gather to thank Tien Hou for granting them a safe journey. In the left-hand hall there is an image of the Lord of Laws (Fa Zhu Gong) while in the right, the Prince of Prominence, Zai Si Xian He. The ubiquitous Kuan Yin, the Goddess of Mercy, also makes an appearance (see page 121. The temples position on the waterfront quickly came to an end, in the 1880s, when one of Singapore's first land reclamation projects, moved the shore several blocks east. Well worth a visit. A little way north of Thian Hock Keng is another much smaller Chinese temple, the **Fuk Tak Chii temple**. This was built in the 1820s and while it is modest - containing just one court and shrine room - it is elegantly proportioned and skilfully decorated.

The Al-Abrar Mosque, also on Telok Ayer Street, was built between 1850 and 1855 by Indian Muslims, who were also responsible for the fancy turrets of the **Nagore Durgha Shrine** - a little further up the street - which was built in 1829. Designated a national monument, the shrine is a blend of architectural styles - Palladian doors and Doric columns combined with more traditional Indian-Islamic touches like the perforated roof grilles ... and then there are the fairy lights. An intriguing architectural sight is the **Telok Ayer Chinese Methodist Church**, 235 Telok Ayer Street. The church was built in 1924 and combines a mixture of eastern and western influences. There is a flat roof with a Chinese pavilion and a colonnaded ground floor. Its all rather odd. During World War Two it was used as a refugee camp.

Tanjong Pagar

The conservation area of **Tanjong Pagar** lies southwest of **Telok Ayer Street**. It is bordered by Tanjong Pagar Road and Neil Road and contains some of the best examples of pre-war shophouse architecture on the island.

In the early 19th century this area was inhabited by *orang-laut*, simple fisherfolk. The name *Tanjong* (cape or promontory) *Pagar* (wooden fence or palisade) may be derived from the fishing stakes that were commonly used to catch fish. With the arrival of the Europeans, it became an area of fruit and nutmeg cultivation. Neil Road was established in the 1830s and at that time was just a track meandering through the nutmeg groves. It was originally called Salat Road and was renamed in 1858 after one of the heroes of the Indian mutiny in Calcutta a year earlier. With the expansion of cultivation, planters and pickers were needed and subsequently hawkers and shopkeepers moved in to supply their needs. The community became dominated by Hokkien and Tamil coolies, with the wealthy merchants living on Duxton and Neil roads. Later in the century, Tanjong Pagar wa ruled by the Triads - or *tongs* (see page 105).

It wasn't very many years after Singapore had been established that a flourishing red light district had also appeared. The reasons are pretty clear in 1824, Singapore had a recorded population of 2,956 Chinese men but jus 361 women, a ratio of 8:1. Ten years later, the combined population ha risen to 10,767,10% of who were female. Amongst the Europeans, the rati in 1824 was slightly more equitable, but even so there were 51 men range against 23 women. With such an imbalance, the area around **Kreta Aye** quickly became a service centre of the red light variety and boatloads o young girls were brought in from China and Hong Kong to provid entertainment for the male population - and with them came their pimps Or perhaps it was the other way around. Teahouses provided 'singing girls and opium dens were commonplace (opium smoking was not prohibite until 1964). Fires were frequent - the tinder-box houses were constructed o wood with flimsy cardboard partitions. In 1830 a disastrous fire raged for days (there were no fire hoses) and in 1917 another fire almost complete destroyed the area.

Between 1900 and 1940 Tanjong Pagar became the 'gateway' fo Chinese immigrants and clansmen took over almost all the shophouses i the area. Consequently, by the 20th century, Tanjong Pagar had becom desperately overcrowded, with houses originally built for one famil housing up to five or six. This was also the constituency where Lee Kua Yew successfully stood in a by-election in 1957.

Redevelopment of Chinatown

Tanjong Pagar was one of the first major projects undertaken by the Urba Redevelopment Authority (URA). They acquired the area in the earl 1980s, realizing that this was a precious piece of Singapore's heritage tha should be retained at all cost. And just in time: the government wished t demolish the area as it had become, by then, little more than a slum Initially, the URA restored and sold off 30 shophouses. Subsequently, the sold the properties unrestored and provided the new owners wit guidelines for restoration. The principal stipulation was that façades mus remain the same, but new owners were given licence to do almost anythin they wanted with the interior, provided that the airwells (an area open to th sky in the middle of the shophouse, which provided light to the back rooms were retained.

Critics of the URA have argued that this process of retaining the façade - the physical fabric - but ripping out the human heart has sanitized the area destroying the character of Chinatown. But to be fair to the URA, th activities that gave old Chinatown its unique character are simply out o step with the new Singapore. Charcoal-making and gunny sack-sewing ar not only unprofitable but young people see their futures in othe occupations. The last craftsmen to work in Chinatown only survive because the colonial rent act meant that they paid S$5 a month in rent. No only do changing economics and expectations pose a formidable challeng to keeping Chinatown preserved for posterity, but many of the traditiona occupations contravene Singapores' health and safety regulations.

One disappointment for the URA is that the 'shophouse' concept, wher a business is run on the ground floor and the owners live upstairs, has no re-established itself. As a result, the area is dead at night. This is something th URA are now addressing, trying - like so many other urban planner worldwide - to encourage people to live in the heart of the city. Many of th plots along Tanjong Pagar remain vacant - suggesting that rates are too high

ea, an appreciation

he health-giving qualities of tea appear lmost unbounded. Tea has been credited vith calming the heart, invigorating the qi nd retarding the ageing process (Shen long's Materia Medica); combating anal stula, expelling phlegm and promoting igestion (T'ang Dynasty Materia Medica), emoving heat from the liver, gall bladder, ungs and stomach (Sui Xi Ju Yinshipu), as vell as reducing cholesterol. It very usefully ures hangovers and "helps to remove rease and stink between the teeth and heeks, [cleansing] the oral cavity giving it fragrance". Oh, and it also quenches the hirst.

low to make a decent (Chinese) cuppa: *nyone visiting the Tea Chapter in hinatown comes away realising that, for he cognoscenti of the tea business, it's ot just a case of chucking a tea bag in a nug with some boiling water. They ecommend that budding tea artistes dhere to the following guidelines when making (Chinese) tea:*

1. Warm the tea pot and the cups
2. Use 3 grammes of tea leaves per 150 cc of water
3. Add the leaves to the pot; half fill with hot water and then immediately pour away (this cleans and warms the leaves). This first brew is usually not drunk
4. Add more hot water and brew for 30-60 seconds
5. For the second brew increase brewing time by 15 seconds (and so on for three to four brews)

Then there is the question of the temperature of the water. This varies according to tea type:
Green teas
under 80°C
Lightly fermented teas
80-90°C
Highly fermented teas
over 90°C

Chinatown

ven so, there are now a number of tea houses, mahjong-makers, eflexologists, calligraphers, lacquer-painters and mask-makers who have set ıp among the advertising agencies, restaurants and bars.

For visitors who are interested in finding out more about conservation reas in the city, the URA are developing their headquarters at 45 Maxwell Road into an Exhibition and Visitors' Centre. A brilliant architectural nodel of the city which they have been piecing together for some time will e moved to the visitors' centre and there will also be various interactive lisplays. The centre is scheduled to open towards the end of 1998. ■ *Admission will be free and opening hours should be office hours, ie Monday-Friday, 0900-1700.*

Tea Chapter

The Tanjong Pagar Heritage Exhibition in the development at 51 Neil Road has a small display of intriguing photographs of old Chinatown, though the accompanying mall and foodcourt, complete with 'authentic' bare brickwork is a little tacky. More interesting is the **Tea Chapter**, almost next door at 9A-11A, where visitors are introduced to the intricacies of tea-tasting in elegant surroundings. Visitors are invited to remove their shoes (sometimes an aromatic experience in itself) and can choose either to sit in one of their special rooms or upstairs on the floor. Relaxing Chinese plink-plink music, muffled feet, a tiny cup of delicious Supreme Grade Dragon Well, Scarlet Robe or Green Iron Goddess of Mercy at your lips and the cool atmosphere (it's air-con upstairs) all contribute towards a soothing experience. As the brochure rather extravagantly puts it "it is a mythical dream come true for those seeking solace from a harsh and unfeeling existence". This is a popular place for young Singaporeans to visit on a Sunday afternoon (see afternoon tea, above). ■ *Monday-Sunday, 1100-2300.*

The white building on the corner of Tanjong Pagar and Neil Road wa the **Jinriksha Station**, built in 1903. It served as the administration centr for the jinriksha pullers. Jinrickshas arrived from Japan via Shanghai in th 1880s and soon became the most popular way to travel. By 1888 there wer 1,800 in use, pulled by immigrants who lived in Sago and Banda streets. A the turn of the century, the fare for a half hour trip would have been 3 cent 20 cents for an hour.

Bird singing

On Sunday mornings bird lovers gather at the corner of **Tiong Bahru** an Seng Poh roads for traditional **bird singing competitions**, where row upo row of thrushes, merboks and sharmas sing their hearts out, in antiqu bamboo cages with ivory and porcelain fittings, hung from lines. The bird are fed on a carefully controlled diet to ensure the quality of their song Owners place their younger birds next to more experienced songsters to tr to improve their voices and pick up new tunes. Birds start twittering at 073 and are spent by 1000. On the opposite side of the road, there's a sho selling everything you need for your pet bird - including porcelain cag accoutrements. Come here early and combine a visit to hear the birds wit breakfast in one of the traditional coffee shops nearby: fresh baked *ro* washed down with sweet black or milky coffee. If you walk on down Sen Poh Road you will come to a fabulous wet **market**; every conceivabl vegetable, fruit, fish, meat, beancurd you could ever want to purchase i available here. ■ *Take the MRT to Tiong Bahru or Outram Park or the bu stops right opposite this spot - bus nos 16, 33 and 36.*

Essentials

Sleeping
■ *on maps*
Price codes:
see inside front cover

Chinatown provides more unusual accommodation than other areas of town, wit several 'boutique' hotels in converted shophouses. These come as a refreshin change from the high-rise anonymity of Orchard Rd or the Colonial core. If you can d without a pool and fitness centre (though some of the new blocks have suc facilities), and don't mind having a small room, but appreciate a little mor individuality, then try here.

L ***Duxton***, 83 Duxton Rd, T2277678, F2271232, duxton@singnet.com.sg, restaura (*L'Aigle d'Or*, page 114). Intimate, stylish 50-room hotel in row of refurbishe shophouses. Deluxe rooms are split level, but even these are small at this price. Guest have use of the large pool at the *Amara Hotel*. Mainly frequented by business peopl as it's convenient for the financial district. Its ambience and size make it stand ou among Singapore's other luxury hotels. Overpriced on the rack rate but goo discounts available either from hotel or from travel agents. Recommended.

A+ ***Amara***, 165 Tanjong Pagar Rd, T2244488, F2243910, reserv@amara.com.sg Several restaurants (with one of the best Thai restaurants in town - *Than Ying* - se **Eating**) and a coffee shop serving a good buffet spread (**3**), decent sized pool, with caf area for steamboat and BBQs. Well maintained with 338 average sized rooms and goo extras such as self-service launderette. 4 tennis courts, jogging track and a gym Business centre with conference room and secretaries on hand. Good location for thos wishing to explore Chinatown or for businessmen, as it lies on the edge of the CBD.

A+ ***Furama***, 60 Eu Tong Sen St, T5333888, F5341489. Grand lobby belies rathe scruffy featureless rooms, it needs a facelift. Restaurant and very basic gym. Th building itself stands out from the crowd for its unusual but rather ugly and date design.

A+ ***Harbour View Dai Ichi***, 81 Anson Rd, T2241133, F2220749, http://www harbourview.com.sg. Good Japanese restaurant, average sized pool and over 40

Large but basic rooms in this high-rise block. Request a harbour view as the view of Tanjong Pagar container port is worth an hour or two's quiet attention. Good location for business district and access to Chinatown. Health centre but no gym, personal safes in more expensive rooms. Business centre with limited secretarial assistance. Meeting room available. Popular with Japanese clients.

A ***The Inn at Temple Street***, 36 Temple Street, T2215333, F2255391. This place opened in 1998. It bills itself as a boutique hotel, and the 42 rooms do have a certain charm: they are well appointed with safes, TVs, Peranakan-style furniture (made in Indonesia) and attached shower (in the standard) or bath (in the deluxe) rooms. On the downside the rooms are very small; not even the deluxe rooms have space for a desk (except in the few single rooms), which will put off business travellers.

A-B ***Chinatown***, 12-16 Teck Lim Rd, T2255166, F2253912. Another shophouse renovation with 40 rooms, a/c, no restaurant but breakfast provided. Small shower rooms and rather bland but, like *Keong Saik* and *The Royal Peacock*, it's an intimate place in an attractive street in the heart of Chinatown. It benefits from a small 'business centre' with a meeting room and secretarial assistance.

B ***Damenlou***, 12 Ann Siang Rd, T2211900, F2258500. A/c, attached bathroom, TV, minibar, cheaper rooms are very small but neat and clean and well presented. Very friendly management and located in an attractive street of shophouses. Recommended.

B ***Dragon Inn Chinatown***, 18 Mosque St, T2227227, F2226116. New hotel with a/c spreading over 4 shophouses on the 2nd and 3rd floors, making it a bit of a warren of a place. Attractive low rise location, but rooms are small and basic. For rooms onto the street with windows, book in advance. *Homely Kitchen* next door is soon to open, providing complimentary breakfast.

B ***Keong Saik***, 69 Keong Saik Rd, T2230660, F2250660. A/c, opened early '97, 25 rooms in a sensitively restored shophouse. Attractive all-wood furniture in immaculately presented but small rooms, with little room for anything other than the bed. Standard rooms have no windows or skylights (attic rooms). An intimate little 'business' hotel, let down by its room sizes.

B ***The Royal Peacock***, 55 Keong Saik Rd, T2233522, F2211770. A/c, charming little restaurant, *Butterfly Pub* (with Karaoke), 79 rooms spread along 10 shophouses, similar standard to *Keong Saik*, rooms marginally larger, but again standard rooms have no natural light and showers only. Price includes continental breakfast. Avoid rooms over the pub. Recommended for general feel of the hotel but not for room size.

B ***Sunshine***, 51-57 Tras St, T2210330, F2211178. Situated in a renovated salmon pink and green shophouse. The 40 a/c, rather small rooms are immaculately presented although some are without windows. Friendly manager, attractive location and close to MRT - no restaurant but there's one next door and many others nearby.

C ***Air View***, 10 Peck Seah St, T2257788, F2256688. Not much to differentiate this from *New Asia*, although it might be marginally cleaner. Outside toilet and unimpressive shower arrangement.

C ***New Asia***, 2 Peck Seah St, T2211861, F2239002. Similar to *Air View* but dingier - a/c, lino floors, smelly rooms, battered furniture ... Bleak.

C ***YMCA***, 70 Palmer Rd, T2224666, F2226467. A/c and basic hot water showers in 50 rooms. Out of the way, at the southern end of Chinatown and the business district, but the rate is good and the rooms are spacious if basic (mostly singles with no toilets). At 40 years old, this must be one of the longest running establishments in Singapore. Friendly manageress - the best place in this price range.

Accommodation west of Chinatown

Between Chinatown and Orchard Rd, along Havelock Rd, there are five 3-4 star hotels grouped together in an area that some rather optimistic locals call 'Riverside'. All these hotels are undergoing facelifts in a desperate bid to win customers. Unfortunately, location is a bit of a drawback: the area is rather isolated (although it is only a few minutes by taxi or bus to Clarke and Boat Quays, Chinatown and Orchard Rd), it is overlooked by some particularly unsightly HDB blocks and there are no shops or restaurants on the doorstep. However, the whole riverside area from here to Clarke Quay is in the process of being 'upgraded' and before long there will be walkways and shopping malls linking these hotels with Clarke Quay.

A+ *Apollo*, 405 Havelock Rd, T7332081, F7331588. Built in 1972, this hotel was showing its age in 1997 but has undergone major cosmetic surgery with a new extension of 135 rooms (making it a 400-room hotel), construction of a sizeable pool tennis court, gym and jacuzzi, the redesign of the lobby area, and renovation of existing rooms. 3 restaurants. Good business centre facilities and larger than average rooms (but featureless).

A+ *Concorde*, 317 Outram Rd, T7330188, F7330989. 3 restaurants, pool, tennis court but no gym. The most stunning design of all the hotels in this area, with a huge circular atrium and exterior bubble lifts. Rooms are being gradually renovated - ask for a new one. Popular tour group hotel, especially for Japanese visitors.

A+ *King's*, 403 Havelock Rd, T7330011, F7325764, Kingstel@singnet.com.sg http://www.asianconnect.com/sha/kings.html. 300 plus rooms in another ugly high-rise block. Initial impressions are favourable but the rooms are an anticlimax Deluxe rooms have balconies and all rooms have personal safes. Family room available. Barren but large pool. Live band every evening, Japanese and Chinese restaurants, business centre with computer available and meeting rooms.

A+ *Miramar*, 401 Havelock Rd, T7330222, F7334027. Restaurants including a 24-hour coffee shop, big pool and paddling pool. Built in 1971, but renovated in 1995, 340 spacious rooms in tower block overlooking the river.

A+-A *River View*, 382 Havelock Rd, T7329922, F7321034. A/c, average restaurant, pool, run by Robert Pregarz, a former Italian sailor and ex-manager of the pre-theme park *Raffles*.

Eating: expensive

● on maps
Price codes:
see inside front cover

5 *L'Aigle d'Or*, *Duxton Hotel*, 83 Duxton Rd, T2277678, **French.** A few Oriental touches and a good vegetarian selection, extensive, expensive menu with wine list to match, sophisticated atmosphere, popular as a business venue at lunch time, booking recommended.

4 *Blue Ginger*, 97 Tanjong Pagar Rd, T2223928. In restored shophouse - good home cooked **Nonya** (Peranakan) food and relaxed atmosphere.

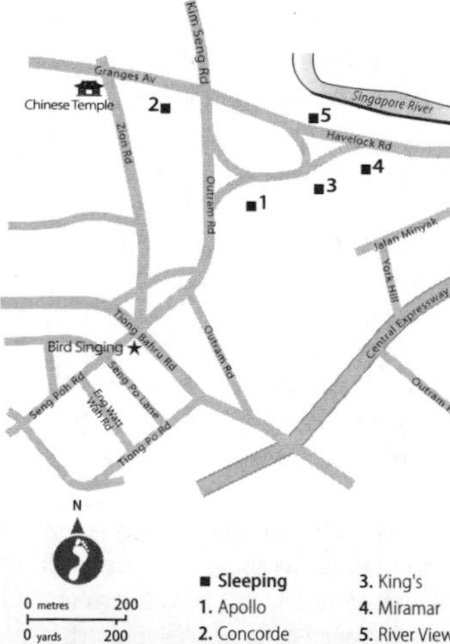

4 *La Cascade*, 7 Ann Siang Rd, T3241808. Attractive and sophisticated little **French** restaurant down a quiet street in Chinatown, serving snails, veal, duck - good menu, recommended.

3 *Chat Point*, Club St. This is a small restaurant-cum-pub serving **Malay/Indonesian/Nonya** dishes. Seafood is best: squid, chilli crab, tiger prawns - and live music.

3 *Clips Wine Bar and Restaurant*, Gemmill Lane (at intersection of Cross St and Club St), **International**. This is more of a wine bar than a restaurant, in an attractive Tuscan-coloured shophouse. The wine list (mostly New World) is considerably longer than the food menu, which is nothing out of the ordinary - steaks, fish, mixed grill and chicken. Closed at lunch.

3 *Orchard Garden*, 4th Floor, Lucky

Chinatown shopping centre, New Bridge Rd, **Chinese**. Dim sum at lunchtime.
4 ***Da Paolo***, 66 Tanjong Pagar Rd, T2247081. One of two *Da Paolo's* in Tanjong Pagar, **Italian**. Both are in restored shophouses decorated in contemporary fashion. Popular with expats, home-made pasta, but over-priced.
3 ***Pasta Brava***, 11 Craig Rd, Tanjong Pagar. Tastiest **Italian** in town in an equally tasty shophouse conversion, fairly expensive but good choice of genuine Italian fare. Recommended.
3 ***Siam's Fins***, 45 Craig Rd (and at other outlets). Hang Khim is a Bangkok chef and he produces the very best shark's fins - along with an assortment of other **Thai** seafoods.
3 ***Swee Kee***, 12 Ann Siang Rd, T2211900. This **Chinese** restaurant has acquired some degree of local reknown due to the owner Tang Kwong Swee - known to his friends as 'Fish-head' - having run the same place for 60 years (although the location has changed). Recommended are the deep fried chicken, Hainanese style, fish head noodle soup and prawns in magi sauce, very popular.
4 ***Thanying***, *Amara Hotel*, T2224688 and at Clarke Quay, T3368146. Provides the best **Thai** food in town, extensive menu and superb food (the 15 female chefs are all said to have trained in the royal household in Bangkok). Specialities include deep fried garoupa, *yam som-o* (spicy pomelo salad), *khao niaw durian* (durian served on a bed of sticky rice - available from May-August) as well as such classics as *tom yam kung* (spicy prawn soup with lemon grass), booking necessary, recommended.

Eating: cheaper

2 ***Fratini***, 1 Neil Rd, T3238088. Cheap and cheerful **Italian** pasta joint in a restored shophouse.
3-2 ***Geah Café***, Gemmill Lane (at intersection of Cross St and Club St), **International**. Small café/bar with a limited menu of sandwiches, fried chicken wings and corn chips, good location for coffee or beer.
2 ***Hillman***, 1st Floor, Block 1 Cantonment Rd, (southern end of Chinatown). Popular good value wholesome **Cantonese** stews served out of earthenware pots.
2 ***New Nam Thong***, 8 Smith St, **Cantonese**, including dim sum from 0400 and a lunchtime menu.
3 ***Sanur***, 3rd Floor, 133 New Bridge Rd. **Malay/Indonesian** restaurant, one of a chain, specialities include fish-head curry and spicy grilled chicken.
2 ***Tai Tong Hoi Kee***, 2 Mosque St, **Cantonese**, dim sum from 0400.
2 ***Tiong Shiang***, corner of Keong Saik and New Bridge Rd, very popular **Hainanese** corner café with tables spilling out onto the street.

Hawker Centres & food courts

1 ***Amoy Street Food Centre***, just south of Al Abrar Mosque at southern end of Amoy St. excellent little centre, worth a graze. **1** ***Chinatown Complex Hawker Centre***, Block 335, 1st Floor, Smith St. Recommended stall: *Ming Shan* (No 179), for its kambing (mutton) soup, famed for decades, though a pretty scruffy food centre. **1** ***Maxwell Road Hawker Centre*** (corner of Maxwell and South Bridge roads), Tanjong Pagar, mainly Chinese, best known for its two chicken rice stalls.

Tea, cakes & coffee shops

Tea Chapter, 9A-11A Neil Rd, Chinatown, T2261175. An excellent little place on 3 floors with a choice of seating (on the floor or at tables), a peaceful atmosphere, plenty of choice of teas as well as sweet and savory snacks, games for those who want to tarry, and the director, Lee Peng Shu, and his wife enthusiastically talk you through the tea tasting ceremony (if you wish). Recommended. See page 111 for further details.

Bars

There are several quiet bars on ***Duxton Hill***, Chinatown, in a pleasant area of restored shophouses - a retreat from the hustle and bustle of Boat Quay or the city. ***Duxton Road*** and ***Tanjong Pagar Road*** (both in Chinatown) also provide a dozen or so bars in restored shophouses. ***JJ Mahoney's***, 55 Duxton Rd, T2256225. Not quite the Irish bar the name might suggest, beer and karaoke. ***Elvis Pub***, 1A Duxton Hill, T2201268. Here the name does say it all: nothing but Elvis played all night, Friday is particularly lively. ***Beaujolais Winebar***, 1 Ann Siang Hill, T2242227. Very pleasant winebar in restored shophouse, serves reasonably-priced wine, candles in winebottles on the window-sills, atmospheric, good cheese and charcuterie platters. Recommended. ***Lone Star Bar***, 54 Tanjong Pagar Rd, run by Mike Brenders, a Texan (ex-US Navy) country and western music, darts, friendly and fun.

Clubs ***Moondance***, Tanjong Pagar Rd, Chinatown. S$13 cover charge (S$16 at the weekends), 25% off happy hour from 1900-2100, karaoke from 1900-2200.

Little India

This area remains the heartland of Indian Singapore and on Sundays it can seem as though a significant proportion of the sub-continent's population has miraculously congregated here. Sunday is the day when migrant workers from South Asia come here to eat, chat, shop and worship, revelling in their cultural ties.

Ins and outs

Getting there

Bugis is the most convenient MRT stop for Little India, although a 10 minute walk is required to get into the heart of the area. Numerous buses run up Serangoon Road including nos 64, 65, 106, 111 and 139 direct from Orchard Road. (A new MRT line currently under construction will run along Race Course Road - which runs parallel to Serangoon Road.)

Getting around

Serangoon Road is Little India's main artery and it stretches some 1.5 km from Rochor Canal Road up to Lavender Street - reasonably easily negotiable on foot.

The area

Little India encompasses the area straddled by three parallel roads: Serangoon Road, Jalan Besar and Race Course Road. It is largely concentrated to the north of the Rochor Canal and has petered out by the time one reaches Rangoon and Kitchener roads.

Throughout the week, the fragrance of incense and freshly cut jasmine hangs over the area and with the sound-tracks of Tamil epic-musicals blaring from the video shops, the pan salesmen on the sidestreets and colourful milk-sweets behind the glass counters of dosai restaurants, Little India - as the name implies - is the sub-continent in microcosm. Every Indian product imaginable is for sale: lunggyis, dotis, saris and spices, sweetmeats, flower garlands, nostril studs, bidis and stalls with mounds of dried beans, rice and back-copies of *India Today*. Little India can be explored reasonably comfortably in half a day, but it is easy enough to spend a full day here mosying down the attractive side streets and sampling the wealth of Indian dishes available from the simplest coffee houses to sophisticated restaurants. (For more background on Singapore's Indian population see page 184.)

Little India is unusual in that it was never designated as an ethnic quarter - as were, for example, Chinatown and Kampong Glam (Arab Street). Instead, it emerged as the centre of Indian culture and life in Singapore through a natural process of evolution, rather than through administrative diktat.

Sights

Serangoon Road

If Little India is the heartland of Indian Singapore, then Serangoon Road is its soul. Serangoon Road was named after the Rongong stork which used to inhabit swampland in the area. By 1828, Serangoon Road was established as "the road leading across the island", but the surrounding area remained swampland until the 1920s when its brick kilns and lime pits attracted Indian (mainly Tamil) labourers to the area. In 1840 the race course was completed, which drew Europeans to settle here. (The road names Cuff,

Dickson and Clive would have been private lanes to the European residences.)

Architecture The Indians introduced a traditional technique of external plasterwork *Madras chunam*, which gave Serangoon Road's shophouses their ornate plasterwork façades (see Late Shophouse style, page 120). Some of the best examples can be found on Jalan Besar and along the cross streets which link Jalan Besar and Serangoon Road. This style of shophouse has come to be known as *Singapore Eclectic*. House numbers 61-69 Syed Alwi Road display some of the finest plasterwork in Singapore and a few roads further north, 10-14 Petain Road, built in the 1930s, show exceptionally ornate tiles and plasterwork. This latter row of shophouses is possibly the last intact group of eclectic style terracing remaining in Singapore. The ceramic tiles were imported from Europe and are a distinct feature of the Straits Chinese house.

The majority of Indians in this area are Chettiars - a money-lending caste from South India (and there are still money changers in many of the shops on Serangoon Road - one optimistically advertises "gold bars accepted") but there are also Tamils, Bengalis and Sikhs, among other groups. Along the southern end of Serangoon Road is a collection of gold shops selling finely-wrought jewellery. Also look out for the birdmen who practice parrot astrology. They whisper your name and birth date to the bird, which then picks out a card with the 'right' fortune on it.

Markets The lively **Zhujiao** (previously **Kandang Kerbau** or **KK**) **Market** on the corner of Buffalo and Serangoon roads is an entertaining spot to wander. Spices can be ground to your own requirements. Upstairs there is a maze of shops and stalls; the wet market is beyond the hawker centre, travelling west along Buffalo Road. New legislation introduced in 1993, which ruled that no animals could be slaughtered on wet market premises, saw the end of the chicken-plucking machine. It used to do the job in 12.4 seconds.

Kandang Kerbau - Malay for corral - was the centre of Singapore's cattle-rearing area in the 1870s. The cattle trade was dominated by Indians and among them was IR Belilios, a Venetian Jew from Calcutta who gave his name to a road nearby. The roads around KK have names connected to the trade: Lembu (cow) Road and Buffalo Road. With the boom in the cattle trade, related activities established themselves in the area; the cattle provided power for wheat-grinding, pineapple preserving and so on.

Opposite the market on Serangoon Road is the **Little India Arcade**, another Urban Redevelopment Authority (URA) project. This collection of handicraft shops is a great place to pick up Indian knick-knacks: leather sandals and bags, spices and curry powders, incense, saris and other printed textiles. There is also a food court here. On the north side of Campbell Road facing onto the Little India Aracade is *Kunas*, an excellent little handicraft shop, and *Jothi's Flower Shop* where garlands of jasmine flowers are strung for Hindu devotees to take to the temple. Hindu holy days are Tuesday and Friday when business is particularly brisk. Down Dunlop Road, named after Mr AE Dunlop the Inspector General of Police whose private road this was, is the **Abdul Gaffoor Mosque**. A mosque was first built on this site in 1859 by Sheikh Abdul Gaffoor bin Shaikh Hyder although the current brick structure was erected in 1910. It is hardly a splendid building but nonetheless has been gazetted as one of Singapore's 32 national monuments. Avoid visiting the mosque during Friday prayer day and in the evenings. Just off Dunlop Road, on Perak Road, is the equally architecturally unremarkable **Church of True Light** which was erected in 1850 to serve Little

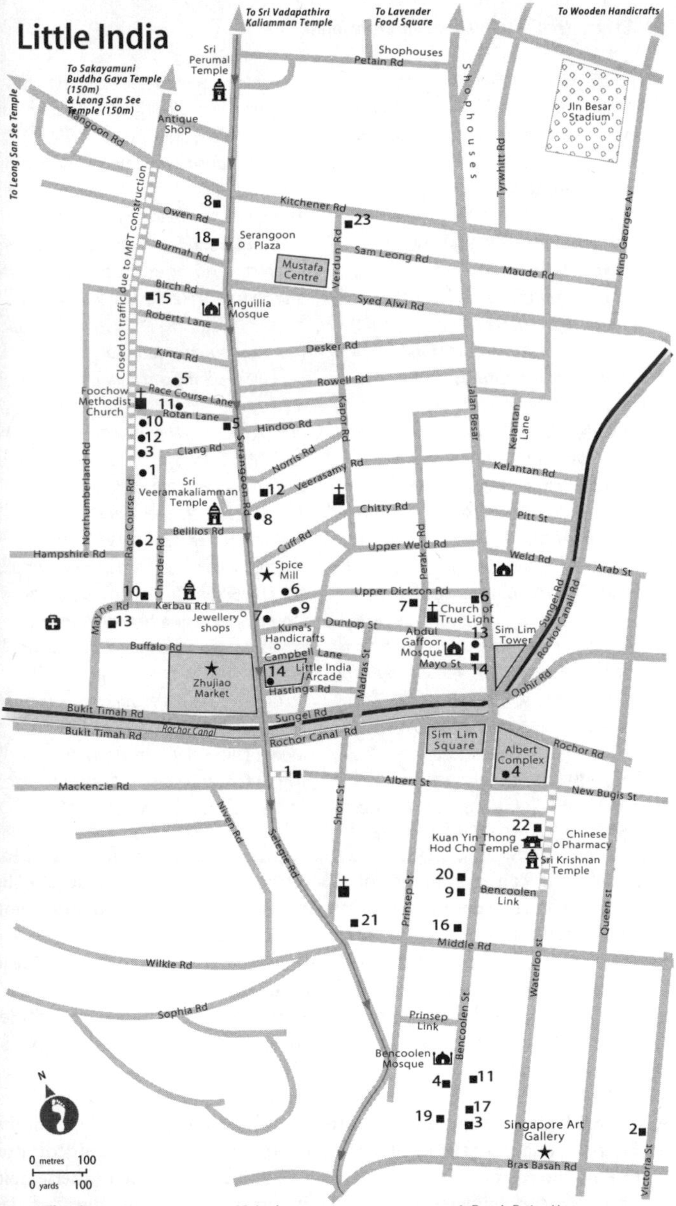

Little India

To Sri Vadapathira Kaliamman Temple
To Lavender Food Square
To Wooden Handicrafts
To Sakayamuni Buddha Gaya Temple (150m) & Leong San See Temple (150m)
To Leong San See Temple

0 metres 100
0 yards 100

■ **Sleeping**
1. Albert Court & Restaurants
2. Allson
3. Bayview Inn
4. Bencoolen
5. Broadway
6. Budget Boarding House
7. Dickson Court
8. Fortuna
9. Goh Homestay & Hawaii Hostel
10. Karbau
11. Lee Boarding House
12. Little India Guesthouses
13. Lucky
14. Mayo Inn
15. Penta
16. Peony Mansions
17. San Wah
18. Starlet
19. Strand
20. Summer View
21. Sun Sun
22. South East Asia
23. Tai Hoe

● **Eating**
1. Banana Leaf Apolo
2. Deli Pub & Restaurant
3. Delhi
4. Fatty's Eating House
5. Kaaraikubi & Amaravathi
6. Komala's Fast Food & Fine Dining
7. Komala Vilas
8. Madras Coffee House
9. Madras New Woodlands
10. Muthu's Curry
11. No Signboard Seafood
12. Nur Jehan
13. Ponthuk Bawean
14. Taj Jazzaraunt

Route of Thaipusam procession

Related maps:
Colonial core
(to the south), page 70
Coloured map
inside back cover

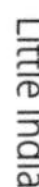

An architectural walkabout in Little India

*The shophouses of Little India have a character of their own, with the earliest examples being some of the plainest and humblest on the island. This **Early Shophouse Style** spans the period between 1840 and 1900. The buildings were generally 2-storey affairs, with Doric columns and minimal ornamentation; there are examples at 127 and 159 Dunlop Street. The early 1900s saw the emergence of the so-called **First Transitional Shophouse**. These were less squat in design and incorporated more decorative elements. Vents, often quite elaborate, were now included above or between the windows, while columns were Corinthian rather than Doric. Examples of this style can be seen at 61 Serangoon Road and 39 Campbell Lane. The **Late Shophouse Style** (1900-1940) overlapped with the First Transitional; of all the styles to be found in Little India these are without doubt the most interesting. The entire surface is elaborately decorated with plasterwork and ceramic tiles, the upper floor is divided into three, making a greater window area, and there are balustrades on the upper floor, creating shade for these rooms. Some of the best examples can be seen at 109-117 Jalan Besar and at the eastern end of Jalan Petain. The **Second Transitional Style** was relatively short-lived, dating essentially from the late 1930s. Architects and art historians have seen the Second Transitional as something of a reaction to the exuberance of the **Late Shophouse Style**. Designs were much simpler, though they still used ceramic tiles and some ornamentation. It is also possible to see the beginnings of Art Deco influences in these buildings. An example of a Second Transitional shophouse can be seen at 15 Cuff Road. Finally, the **Art Deco Style** emerged at the beginning of the 1930s and shophouses continued to be built in this style into the 1960s. Art Deco shophouses represent a logical progression from the Second Transitional style. Designs were simpler still, with proportions being more important than detail. In addition architects began to design groups of buildings rather than individual structures – with particular interest in corner sites. Many of these buildings were dated, so they are easily identified. An example can be found at 22 Campbell Lane.*

India's Anglican community of Hock Chew and Hinghwa descent. The church is open on Saturday and Sunday between 0900-1300 and should you pass by at this time it is worth entering for a few minutes.

Walking up Serangoon Road, take a right at Cuff Road to see Little India's last **spice mill** at work in a blue and mustard yellow shophouse - P. Govindasamai Pillai's. It's hard to miss the chugging of the mill, let alone the rich smells of the spices. Here spices are ground for use on the day of cooking.

Sri Veeramakaliamman Temple

The **Sri Veeramakaliamman Temple** on Serangoon Road was built for the Bengali community by indentured Bengali labourers in 1881 and is dedicated to Kali, the ferocious incarnation of Siva's wife. The name of the temple means Kali the courageous. It is similar in composition to most other temples of its kind and has three main elements: a shrine for the gods, a hall for worship and a *goporum* (or tower), built so that pilgrims can identify the temple from afar. The gopuram of this temple, with its cascade of gaudy, polychromed gods, goddesses, demons and mythological beasts, is the most recent addition and was only completed in 1987. Worshippers and visitors should walk clockwise around the temple hall, and for good luck an odd number of times. The principal black image of Kali in the temple hall (clasping her club of destruction - not a women to get on the wrong side of) is flanked by her sons, Ganesha and Murugan.■ *The temple is closed*

The Story of Kuan Yin

Turned onto the streets by her husband for some unspecified wrong-doing, Kuan Yin (sometimes Quan Am), disguised herself as a monk and took refuge in a monastery. She was then accused of fathering, and then abandoning, her child. Accepting the blame (why is unclear), she was again turned out onto the streets, only to return to the monastery much later when she was on the point of death – to confess her true identity. When the Emperor of China heard the tale, he made Kuan Yin the Guardian Spirit of Mother and Child, and childless couples now pray to her. Kuan Yin's husband is sometimes depicted as a parakeet, with the Goddess usually holding her adopted son in one arm and standing on a lotus leaf (the symbol of purity).

Monday-Sunday, 1230-1600.

Further up Serangoon Road is another Indian temple, **Sri Perumal**, with its high goporum sculptured with five manifestations of Vishnu. The temple was founded in 1855, but much of the decoration is more recent. This carving was finished in 1979 and was paid for by local philanthropist P. Govindasamy Pillai, better known as PGP, who made his fortune selling saris. Like other Hindu temples, there is greatest activity on the holy days of Tuesdays and Fridays. For the best experience of all, come here and to the Sri Veeramakaliamman and Hindu Chettiars (see page 120) temples during the two day festival of **Thaipusam**, generally held in January (see page 52), which celebrates the birthday of Murugan, one of Kali's sons. ■ *Monday-Sunday, 0630-1200, 1800-2100.*

Sakayamuni Buddha Gaya Temple

Further north at 366 Race Course Road (parallel to Serangoon Road) is the Buddhist **Sakayamuni Buddha Gaya Temple** or Temple of One Thousand Lights dominated by a 15m-high, 300 tonne, rather crude, statue of the Buddha surrounded by 987 lights (the lights are turned on if you make a donation). The image is represented in the attitude of subduing Mara - the right hand touches the ground calling the Earth Goddess to witness the historic Buddha's resistance of the attempts by Mara to tempt him with her naked dancing daughters. At the back of the principal image is a smaller reclining Buddha. Devotees come here to worship the branch of the sacred Bodhi tree - under which the Buddha gained enlightenment - and a replica mother-of-pearl footprint of the Buddha showing the 108 auspicious signs of the Enlightened One. ■ *0730-1645 Monday-Sunday, remove shoes before entering.* Across the road is the Chinese Mahayana Buddhist **Leong San See Temple**, or Dragon Mountain Temple, with its carved entrance, (where you don't have to remove your shoes). It is dedicated to Kuan Yin (the goddess of mercy) who had 18 hands, which are said to symbolize her boundless mercy and compassion. The principal image on the altar shows her modelled, as usual, in white surrounded by a mixed bag of Chinese Mahayana folk gods and Theravada images of the Buddha.

Essentials

Sleeping

■ *on maps*
Price codes: see inside front cover

Most of Singapore's budget accommodation (such as it is) is to be found in the Little India and Arab Street areas to the north of town. Little India is probably a more interesting place to stay but the accommodation in the Arab Street area is a trifle cheaper. (See the Arab Street section for accommodation there.) Cheap accommodation is very limited in Singapore and many of the backpackers' haunts are to be found in apartment blocks and do not have much to recommend them - othe than price.

A+-A ***Albert Court***, 180 Albert St, T3393939, F3393252, http://www.fareast.com sg/hotels. An unusually designed hotel (a mixture of western and Peranakan), lying behind a courtyard of renovated shophouses. This is an intimate place built to high specifications, with attractive extras. Ask for a room with big windows. Restaurant but no other facilities. Right next to a good range of restaurants in Albert Court Recommended.

A ***City Bayview***, 30 Bencoolen St, T3372882, F3382880. A/c, restaurant, leafy rooftop pool. Neat little hotel block with business facilities, personal safes in rooms, attentive and friendly service, popular with tour groups. The rooms are smallish but the hotel is competitively priced and well-run.

A ***Bencoolen***, 47 Bencoolen St, T3360822, F3362250. The hotel that was here in 1997 has been pulled down - and not a toilet flush too soon - and in mid-1998 a new edifice was in the process of going up. The picture is impressive enough and they are advertising such refinements as a health centre. The hotel should be completed either late 1998 or 1999.

B ***Dickson Court***, 3 Dickson Rd, at Jl Besar end, T2977811, F2977833. Price includes simple buffet breakfast. New, clean and smart, with friendly management.

B ***Summer View***, 173 Bencoolen St, T3381122, F3366346. Compact and quite wel designed modern block with 80 very small rooms and no restaurant. Popular with regional businessmen and during early/mid-1998 was offering room discounts that brought it down just into our **C** category - and with breakfast thrown in as a reckless gesture.

B-C ***Broadway***, 195 Serangoon Rd, T2924661, F2916414. A/c, restaurant, ugly hote block stuck on its own, Indian-run and Indian patronized establishment with clean rooms and friendly management, excellent Indian restaurant downstairs (*New Delh Restaurant*): 'we know the way to your heart is through your stomach'.

C ***Kerbau***, 54/63 Kerbau Rd, T2976668, F2976669. A/c, small hotel in modernised shophouse on this quiet dead-end street. The rooms are hardly spacious and nothing special, but they are clean with attached showers and if you get one looking out onto Kerbau Road it is possible to open the shutters in the evening and watch Indian life from above. Good value. Recommended.

C ***Little India Guesthouse***, 3 Veerasamy Rd, T2942866, F2984866. Some a/c, no private bathrooms, but spotless male/female shower areas and immaculate rooms. No food served here, but plenty on the street. Good location if you want to be in the heart of Little India and all in an attractive salmon-pink shophouse. Recommended.

C ***Lucky***, 18 Race Course Rd, T2919122, F2919391. Small rooms, basic but clean. Good price for location.

C ***Mayo Inn***, 9A Jalan Besar, T2956631, F2958218. A/c, this little converted shophouse on the corner of Jalan Besar and Mayo Street opened in 1996. Rooms are small but are clean and have attached bathrooms.

C ***South East Asia Hotel***, 190 Waterloo Street, T3382394, F3383480, seahotel@ mbox2.singnet.com.sg. A/c, rooms here are clean enough, with attached showers, but they are also a trifle musty. The fact that the hotel seems to be tiled from floor to ceiling is presumably a throw back to the Jurassic period in interior decoration.

C ***Strand***, 25 Bencoolen St, T3381866, F3381330. A/c, attractive café and refurbished rather trendy lobby raises expectations which are then dashed by poor rooms; they are big though and it's quite good value. Popular weekend buffet.

C ***Tai Hoe***, 163 Kitchener Rd, T2939122, F2984600. A/c, hot water bath, not visited on our last visit but recommended by a traveller.

C ***Waterloo Hostel***, 4th, 5th and 7th Flr, 55 Waterloo St, T3366555, F3362160. A/c, centrally located, big rooms with TVs and telephones, complimentary tea/coffee and basic breakfast, very pleasant, friendly atmosphere, run by Catholic Welfare Centre. Recommended. If the hostel is full and you are offered rooms in their 'homestay' - avoid, as the rooms are noisy and not recommended.

C-D ***Peony Mansion Travellers' Lodge***, 4th Flr, 46-52 Bencoolen St (lift round back of building), T3385638, F3391471. Another place in the same block as the *Lee Boarding House*, marginally better than the *Peony Mansions* across the road. Has the advantage of two good and cheap Muslim restaurants at ground level.

C-D ***San Wah***, 36 Bencoolen St, T3362428, F3344146. Some a/c, public showers, 10 rooms in one of the very few remaining family-run Chinese hotels in Singapore. The lovely villa, more than 50 years old, is set rather incongruously in a largish compound surrounded by new blocks or empty plots. It is run by the elderly Mr Chao Yoke San and his son. While the hotel may not be very clean, and is often noisy, it has a character and ambience that others cannot match.

C-D ***Sun Sun***, 260A-262A&B Middle Road, T3384911. Some a/c, this is a great little hotel, up a flight of stairs at the southern edge of Little India, run by a Chinese gentleman. All rooms have communal facilities but the showers and toilets are very clean. The rooms are large but plain, with a sink in one corner, and an extra few S$ buys you a/c. Recommended.

D ***Goh's Homestay***, 4th Flr (no lift), 169D Bencoolen St, T3396561, F3398606. Tiny rooms with separate showers but an immaculately clean, friendly place with nice snack bar and fax/storage/washing facilities, only 20 rooms so booking is advisable. Recommended.

D ***Hawaii Hostel***, 2nd Flr, 171B Bencoolen St, T3384187. In same block as *Goh*, but not quite as good. 27 small and rather dirty rooms (and an 8 bed dorm for S$18). Simple breakfast included in room rate, washing facilities available, friendly manageress.

D ***Lee Boarding House***, 7th Flr, 52 Peony Mansion, 46-52 Bencoolen St, T3383149, F3365409. Calls itself 'the exclusive club for travellers' but it seems pretty grim. 100 rooms, some a/c, some with bathrooms, complimentary breakfast of sorts, travel information service, **E** for dorm beds.

D-E ***Peony Mansions***, 2nd Flr, 131A Bencoolen St, T3385638, F3391471. Windowless rooms with only beds in them (no space for anything else). Outside cold (broken?) showers. Dirty. For double the money you can have same size room and a/c (of sorts) and a hot shower (also broken?). A plus is the good roti man on street below.

Eating: expensive

● *on maps*
Price codes:
see inside front cover

Restaurants here range from sophisticated air-conditioned places to the simplest of banana plate eateries. For North Indian cuisine, the best option is to trot down to the southern end of Race Course Rd, where there are six good restaurants in a row, all competing for business including the *Banana Leaf Apolo*, *Delhi*, *Nur Jehan* and, most famous of all, *Muthu's*. Some of the best vegetarian restaurants - South Indian particularly - are found on the other side of Serangoon Road, along Upper Dickson Street.

3 ***Amaravathi***, 19/20 Race Course Lane, **Indian**. In the same block as *Kaaraikubi* and also air-conditioned but this place serves Mulli cuisine.

3 ***Aziza's***, 02-05 Albert Court, 180 Albert St, T2351130. Renowned for excellent home-cooked **Malay** food. It is said that the Sultan of Brunei eats here when in town.

3 ***Banana Leaf Apolo***, 56-58 Race Course Rd, T2938682. **North Indian** food, another popular fish-head curry spot, air-conditioned and more sophisticated than the name might imply - although the food is still served on banana leaves to justify the name.

3 ***Delhi***, Race Course Road. **North Indian** food including chicken tikka, various tandooris as well as creamy Kashmiri concoctions.

3 ***Kaaraikubi Banana Leaf***, 19/20 Race Course Lane. Air-conditioned **Indian** restaurant without much character but with excellent food on this quiet street off Serangoon Road.

3 ***Komala Vilas***, 76-78 Serangoon Rd, T2936980. **South Indian** thalis and masala dosas, bustling café, with a little more room upstairs, recommended.
3 ***Muthu's Curry***, corner of Rotan and Race Course Rd, T2937029. **North Indian** food reckoned by connoisseurs to be among the best banana leaf restaurants in town. *Muthu's* fish-heads are famous, recommended.
4 ***Taj Jazzaraunt***, Campbell Lane (above the Little India Arcade). This is a slightly different place to eat **Indian** food. Garlic king prawns, tandoori, shashlick and other North Indian delights can be consumed to live jazz. The restaurant stretches along the whole first floor of the shophouse block so it is possible to grab a table on a balcony and watch the Indian life of Serangoon Road.
3 ***Wing Seong Fatty's Eating House***, 01-33 Albert Complex, T3381087. Established in 1926, excellent steamed garoupa, roast duck and pork, peeled chilli prawns and other **Cantonese** dishes. Recommended.

Eating: cheaper

2-3 ***Komala's Fast Food***, Upper Dickson Road. This is the fast food end of the Komala empire - **South Indian** delicacies including thalis, masala dosas and idlis are served in an airconditioned restaurant, very popular and recommended.
2 ***Madras Coffee House***, Serangoon Road (opposite the Sri Veeramakaliamman Temple). This is a great little traditional place with marble tables, fans and stainless steel cups and plates as well as excellent sweet and salt lassis, yoghurt rice, dosas and other **South Indian** dishes. Recommended.
2 ***Madras New Woodlands***, 12 Upper Dickson Rd (off Serangoon Rd), T2971594. Thalis, masala dosa and **vegetarian** curries, good and cheap, recommended.
2 ***New Delhi***, *Broadway Hotel*, 195 Serangoon Rd. Good, cheap vegetarian and non-vegetarian **North Indian** food, specialities are chicken and almond, and seafood curries.
2 ***Ponthuk Bawean Restaurant***, Dunlop Street (at Jalan Besar end). Simple, open-air **Malay** restaurant in a wonderfully gaudy shophouse serving such dishes as beef rendang, chilli eggs, and spicy beans.

Hawker centres & food courts

1 ***Albert Court***, between Waterloo and Queen Sts. There's a huge area of hawker stalls here. **1** ***Lavender Food Square***, Lavender Rd, north of Little India, is one of the best hawker centres in town. **1** ***Paradiz Centre Basement Food Centre***, 1 Selegie Rd, recommended stall: *Mr Boo's Teochew Mushroom Minced Meat Mee* (No 34). **1** ***Zhujiao or Kandang Kerbau (KK) Food Centre***, in the same complex as the wet market, on the corner of Buffalo and Serangoon roads. Wide range of dishes, and the best place for Indian Muslim food: curries, rotis, dosai and murtabak are hard to beat (beer can be bought from the Chinese stalls on the other side).

Cafés

3 ***Café Oriel***, ground floor of Selegie Arts Centre, off Prinsep St. Popular for its pizzas.

Tea, cakes & coffee shops

Zhong Guo Hua Tuo Guan, this traditional Chinese tea house has quite a few outlets including an atmospheric one at 52 Queen St (name above the tea house is in Chinese characters), just by the Albert and Waterloo streets roadside market. Sells Hua Tuo's ancient recipes helpful for 'relieving of heatiness' and 'inhibiting the growth of tumor cells,' amongst other things. Very friendly proprietress will introduce you to wild ginseng and showfrog, or longan herbal jelly and tell you why you will feel better (that's if you can get any of the concoctions down!).

Arab Street

Originally this area was a thriving Arab village known as Kampong Glam (Glam Village). There is some disagreement over the origins of this name. Some commentators have attributed it to the Gelam tribe of sea-gypsies who once lived in the area. More likely, it refers to the glam tree from which Bugis seafarers extracted resin to caulk their ships.

Ins and outs

Getting there

Bugis MRT station is near the southwestern edge of Arab Street while Lavender is on the northeastern fringe of the area. The only bus to run direct from Orchard Road is no 7.

Getting around

Arab Street is the smallest of the areas highlighted in this book and it is easy to explore on foot.

The area

Singapore's Arabs were among the area's earliest settlers, the first being a wealthy merchant called Syed Mohammad bin Harum Al-Junied who arrived in 1819, a couple of months after Stamford Raffles. The Alkaffs were another important local Arab family, who built their ostentatious mansion on Mount Faber (now a restaurant, see page 132). Arab merchants began settling in the area around Arab Street in the mid 19th century.

Arab Street is still the main artery of Muslim Singapore, and is the name applied to the district sandwiched between Rochor Canal Road, Jalan Sultan, Victoria Street and Beach Road. In this area are a number of attractive streets including Kandahar Street, the touristy Bussorah Street, and Arab Street itself. Much of Kampong Glam has been renovated by the Urban Redevelopment Authority (URA) in an attempt to retain some of its architectural heritage. As one would expect, this part of town has the greatest concentration of Muslim restaurants including Indonesian, Malay and Indian. Many of the cheapest - and noisest - are arrayed along busy North Bridge Road. Cut into the Arab quarter and roads like Kandahar, Bussorah and Pahang to find quieter places to eat and drink.

Sights

Mosques

The focal point of the Arab quarter is the **Sultan Mosque**, with its golden domes, on North Bridge Road. Completed in 1928 and designed by colonial architect Denis Santry of Swan & Maclaren, it is an eclectic mixture of Classical, Moorish and Persian. It is Singapore's largest mosque and attracts thousands of the faithful every Friday. The original building, constructed in the 1820s, was part of a deal between the Temenggong of Johor and the East India Company in which the company donated S$3,000 towards its construction and the Temenggong leased the land to the trustees of the mosque. ■ *0900-1300, 1400-1600. NB Visitors in shorts, short skirts or singlets will not be permitted to enter.* Next door is the old **Kampong Glam Istana**, built in the early 1840s as the Temenggong Ali Iskander Shah's palace.

Another popular mosque right at the eastern edge of Kampong Glam is the **Hajjah Fatimah Mosque** on Java Road. Unusually, it was financed by a wealthy Melakan-born Malay woman, Hajjah Fatimah (Hajjah is the femal equivalent of Haji, meaning someone who has made the pilgrimage t Mecca), married to a Bugis merchant who is said in some sources to hav been the Sultan of Gowa in Sulawesi. It was designed by an unknown Britis architect and the work contracted to a French construction company whic employed Malay labour. It was completed in 1846 and has, as a result of it cosmopolitan history, a distinctive flavour. Unfortunately, it is nov dwarfed by surrounding Housing Development Board (HDB) blocks, bu inside there are photographs of its HDB-less hinterland in 1959.

Stalls and shops In the maze of side streets around the Sultan Mosque there is a colourfu jumble of Malay, Indonesian and Middle Eastern merchandise. Excellen selections of batik (which is sold in sarong lengths of just over 2m) jostle fo space with, silk and Indian textiles (especially along Arab Street), wickerware jewellery, perfumes and religious paraphernalia. In the weeks before Har Raya Puasa, Bussorah Street is lined with stalls selling all kinds of traditiona foods - after dark it is a favourite haunt of famished Muslims durin Ramadan. Bussorah Street has been gentrified as part of the URA' redevelopment efforts: it is now a pedestrianised, tree-lined street of elegan

Arab Street

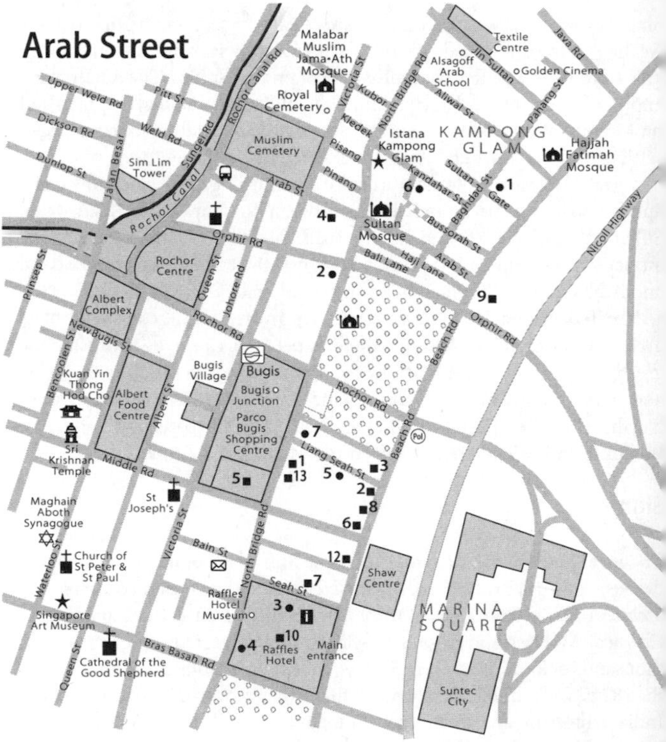

Related maps
Colonial Core,
page 70
Coloured map
inside back cover

0 metres 100
0 yards 100

■ **Sleeping**
1. Ah Chew
2. Beach
3. Cozy Corner Lodge
4. Golden Landmark
5. Intercontinental
6. Lee Traveller's Club
7. Metropole
8. Park View
9. Plaza
10. Raffles
11. Season's Homestay
12. Shang Onn
13. Waffles Homestay

● **Eating**
1. BiBik's Place
2. Blanco Court Food Centre
3. Doc Cheng's
4. Empire Café
5. Pivdofr at Joon's
6. Rumah Mak Minang
7. Wayang Caf

Malaysia Bus terminal

Return from the dead: Bugis Street

One of Singapore's more famous sights used to be Bugis Street, a street where by day hawkers and stalls would congregate but where, at night, transvestites would promenade and noisy bars would stay open until the early morning. Bugis Street was, in a sense, the nemesis of all that Lee Kuan Yew's squeaky-clean Singapore was aiming to become: it was unplanned, anarchic, wild, outrageous. Then, in 1985, Bugis Street was demolished to make way for the Mass Rapid Transit system. As the Economist put it at the time, this was perhaps more than mere coincidence because "Bugis Street represents all that the authorities seem to want to erase".

But the arrival of the demolition ball was not to be the end of Bugis Street. In 1989 it was proposed that the street be recreated in a new, but nearby location. As the project consultant was quoted as saying in the Singapore Bulletin, the new creation would be "right down to the toilet building ... it will be back with smell and all". But, it would, at the same time, be "absolutely safe in terms of hygiene and personal safety". The buildings were rebuilt to the same dimensions and style, even posters from the 1960s were painted onto walls to give the ambience of the old street. But as this was a place for families and wholesome entertainment, the transvestites that made the old Bugis Street what it was, were banned. The irony, though, was that the upmarket 'retail and food and beverage outlets' that occupied the reconstructed shophouses complained of poor business and were allowed to hire transvestites as customer relations officers to explain the history of the street. But, the Straits Times Weekly reassured its readers, they would be watched by closed circuit television and plain clothes men to ensure that they did not solicit. When the Singapore Tourist Board put on a show in Hong Kong to promote the Republic they used transvestites. Local journalists asked how this could be justified in Singapore terms, and they were told that the performers were not transvestites but "female impersonators, professional artistes". New Bugis Street has, in the process of this transformation, become more authentic of modern Singapore than the old Bugis Street was of the Singapore of the 1960s and 1970s. The latter was anachronistic ... an oddball place that had to be worn down.

shophouses. Tombstone-makers are based along Pahang Street. Nearby at the junction of Jalan Sultan and Victoria Street is the **old royal cemetery** which was marked on maps as such from the 1930s. The associated mosque is the **Malabar Muslim Jama-Ath mosque**, which was built in the 1920s. The architect, an Indian named A.H. Siddique, was unusual in two respects: first he learnt his architectural skills through a correspondence course; and second, it is said he never took a fee for any religious building he designed (Muslim or other).

Bugis Street

Bugis Street is southwest of Arab Street, right across the road from the Bugis Street MRT station. It is packed with stalls selling cheap T-shirts, copy watches, handicrafts - like a street market you might see in Thailand or Malaysia, but something that seems rather out of place in modern day Singapore. For those who like to see Singapore not just as a giant shopping plaza but also as a real life experiment in ersatz existence, then Bugis Street offers more than key rings and Oriental flim-flam. The whole street has been re-created from a road that was demolished to make way for the MRT in the mid-1980s. Some people maintain that the reason it was demolished, and then brought back from the dead, sums up Singapore's approach to life (see box). On the opposite side of Victoria Street is the new Parco Bugis Centre, a high-tech shopping plaza (in reconstructed air-conditioned shophouses) bustling with life and containing restaurants, shopping mall and yet another of Singapore's fabulous fountains.

Temples **Waterloo Street**, much of which has been pedestrianised, cuts across New Bugis Street and is also worth a modest detour. The **Sri Krishnan Temple** at 152 Waterloo Street dates back to the 1870s when a simple attap hut protected two Hindu images (Krishna didn't arrive until the 1880s). Over the years it has been expanded and refined as the Hindu population of the surrounding area has prospered. Almost next door is a large, modern Mahayana pagoda dedicated to **Kuan Yin** - the **Kuan Yin Thong Hod Che Temple**. This temple is particularly popular - try visiting around lunch time (1200-1300) when scores of worshippers come here to pray for good fortune. The central image is of multi-limbed Kuan Yin (see page 121) while on either side are Ta Ma Tan Shith and Hua Tua. The latter was an important Han Dynasty fingure (3rd century BC) who is now the patron saint of Chinese medics. Perhaps not coincidentally, on the other side of the street in Cheng Yan Court, is a collection of **traditional Chinese pharmacies** selling the usual range of dried fungi, antlers, bones, herbs roots like ginseng, dessicated sea horses, and other unidentified body parts

Essentials

Sleeping
■ *on maps*
Price codes: see inside front cover

The Arab Street area and Little India are the two centres of budget accommodation in Singapore. In Arab Street they are centred on, or close to, Liang Seah Street, a narrow street of shophouses that are gradually being gentrified. There is a good range of restaurants here from trendy cafés to cheap Chinese and Muslim restaurants. It lies between the Arab and Indian quarters so is also quite convenient for these two areas of town. It is about a 15 min walk from the Colonial core.

A+ *Golden Landmark*, 390 Victoria St, T2972828, F2982038. This 400-room tower block (with Arabic overtones) is looking older than its 1980s birthdate would indicate. It has an Indonesian restaurant, a big pool, corporate floors and a business centre. Caters mainly for tours and corporate clients - not many Europeans stay here.

A-B *Park View Hotel,* 81 Beach Road, T3388558, F3348558, http://www.parkview.com.sg. A/c, new medium-sized hotel. There is no pool or gym but the rooms are well appointed - the deluxe rooms are a good size and better value than the slightly cramped standard (no windows) and superior rooms.

B *Dickson Court*, 3 Dickson Rd, at Jl Besar end, T2977811, F2977833. Price includes simple buffet breakfast. New, clean, smart, with friendly management.

C *Beach*, 95 Beach Rd (corner of Liang Seah St), T3367712, F3367713. A/c, basic but clean rooms in an ugly block.

C *Tai Hoe*, 163 Kitchener Rd, T2939122, F2984600. A/c, hot water bath, not checked on our last visit but recommended by a traveller.

C-D *Ah Chew Hotel*, Liang Seah Street, T3375285. Old hotel in an unrenovated shophouse and the 14 rooms are much as you would expect: old and unrenovated but with some character - cash only.

D *Shang Onn*, 37 Beach Rd, T3384153. 10 rooms in another ugly apartment block, no breakfast, but efficient service and rooms are adequate (fan only), no dorms, long term visitors encouraged, not very friendly but recommended.

D-E *Lee Travellers' Club*, 6th Flr of the Fu Yuen apartment block (and next to the *Park View Hotel*), 75 Beach Rd, T3395490. Some a/c, breakfast included, short on bathrooms, but clean rooms, cooking and storage facilities, owner prides himself on security, **E** for dorms.

D-E *Waffles Homestay*, 2/F, 490 North Bridge Rd. Great little place, friendl

Arab Street

Win

a 7 night 'Bangkok & Beach' holiday for two courtesy of Hayes & Jarvis

20 runners up to win a Footprint Handbook of their choice

Footprint Handbooks are the most accurate and up-to-date travel guides available. There are over 38 books in the series and more in the pipeline. You can find out more by contacting us:

T +44 (0) 1225 469141

E handbooks@footprint.cix.co.uk

www.footprint-handbooks.co.uk

Well established as one of the UK's leading tour operators Hayes & Jarvis has been selling long haul holidays to the discerning traveller for over 40 years. Every Hayes & Jarvis holiday is the product of careful and meticulous planning where good quality and reliability go hand in hand with value for money.

To enter the Prize Draw fill in this form using a ball-point pen and return to us.

Mr ☐ Mrs ☐ Miss ☐ Ms ☐

First name ____________________

Surname ____________________

Permanent Address ____________________

____

____

Postcode/Zip ______________ Country ______________

Email ____________________

Occupation ______________ Age ______________

Title of Handbook ____________________

If you have any friends who would like to hear about Footprint Handbooks, fill in their details below.

Mr ☐ Mrs ☐ Miss ☐ Ms ☐

First name ____________________

Surname ____________________

Permanent Address ____________________

____

____

Postcode/Zip ______________ Country ______________

Which two destinations would you like to visit in the next two years?

____

If you do not wish to receive information from other reputable businesses, please tick box ☐

Footprint Handbooks

Travel guides for free spirits

Affix
Stamp
Here

Footprint Handbooks
6 Riverside Court
Lower Bristol Road
Bath
BA2 3DZ
England

RCS99

management, lovely roof terrace, access through an Indian restaurant - the *Haj*. Recommended.

D ***Season Homestay***, 26A Liang Seah St, T3372400, http://www.sgweb.com.sg/homestay. Some a/c, this place opened in 1997, rooms are small (or cozy as they bill them) and can be stuffy, but also clean. Breakfast is included in the rate and dorm beds (**E**) are also available.

D-E ***Cozy Corner Lodge*** (formerly the *Backpackers Cozy Corner*), 2a Liang Seah St, T3348761. Located above a restaurant, dorm beds available, this is a cheap option, but the rooms are cramped - sardines come to mind. One dorm room doubles up as the reception, remains popular.

Eating

● *on maps*
Price codes: see inside front cover

Arab Street is the best area for Muslim food of all descriptions - Malay, Indonesian, Indian or Arabic. There are some good restaurants around the Sultan Mosque and many more on noisy North Bridge Road. Try the Parco Bugis Shopping Centre for non-Muslim restaurants including good Italian and New Bugis Street for simple open-air fare and jugs of cold beer.

3 ***Bibik's Place***, Pahang St. Upmarket little place in a renovated shophouse, excellent **Nonya** dishes.

4 ***Masakatsu***, 80 Middle Rd, Ground Floor, Parco Bugis Junction, T3348233, **Japanese**. Known for its hotpot. Book at weekends.

4 ***Pasta Fresca da Salvatore***, Shaw Centre, **Italian**. Fresh, tasty pizzas and a good range of pasta dishes, open 24 hours.

3 ***Pivdofr at Joons***, Liang Seah St, **International**. Another café serving sandwiches and salads although it also has a good set lunch menu.

2 ***Rumah Makan Minang***, Kandahar St (facing onto the Istana Kampong Glam). Small restaurant serving cheap Padang (West Sumatran) dishes including beef rendang (dry beef curry), spicy grilled fish and kangkung.

2-3 ***Zam Zam Restaurant***, junction of Arab St and North Bridge Rd. **Muslim Malay-Indian** dishes served in busy and chaotic coffee shop. Very popular and recommended for a taste of the other Singapore - spicy meats, char-grilled seafood, creamy curries.

Clubs

Boom Boom Room, 3 New Bugis St, T3398187. Cabaret and stand up comedy shows. Popular with locals; tame by international standards.

Marina South and the Port

*To make something out of nothing, **Marina Village** was built, complete with restaurants, bars, concert venues, discos, a night bazaar and a 24 hour bowling alley. It was, however, a complete flop, and the ebullient Moroccan businessman who financed it has fled the country. It has now become rather more popular as a place to relax, especially at the weekend.*

Ins and outs

Getting there Marina South is rather isolated from the rest of the city - which probably explains why it is taking some time to get established. To get there, take the MRT to Marina Bay and then the shuttle bus to Marina South. Bus or taxi is the most convenient way to get to the World Trade Centre. Bus nos 65 and 143 run direct from Orchard Road. (A new MRT line currently under construction will terminate at the World Trade Centre.) Ferries for the southern islands group including Pulau Kusu and St John's leave from the World Trade Centre - as do international ferries for Indonesia's Riau Islands. Tanjong Pagar is the nearest MRT stop to the Tanjong Pagar container terminal.

Getting around This is not really an area that one 'explores' on foot.

The area

Marina South, east of the city proper, is a vast expanse of land reclaimed from the sea in the 1970s and 1980s as an overspill area for the envisaged spread of Singapore's financial district. Locals come here to jog along the

Marina South & the Port

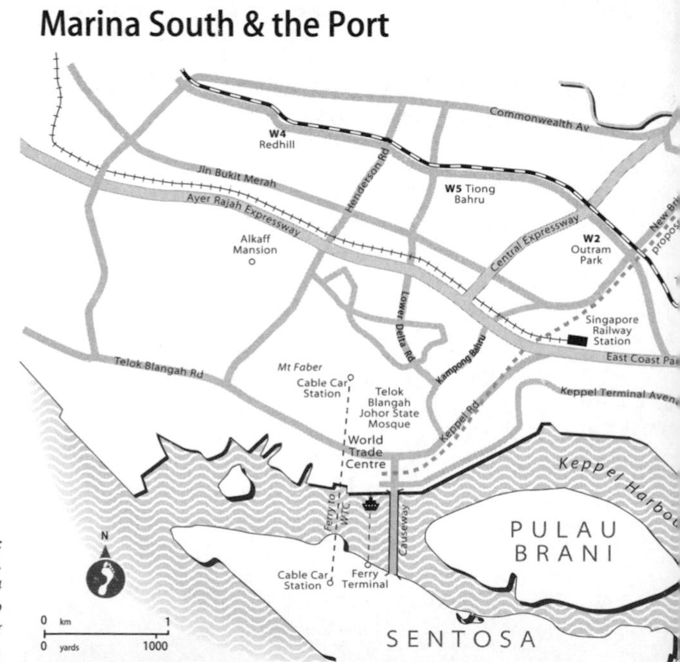

Related maps: Sentosa, *page 134* *Coloured map* *inside back cover*

promenade, roller blade, or fly kites. In the evening the outdoor seafood restaurants are popular. For Singapore's developers, Marina South's progress has been disappointing and it has not taken off as envisaged.

The world's busiest port

Singapore port is strategically located at the southern end of the Strait of Melaka, half way between China and India. It is a free port, open to all maritime nations. Largely sheltered from the city, it has seven gateways; the biggest - the container port - is the **Tanjong Pagar terminal**. In 1820 the first resident governor, Colonel William Farquhar, realising the advantages of Keppel Harbour's deep and sheltered water, began to develop it as a port. In 1864 the Tanjong Pagar Dock Company was formed and in 1972 the first container terminal was established.

There are usually 800 or more ships in port at any one time - one arrives, on average, every 5 minutes. In 1995 104,014 vessels called here making it, in terms of shipping tonnage, the busiest port in the world (overtaking Rotterdam). It is also the world's busiest container port, overtaking Hong Kong in 1990. Singapore port has attracted admiring comment ever since it was founded. In 1934, Roland Braddell described the harbour as a "Clapham Junction of the World" - referring to the world's busiest railway junction in London. For the best views of the port, the *Harbour View Dai-Ichi Hotel* must win the prize.

World Trade Centre

To the west of Tanjong Pagar port, on Keppel Road, is the World Trade Centre. Most people visit the World Trade Centre either to get to Sentosa (see page 133), to take the boat to Batam and Bintan islands in Indonesia's Riau Archipelago, or to climb aboard the cable car which connects Sentosa with Mount Faber. Also here is the **Singapore Maritime Showcase**. This is a museum devoted to Singapore's role as one of the world's largest and most efficient ports. A 12-minute *Maritime Odyssey* transports you rather jerkily in a container through past, present and future Singapore. An extensive model of the port gives some idea of its size, a video wall describes the process of loading and unloading, there are banks of computers providing touch screens for maritime information and a game, and some basic Lego to construct your own port. Neptune Topaz provides a bridge and control panels for potential naval recruits and a short unexciting film about key ports of the world. The wooden models of ships are more fun. A cheap way to spend a rainy afternoon with bored children, but not worth a special visit. ■ *Free except for the Maritime Odyssey which costs S$2, S$1 children. 1030-1830 Tuesday-Friday, 1030-2030 Saturday and Sunday. Numerous buses stop at the World Trade Centre including numbers 10, 30, 61, 84, 93, 97, 100, 131, 143, 145 and 166.*

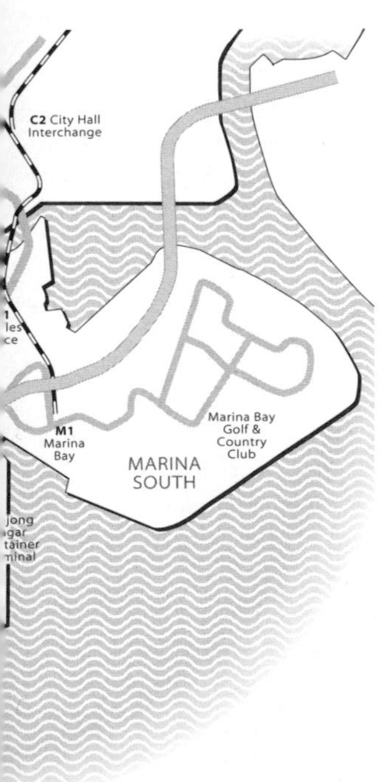

Opposite the exhibition halls of the World Trade Centre, lies the **Telok Blangah Johor State Mosque**, dating from the 1840s. It was the focal point of the pre-Raffles Malay royalty in Singapore. The tomb of the Temenggong Abdul Rahman - the *Tanah Kubor Rajah* or *Tanah Kubor Temenggong* - is nearby; he was partly responsible for negotiating Singapore's status as a trading post with Stamford Raffles. The Johor royal family lived at Telok Blangah until 1855 when the town of Iskandar Putri was founded on the other side of the straits; it was renamed Johor Bahru in 1866.

Essentials

Sleeping Staying in this area of town is inconvenient and there are, in any case, no hotels. The closest centres of accommodation are the Colonial core and Sentosa Island.

Eating

● *on maps*
Price codes: see inside front cover

4 ***Alkaff Mansion***, Mount Faber Ridge, 10 Telok Blangah Green, T2786979. Built in the 1920s, this huge house has undergone a S$3mn refurbishment and makes a magnificent restaurant surrounded by parkland. Go here for the atmosphere, not the food, which is very average. If you do eat, the **continental** cuisine is better than the **Indonesian**.

4 ***Long Beach Seafood***, 31 Marina Park, Marina South, T3232222. One of the island's most famous **seafood** restaurants, specializing in pepper and chilli-crabs, drunken prawns and baby squid cooked in honey.

4 ***Prima Tower Revolving Restaurant***, 201 Keppel Rd, T2728822. Revolving restaurant atop a huge silo looks out over the harbour and city, established 20 years ago and with the same chef still working here. **Beijing** cuisine, particularly good Peking Duck, book in advance.

1 ***Dotty Café***, Bukit Chermin Rd, off Keppel Marina, T2708575 and Telok Blangah Rd, just west of where the cable car goes over the road. Call Dorothy before you go and plan your **seafood** menu to get the best catch of the day. Eat under fairy lights, right on the sea, and admire yachts moored next door, very quiet and peaceful.

Eating: cheaper ***Han's***, 8 branches around the city including Harbour Promenade World Trade Centre (WTC). This chain of restaurants is Singapore's answer to the Greasy Spoon - cafes without the acute accent on the 'e', single dish **Chinese** meals, simple (largely fried) breakfasts, some **European** food including such things as steaks, burgers and fries all served in large helpings at very competitive prices.

Bars ***Alkaff Mansion***, Mount Faber Ridge, 10 Telok Blangah Green, perfect for sundowner 'stengahs' on the terrace with an excellent view of the harbour.

Sentosa

A British military base until 1970, Sentosa - formerly Pulau Belakang Mati - is now an elaborate pleasure resort. With four hotels, a youth hostel and camp site, it is possible to by-pass reality and spend days in a fantasy land of exploding volcanoes, ferro cement geology and enchanted groves.

Ins and outs

Getting there

Bus: service 'A' operates from the World Trade Centre bus terminal to Sentosa from 0700-2000, Monday-Thursday, 0700-2300 Friday-Sunday. To get to the World Trade Centre take buses 65, 167 or 143 from Orchard Road; 61, 84, 143, 145, 166 and 167 from Chinatown (the nearest MRT station is at Tanjong Pagar, from which buses 10, 97, 100 and 125 go to the World Trade Centre). Bus 'C' leaves from the Tiong Bahru MRT station for the ferry terminal and Musical Fountain and operates 0700-2200 Monday- Thursday, 0700-2300 Friday-Sunday. Service 'E' plies Orchard Road, Bras Basah Road and Marina Square, stopping at Lucky Plaza, *Mandarin Hotel*, Peranakan Place, *Meridien Hotel*, Plaza Singapura, Bencoolen Street, POSB Headuarters, Raffles City and *Pan Pacific Hotel*, 1000-2000. Bus services 'A' and 'C' cost S$6 (S$4 for children). Bus service 'E' is S$7 (S$5 for children). These are return fares and include entrance to Sentosa (normally priced at S$5). **Taxis**: are charged a toll of S$3 and can only drop off/pick up at the hotels on Sentosa. **Cable Car**: an alternative way to reach Sentosa is via the Cable Car. There are three stops: Mount Faber (the highest point in Singapore, with scenic views and seafood restaurants - worthwhile), the Cable Car Tower adjacent to the World Trade Centre, and the Cable Car Plaza on Sentosa. Fares: one way S$5.90, return S$6.90. Admission to Sentosa is in addition to these fares. Cable car operates: 0830-2100 Monday-Sunday. **Ferry:** The ferry from the World Trade Centre leaves every 20 minutes from 0930-2100, every 15 minutes 0830-2100 Saturday and Sunday. Fare USS$1.30 return (with entrance to Sentosa, USS$6.30). **MRT**: a new MRT line is under construction which will terminate at the World Trade Centre.

Getting around

On Sentosa **free buses** (operating every 10 minutes, 0900-2230 Monday-Sunday) link the ferry terminal, Underwater World, Fort Siloso, and Images of Singapore. The free night bus (1930-2230 Monday-Sunday) runs between the *Beaufort* and *NTUC* hotels and the Musical Fountain and ferry terminal. The **monorail**, also free, links all the island's attractions and runs at 10-minute intervals (0900-2200 Monday-Sunday). **Bicycles**, **tandems** and **trishaws** for hire from the ferry terminal. For biking enthusiasts, there is a 6 km cycle track around the island.

The island

The name chosen for the island is hardly appropriate: *Sentosa* means 'peace and tranquillity'. In 1990, Sentosa welcomed a million visitors, about 45 per cent of whom were foreign tourists. It is guaranteed to provide plenty of entertainment for children, and adults may be pleasantly surprised with one or two attractions. On weekends, Sentosa can be a nightmare, as crowds converge on the island's attractions. In short, it is not the sort of island escape one would choose to 'get away from it all' and the words 'peace' and 'tranquillity' are certainly not the first to spring to mind.

A second word of warning is that a day at Sentosa tends to be an expensive as well as an entertaining experience. A family of four can easily get through S$200. Basic admission is S$5 (S$3 for children) but there is a charge for each attraction. There are various combination tickets tha include admission to Sentosa and to selected attractions. It is slightl cheaper to buy tickets this way at the World Trade Centre or on Moun Faber at the cable car entrance, rather than purchasing tickets at individua attractions after arrival (see each entry for admission charges). Th disadvantage of purchasing tickets in this way is that it commits you befor seeing what is on offer. Some combination tickets also tie you in to a tour ■ *Sentosa is open 0730-2300, Monday-Thursday, 0730-2400 Friday-Sunda and public holidays. Note that some attractions close before 2300 - many a 1900.*

Attractions

Images of Singapore, **Pioneers of Singapore** and the **Surrende Chambers** offer a well-displayed history of Singapore focusing on ke figures from the origins of the city state as an entrepôt through to th modern period and also telling the traumatic World War Two story. Th wax models are not up to Madame Tussaud's standard but the history i well told for those interested in such things. ■ *S$5 (S$3 for children) 0900-2100. monorail station 4, bus numbers 2 and A.*

Fort Siloso is Singapore's only preserved coastal fort, built in the 1880 to guard the narrow west entrance to Keppel Harbour. It has been recentl renovated and is a very informative visit, especially if you are interested i the fall of Singapore. It is possible to explore the underground tunnels artillery nests and bunkers, experience a mock firing of a 7-inch gun, ru riot over the assault course and play various interactive computer game with a martial tinge. The fort was built to guard against a seaward attack but as every amateur student of Singapore's wartime history knows, th Japanese assault was from the north. The guns of Fort Siloso were turne landwards but could do little to thwart the Japanese advance. When news o the surrender came through, the soldiers of the Royal Artillery (many from the Indian sub-continent) sabotaged the guns to prevent them falling int

Related maps:
Marina & port (to the north), page 104
Coloured map page 1

Sentosa's most unlikely visitor

For many years, Sentosa's most unlikely (long-term) visitor was Chia Thye Poh, Singapore's very own Nelson Mandela. Chia, an opposition MP, was arrested in 1966 for organizing an anti-Vietnam rally. For a while he was incarcerated in a cell in a standard prison but was eventually transferred to a guardhouse near stop number 6 of Sentosa's monorail system. He was permitted freedom of movement during the day, but had to return to his room in Fantasyland at 2100 and remain there until 0600.

enemy hands. ■ *S$3 (S$2 for children) 0900-1900 monorail station 3, bus numbers 2 and A.*

The **Maritime Museum** is housed in a building in the shape of a boat and traces the development of marine vessels from the earliest fishing boats through to the modern day. It also tells the history of Singapore as a port. ■ *S$2 (S$0.50 for children). 1000-1900 Monday-Sunday. Monorail station 7, bus Numbers A, C, E and M.*

The **Asian Village**, is a short walk from the ferry terminal. It opened before it was fully completed in 1993 and has had difficulty attracting patrons. The idea was to construct three theme villages for East Asia, South Asia and Southeast Asia. They're pretty dismal, although some quality souvenirs are for sale. Adventure Asia - a rather half-hearted attempt at an all-Asian kiddies' funfair - was added for good measure. This part of the village is open 1000-1900, and the rides are individually priced from S$2 to S$3, or S$5 for the paddle boats. An all-Asian restaurant and a village theatre, built up a hillside and capable of seating up to 800 people, are other attractions. This is Singapore's attempt at virtual reality: rather than having to travel to these places, the sights are all conveniently brought together on a single site. ■ *Free but the various shows have an entrance charge. 1000-2100 Monday-Sunday. Monorail station 1, bus Numbers 2 and C.*

Not far away is the **Enchanted Grove of Tembusu**. The name is the most exciting thing about this attraction; but then admission is free. ■ *0900-2300. monorail station 1, bus numbers 2 and C.*

The **Butterfly Park and Insect Kingdom Museum** is a 1 hectare park containing 2,500 butterflies at all stages in their life cycle. Also here is a rather anti-septic museum of dead butterflies and insects. ■ *S$5 (S$3 for children) 0900-1900. Monorail station 4, bus numbers 2 and A.*

Underwater World, the largest walk-through oceanarium in Asia, is highly recommended. A 100m tunnel, with a moving conveyor, allows a glimpse of some of its 350 underwater species and 5,000 specimens. Giant rays glide overhead while thick-lipped garoupa and spooky moray eels hide in caves and crevices. A new exhibit is the so-called 'creatures of the deep' tank with giant octopus and spider crabs - brace yourself, as they put it, for an encounter with the world's ugliest eel and creepy crabs. Other smaller tanks house cuttlefish, turtles, reef fish, sawfish, corals, sea urchins and other marine creatures. ■ *Feeding times are well-worth arriving for: 1130, 1430, 1600 and 1630. S$13 for adults, S$7 for children. 0900-2100. monorail station 2, bus numbers 2 and A.*

The **Musical fountain** is a disco-lit fountain which gyrates, together with a rather unorchestrated laser light show, to everything from *Joan Jett and the Blackhearts* to the *1812* overture. Shows at 1630, 1700 and 1730. Later in the evening the Musical Fountain is joined by one of Sentosa's more recent attractions - a 37m, 12 storey-tall **Merlion**. This stupendous, laser-emitting symbol of Singapore joins with the fountains to create the

Musical Fountain and Rise of the Merlion Show. Each performance lasts 30 minutes and they kick off at 1930, 2030 and 2130 Monday-Sunday. At other times of day the merlion can be climbed either up to its mouth or its crown for views over Sentosa, the city and port. The shop here (nothing can be built on Sentosa without some merchandising outlet) is themed as a Bugis shipwreck. The Bugis were the feared Malay seafarers who sailed from Sulawesi and controlled the seas of the Malay archipelago before the European period. They have often been likened to the Vikings and, like the Vikings, they were famed for their fearlessness and for their seafaring skills - and for the terror they instilled in the hearts of coastal communities. (The word bogey is said to be derived from bugis, and was first used in 1836 as another term for the devil. Thackeray wrote: The people are all naughty and bogey carries them off. In 1865 the word was bastardized once more into bugbear, a hobgoblin reputed to devour naughty children.) ■ *S$3 (S$2 for children). Merlion open: 0900-2200, last admission 2130. Monorail station 1 and 4, bus numbers 2, A, C.*

Volcanoland, a 'multimedia entertainment park', is another of the newer attractions: it takes you on a subterranean journey into the earth and is supposed to trace the evolution of life - although your children will pass no exams with this rubbish. The main show is entertaining enough, but the rest of the complex is rather disappointing and, as with so much on Sentosa, the visitor exits from the multi media extravaganza, no doubt filled with grand - but erroneous - thoughts about the origins of life, straight into a shop. There are also occasional Mayan dances, although these are in no sense authentic; time your visit to coincide with these shows if desired. ■ *Eruption of volcano takes place every half hour from 1030. S$10 (S$6 for children). 1000-1900 Monday-Sunday. Bus numbers A, C.*

The **Sentosa Orchid Gardens**, very close to the ferry terminal, are planted out with 10,000 plants and over 200 species of orchid. Within the gardens is a restaurant, a fish pond with koi carp, a Japanese tea room, and various other gazebos, boulders and associated paraphenalia and - yes, you've guessed it - a souvenir ship. ■ *S$3.50 (children S$2). 0900-1800, last visitor 1800. Monorail stations 1 and 7; bus numbers 2, A, C, E.*

Sunbathing or swimming at the lagoons and nearby **'beach'** is possible at **Sun World**. You can hire pedal boats, windsurfers, canoes or aqua bikes. **Siloso Beach**, at the west end of the island, has been redeveloped by the Sentosa Development Corporation. Tens of thousands of cubic metres of golden sand were shipped in, as were 300 mature coconut palms and over 100 ornamental shrubs and flowering trees. The island has four **beaches**: Central, Beach Monkeys, Siloso and Tanjong. ■ *Monorail station 5 for Central and Beach Monkeys, station 2 for Siloso, bus numbers 2, A and M or the Beach Train.*

Fantasy Island, advertised as the 'ultimate water adventure' this is a must for children: white water river rapids, play areas in the water and aquatic slides are fun and well-designed. The various slides and chutes are graded from 1 to 4 and there is an area reserved purely for smaller children with life guards keeping a wary eye out. Public lockers and changing rooms, but no towels provided. Various snack bars on site. A sunny day here can turn a pallid European into a lobster in less time than it takes to say thermador. At weekends it is packed. ■ *S$20 (S$12.50 for children). 1000-1900 Monday-Sunday. Monorail stations 1 and 7; bus numbers 2, A, C, E, and M.*

Close to Fantasy Island is Sentosa's latest attraction: **Cinemania**. This is a high tech movie extravaganza. Combining high definition film with state of the art sound and seats raised on hydraulic jacks, it creates what is rather ambitiously called hyper reality. The blurb warns that you should give this a miss if you have back, neck or heart problems, are pregnant, suffer from epileptic fits, or have a surname beginning with B. ■ *Shows every 30 minutes, 1100-2000. S$10 (S$6 for children). Monorail stations 1 and 7, bus numbers 2, A, C, E and M.*

At **Fun World** you can go cycling, roller-skating or play golf on the 18-hole course and there is also a maze. The **WonderGolf** course is fun: 45 mini-holes each with some novel obstruction to surmount. ■ *S$8 (S$4 for children). 0900-2100.*

Sentosa Island Tour S$28 from the following hotels: *Sheraton Towers, Mandarin, Boulevard, Shangri-La, Orchard, Hilton International.*

Essentials

Sleeping

■ *on maps*
Price codes:
see inside front cover

Contrary to first impressions, it is possible to escape from Sentosa's hoardes, thanks to the construction of three hotels. The hotels are good, and it is easy enough to get to town from here (complimentary shuttle buses are provided) but, as Stan Sesser put it in the title of his *New Yorker* piece on Singapore, it is rather like being a prisoner in a theme park.

L-L+ ***Beaufort***, Bukit Manis Rd, T2750331, F2750228, Beaufort@singnet.com.sg. A/c, restaurants, large (33 metre) pool, gym, tennis courts, archery, volley ball court, squash courts, access to the 18-hole Tanjong golf course, and 27 acres of grounds. The most refined of the hotels on Sentosa, smaller, quieter and more elegant than the *Rasa Sentosa*, with excellent service.

A+ ***Rasa Sentosa (Shangri-La)***, 101 Silosa Rd, T2750100, F2750355 (or in the UK on T0181 747 8485). At the southern tip of the island, fronting the beach, a/c, restaurant, freeform pool, sports facilities, creche, clean beach (sterilized sand imported from Indonesia) and the water is OK for swimming. The hotel is built in a curve, behind Fort Siloso, it has 1st class facilities and an unsurpassed view of the oil refinery just across the water, competitive weekend package deals available - though it can get very busy then.

A ***Sijori Resort***, situated close to the action by the 37m-high Merlion. This hotel/resort opened in early 1997 and is clearly positioned to tempt those people who wish to make full use of Sentosa's attractions.

Sentosa Youth Hostel (next to the lagoon), bookings can be made up to 6 months in advance T2707888 or 2707889. The hostel is really meant for local youth and community groups, but an a/c room accommodating up to 12 costs S$110 a night during the week and S$120 on weekends. Bedding is provided, there are clean and adequate toilet and shower facilities and BBQ pits.

NTUC Sentosa Beach Resort, 10 a/c chalets housing 6-10 people, with own bathroom and sitting room, also provides 15 camp shelters with attap roofs, for up to 4 per shelter, pool cafe and barbecue area.

Sentosa Holiday Chalets, to book call Sentosa Information Office at T2707888 or 2707889. Chalets come in 4-, 6- and 12-bed sizes. Minimum stay in the 4-bed chalet is 2 nights (S$70 non-peak, S$100 peak), while the 6- and 12-bed chalets are available for a minimum of 3 nights. The chalets - which are renovated pre-War era officers quarters - contain a/c bedrooms, basic kitchen facilities, toilets and showers.

Sentosa Campsite, close to Central Beach (monorail station 5) and can accommodate 300 people. To book call Sentosa Information Office at T2707888 or 2707889. 4- (S$12), 6- (S$14.50) and 8-person (S$19) tents are available while camp beds are rented out at S$0.50 a night. BBQ pits and toilet and shower facilities provided.

Eating

● *on maps*
Price codes:
see inside front cover

There are fast-food outlets and restaurants dotted around the island. The ***Sentosa Food Centre*** close to the ferry terminal is a squeaky-clean hawker centre, serving Malay, Chinese, Peranakan, Indian and Western cuisine. The dishes are pricier than elsewhere in Singapore and the food is sometimes disappointing, open 1100-2200. Other restaurants at the ferry terminal include a ***Burger King***, ice cream parlour, the ***Singapore Riverboat*** (a paddlewheel steamer) and the ***Camellia Restaurant***. Beside the Merlion is ***Sir Basil's Café and Bar*** and there are also several burger outlets and snack bars at Siloso, Central and Tanjong beaches as well as those associated with many of the individual attractions. In short, visitors will not starve during their visit. There are more elegant restaurants at the hotels of which the best is ***Siggi's*** at the *Beaufort*, T2750331. Worth splashing out on the **New Asia** buffet while sitting on the terrace *al fresco*.

Singapore West

The western portion of Singapore has been transformed since independence. Not long ago it was an out-of-the-way spot; now it is dotted with new towns and housing developments and is linked to the city via the western line of the MRT, which extends all the way to Boon Lay. Further west still is Singapore's industrial hub - the Jurong Industrial Estate. And right at the western tip of the island is the old fishing settlement of Tuas, now virtually obliterated by the industrial developments that surround it.

Ins and outs

Getting there

The MRT West line runs all the way from the city to Boon Lay, with nine stops in between. However a number of the main sights in this part of the island are (for Singapore) distant from any MRT station and it is best either to take a bus or taxi. Jurong East Interchange links the MRT West line with the MRT North line.

Getting around

This area is spread out and bar a handful of sights which are within walking distance of one another it is usually necessary to catch a train, bus or taxi.

The area

This is an area of contrasts. From east to west, there are the hideous Haw Par Villas, better known as the Tiger Balm Gardens, the excellent Jurong Bird Park and its sister Reptile Park, the rather moth-eaten Tang Dynasty Village, the Science Museum and, newest of all, the propogandist Singapore Discovery Centre. Also in this part of the island are glimpses of a Singapore which is largely absent from the city centre. Tree-lined streets like the western end of Jurong Road and its continuation, Upper Jurong Road, laid out like much else of Singapore by that most visionary of colonial city planners, John Turnbull Thomson. Also here is Holland Village with its attractive Mediterranean ambience.

Sights

Haw Par Villa

Haw Par Villa (formerly Tiger Balm Gardens) is at 262 Pasir Panjang Road, on the way out to Jurong. Built by Aw Boon Haw and Aw Boon Par, brothers of Tiger Balm fame, it was their family home until they opened it to the public. The delightful estate was finally sequestrated by the Singapore government in 1985 and turned into the island's most revolting theme park, a gaudy adventureland of Chinese folklore - the biggest Chinese mythological theme park in the world. Boon Haw originally designed the gardens for his family's enjoyment. But his gory sculptures have instilled a sense of traditional morality in generations of Singaporeans. Sequences depict wrongdoers being punished in creative ways, most notably in the Ten Courts of Hell (which is reached along the Alley of the Ten Shops of Tack): one is having his tongue cut out, another is galled by a spear, others are variously impaled on spikes, gnawed by dogs, boiled in oil, bitten by snakes, sliced in two, drowned in the Filthy Blood Pond or ground into paste by enormous millstones. Some of the allegories and stories are obscure to say the least: a pig dressed in what appears to be a forerunner to the 'Y' front; acrobatic mermaids; and tangoing fowl. Though doubtless highly significant to the cognoscenti of Chinese mythology, many of the stories will be lost on the uninitiated.

Consider the story of the great Jiang Zi Ya who can be seen bearded and clasping a fishing rod towards the top of the complex. Apparently Zi Ya held the un-baited rod above a river for 8 years because, so he said to a perplexed passer-by, he was not trying to catch fish but was awaiting 'the arrival of a great leader'. His patience was rewarded when King Wen chanced upon Zi Ya still fishing after almost 100 months. Rather than being appalled at the man's foolhardiness, King Wen was singularly impressed and appointed him his Prime Minister. The moral of this story, unsurprisingly, is that "All good things come to those who wait". Perhaps it should be, "When you go fishing with Zi Ya, remember to take lots of sandwiches and orange squash".

Its 9 hectares site is five times the size of the original villa and its grounds. There is a large section on ancient China, with pagoda-roofed buildings, arts and crafts shops and restaurants serving authentic cuisine as well as traditional theatre - in which lion dances and wayangs are performed. The 'Creation of the World Theatre' tells classic tales from the Qin Dynasty; in the 'Legends and Heroes Theatre' a life-like robot is programmed to relate stories, and a video in the 'Spirit of the Orient Theatre' explains Chinese folklore, customs, traditions and festivals. At the beginning of 1998 there arose the possibility that these venerable gardens might close. The number of employees has been slashed and some attractions have been closed to save money. ■ *S$5 (it was sharply reduced in 1998 from S$16.50). 0900-1800 Monday-Sunday.* **NB** *Do not even think about visiting Haw Par Villa over Chinese New Year - each year about 12,000 people saunter around it in the space of about 4 days. MRT west-bound to Buona Vista, then bus 200; or to Clementi and then bus 10. Direct buses to the Haw Par Villas are 10, 30, 51, 143 (runs from Orchard Road), 176 and 200.*

Holland Village is especially worth visiting at the weekend. This is really a residential area - and was once the home to the British forces

Related map: Coloured map page 1

Singapore Island West

barracked in Singapore - but it also developed into one of the trendier parts of suburban Singapore. There are restaurants and bars, small craft and antique shops, and a good wet market - Pasar Holland. The Holland Village Shopping Centre on Holland Avenue is the best stop for Asian arts and crafts and there are ample places to eat and relax while exploring the area. ■ *Take the MRT to Buona Vista and then walk up Commonwealth Avenue to Holland Avenue (about 15 mins) or take buses 106 or 200.*

The west coast is dominated by the industrial district of **Jurong**, where about two-thirds of the island's industrial workforce is employed. Jurong is the product of Singapore's first big state-supported industrialization programme in the 1960s and early 1970s. It now supports a large shopping complex, complete with cinemas, bowling alleys, skating rinks, hawker stalls as well as parks and other attractions.

Jurong Bird Park

Jurong Bird Park, on Jalan Ahmad Ibrahim (T2650022), is a beautifully kept 20 hectare haven for more than 8,000 birds of 600 species from all over the world, including a large collection of Southeast Asian birds. As it is now difficult to see most of these birds in the wild in Southeast Asia, a trip here is well worthwhile. Highlights include the world's largest collection of Southeast Asian hornbills and South American toucans and an entertaining air-conditioned penguin corner, complete with snow. Another main attraction is one of the largest walk-in aviaries in the world, with a 30m-high man-made waterfall and 1,500 birds. There is also an interesting nocturnal house with owls, herons, frogmouths and kiwis and bird shows throughout the day (the birds of prey show - at 1000 and 1600 - is particularly good). There is a monorail service round the park for those who find the heat too much (S$2.50, S$1 for children). ■ *S$10.30 (S$4.12 for children under 12), family tickets available for S$20. 0900-1800 Monday-Friday, 0800-1800, weekends and public holidays. MRT west-bound to Boon Lay then SBS bus 194 or 251 from Boon Lay interchange.*

Jurong Reptile Park, Jalan Ahmad Ibrahim, is next to Jurong Bird Park. This was formerly called the Jurong Crocodile Paradise but after renovation in 1997 has re-emerged under a new name. The name really says it all: 100 reptilian species with an emphasis on poison and danger - cobras, crocodiles, poison arrow frogs, and iguanas (not so scary). ■ *S$7 (S$3.50 for children under 12). 0900-1800 Monday-Sunday. MRT west-bound to Boon Lay; bus numbers 194 or 251 from Boon Lay Interchange.*

Tang Dynasty City

Tang Dynasty City, Jalan Ahmad Ibrahim/Yuan Ching Road, Jurong (T2611116), covers 12 hectares and is a recreation of the ancient Chinese capital of Chang An. Developers worked for 3 years to build this

The Tiger Balm story

In the latter years of the 19th century, a Chinese herbal doctor called Aw Chu Kin left China for Burma, where he hoped to make his fortune. In Rangoon he peddled his concoctions to ailing Burmese. Before his death in the early 1920s he invented a balm which he claimed was a miracle-cure for insect bites, stomach aches, colds, headaches, bonchial problems and muscle strain. Nobody believed him and when old Mr Aw died, his wife had to pawn all her jewellery to cover his funeral costs.

The only thing his sons Boon Haw (Haw means 'tiger') and Boon Par inherited was his secret recipe, but being entrepreneurs, they decided to market their birthright and rename it Tiger Balm. It became so well known in Rangoon that Boon Haw decided to try his luck in Singapore while Boon Par struck out for Hong Kong. Within a few years, the balm empire had expanded to Malaysia, Hong Kong and China. In 1926 Boon Haw built a magnificent villa on Nassim Road, Singapore, which the Urban Redevelopment Authority demolished in 1990. In 1931 he began work on Haw Par Villa, commissioning an artist from Swatow, China to landscape the gardens. The Japanese wrecked the place during the war and Boon Haw died in Honolulu in 1950 before it was restored to its lurid splendour. Tiger Balm, which is manufactured by the company Haw Par Brothers (despite the fact that the family no longer has any interest in it), now cures people all over the world. A small dab ot it on a mosquito bite works wonder.

S$70mn theme park. The City includes 100 shophouses and a temple, with carvings by workmen from China, and a 600m-long, 10m-high model of the Great Wall of China, built with bricks imported from Shenzhen. There is also a 7-storey pagoda, housing the monkey god and an impressive artificial waterfall. The main attraction, though, is an 'underground palace', with replicas of the 1,500 terracotta warriors found in the tomb of Shih Huang Ti in Xian, China. Visitors are ushered into a small theatre where a short and bloody film of the emperor's life provides a simple historical background before an entirely irrelevant natural event ends the film show and visitors enter the reconstruction of the tomb to view the arrayed ranks of warriors illuminated by lasers.

Other key attractions include a ghost mansion and a tacky and rather musty museum where notables from Chinese history are poorly modelled from wax. There are also various shows and events staged through the day from noodle-making demonstrations to juggling and martial arts and a traditional wedding procession. The City doubles as a huge movie studio and the Tang Dynasty Motion Picture company plans to make three feature films a year. The place has been half finished for years and judging by the undergrowth at the back of the lot it seems as though the enterprise is running low on funds. Indeed the general tenor is one of over-ambition: though S$70 million may have been spent on the place, it would have been better to have envisaged something less grandiose and at least have done it well. There is a restaurant on site and a better and cheaper food court across the road in the Jurong Bowl complex. Given these quibbles, the entrance fee is steep for something still half baked. ■ *S$15.45 (S$10.30 for children) but advance tickets at slightly reduced rates available from travel agents and other outlets in town. 1000-1830, Monday-Sunday. MRT to Lakeside and then bus 154, or to Boon Lay and then bus 178.*

The **Chinese and Japanese Gardens** are on Yuan Ching Road, Jurong (T2643455). These gardens extend over 13 hectares on two islands in Jurong Lake. The Chinese garden - or Yu-Hwa Yuan - is said to be modelled on an imperial Sung Dynasty garden, and specifically on the classical style of Beijing's Summer Palace. There are artfully scattered boulders, Chinese pavilions, and a brace-and-a-half of pagodas to give it that Oriental flavour but it is hard to believe that the Sung emperors would have been happy with this. Rather more refined is the Penjing Garden (Yun Xiu Yuan - or Garden of Beauty), a walled bonsai garden, which reputedly cost S$6 million to develop. The garden contains 3,000 miniature potted penjing (bonsai) trees, sourced from all over Asia. The two outside the entrance are said to come from Sichuan and to be over 280 years old. They symbolize male and female lions guarding the entrance, but just in case these arboreal defenders should fail, there is also a pair of stone lions to act as back-stops. Close to the main entrance is a large statue of the sage Confucious (551-479BC), looking suitably studious and wise, and a stone boat craftily concealing an F&B outlet. On a small rise in the middle of the Chinese garden is the main pagoda which towers up through six levels. It is possible to sweat your way to the top for a great view of HDB blocks.

The **Double Beauty Bridge** leads to the more peaceful Japanese garden, said to be one of the largest such gardens outside Japan. The Seiwaen or garden of tranquility is based on Japanese landscaping techniques that were practised from the 14th to 17th centuries, characterized by sweeping lawns and gently flowing streams. It is designed to mirror the natural order. Frankly it is hard to see that much difference between this garden and the Chinese garden but overall they are well kept and peaceful (at least early in the morning) though there is not much here to really excite the botanist. However, children will have fun hiding behind boulders and rolling down hills. **Fishing**: two lakes are open for fishing and are stocked with snakehead, tilapia, grass carp, red tilapia and toman. S$30 per rod on the big pond, S$50 per rod on the small pond (Sundays only on the small pond). **NB** If you want to enjoy the peace it is best to arrive at the gardens when they open at 0900 and there are few people about - avoid weekends when they are crowded. You also stand more chance of seeing the large monitor lizards and turtles that live in the lake. ■ *S$4.50 (S$2 for children). 0900-1900 Monday-Saturday, 0830-1900 Sunday and public holidays. Last admission 1800. MRT to Chinese Gardens (W10) and then walk the 200m across the open grassed area to the east gate. Alternatively, take bus nos 335 or 180 which also run to the MRT stop and the east gate, or 154 which run past the main west gate.*

Not far west of the Chinese and Japanese Gardens is the **Singapore Mint Coin Gallery** at 20 Teban Garden Crescent (T5662626). This is hardly a major attraction and because it is rather out of the way few people, bar the truly committed, make it here. There is a modest exhibition of coins and medals, most of Singapore origin. ■ *Free. 0900-1630 Monday-Friday. Bus number 154 stops opposite the Singapore Mint (on Jl Ahmad Ibrahim) or take the MRT to Boon Lay and walk.*

The Science Museum

The **Science Centre**, on Science Centre Road, Jurong, might be aimed more at children than adults - it is usually packed with school children enjoying a few hours away from cramming - but there is plenty of fun for grown-ups too. The central hub of the museum has a figure of Einstein talking in a rather forced German accent, hatching chicks and various other exhibits including a computer screen where it is possible to conduct plastic surgery on your face. From this hub radiate the Hall of Life Sciences, a Virtual Science Centre, the Aviation Centre, a children's Discovery Centre and a Physical Science Hall. In the Aviation Centre, where Changi Airport makes a predictably significant appearance, visitors are guided around the wonders of flight by Archie the Archaeopteryx - a sort of avine dinosauri maitre d'. For an extra S$3 (S$2 children) it is possible to fly a simulator. Th Hall of Life Sciences theme is humanity's impact on the earth and here ther are some live animals along with a few talking dummies including dinosaur (spouting surprisingly unscientific rubbish), and Charles Darwi (far too thin) talking with an American accented gorilla. Disney's *Jungl Book* has a lot to answer for. Overall the centre succeeds in its mission t make science come alive, with plenty of gadgets and hands-on exhibits. I makes most sense to come here with children who will be able to spen several hours having fun and maybe even learning something. ■ *S$. (S$1.50 for children). 1000-1800 Tuesday-Sunday.*

In the **Omni-theatre** (T5603316/5641432) next door, the marvels o science, technology and the universe can be viewed in a 284-sea amphitheatre with a huge hemispherical (3-D) screen and a 20,000 wat sound system. Take a seat-of-your-pants thrill ride while learning about th science of roller coasters, climb Everest or experience an exploding volcan (films change periodcally). Excellent films and very popular. ■ *S$10 (S$ for children) for Omninax movies (screened 1000-2000, Tuesday-Sunda every hour); S$6 (S$3 for children) for Planetarium show at 1000 and 1100 Tuesday-Sunday 1000-2100, T5689100 for film schedules. Take the MRT t Jurong East, and walk the last 300m through the HDB block and acros Townhall Road to the museum. Bus nos 66, 198, 335 and TIBS bus No 178 ru direct to the the museum. Alternatively get bus nos 51, 78, 97 or 147 to th Jurong East Interchange and then change to a 335 or walk the last 10 mins.*

Ming Village

The **Ming Village**, 32 Pandan Road (T2657711) (not to be confused with the Tang Dynasty City) is one of the last factories in the world that faithfull reproduces Chinese porcelain antiques using traditional methods - from mould-making to hand-throwing - dating from Sung, Yuan, Ming and Qi dynasties. All the pieces are painted by hand and the factory blur maintains that traditional methods of craftsmanship are scrupulousl followed. It is possible to take a guided tour around the factory premise and seeing the work that goes into the pots certainly helps explain why th prices are so high in the showroom. The shop has an export departmen which will pack items for shipment. The Village also runs traditiona pottery and painting classes for long-stay and short-stay group visitors. Th **Pewter Museum** which has moved to the Ming Village has daily demonstrations of traditional pewter making processes. ■ *Free. 0900-173 Monday-Sunday. MRT to Clementi, then bus 78. Or take the free Trolle Ming Village Shuttle Service which picks up at Paragon By Sogo (opposite th Crown Prince Hotel) at 0920 and 1030 and at City Hall-Bras Basah Roa* (Raffles Hotel *bus stop) at 0930 and 1040.*

Singapore Discovery Centre

Singapore's latest attraction, right at the western end of the island, is the **Singapore Discovery Centre**. This is really an epic, S$70mn PR exercise for Singapore Inc concocted by the Singapore Defence Forces. A fair number o the attractions are military. For example, there is a shooting gallery, a military tactics gallery, an array of military equipment from aircraft to night vision goggles - you can even make a simulated parachute jump, manoeuvring to your landing spot. There is also a good children's adventure playground, a recreation of significant events from Singapore's history with a walk-through gallery of shophouses and early HDB flats, and a stomach-churningly realistic motion simulator where, for example, you can follow a missile in flight. It is, as one might expect, well done with lots o ands-on interactive computer exhibits. It is also fascinating as an llustration of nation-building. The two main lessons to be learned here are: . That Singapore is dedicated to world peace and constructive ngagement; 2. That if you mess with Singapore you'll be in for a shock. 'here is also, of course, a food court and retail outlet for those who are mpty of stomach or would like to be of pocket. http://www.asianconnect. om/sdc. ■ *S$9 (children, S$5), extra charge for motion simulator (S$4) and hooting gallery (S$3). 0900-1900 Monday-Friday (last admission, 1800), 900-2000 Saturday-Sun and Public Holidays (last admission, 1900), closed n Monday. West-bound MRT to Boon Lay (W12) and then connecting SBS us numbers 192 and 193 from the Boon Lay interchange or direct on SBS bus umbers 192 and 193.*

:ssentials

Eating

● *on maps*
Price codes: see inside front cover

'hese are really two areas in the western portion of the island where more unusual estaurants are concentrated. Pasir Panjang Village, close to the University, and Iolland Village, not far to the north.

4 ***Brazil Churrascaria***, 14-16 Sixth Ave, T4631923. If carnivore-style is your thing, this **Brazilian** restaurant - with its huge skewers of barbecued (*churrascaria* is portuguese or barbecue) meat - is for you, as much meat as you can eat.

4 ***El Felipé's***, 34 Lorong Mambong, Holland Village, T4681520, **Mexican**.

4 ***Gerry's Fine Foods***, Lorong Mambong, Holland Village. A **steak and ribs** place, great ries, cold beer.

4 ***Hazara***, 24 Lorong Mambong, Holland Village, T4674101, **Indian**. Sister restaurant o *Kinara* at Boat Quay, specializing in northwest Frontier cuisine (tandooris etc), particularly good tandoori leg of lamb, splendid decor with genuine frontier feel, service can be slow.

5 ***Hot Stones Steak and Seafood***, 22 Lorong Mambong, Holland Village, **nternational**. Another restaurant at 53 Boat Quay (T5355188). Speciality: cooking slabs of meat or seafood on baking-hot Serpentine rock at the table.

4 ***Cha Cha Cha***, 32 Lorong Mambong, Holland Village, T4621650. Small and informal **Mexican** restaurant with some outdoor seating, extensive menu.

4 ***Restaurant Lucerne***, Pasir Panjang Village, T7761221. Sophisticated **Swiss** restaurant.

5 ***Wala-Wala***, 31 Lorong Mambong, Holland Village T4624288, **Mexican**. Buzzy atmosphere and pretty tiles on the tables, good, honest, no pretentions.

Bars

There are a number of pubs and bars in a row of restored shophouses in Pasir Panjang Village along what is known as ***The Pub Row.***

East Coast

Although the east coast may not be what it was, those who want a change from the order and glitz of Orchard Road could do worse than simply hop on the 16/14 bus which runs along Joo Chiat Road and then onto the East Coast Road. There are good eating places, side streets and interesting shops (antiques, crafts etc), and even a village feel.

Ins and outs

Getting there The MRT East line runs all the way to Pasir Ris. For Joo Chiat Road, alight at Paya Lebar MRT station. For the coast it is best to take a bus (No 16 from Orchard and Bras Basah roads) or taxi.

Getting around This area is too large, and the sights too spread out, to explore on foot. However some parts, like Joo Chiat Road, are sufficiently compact to walk.

The area

The eastern part of the island used to be dotted with small Malay fishing kampungs, most of which have now been demolished and replaced by Housing Development Board tower blocks. Great chunks of land have been reclaimed from the sea and carefully landscaped beaches now line the coast up to Changi. Just off the city end of the East Coast Parkway is the National Sports Stadium.

Sights

Katong and Geylang Serai Katong is an enclave of Peranakan architecture and there are still streets of well-preserved shophouses and terraced houses in their original condition. **Joo Chiat Road** gives a good feel of old Singapore, sandwiched between the upmarket residential districts and government Housing Development Board projects. While most of the traditional businesses here have closed down or moved out, there are still some candle makers struggling to make a living and a few other craftemen. On Koon Seng Road, many of the houses have been carefully restored and it is less touristy than Emerald Hill and Tanjong Pagar. European civil servants and Straits Chinese mandarins had grand houses along the waterfront, a handful of which still stand today among the HDB blocks and condominiums. Restaurants in Katong serve some of the best Peranakan food in Singapore including delicious pastries and sweets. A little further away is **Geylang Serai** (on Geylang Road) considered the heart of Malay culture in Singapore; it was once an agricultural area but has been transformed into a modern industrial zone. Geylang market is well-stocked with Malay food and this is a good place to come for Indonesian and Malaysian cuisine. ■ *For Katong take bus 14 or 16 from Orchard Road; for Geylang take the MRT to Paya Lebar.*

The **Malay Cultural Village**, Geylang Serai (T7484700, F7411662), is on a 1.7 hectares site between Geylang Serai, Sims Avenue and Geylang Road. But the Malay answer to the new Tang Dynasty City, with its mock-kampung houses, Malay foodstalls and shops has failed to draw many visitors. The irony of it is not lost on Singapore's Malay community, who have been resettled from their kampungs into HDB flats over the past 20 years. Malay cultural identity is better characterized in the stalls at

Geylang market than in the cultural village. In an attempt to claw back visitors from other rival attractions there is a new Lagenda Fantasi presentation which introduces people to legends which could only very loosely be described as Malay - Aladdin, Ali Baba and the like. ■ *0900-1730, Monday-Sunday. Bus, SBS 2, 7; MRT to Paya Lebar, followed by 5 minutes walk.*

Joo Chiat Road, which runs south down to the sea, is interesting for its unchanged early 20th century shophouse fronts. The extravagant façades, found both here and on Koon Seng Road are an excellent example of the Singapore Eclectic Style which evolved in the 1920s and 1930s. This whole area was originally a coconut plantation owned by a family of Arab descent - the Alsagoffs. A portion was purchased by a wealthy Chinese, Chew Joo Chiat, after whom a number of the roads are named (not just Joo Chiat Road; also Joo Chiat Lane, Joo Chiat Terrace and Joo Chiat Place). bus no 16 from Orchard Rd runs down Joo Chiat Road, as does no 33. Peter Wee's Katong Antique House at 208 East Coast Road is well worth a visit if you are in the area, with its unsurpassed collection of Peranakan antiques and an owner who is probably the most knowledgeable person in Singapore on the Peranakan culture.

East Coast Park

East Coast Park is a popular recreation area with beaches and gardens as well as a tennis centre, driving range, sailing centre (see page 57), the **Big Splash** and a food centre. ■ *S$3, S$2 for children. 1200-1745 Monday-Friday and 0900-1745 Saturday and Sunday.* In fact there are assorted sports and entertainment facilities strung out over several kilometres - although they are largely patronised by locals rather than foreign visitors. The sand along these beaches was imported from near-by Indonesian islands. The **East Coast Recreation Centre**, in East Coast Park, has the usual array of crazy golf, foodstalls, cycling, canoes and fun rides. ■ *Getting to the East Coast Park is a little tricky by public transport during the week as there is no direct bus. Either take bus 16 from Orchard Road (the aiport bus) and get off at Marine Parade or bus number 197 which runs down North*

Related map: Coloured map, page 1

Bridge Road and South Bridge Road. From Marine Parade, walk towards the park and the sea, crossing the expressway. On weekends and public holidays bus number 401 runs from the Bedok MRT station to the East Coast Park, passing many of the attractions, using the service road.

The **Crocodilarium**, 730 East Coast Parkway, T4473722, has over 1,200 inmates, bred in pens. Note that it is a commercial operation, not a zoological centre and the animals here will end up as shoes and handbags. The best time to visit is at feeding times (1100 Tuesday, Thursday and Saturday) - the Crocodilarium also stages crocodile-wrestling bouts; ring for times. Crocodile-skin goods are for sale. ■ *S$2 (S$1 for children) 0900-1700 Monday-Sunday. No direct buses. Take the MRT to Paya Lebar or Eunos and then take a taxi.*

The **Singapore Crocodile Farm** at 790 Upper Serangoon Road is, like the Crocodilarium on the East Coast, a commercial set-up. Here, visitors can learn about skinning techniques and various other methods of transforming scary reptiles into quiescent handbags and shoes. This farm with its population of about 800 crocodiles, has been on the same site since 1945, importing crocodiles from rivers in Sarawak. ■ *0830-1730 Monday-Sunday. Buses 81, 84, 97, 111, 153 all run along Upper Serangoon Road and stop opposite the farm.*

The **Air Force Museum** is at Blk 78 Cranwell Road (T5401537), which runs off Loyang Avenue. Assembled here are some aircraft as well as lots of aeronautic paraphenalia ranging from helmets to missiles providing a showcase illustrating the development of the Singapore Air Force (and its predecessor, the Malayan Volunteer Air Force) from its inception in 1939. ■ *Free. 1000-1630 Tuesday-Sunday. MRT to Tanah Merah (E9) and the SBS bus 9 or 2 both of which run down Loyang Avenue.*

Changi

Changi Prison is on Upper Changi Road. The prison, as featured on the 'Go to Jail' square in the Singapore version of *Monopoly*, is where Singapore's hangman dispenses with drug traffickers - with gruesome regularity. It was originally built to house 600 prisoners but during the war, more than 3,500 civilians were incarcerated here. In 1944, POWs were moved into the prison, and 12,000 American, Australian and British servicemen were interned in and around it. It is mostly visited by World War Two veterans - there is a small museum with reproductions of WRM Haxworth's paintings and the then 17-year-old trooper George Aspinall's photographs, which record the misery of internment. A replica of the atap-roofed Changi Prison chapel stands in the prison yard. The memorial chapel's original altar cross, whose base was made from a Howitzer shell casing, was returned to the chapel in 1992. James Clavell's novel *King Rat* is more enlightening than a visit to Changi. To view the murals, a weeks notice is required, T7437885/5430893. 0930-1630 Monday-Saturday. The Chapel holds a service on Sunday evening, 1730, T5451411. The Prison Museum has an interesting display. ■ *MTR to Tanah Merah and then bus number 2 or bus 2 direct from Orchard Road.*

Less than a generation ago, **Changi Village** was a sleepy backwater of Singapore, with a good beach and a few sailors' bars. Now it is dwarfed by its housing estate and has one of Asia's busiest airports in its back yard. The photo shop, *George Photo*, on Changi Village Road, is named after wartime photographer George Aspinall, who learned how to process film in the shop's darkroom in 1941. There is also a wet market and a hawker centre here as well as a number of restaurants along the main street. **Changi Beach** is packed at weekends. Singaporeans come to enjoy the beach, pitching their tents, setting up barbecues and turning it into an Oriental Malaga for 48 hours; surprisingly - for Singapore - the beach is covered in rubbish. From **Changi Point**, bumboats leave for Pulau Ubin every 15 minutes, (see page 158) and for various destinations in Johor, just across the straits. There are also boats to Singapore's northeast islands. ■ *Take the MRT to Tanah Merah (E9) and board SBS bus 2 opposite the station. Alternatively take SBS bus 2 all the way - it runs along Victoria Street through the Arab quarter and then onto Kallang Road. SBS bus 29 also goes to Changi Village; board at Tampines (E11) MRT station.*

Essentials

Sleeping

■ *on maps*
Price codes: see inside front cover

There are a handful of reasonably priced places to stay in this area of the city, along Geylang Road and down Joo Chiat Road; the Tourist Office provides a listing. On the whole, the hotels are patronised by Asian businessmen, but if you are looking for an alternative to the bustle of the city, and don't mind having to walk and take the MRT or bus into town, this is an option.

B ***Hotel 81***, 305 Joo Chiat Road, T3488181, F3486960, hotel81@pacific.net.sg, http://www.hotel81.com.sg. Good value place to stay for the businessman or woman on a budget. Attractive shophouse hotel. With reasonable rooms.

B ***Chancellor***, 181 Joo Chiat Road, T7422222, F3488677, intercon@signet.com.sg, http://www.asiabiz.com/chancellor. Smallish rooms in shophouses, but nice showers and clean and efficient. Pastel shades and a huge TV in each room. Good value but 10 minutes walk from the MRT.

B ***Sea View***, 26 Amber Close, T345222, F3484335, ugly great block and not particularly friendly. Note that this place is considerably cheaper if booked from the airport hotel desk.

C ***Amber***, 42 Amber Road, T3445255, F3451911, a/c. 21 comfortable rooms with TV and attached bathrooms.

C ***Malacca***, 97-99 Still Road, T3457411, F4405121, a/c. Another good value business hotel in this area of town, 20 minutes walk from nearest MRT station (Eunos). Rooms are very well appointed at the price with a/c, TV, and attached bathrooms - cash only.

Eating

4 ***Chao Phaya Thai Seafood***, Block 730, 2nd Floor, Ang Mo Kio Ave 6, T4560118. Enormous informal restaurant with huge choice of authentic **Thai** dishes including chilli crab, *tom yam kung* and green, yellow or red curried fish.

2 ***Charlie's***, Block 2, 01-08, Changi Village, T5420867. Charlie's folks, who were first generation immigrants from China, set up the *Changi Milk Bar* in the 1940s, then Charlie's Corner became the favoured watering hole and makan stop for sailors and riggers for decades. His mum still fries up the chips that gave them the reputation as the best chippies east of London's Isle of Dogs, excellent chilli-dogs, spicy chicken wings and 70 beers to choose from, closed weekends, recommended. Bus to Changi Point from Tampines MRT.

There are several **seafood** restaurants on Mount Faber hill, with a good view - they are not that popular and the seafood is far from being the best in town, but it's a pleasant location.

3 ***House of Sundanese Food***, 218 East Coast Road, T3455020. Typical ***Sundanese*** dishes from West Java include spicy salad (*keredok*), charcoal-grilled seafood (*ikan sunda, ikanemas*) and curries, a/c restaurant with real home-cooked food.

3 ***Kim's Seafood Restaurant***, 477 Changi Road, T7421119. Claypot pepper crabs are the speciality in Mr Tan's cheap and informal seafood restaurant, open to 0130 weekdays and 0230 on Saturday.

3 ***Palm Beach Seafood Restaurant***, Palm Beach Leisure Park, 1st and 2nd floors, 5

Stadium Walk, T3443088. Located near the International Building and the Nationa Stadium, spread over four a/c floors, basic decor; tiled flooring and melamin crockery, good shellfish at a fair price - the chilli crab is a speciality.

UDMC Seafood Centre, 1000 East Coast Parkway. There are 10 outlets here an they're all good. In particular - **3** ***Gold Coast Live Seafood***, T4482020 and **3** ***Jumb Seafood***, T4423435. Serving Singapore specialities like chilli crabs and black peppe crayfish. **3** ***International Seafood Centre***, also on the ECP, provide trolleys to choos your fish pre-cooking. Not for the squeamish. Recommended.

Bars **1** *Changi Sailing Club*, Changi Village, pleasant and, surprisingly, one of the cheapes places for a quiet beer, overlooking the Strait of Johor. **1** ***Charlie's***, Block 2, 01-08 Changi Village. Charlie Han describes his bar as "the pulse of the point", tucked awa behind the local hawker centre, he is a teetotaller but serves 70 brands of beer from a over the world, which you can sip as you watch the red-eyes touchdown on runwa one, Charlie's is best known for its fish and chips, closed over the weekend (se *Restaurants*). Recommended.

North of the Island

The north of the island is Singapore's back garden: in between the sprawling new housing estates there are areas of jungled wilderness, mangroves, lakes and landscaped gardens.

Ins and outs

Getting there

The MRT North line loops right around this part of the island and has 23 stops. TIBS buses - the Trans-Island Bus Service - are also useful.

Getting around

This is the largest of the areas designated in this book and generally the places mentioned are too far apart to walk between. Take a taxi, bus or the MRT.

The area

Immediately north of the city is the suburb of Toa Payoh, one of the first new towns to be built in Singapore and the first to have its own town centre. Since the construction of Toa Payoh in the 1960s the Housing Development Board has built a string of other new towns outside the central area: **Queenstown** - also in the 1960s - **Ang Mo Kio** and **Bedok** in the 70s, and **Hougang** and **Tampines** in the 80s. Ang Mo Kio - literally "bridge of the red-haired foreign devil" - was named after John Turnbull Thomson, the

Related map: Coloured map, page 1

19th century government surveyor who was responsible for extending Singapore's road network into the interior.

The northern loop of the MRT links these new towns both with the city centre and with the west of the island. However many of the places of interest are situated away from the MRT and are accessible only by bus or taxi. These include the excellent Singapore Zoological Gardens and Night Safari, the Bukit Timah Nature Reserve, the Seletar and MacRitchie reservoirs, as well as a number of suburban Chinese pagodas which are fascinating more for the insight they offer into local beliefs than for any architectural merit.

Sights

Just outside the city limits, on Tai Gin Road (which runs of Balestier Road) is **Sun Yat Sen's Villa**. Sun Yat Sen was an early Chinese republican leader and he is a figure of some reverance among Chinese - a sort of Chinese Gandhi. He visited Singapore on a number of occasions and when here stayed at this villa. It became the headquarters of the Tung Ming Hin in Singapore, dedicated to the overthrow of the Manchus. The villa - which dates from the 1880s - is currently closed and undergoing renovation and expansion. The Chinese Chamber of Commerce, who own and maintain the villa, say that when it is finished it will not be a museum but a memorial hall to the great man. They also, and rather disarmingly, admit that it wont be of much interest to Westerners - it is mainly for the benefit of Chinese on pilgrimmage. It is expected to reopen to the public in 2000. ■ *Opening hours and admission fees are still to be decided. take a bus (numbers 131 and 145 are most convenient) travelling down Balestier Rd and alight at the Jalan Dusun stop. From here walk up Ah Hood Rd past the Lee Kuo Chuan Primary School to get to the villa - about a 5 minute walk. Alternatively, take a taxi.*

Siong Lim Temple

The **Siong Lim Temple** at 184 Jalan Toa Payoh lies due north of the city within the modern suburb of Toa Payoh. This Fujian temple's full name is Lian Shan, Shuang Lin which means Lotus Hill, Twin Groves, referring to the *sal* grove in Kunisnara, near Patna, where the Buddha attained enlightenment. It is the largest Buddhist temple in Singapore and was originally built between 1898 and 1905. However since then Singapore's urban expansion has enveloped it. Chunks of its original 4 hectares have been chipped away for housing development and, perhaps to atone for the effrontery, the Singapore Tourist Board gave the temple its Suzhou-style rock garden. Despite the redevelopments the temple retains its excellent wood carvings and some fine Thai images of the Buddha. There is also an statue of Kuan Yin and a corpulent image of the Maitreya Buddha. ■ *Take the MRT to Toa Payoh. Then take bus numbers 8 or 26 getting off at HDB block 195, one stop past the Toa Payoh stadium.*

Kong Meng San Phor Kark

Kong Meng San Phor Kark See Chinese Temple Complex (Bright Hill Drive) has, since its construction in 1989, grown into a sprawling, million dollar religious centre whose golden roofs spread over 7½ hectares. Fed up with tastefully mouldering 19th century Chinese temples? Then this is the place for you. This is Chinese temple garishness on a truly gargantuan scale. Restrained was clearly not a word in the architect's vocabulary. The complex has been the backdrop for many kung-fu movies and is one of the largest such complexes in Southeast Asia. From the main entrance on Sin Ming Avenue pilgrims climb up through a series of halls with images of the historic Buddha and various other gods and goddesses from Chinese Mahayana Buddhism's extensive repertoire. There are halls for prayer and meditation, a pool containing thousands of turtles, a Buddhist library, an old people's home (and, appropriately, a crematorium), as well as a 9m-high marble statue of Kuan Yin, the 15-headed goddess of mercy, carved by Italian sculptors. At the top of the complex is a regular office block surmounted by a large gold stupa. The walkways are crowded with hawkers selling jade bangles, Buddhist icons and dubious medicinal remedies. Resident geriatrics in the old people's home spend their last days making paper cars and other worldly symbols which are torched after their deaths and, they hope, follow them into the next world. As you wander around this fantastic complex three things may strike you as odd: 1. There are virtually no Europeans in sight; 2. Almost every visitor is female and aged 60 or over; 3. Of these female pilgrims, the majority are wearing traditional Chinese-style pyjama suits. Which begs a number of questions. Is this where women, but not men come to cash in their merit chips prior to earthly departure? Is the pyjama suit a necessary fashion accoutrement for visiting? People in Singapore City certainly don't wear them. Or are these visitors from mainland China or Taiwan? ■ *Take bus number 130 from Raffles City or Clifford Pier; alight at the Sin Ming Drive stop which stops opposite the crematorium. The walk on to the T junction and turn left down Sin Ming Avenue to the main entrance. Alternatively, take the MRT to Ang Mo Kio, cross the road to the Ang Mo Kio bus interchange and board bus number 130. The golden stupa of the temple can be seen from some way off.*

On the north coast of the island is the **Singapore Navy Museum** at Endurance Block, Sembawang Camp (T 7505585). There's not a great deal here to warrant the long trip out: some historic photographs and navigation equipment, and a few more contemporary bits and pieces. ■ *Free. 0830-1630 Monday-Friday, 0830-1200 Saturday. MRT to Yishun (N12) and then TIBS bus 856 from the Yishun Interchange. This runs down Yishun Avenue, onto Sembawang Road and then Canberra Road before turning left onto Admiralty Road West. Alight at the second stop on Admiralty Road West, opposite the entrance to Sembawang Camp and obtain a pass at the gate.*

The Singapore Zoological Gardens

The **Singapore Zoological Gardens**, 80 Mandai Lake Road (T2693411), is one of the world's few open zoos (moats replace bars), making it also one of the most attractive zoos in the world, with animals in environments vaguely reminiscent of their habitats. In its promotional brochure, the 20-hectares zoo claims that its open-design concept has paid off: "Our reward is happy animals. The proof lies in the zoo's good breeding record: unhappy animals do not make love!". Only the polar bears and the tigers seemed unhappy in their surroundings. It contains over 170 species of animals (about 2,000 actual animals), some of them rare - like the dinosauric Komodo dragons and the golden lion tamarin - as well as many endangered species from Asia, such as the Sumatran tiger and the clouded leopard. The pygmy hippos are relatively recent newcomers; they live in glass-fronted enclosures (as do the polar bears), so visitors can watch their underwater exploits. Animals are sponsored by companies - *Tiger Beer*, for example, sponsors the tigers and *Qantas* the kangaroos.

There are animal shows throughout the day carrying a strong ecological message: primates and reptiles (at 1030 and 1430) and elephants and sealions (at 1130 and 1530). Animal feeding times are provided upon arrival. The latest addition to the zoo is a Treetops Trail where visitors can view primates, crocodiles, squirrels and pheasants from a 6 metre-high boardwalk. There is a children's area too with farm animals, a miniature train and play equipment. There are tram tours for those too weary to walk (S$2.50 and S$1), with recorded commentaries, and several restaurants. Elephant, camel and pony rides are on offer at various times each afternoon. A shop sells environmentally sound T-shirts and cuddly toy animals. Overall, a well-managed and informative zoo; it's well worth the trip out there (Website: http://www.asianconnect.com/zoo/). Video cameras can be hired (S$10/hour). ■ *S$10.30, S$4.60 for children 0830-1800 Monday-Sunday, T2693411. MRT to Ang Mo Kio and then SBS 138 from the Ang Mo Kio interchange or MRT to Choa Chu Kang and then TIBS 927. Alternatively take bus No 171 to Mandai Road and then cross the road to board the SBS 138 to the zoo. On Sundays and public holidays Trans-island bus service (TIBS) number 926 runs from the Woodlands bus interchange direct to the zoo. Taxis cost about S$10 to the zoo from the Orchard Road area. A bus service runs every 30 minutes from 0730 until 2300 from Orchard and Scott Roads (ask at your hotel), S$5 one way. Another option is to book a ticket on the air-con Zoo Express which provides guided tours on demand (contact Elpin, T7322133).*

Night Safari

The unique **Night Safari** is situated adjacent to the zoo, covering 40 hectares of secondary growth tropical forest. The area has been cunningly converted into a series of habitats populated with wildlife from the Indo-Malayan, Indian, Himalayan and African zoogeographical regions. The park supports 1,200 animals belonging to 110 species including the tiger, Indian lion, great Indian rhinoceros, fishing cat, Malayan tapir, Asian elephant, bongo, striped hyaena, Cape buffalo, and giraffe. Visitors can either hop on a tram to be taken on a 40-minute guided safari through the jungle lit by moonglow lighting and informed by a rather earnest commentary, or they can walk along three short trails at their own pace - or they can do both. The whole affair is extremely well conceived and managed, and the experience is rewardingly authentic - possibly because the night-time ambience hides the seams that are usually so evident in orthodox zoos. Children love the safari experience believing that they truly are chancing upon animals in the jungle. At the entrance "lodge" there is a good noodle bar as well as a *Burger King*. There is also another small café, at the East Lodge. ■ *S$15.45, children S$10.30. 1830-2400. Safaris start at 1930 but restaurants are open from 1630. The last tram leaves at 2315. NB No flash cameras permitted. Bus take the trans island bus number 171 (it stops at Orchard Boulevard and Scotts Roads) to Mandai Road and then cross the road and board the SBS 138 which goes direct to the Night Safari. By MRT, either get off at Ang Mo Kio and then board the SBS 138, or alight at Choa Chu Kang and board the TIBS 927. A taxi from the city will cost around S$12 and takes 30 minutes.*

The Mandai Orchid

The Mandai Orchid Gardens, Mandai Lake Road (T2691036), next to the zoo, is Singapore's largest commercial orchid farm and started life in 1960 as a hobby for orchidologists John Ede and John Laycock. The rare black orchid of Sumatra blossoms in July. ■ *S$2, S$0.50 for children under 12. 0830-1730 Monday-Sunday. Take the MRT to Ang Mo Kio, and bus 138 from the interchange.*

The Kranji War Memorial and Cemetery

The **Kranji War Memorial and Cemetery**, Woodlands Road, on a gentle hillside overlooking the Straits of Johor, is where Allied soldiers killed in Singapore in World War Two are buried. In the heart of the cemetery is the War Memorial, bearing the names of 24,346 Allied servicemen who died in the Asia-Pacific region during the war. The design of the memorial is symbolic, representing the three arms of the services - the army, navy and airforce. The upright section represents a conning tower, the lateral elements are wings, and the walls symbolize army lines. Flowers are not allowed to be placed on graves, in case tiger mosquitoes breed in the jars. ■ *Bus number 170 goes direct from Rochor Road; alight opposite the entrance to the cemetery. On weekends bus number 181 also stops here.*

Nature reserves

Sungei Buloh Nature Park, Neo Tiew Crescent (T6690377), is Singapore's first designated wetland nature reserve. It is an important stop-over point for birds migrating along the East Asian Flyway. The best time to visit is in November. Carefully constructed hides throughout 87 hectares provide excellent observation points for visitors to view birds like sea eagles, kites, and blue herons. There is also a mangrove swamp to walk through. ■ *S$1, children S$0.50. 0730-1900 Monday-Friday, 0700-1900 weekends and public holidays. Binoculars for hire. Audiovisual show 0900, 1100, 1300, 1500 and 1700 Monday-Saturday, every hour between 0900 and 1700 on Saturday & Sunday. Take MRT to Kranji or Woodlands stations. Alternatively take TIBS bus 170 from Queen's Street to the Woodlands interchange. At Kranji or Woodlands, board TIBS bus 925 to Kranji Reservoir. On weekends bus 925 runs all the way to the Park entrance but on weekdays it is a further 20-minute walk to the park.*

Bukit Timah Nature Reserve, on Hindhede Drive off Upper Bukit Timah Road (T4709900), nestles in the centre of the island and has a resident population of wild monkeys, pythons and scorpions. It was one of the first Forest Reserves established in 1883 for the purposes of protecting the native flora and fauna. The naturalist Alfred Russel Wallace collected beetles at Bukit Timah in 1854. Jungle trails go through the forested terrain (130 million-year-old tropical rainforest) that once covered the whole island. The artificial lakes supply the city with much of its water. Clearly marked paths (one of them metalled) in the 81-hectare reserve lead to Singapore's highest point (164m) for scenic views. A visitors' centre includes an informative exhibition on natural history (open 0830-1800). The nature reserve is at its quietest and best in the early mornings. It is a wonderful contrast to the bustle of modern Singapore. ■ *Take the MRT to Newton Station, then TIBS bus 171 or TIBS bus 181.*

At **Bukit Batok**, there is what little remains of a Japanese Syonan Shrine, built by Australian and British POWs. All that still stands are the 125 stone steps leading up to the shrine sight. The shrine's demise is attributed to the termites which the POWs reportedly placed in the materials they used to build it. From here you can walk to the rock formations known as Little Guilin. ■ *Entrance is at Bukit Batok on top of the hill at Larong Sesuan off Upper Bukit Timah Road. MRT to Bukit Batok and then bus 365 from the Bukit Batok interchange.*

MacRitchie and Seletar Reservoirs on Lornie and Mandai roads, are popular for joggers and weekend picnickers. Jungle paths surround the reservoirs. The entrance to MacRitchie Reservoir is on the south-east side. ■ *Buses 132 and 167 run from Scotts Road or Orchard Boulevard. The entrance to the Seletar Reservoir is on the east side, the other side from the zoo. Bus numbers 138 and 171 both stop opposite the entrance; 171 runs down Scotts Rd.*

Singapore's Islands

Ins and outs

Getting there Ferries for Pulau Kusu and St John's leave from the World Trade Centre; for Pulau Ubin bumboats depart from Changi Point; and for Sisters Island by privately hired boat from Jardine Steps or Clifford Pier.

Getting around Pulau Ubin is by far the largest of these islands and many visitors hire mountain bikes to get around.

The area

The less accessible islands are a welcome break from the city and offer a pleasing contrast to everything that modern Singapore stands for. There are around 40 neighbouring small islands, the largest of which is **Pulau Tekong**. The group of islands west of Sentosa - **Pulau Brani, Bukom** and **Sambol** - are industrial adjuncts of Singapore proper. Pulau Brani was the site of Singapore's first tin smelter, built in 1890 by the Straits Trading Company. Later, it became popular as a coaling depot for British naval vessels, due to its sheltered position. You can get a scenic view of the oil refinery on Pulau Bukum from Sentosa's swimming lagoon. Ferries link the city with all its surrounding islands but for more obscure spots it's necessary to hire a boat from Clifford Pier. This is an expensive business: expect to pay around S$60 per hour. **NB** Avoid going to the islands on public holidays.

St John's Island

Happily, developers have been less active on Singapore's other southern islands than they have on Sentosa, although they are popular city escapes. **St John's** is the largest with a few holiday camps and swimming lagoons. It used to be a quarantine station and an opium addiction treatment centre. When Stamford Raffles first approached Singapore, his six ships anchored off St John's. The Malays called it Pulau Si-Kijang - barking deer island. The English sailors could not pronounce it, and corrupted it to St John's. There are plans to build a causeway linking St Johns with Lazarus and Serengat islands but this is probably some way off (see below).

Eating and Sleeping A few holiday bungalows here, and camping is permitted; there is a cafeteria and shop; contact the World Trade Centre T2707888 or 2707889 for details.

Kusu Island

It is possible to walk around **Kusu**, or Turtle Island, in a few minutes. *Kusu* means turtle in Malay and according to legend, a giant turtle turned itself into an island in order to save two shipwrecked sailors, a Malay and a Chinese, who lived here peacefully until they died. Kusu has a Chinese temple and Malay shrine (see Festivals, page 52) where the Malay/Chinese god *Datok Kung* is worshipped. This god is an amalgum of the Chinese God of the Soil, *Ta-po-kung*, and a Malay spirit, *Datok*. Like most such gods, he is thought to bring good fortune to his supplicants and is depicted bearded and smiling. There is a ferry to both islands from the World Trade Centre, 30 minutes to Kusu, 1 hour to St John's (S$6.20 return, S$3.10 for children). Monday-Saturday ferries leave the World Trade Centre at 1000 and 1330; on Sunday and public holidays there are 6 departures the first at 0945 and the last at 1715. The last boat back from St John's leaves the jetty at 1445 (Monday-Saturday), and at 2030 on Sunday and public holidays. T2703918 for details.

Southern Island group

Pulau Hantu, **Sister's Islands** (Subar Laut and Subar Darat), **Pulau Seringat** and **Lazarus Island** , like Pulau Biola near Raffles Lighthouse, are popular for snorkelling and fishing.

The Sentosa Development Corporation have big plans for Pulau Seringat and Lazarus Island. The intention is to merge the islands by reclaiming two shoals. Over 1,000 homes will be built and two hotels - a tiered *Hilltop Hotel* and a *Beach Hotel* with around 500 rooms in total. There will be no cars on the island, only electric trolley buses, and the intention is to create a lifestyle resort with a Mediterranean flavour. The plans also include the construction of a 600 metre-long beach. A causeway will link this new development with nearby St John's Island. The project is still under discussion so is unlikely to be completed in the near future.

Pulau Seking is slightly further away and village life here is still just about intact although the population of less than 50 inhabitants, living in a traditional fishing village on stilts, is rapidly dwindling. There are no regular ferry services to these islands. Charter a boat from Clifford Pier (from around S$60 per hour for 6-12 passengers) and stock up on food and water before you go. Many tour operators have snorkelling equipment for hire.

Islands to the northeast

Pulau Ubin is a great - but little-known - awayday from concrete and capitalism. This island is the source of granite for the causeway and Singapore's earlier buildings and skyscrapers. Its name derives from the Javanese word for 'squared stone'. Ubin village affords a taste of Singapore in bygone days, with dilapidated wooden shophouses, coffee-shops and community spirit. The island, with its beaten-up cars and old taxis, quarry pits, jungle tracks, hills, beaches and challenging trails, is a mountain-biker's paradise and has become a popular destination for that reason, as the trails are quite challenging; it is possible to hire bicycles in the village. There is also an outward bound centre on the island and students come here to experience outdoor living.

This vision of Pulau Ubin might be about to change as the island's first holiday resort is due to open at the end of 1998 (see Accommodation, below). The Urban Redevelopment Authority has also published plans to reclaim an additional 2,694 ha on Pulau Ubin and Pulau Tekong (the majority on Tekong).

The best restaurant on the island - which doubles as one of the best restaurants in Singapore - is *Ubin Seafood*, on the northeast shore at the end of a pot-holed jungle track (see below).

Sleeping **A-B** ***Ubin Lagoon Resort***, new resort which is scheduled to open at the end of 1998, 150-odd kampung-style a/c chalets with lots of water (jet skis, snorkelling, scuba diving) and other sports facilities (bicycling, tennis) as well as a camp site with BBQ pits, seafood market, and a large marine lagoon stocked with fish where novice divers will be able to dive with safety. The idea is to create a back-to-nature resort at an affordable price.

D ***Nature Traveller House***, 8Y Pulau Ubin, T5426154. Run by Thian, the owner of the biggest mountain-bike shop. Rooms are fan-cooled only, kitchen facilities available. **Bungalows**: the National Trades Union Congress (NTUC) are building some bungalows and these should be available for non-NTUC members to rent. **Camping**: tents available for rent on the island, contact *Universal Adventure* on T7206639.

Eating **3** ***Ubin Seafood***, T5458202/5426215 (ask for Liang), is on the northeast shore of Pulau Ubin, at the end of a jungly track, and is one of the best seafood restaurants in Singapore. It is best to book - not because it is always crowded, but to ensure they have stocked up on all the crabs, fish, mussels and Tiger beer you need; recommended. Note: in 1998 *Ubin Seafood* was shut, but probably only temporarily.

Sport Canoes, kayaks and mountain bikes all available for hire on the island. Mountain bikes can also be hired from Changi Village - S$20/day (S$10 returnable deposit).

Transport From Changi Point it costs S$1.50 to go to Pulau Ubin; bumboats go when they're full - very frequently at the weekends - and operate between 0600 and 2200. It is possible to charter the whole vessel if you want to be alone, or are bored waiting for the boat to fill up. (For transport to and from Changi Village, see page 149.)

Background

Background

Singapore: a Brave New World

Singapore is difficult to fathom, especially from afar. Beneath its slick veneer of westernized modernity, many argue that Singapore's heart and soul are Asian. Behind the computers, hi-tech industries, marble, steel and smoked-glass tower blocks, highways and shopping centres is a society ingrained with conservative Confucian values.

A few years back, an editorial in the pro-government Straits Times *said: "Values are the software which makes the nation's social and economic hardware tick." Singapore still believes in extended families, filial piety, discipline and respect but above all, it believes in the Asian work ethic. The man who has instilled and preserved these values is former Prime Minister Lee Kuan Yew - a man who has been characterized as the "Thomas Jefferson of the Pacific Rim" and "Asia's Moses". But, to some – and it should be added that most of these are non-Singaporeans – his far-sighted vision has transformed this clockwork island into a regimented city state. In this view of things, modern, automated Singapore has spawned a generation of angst- ridden, over-programmed people who have given their country the reputation of being the most crushingly dull in Asia. But now, all that is changing. The architect of modern Singapore has allowed a new generation of Singaporeans to step up to the drawing board.*

History

Early records

Although Singapore has probably been inhabited for the past two millennia, there are few early records. In the 3rd century, Chinese sailors mention *Pu-luo-chung,*"the island at the end of the peninsula" and historians speculate that this may have been Singapore. Even its name, *Singapura*, from the Sanskrit for "Lion City", is unexplained - other than by the legendary account in the *Sejara Melayu*. It was originally called Temasek - or 'Sea Town' - and may have been a small seaport in the days of the Sumatran Srivijayan Empire. Following Srivijaya's decline at the end of the 13th century, however, Singapore emerged from the shadows to become, for a short while, a locally important trading centre in its own right.

Marco Polo, the Venetian adventurer, visited Sumatra in the late 1200s and referred to *Chiamassie*, which he says was a "very large and noble city". Historians believe this was probably Temasek. According to the 16th century *Sejara Melayu*, Temasek was a thriving entrepôt by the 14th century, when it changed its name to Singapura. Another contemporary account, however, by the Chinese traveller, Wang Ta-yuan, noted that the island was a dreaded pirate haunt. Whatever prosperity it may have had, did not last. In the late 1300s, it was destroyed by invading Siamese and Javanese, for Singapura fell in the middle ground between the expanding Ayutthaya (Siamese) and Majapahit (Javanese) empires. The ruler - called Parameswara, who was said to be a fugitive prince from Palembang in Sumatra - fled to Melaka, where he founded the powerful Malay sultanate in the 1390s. Following Parameswara's hasty departure, Singapura was abandoned except for a few *Orang Laut* ('Sea People'), who made a living from fishing and piracy. While trade flourished elsewhere in the region, the port which today is the busiest in the world, was a jungled backwater and it remained that way for four centuries.

Raffles steps ashore

In the early 1800s, the British East India Company occupied Dutch colonies in the east to prevent them falling into French hands: Napoleon had occupied Holland and the Dutch East India Company had gone bankrupt. In January 1819 Sir Thomas Stamford Raffles arrived in Singapore with the hope that he could set up a trading post at the mouth of the Singapore River. On 31 January he wrote to Sir William Marsden: "Here I am in Singapore, true to my word, and in the enjoyment of all the pleasures which a footing on such classic ground must inspire. The lines of the old city, and of its defences, are still to be traced, and within its ramparts the British Union waves unmolested". He was relieved to hear that the Dutch had never been there and promptly struck a deal with the resident *temenggong* (Malay chief) of the Riau-Johor Empire. To seal this agreement he had to obtain official approval from the Sultan of Riau-Johor.

Due to a succession squabble following the previous sultan's death in 1812, there were two claimants, one on Pulau Lingga (far to the south), who was recognized by the Dutch, and one on Pulau Bintan. Realizing that the Dutch would bar the Lingga sultan from sanctioning his settlement on Singapore, Raffles approached the other one, flattering him, offering him money and pronouncing him Sultan of Johor. He agreed to pay Sultan Hussein Mohammad Shah 5,000 Spanish dollars a year in rent and a further 3,000 Spanish dollars to the temenggong. The Union Jack was officially raised over Singapore on 6 February 1819 and Raffles set sail again the next day - having been there less than a week - leaving in charge the former Resident of Melaka, Colonel William Farquhar. It was this act of Raffles' that led to him being accorded the title "Founder of Singapore". Yet some historians would give the title to another great, although lesser known, British colonialist, Sir John Crawfurd. Ernest Chew, Professor of History at the National University of Singapore, argues that all Raffles secured in his negotiations was permission to establish a trading post. It was not until Crawfurd became the second Resident of Singapore in 1824 that Britain acquired the island by treaty. Such details of history could not, however, dampen or detract from the celebrations marking the 175th anniversary of the 'founding' of Singapore by Sir Stamford Raffles in 1994.

The Treaty of London

The Dutch were enraged by Raffles' bold initiative and the British government was embarrassed. But after a protracted diplomatic frisson, the Treaty of London was finally signed in 1824 and the Dutch withdrew their objection to the British presence on Singapore in exchange for the British withdrawal from Bencoolen (Benkulu) in Sumatra, where Raffles had served as governor. Seven years later, the trading post was tied with Penang (which had been in British hands since 1786) and Melaka (which the Dutch had had swapped with Bencoolen). They became known as the Straits Settlements and attracted traders and settlers from all over Southeast Asia, and the world.

Raffles' vision

Although Sir Thomas Stamford Raffles spent little time in Singapore, his vision for the city can still be seen today. "Our object is not territory but trade; a great commercial emporium and a fulcrum whence we may extend our influence politically as circumstances may hereafter require." Each time Raffles departed he left strict instructions on the layout of the growing city, stipulating, for example, that the streets should be arranged on a grid structure wherever possible. Houses were to have a uniform front and "a verandah open at all times as a continued and covered passage on each side of the street" (the so-called 'five-foot ways') - stipulations which resulted in the unique character of Singapore and later Malaya. During his second visit in 1819, he divided the town into distinct districts or kampungs (the Malay word for village). Raffles firmly believed that the different ethnic groups should be segregated. The Europeans were to live in the Beach Road area between Stamford canal and Arab Street, the Chinese were to live south of the river (and in fact, Chinatown was divided into three separate areas for the different dialect groups), the Temenggong and the 600-odd Malays were to live along the upper reaches of the river. To the northeast of the European enclave, Kampung Glam housed Sultan Hussein and his Arab followers. The land on the north side of the river was set aside for government buildings. A mere six months after Raffles had landed, more than 5,000 people had settled around the mouth of the river. Much of the area to the south was mangrove swamps, but that was reclaimed and settled too.

European merchants soon realized that the beach was inappropriate as a landing area because of the swell. In agreement with Farquhar, they started to unload from the north bank of the river. When Raffles returned for his third and final visit in October 1822, he was horrified by the chaos of the town. He fell out with Farquhar and had him replaced by John Crawfurd.

Thomas Stamford Raffles: architect of Singapore

"It is a pity to my mind that when Thomas Stamford Raffles... was knighted by his friend the Prince Regent in 1817, he chose to be dubbed Sir Stamford," writes Jan Morris in her introduction to Maurice Collis' biography of Singapore's founding father. "Tom Raffles was much more his style."

Raffles was the son of an undistinguished sea-captain, and was born in 1781 aboard his father's West Indian slaving ship somewhere in the mid-Atlantic. He joined the East India Company as a clerk aged 14 when his father could no longer afford his school fees. Ten years later, in 1805, he was posted to Penang as an assistant secretary to the government, getting a 21-fold salary rise in the process. On the journey out, he learned Malay and was accepted as an expert within a few months of his arrival.

On a visit to Calcutta in 1810, the Governor-General of India appointed him Governor of Java, a post he held from 1811-1816. The British Governor of India described Raffles as "a very clever, able, active and judicious man". In 1814 his wife, Olivia, died. Raffles was devastated, but occupied himself researching A History of Java, *which was published in 1817, and is considered a landmark study.*

As an administrator, Raffles was well-liked. He was known as a fair and reasonable man; he had a forceful character and opportunistic streak but few social pretentions. He battled to suppress piracy and slavery and was a close friend of William Wilberforce, the social reformer. He became convinced of the virtues of free trade. In the words of Jan Morris, "he was only the instrument of inexorable geo-political forces ... [although] he believed in his country as the chief agent of human progress."

After five years in Java, Raffles returned to England where, in 1817, he married for the second time to an Irish woman, he described as "affectionate and sensible, though not very handsome". He took her back to the East, where he was appointed Lieutenant-Governor of Bencoolen (Sumatra) in 1818. The same year, while on a visit to Calcutta, Raffles persuaded the Governor-General of India, Lord Hastings, to sanction a mission to set up a trading post at the southern tip of the Strait of Melaka. On 28 January 1819, after casting around some other islands in the area, he headed for Singapore, anchoring off St John's Island before sailing up the Singapore River the next day.

After stepping ashore, and claiming Singapore for Britain he did not return again until September 1822, by which time it was a booming port with 10,000 inhabitants. Raffles noted with satisfaction that in the first 2½ years, 2,839 vessels had entered and cleared the harbour; the total turnover was 8 million Spanish dollars. It was an omen of things to come. Raffles allowed unrestricted immigration and free trade. During this third (and final) visit, Raffles quarrelled with Farquhar, took over the administration himself, wrote a constitution and drew up a street plan.

Sir Stamford returned to England and having founded Singapore, went on to found London Zoo. But he was far from well; for some time he had been suffering from terrible, unexplained headaches. He fell out with the East India Company and died the day before his 45th birthday in Hendon, North London from a suspected brain tumour. His funeral was virtually ignored by London society and the local vicar refused permission for a plaque to be erected in his memory. Eight years later, his friends and admirers commissioned a marble statue of him which was placed in the north aisle of Westminster Abbey. Jan Morris writes that despite Raffles' short sojourn in Singapore, "he is honoured still in the Lion City as no other western imperialist is honoured in the East". On 30 January 1994, Singapore celebrated the 175th anniversary of Raffles' first landing.

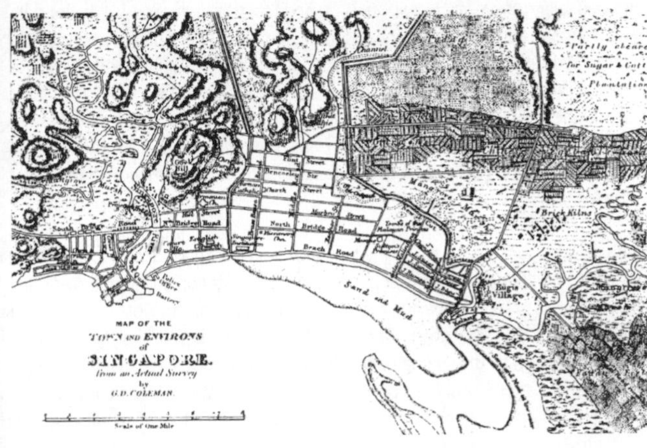

Map of Singapore town and surrounds based on an 1839 survey by GD Coleman

Fishing village to international port

Economic expansion

Within 4 years of its founding, Singapore had overshadowed Penang in importance and had grown from a fishing village to an international trading port. Thanks to its strategic location, it expanded quickly as an entrepôt, assuming the role Melaka had held in earlier centuries. But by 1833, the East India Company had lost its China trade monopoly and consequently its interest in Singapore and the other Straits Settlements declined. Their status was downgraded and their administration trimmed. Whilst Penang and Melaka declined, however, Singapore boomed. It had benefited from the abolition of the East India Company's monopoly. When the Dutch lifted trade restrictions in the 1840s, this boosted Singapore's economy again. New trade channels opened up with the Brooke government in Sarawak and with Thailand. The volume of trade increased fourfold between 1824 and 1868. However, the lack of restrictions and regulation descended into a state of commercial anarchy and in 1857 the merchants, who were dissatisfied with the administration, petitioned for Singapore to come under direct British rule.

Ten years later, the Colonial Office in London reluctantly made Singapore a crown colony. Then, in 1869, the Suez Canal opened which meant that the Strait of Melaka was an even more obvious route for east-west shipping traffic than the Sunda Strait, which was controlled by the Dutch. 5 years after that, Britain signed the first of its protection treaties with the Malay sultans on the peninsula. The governor of Singapore immediately became the most senior authority for the Straits Settlements Colony, the Federated Malay States and the British protectorates of Sarawak, Brunei and North Borneo. In one stroke, Singapore had become the political capital of a small empire within an empire. As Malaysia's plantation economy grew (with the introduction of rubber at the end of the 19th century) and as its tin-mining industry expanded rapidly, Singapore emerged as the expanding territory's financing and administrative centre and export outlet. By then Singapore had become the uncontested commercial and transport centre of Southeast Asia. Between 1873 and 1913 there was an eightfold increase in Singapore's trade. Joseph Conrad dubbed it "the thoroughfare to the East".

Historian Mary Turnbull writes, "Growing Western interests in Southeast Asia and the expansion of international trade, the liberalizing of Dutch colonial policy in the Netherlands East Indies, the increasing use of steamships (which from the 1880s replaced sailing ships as the main carriers) and the development of telegraphs all put Singapore, with its fine natural sheltered harbour, at the hub of international trade in Southeast Asia. It became a vital link in the chain of British ports which stretched from Gibraltar, through the Mediterranean Sea and the Indian Ocean to the Far East. The 60 years from the opening of the Suez Canal to the onset of the Great Depression in 1929 were a time of unbroken peace, steady economic expansion and population growth in Singapore, with little dramatic incident to ruffle the calm."

Social welfare Though Singapore quickly made the transition from colonial outpost to commercial entrepôt, conditions for many people were harsh. Sanitation and health were abysmal for all except the wealthy, education was limited, and work was hard and poorly paid. In 1910 over one third of children born died before their first birthday. Death rates, even by the standards of other colonial outposts, were high. Brenda Yeoh observes that Singapore's population during the late 19th and early 20th centuries was only sustained by immigration - the "appallingly high mortality rates", she writes, outstripped the birth rate. Needless to say, it varied considerably between the races. Among Europeans the death rate averaged 14 per 1,000 between 1893 and 1925. But for Malays and Chinese it was three times higher at 40 per 1,000. The diseases that wrought such havoc represent a veritable compendium of tropical ailments and included malaria, smallpox, beri-beri, cholera, enteric fever and bubonic plague.

By the mid-19th century it was accepted by some people that only a clean and safe water supply would make Singapore a healthier place to live and the *Straits Times* and medical men like Dr W.R.C. Middleton, the Municipal Health Officer, began to press the municipal authorities to make improvements. The first municipal water works was opened in 1878 near Thomson Road. This was financed with a gift of S$13,000 from Tan Kim Seng, a wealthy Straits Chinese merchant, who gave the money in 1857 on the condition that the water would be available to all, free of charge. There is a fountain dedicated to his memory on the Padang (see page).

For the colonial authorities and most Europeans the poor health of the Chinese and Malay populations was due, in large part, to "Asiatic" habits. As Brenda Yeoh has uncovered in documents from the end of the 19th century, it was widely accepted that the Asiatics had "incurably filthy and disorderly habits" and "a scant love for water and soap". With such ingrained beliefs it took many years before the authorities saw a need to provide a comprehensive system of urban sanitation and water supply. As a result, it was not until the late 1920s that mortality rates began to show a sustained decline.

629AD	1330	1819, January	1821	1822	1824
Probable mention of Singapore as a suzerain territory of Funan (present day Cambodia) in Liang Shu, a Chinese account	Temasek, or Singapore, mentioned in *Tao Yi Tchih Lueh*, a Chinese account of the war between Siam (Thailand) and the island		The first junk-load of Chinese immigrants arrives from Amoy (Xiamen)	Singapore's first school (six girls, six boys) opens for business	Treaty of London signed with the Dutch and Britain formally acquires the island The first gas street lamps begin to glo and Singapore's firs newspaper, The

The Japanese invasion and occupation

World War One gave Singapore a measure of strategic significance and by 1938 the colony was bristling with guns; it became known as Fortress Singapore. Unfortunately, the impregnable Fortress Singapore had anticipated that any attack would be from the sea and all its big guns were facing seawards. The Japanese entered through the back door. Japan attacked Malaya in December 1941 and having landed on the northeast coast, they took the entire peninsula in a lightning campaign, arriving in Johor Bahru at the end of January 1942.

The invasion

The Japanese invasion of Singapore was planned by General Tomoyuki Yamashita and was coordinated from the Sultan Ibrahim tower in Johor Bahru, which afforded a commanding view over the strait and north Singapore. Yamashita became known as the Tiger of Malaya for the speed with which the Japanese 25th Army over-ran the peninsula. The northeast coast of Singapore was heavily protected but the northwest was vulnerable and the Japanese attacked in a three pronged offensive by the 18th Division, 5th Division and the Imperial Guard. About 20,000 Japanese landed on the northwest coast, surrounding the Australian 22nd Brigade and wiping them out. The 27th Australian Brigade fared much better and was beating back the Japanese at Kranji when orders were misunderstood and the Australians retreated, to the bemused delight of the Japanese. There were three main battlefronts at Sarimbum Point, Bukit Timah, Mandai and Pasir Panjang; in each case, the Allies were out-manoeuvred, out-numbered and out-gunned. Towards the end, the battle became increasingly desperate and degenerated into hand-to-hand combat. On 13 February 1942 the Japanese captured Kent Ridge and Alexandra Barracks on Alexandra Road. They entered the hospital where they bayoneted the wounded and executed doctors, surgeons and nurses. The Allies and the local people were left in little doubt as to what was in store.

The surrender

With their water supplies from the peninsula cut off by the Japanese, and facing an epidemic because of thousands of rotting corpses, British Lieutenant-General Arthur Percival was forced to surrender in the Ford Motor Company boardroom on Bukit Timah Road at 19.50 on 15 February 1942. The fall of Singapore, which was a crushing humiliation for the British, left 140,000 Australian, British and Indian troops killed, wounded or captured. Japan had taken the island in one week.

There were more than a few sparks of heroism during the Fall of Singapore - the British Empire's greatest ever defeat. Take the case of the small, 700-tonne auxiliary ship *HMS Li Wo* commanded by Lieutenant T Wilkinson. This tiny vessel set sail from Singapore on 13th February and soon afterwards spotted - and was spotted by - a Japanese invasion fleet steaming towards the Dutch East Indies. Unable to escape,

1828, June 26th — The first two executions are carried out in Singapore

1831 — The Singapore Chronicle records the first sighting of a tiger

1852 — The first cricket match is played on the Padang

1869 — Completion of Suez canal strengthens Singapore's strategic and trading importance

1880 — The rickshaw makes it's first appearance

Wilkinson ordered the battle ensign raised, and prepared the ship's single four inch gun for battle. With his ship hit numerous times, he rammed the *Li Wo* into a transport ship before his own vessel sank. He was awarded a posthumous VC - the fourth and last of the inglorious Malayan campaign.

Following the defeat there were accusations that Churchill had 'abandoned' Singapore and let it fall to the Japanese when reinforcements were diverted elsewhere. The motivation for this, it has been suggested, was to get America to join the war. It is significant that Churchill never pressed for an inquiry into the fall of Singapore - the historian Peter Elphick suggests that Churchill was worried that he would emerge as the prime factor behind the capitulation. Significantly, the War Office files concerning the inquiry have still to be released. There is also little doubt that the defence of Singapore itself, and Malaya more widely, was poorly handled. The two commanding officers, generals Percivall and Heath, were often at odds. There was a widespread lack of appreciation of the martial skills of the Japanese. The forces defending Singapore lacked sufficient air cover and were poorly equipped. And training and morale were poor. There were also accusations of mass desertion and drunkenness on the part of the defending force. As many of the soldiers were Australian this became - and remains - a highly sensitive subject with at least some of the hallmarks of Gallipoli. Major Westall is quoted in the British Official History as estimating that 80 percent of desertions were from Australian units. There were, in short, manifold reasons why Singapore fell. The massive surrender certainly stands in stark contrast to Churchill's orders issued to General Wavell on the 10th February:

> *"There must at this stage be no thought of saving the troops or sparing the population. The battle must be fought to the bitter end at all costs...Commanders and senior officers should die with their troops. The honour of the British Empire and of the British Army is at stake."*

Colonel Phillip Parker, in his diary account of the defence of Singapore describes the moment of defeat: "The end - and inglorious end - had come. No last desperate struggle; no Dunkirk or Crete. Just the pathetic fizzle and splutter of a damp squib". Even at the end, Peter Elphick contends in his book *Singapore: the pregnable fortress* (1995), Singapore could have been saved. The Japanese had run critically short of ammunition and were outnumbered.

The occupation The Japanese ran a brutal regime and their occupation was characterized by terror, starvation and misery. They renamed Singapore *Syonan* - meaning 'light of the south'. The intention was to retain Syonan as a permanent colony, and turn it into a

1906	Singapore town is turned on by electric lights
1915	The first Singapore Sling is slung
1941, December	Japanese attack Malaya
1942, February 15th	General Percival surrenders to the Japanese and Singapore falls
1945, September 12th	The Japanese surrender
1948	The British create the Federation of Malaya
1949	The Singapore Family Planning Association open

military base and a centre in its 'Greater East Asia Co-Prosperity Sphere'. During the war Singapore became the base of the collaborationist Indian National Army and the Indian Independence League.

In the fortnight that followed the surrender, the Japanese required all Chinese males aged 18-50 to register. 'Undesirables' were herded into trucks and taken for interrogation and torture by the Kempetai military police to the old YMCA building on Stamford Road or were summarily bayoneted and shot. The purge was known as *sook ching* - or 'the purification campaign'. Thousands were killed (Singapore says 50,000, Japan says 6,000) and most of the executions took place on Changi Beach and Sentosa. The sand on Changi Beach is said to have turned red from the blood.

Allied prisoners-of-war were herded into prison camps, the conditions in which are vividly described in James Clavell's book *King Rat*; the author was himself a Changi POW. Many of the Allied troops who were not dispatched to work on the Burma railway or sent to Sandakan in North Borneo, where 2,400 died, were imprisoned in Selarang Barracks on the northeast side of the island. On the site of Changi Airport's Runway No 1, four men who attempted to escape were summarily executed. Three and a half years later, a Japanese commander, Major General Shempei Fukuei was sentenced to death for ordering the killings and executed on the same spot.

After Hiroshima and Nagasaki

Following the dropping of atomic bombs on Hiroshima and Nagasaki, the Japanese surrendered on 12 September 1945. The Japanese 5th and 18th Divisions which had spear-headed the invasion of Singapore and had carried out the massacres of civilians were from the towns of Hiroshima and Nagasaki respectively. Lord Louis Mountbatten, who took the surrender, described it as the greatest day of his life.

In the wake of the war, the Japanese partially atoned for their 'blood debt' by extending 'gifts' and 'special loans' to Singapore totalling some US$50 million. But Japanese war crimes were neither forgiven nor forgotten. When the head of Sony, Morita Akio and Japanese parliamentarian Ishihara Shintaro wrote in their 1990 book *The Japan that can say "No"* that the countries occupied by Japan during the war had become the best performing economies in Asia, it caused outrage and old wounds were reopened. They wrote: "We have to admit that we have done some wrong there ... but we cannot deny the positive influence we had". Older Singaporeans also noted with dismay and concern how Japan had rewritten its historical text-books to gloss over its wartime atrocities and many Singaporeans harbour a deep-seated mistrust of the Japanese. Among the most outspoken of them is former Prime Minister Lee Kuan Yew. This mistrust remains despite former Japanese Prime Minister Toshiki Kaifu's public apology in 1991 for what his countrymen had done half a century before.

1959 General elections held and Lee Kuan Yew becomes the first Prime Minister of an independent Singapore

1963 Singapore joins the Federation of Malaysia

1965 Singapore leaves the Federation of Malaysia

1971 Britain withdraws from it's base in Singapore

1983 Singapore's first three cases of AIDS are diagnosed

1993 Mr Ong Teng Cheong becomes Singapore's first elected President

After the war

Following a few months under a British military administration, Singapore became a crown colony and was separated from the other Straits Settlements of Penang, Melaka and Labuan. The Malay sultanates on the peninsula were brought into the Malayan Union. The British decision to keep Singapore separate from the Malayan Union sparked protests on the island and resulted in the founding of its first political party, the Malayan Democratic Union (MDU), which wanted Singapore to be integrated into a socialist union. The Malayan Union was very unpopular on the mainland too, and the British replaced it with the Federation of Malaya in 1948. Singapore was excluded again because Malaya's emergent Malay leaders did not want to upset the peninsula's already delicate ethnic balance by incorporating predominantly Chinese Singapore.

The same year, elections were held for Singapore's legislative council. The MDU, which had been heavily infiltrated by Communists, boycotted the election, allowing the Singapore Progressive Party (SPP) - dominated by an English-educated élite - to win a majority. The council was irrelevant to the majority of the population however and did nothing to combat poverty and unemployment and little to promote social services. When the Communist Emergency broke out on the peninsula later the same year, the Malayan Communist Party of Malaya (CPM) was banned in Singapore and the MDU disbanded.

Harry Lee returned from study in England in 1950. In 1954, as his political aspirations hardened, he let it be known that he wished to be called Lee Kuan Yew. Ten years later the British foreign secretary George Brown is still alleged to have remarked to him: "Harry, you're the best bloody Englishman east of Suez".

Political awakening

In 1955 a new constitution was introduced which aimed to jolt the island's apathetic electorate into political life. Two new parties were formed to contest the election - the Labour Front under lawyer David Marshall (descended from an Iraqi Jewish family) and the People's Action Party (PAP), headed by Lee Kuan Yew (see page 200). These two parties routed the conservative SPP and Marshall formed a minority government. His tenure as Chief Minister was marked by violence and by tempestuous exchanges in the Legislative Assembly with Lee. Marshall resigned in 1956 after failing to negotiate self-government for Singapore by his self-imposed deadline. His deputy, Lim Yew Hock (who later became a Muslim) took over as Chief Minister and more Communist-instigated violence followed.

The rise of the PAP

The influence of the PAP grew rapidly, in league with the Communists and radical union leaders, and through the Chinese-language schools and trades unions. For Lee, who hated Communism, it was a Machiavellian alliance of convenience. He mouthed various anti-colonial slogans but the British, at least, seemed to realize he was playing a long, and cunning, game. The Communists came to dominate the PAP central committee and managed to sideline Lee before their leaders were arrested by Marshall's government. At the same time, Singapore's administration was rapidly localized: the four main languages (Malay, Chinese, Tamil and English) were given parity within the education system and locals took over the civil service. In 1957, as Malaya secured independence from the British, Singapore negotiated terms for full self-government. In 1959 the PAP swept the polls, winning a clear majority, and Lee became Prime Minister, a post he was to hold for more than three decades.

The PAP government began a programme of rapid industrialization and social reform. Singapore also moved closer to Malaysia, which Lee considered a vital move in order to guarantee free access to the Malaysian market and provide military security in the run-up to its own independence. But the PAP leaders were split over the wisdom of this move, and the extreme left wing, which had come to the orefront again, was becoming more vociferous in its opposition. Malaysia, for its part, felt threatened by Singapore's large Chinese population and by its increasingly Communist-orientated government. Tunku Abdul Rahman, independent Malaysia's irst Prime Minister, voiced concerns that an independent Singapore could be 'a econd Cuba', a Communist state on Malaysia's doorstep. Instead of letting the ituation deteriorate, however, Tunku Abdul Rahman cleverly proposed Singapore's nclusion in the Federation of Malaysia.

The Federation of Malaysia and independence

He hoped the racial equilibrium of the Federation would be balanced by the nclusion of Sarawak, Brunei and North Borneo. Lee liked the idea, but the radical eft wing of the PAP were vehemently opposed to it, having no desire to see ingapore absorbed by a Malay-dominated, anti-Communist regime, and in July 961 they tried to topple Lee's government. Their bid narrowly failed and resulted n the left-wing dissenters breaking away to form the Barisan Sosialis (BS), or ocialist Front. Despite continued opposition to the merger, a referendum showed hat a majority of Singapore's population supported it. In February 1963, in *Operation Coldstore*, more than 100 Communist and pro-Communist politicians, rades unionists and student leaders were arrested, including half the BS Central xecutive Committee.

On 31 August 1963, Singapore joined the Federation of Malaysia. The following month, during a delay in the implementation of the Federation while the wishes of he Borneo states were being ascertained, Singapore declared unilateral ndependence from Britain. The PAP also won another resounding victory in an election and secured a comfortable majority. Almost immediately, however, the new Federation ran into trouble due to Indonesian objections, and Jakarta launched its *Konfrontasi* - or Confrontation. Indonesian saboteurs infiltrated Singapore and began a bombing spree which severely damaged Singapore's trade. In mid-1964 ingapore was wracked by communal riots which caused great concern in Kuala umpur, and Lee and Tunku Abdul Rahman clashed over what they considered undue interference in each others' internal affairs. Tensions rose still further when he PAP contested Malaysia's general election in 1964, and Lee attempted to unite all Malaysian opposition parties under the PAP banner. While the PAP won only one of the 10 seats it petrified many Malay politicians on the mainland. Finally, on 9 August 1965, Kuala Lumpur forced Singapore to agree to pull out of the Federation, and it became an independent state against the wishes of the government. At a press conference announcing Singapore's expulsion from the Federation, Lee Kuan Yew wept. In the first volume of his memoirs, published towards the end of 1998, Lee writes of his "heavy sense of guilt" over Singapore's expulsion from Malaysia. "I elt I had let down several million people in Malaysia, immigrant Chinese and ndians, Eurasians, and even some Malays ..."

As a footnote to Singapore's expulsion from the Federation, in June 1996 Lee Kuan Yew suggested in an interview with local and foreign journalists that the sland republic might rejoin the Federation should certain conditions be met - like no racial favoritism. Few other politicans, either in Singapore or Malaysia, took the proposal seriously. The Malaysian cartoonist Lat drew an image of the managers of Malaysian chewing gum factory pounding the board room table as they onsidered the possibility of Singapore's chewing gum ban being extended to Malaysia.

Singaporeans and their history

What is perhaps unusual is the ease with which Singaporeans have come to terms with their history. The psychology of decolonization, so evident elsewhere, seems not to have afflicted the average Singaporean. Perhaps this is because all the population are the sons and daughters of relatively recent immigrants. Perhaps because of the self-evident social and economic achievements of the country. Or perhaps it is because there is general acceptance that the colonial experience was beneficial. It is reflected in such things as place names. After independence there was no rush to rename streets after resistance fighters and nationalist figures from history. Empress Place, Connaught Drive, Alexander Road, Clive Street and Dalhousie Pier remain with the names that the British gave them.

Land and environment

Geography

Singapore is a small, roughly diamond-shaped island at the end of peninsular Malaysia and is not much bigger than Britain's Isle of Wight or about the size of the Bronx. It occupies a strategic position at the turning-point for shipping on the shortest sea route between the Indian Ocean and the South China Sea. It is separated from Malaysia by the narrow Strait of Johor, but the two are linked by a 1.2 km-long causeway. To the south, Singapore is separated from the north islands of the Indonesian Riau Archipelago by the Strait of Singapore, which has been a favoured pirate haunt for centuries. The country includes 58 other small islands, islets and reefs which lie a little over one degree (137 km) north of the equator. The biggest of Singapore's other islands are Pulau Tekong (18 sq km) and Pulau Ubin (10 sq km), both to the northeast. Singapore island itself measures 23 km north to south and 42 km east to west and has an area of around 600 sq km, although this is increasing thanks to ambitious land reclamation schemes. After 1961 large areas of land were reclaimed from mangrove swamps to provide the Jurong industrial estate. There has been further reclamation along the east coast and at Marina Bay.

Singapore's skyscrapers are mostly taller than the island's highest point, Bukit Timah Peak (Tin Hill), whose summit is just 165m. (The three tallest buildings are the UOB Plaza, the OUB Centre and the Republic Plaza which all rise to 280m.) Most of the island is about 10m above sea-level, although there are scattered undulating hillocks and ridges - such as the one ending at Mount Faber, where the cable car goes across to Sentosa. The hillier areas at the centre of the island are mainly made up of granite and other igneous rocks. The west of the island is composed of sedimentary shales and sandstones while alluvial deposits cover the east end. Singapore's foreshore provides a superb, sheltered deep-water anchorage, in the lee of two islands - Sentosa (formerly Pulau Blakang Mati) and Pulau Brani (now a naval base).

Climate

Singapore's climate is uniformly hot and sticky throughout the year, although the northeast monsoon, which blows from November to January, gives some respite. These 'winter' months are also the wettest. The average daily maximum temperature is 30.7°C which drops to an average minimum of 23°C. The hottest months are March to July; the highest temperature on record is 35.8°C recorded in April 1983. The coolest month is January and the coldest temperature recorded this century is 19.4°C. Relative humidity peaks at over 96 percent just before dawn, while the daily average is about 84 percent. Most Singaporeans prefer their air-conditioned microclimates to their balmy equatorial air and frequently catch colds from rushing between the two.

The haze

The stupendous fires that blazed across the Indonesian island of Sumatra and Indonesian Borneo in 1997 brought hazardous conditions to large swathes of Southeast Asia – as far north as southern Thailand. Although Singapore was less affected than neighbouring Malaysia where the Air Pollution Index broke through the 'hazardous' 300 mark, even here the air became unpleasant to breathe. Rosemary Richter reported from Singapore that the experience of breathing the polluted air was like "inhaling hot cotton wool fibres" and "living inside a wet blanket redolent of a refuse tip". Other correspondents noted the bitter smell, oppressive darkness and watering eyes.

What may be remarkable to many Westerners was the time it took before the politics of blame took hold. Criticism from Singapore and Malaysia, the two countries most affected after Indonesia, was astonishingly muted. It was the media in the two countries, chivvied on by an irate public making their feelings known through newspaper letter columns and radio talk shows, that encouraged the governments of Singapore and Malaysia to take a more forthright stance. Warren Fernandez in Singapore's Straits Times *wrote at the peak of the crisis that it was time to put aside Asean's usual chumminess: "This will entail their being able to set aside traditional inhibitions – diplomatic niceties, worries about national sensitivities, the so-called 'Asean-way' of not interfering in each other's affairs – to take steps to deal with a common problem that transcends national borders".*

The Indonesian government argued that the ultimate cause of the fires was linked to the periodic droughts associated with changes in the El Niño Southern Oscillation, off Peru. But critics pointed the finger of blame at the lax forest management policies of the Indonesian government and the cronyism endemic in the logging industry there.

In normal years the fires come to an end with the onset of the rainy season in Sumatra and Kalimantan towards the latter months of each year. But in 1997 the rains did not come and the fires were already raging again in early 1998. In April there were reports that an area of forest three times the area of England was threatened with destruction. Professor Klaus Topver, the head of the UN action team set up to deal with the fires, said: "I would describe this as one of the worst environmental disasters of the last decade of the century". The Worldwide Fund for Nature put the cost of haze-related damage during 1997 at US$4.5bn.

It rains throughout the year, but the northeast monsoon brings the most prolonged downpours. The average annual rainfall is 2,369 millimetres; the wettest month is December, with an average of 277mm and the driest is July with 159 millimetres. The most rain ever recorded in a single day fell on 2 December 1978, when Singapore received 512 millimetres of rain. Sometimes it rains for several days continuously and on these occasions there is often serious flooding. Between monsoons, from April to November, there are regular pre-dawn thunderstorms which strike with frightening intensity three or four times a month; they are called Sumatras. Dramatic thunderstorms are fairly common at other times of year too; Singapore has an average of 180 lightning days a year. The sunniest month is February and the cloudiest, December.

Flora and fauna

When Stamford Raffles first arrived, Singapore was blanketed in dense jungle and skirted by mangroves. An 1825 account of Bukit Timah (in the centre of the island), which appeared in the *Singapore Chronicle*, gives a graphic impression of what Singapore must have been like in those days. "Bukit Timah, although not above

lower power

he Vanda Miss Joaquim orchid was amed after an Armenian woman, Agnes oaquim, who found the orchid – a atural hybrid' – growing in her garden in 893 and presented it to the Botanic ardens. In 1981 it was chosen as ngapore's national flower and then became the motif on Singapore's national costume – the flowery shirts sported by politicians. The purple and white orchid is on sale in all Singapore florists and can also be seen at the orchidarium in Singapore's botanic gardens (see page 95) and at the Mandai Orchid Gardens (see page 154).

even or eight miles from the town, has never been visited by a European, seldom y a native; and such is the character of the intervening country, that it would be most as easy a task to make a voyage to Calcutta as to travel to it." Originally the land was over 80 percent forested; but by the 1880s, about 90 percent of that had ready been cleared. Today virtually all the jungle has disappeared and 49 percent f Singapore's land area is concreted over. Many endemic plant species have sappeared too, including more than 50 species of mangrove orchid. Bukit Timah ature Reserve has 62 hectares of mature rainforest, however, and there is a total of .796 hectares of forest reserve under management - including 15 sq km of angrove along the north coastline.

Singapore is one of only two cities in the world to have genuine tropical inforest - the other being Rio de Janeiro in Brazil. Although few tourists come to ngapore to see wildlife, the tourism board is promoting ecotourism at Bukit Timah ature Reserve and at Kranji, MacRitchie, Seletar and the Upper and Lower Peirce eservoirs. All have areas of primary rainforest and contain more plant species than e whole of North America - a mere 45 minutes from the centre of the city. odern Singapore is a big, carefully planned landscaped garden. About 80 percent f its trees and shrubs are imported, however. Even frangipani - with its fragrant hite blossoms - was originally introduced from Mexico. Bougainvillaea was nported from South America and the travellers' palm, so often associated with old ngapore, is a native of Madagascar. It is not actually a palm, being related to the anana tree and was introduced to Singapore in the early 1900s.

Merlions and tigers

espite the name *Singapura* - 'Lion City' - there have been no reported sightings f lions since the 13th century, when, according to the *Sejara Melayu* (the 16th entury *Annals of the Royal Court of Melaka*), Sri Tri Buana, the ruler of Palembang Sumatra) mistakenly thought he saw one while sheltering from a storm on the land.

"The King [Sri Tri Buana] then went inland for sport on the open ground at Kuala Temasek [the Padang] and they beheld a strange animal. It seemed to move with great speed; it had a red body and a black head; its breast was white; it was strong and active in build, and in size was rather bigger than a he-goat. ... Sri Tri Buana inquired of all those who were with him, 'What beast is that?' But no one knew. Then Demang Lebar Daun said, 'Your Highness, I have heard it said that in ancient times it was a lion that had that appearance. I think that what we saw must have been a lion [Singha] ...' ...Singhapura became a great city, to which foreigners resorted in great numbers, so that the fame of the city and its greatness spread throughout the world".

lany of Singapore's bigger mammals and more exotic species have long-since isappeared, along with their habitat. The largest mammal still surviving in the vild' - other than the ubiquitous human - is the wild pig (found on Pulau Ubin and ulau Tekong).

Man-eating tigers provoked a national emergency in 1855 and created a furore in the *Raffles Hotel* in 1902; but the last wild tiger was shot in Singapore by a Mr Ong Kim Hong in October 1930. Sambar deer, barking deer, wild boars and wild cats, which were once common, have all now gone. But flying lemurs (*Cynocephalus cariegatus*), flying squirrels (*Callosciurus notatus* and *Sandasciurus tenuis*), flying lizards and flying foxes still inhabit the protected forests where there are also small populations of mouse deer, porcupines and pangolins (scaly anteaters). Singapore also has many reptiles - the most common being lizards and snakes - but there are also crocodiles, whose fertilized eggs have been found in Seletar Reservoir. In 1989 a Thai construction worker was bitten by one while fishing. More than 300 bird species have been recorded in Singapore; the government has established a small bird sanctuary in mangrove swamps at Sungei Buloh (near Lim Chu Kang on the north coast) where there are many migratory birds.

Art and architecture

Among the first things a visitor notices on arrival in Singapore - indeed even before arrival, on the final approach to Changi International Airport - are the towering modern high-rise buildings. Many of these are public Housing Development Board (HDB) blocks, but there are countless luxury condominium developments and, in the city, huge office towers. The rush to modernize the city skyline and clear the urban slums resulted in what is now dubbed the 'architectural holocaust' of the 1960s and 1970s. When Singapore's older colonial buildings fell into disrepair, and the old shophouses had become squalid, decaying wrecks, they were demolished, instead of being gutted and restored. Other old buildings - perhaps most notably, the Raffles Institution - were torn down to make way for gleaming skyscrapers.

Public housing

That Singapore at independence was a squalid place, where a large number of people lived unhealthy lives in cramped conditions with poor sanitation is beyond question. The Housing Development Board (HDB) was established soon afterwards to deal with the problem and is a model of its type: between 1960 and 1990, 630,000 apartments were built and today 86 percent of the Republic's population live in HDB housing. They are still being built at a rate of 30,000 a year. Over time, though, the HDB's building rationale has changed. To begin with it was a case of building cheap, basic accommodation as quickly as possible. Almost all these original developments have since been torn down, although a few older HDB blocks are used to house Singapore's army of guest workers. As Singapore's population has become more and more affluent, the HDB has moved increasingly upmarket. Its mission is now to meet the needs and aspirations of a population which is one of the best paid in Asia.

Conservation and the Urban Redevelopment Authority

However, the HDB building frenzy did have one side effect which only the luxury of affluence revealed. During the 1980s the government began to realize that in tearing down the squalid it was also tearing down the old. The turning point came with the impending demolition of the Raffles Institution set up by Sir Stamford Raffles in 1823. Perhaps not coincidentally, Lee Kuan Yew was educated here between 1936 and 1939. Just before it was too late - but not for the Raffles Institution - the Urban Redevelopment Authority (URA) was set up to identify and gazette buildings of historic and architectural value. In one of its pamphlets the URA intones: "A nation must have a memory to give it a sense of cohesion, continuity and identity. A sense of a common history is what provides the links to hold together a people who came from the four corners of the earth". It is typically Singaporean that the preservation of the island's architectural heritage is primarily justified not on artistic grounds, but as an exercise in nation-building.

Since the URA was established, great effort has been put into restoring shophouses to their former glory. By 1996 the URA had gazetted 5,320 buildings in 10 different areas of the city for conservation. These included four separate areas of

Chinatown, the former Malay quarter of Kampong Glam, Little India and several of the quays along the Singapore River. Among the buildings declared national monuments are many old churches, temples, mosques, markets and even hotels (notably the *Raffles Hotel* - see page 73 - and the *Goodwood Park Hotel*). About a quarter of the 5,000-odd listed buildings have so far been renovated and given that shophouses are changing hands for up to S$2 million, there seems to be money and profit in climbing aboard the architectural aesthetes' bandwagon.

Museum-izing Singapore

To the cursory observer, Singapore is doing much to restore the past and to protect the architecturally valuable. Some conservationists, however, argue that this rush to renovate and conserve Singapore's fast-disappearing architectural heritage is surface treatment. The façades may have been restored, but the interiors are ripped out in the interests of efficiency and economy. (The URA stipulates that the original façade and roof form must be preserved, but the interior can be changed.) The former functions of the buildings as brothels, warehouses and trading emporia are lost from view as advertising agencies, fancy restaurants and trendy bars take over. To the purist, this is Micky Mouse restoration for the Singapore yuppie who likes to sip beer in tasteful surroundings. Other renovation efforts have notably lacked even good taste. The Convent of the Holy Infant Jesus on Victoria Street is a classic example: it has been renovated and turned into a shopping complex - CHIJMES - with 70 retail units. (Plans to turn the chapel into a disco were abandoned.) Nor do all gazetted buildings have a copper-bottomed guarantee of protection. In March 1993, a contractor demolished a pre-war row of shophouses - earmarked by the URA for conservation - 'by mistake'. His defence was that because he could not read English, he could not understand the URA's plans or instructions. He was fined S$2,000.

Singapore is being 'museumized' or 'spectacle-ized'; it is becoming a showcase. Boat Quay, Bugis Street, Lau Pa Sat (Telok Ayer) Market, Clarke Quay - all these historic places, having been turned into conservation areas, and turned over to new owners and functions, have had their historical links severed. Heritage and history are being manipulated and transformed. Radicals would say that this is ideologically driven, and that it cannot be divorced from what the government would like Singaporeans (and visitors) to think about themselves and about their roots. Brenda Yeoh and Lily Kong, two geographers at the National University of Singapore, wrote in a paper in 1994 that:

> *"The re-creation of the past in a place gives the state the opportunity to filter out what it deems undesirable and to retain what it considers beneficial to cultivating a sense of cohesion and national identity. History is thus recycled as nostalgia."*

Koh-Lim Wen Gin, the Urban Redevelopment Authority's director of conservation and urban design, has accused the architectural 'purists' who have criticized the URA's efforts, as simply living in Wonderland. As she points out, to have returned the warehouses and godowns of Boat Quay back into places to store rubber and rice is patently barmy. The companies that have invested in renovating this previously run-down area must be given some latitude when it comes to deciding on their use and this will be driven by that use which yields the highest return. Defenders of the policy also point out that few 'ordinary' people - who were the original residents of these shophouses - wish to live there, even if they could afford the sky-high rents. Times have moved on, the people have moved on and out to HDB developments, and the notion that these buildings could be restored not just to their former glory but also to their former use does not stand up to scrutiny.

Colonial architects

The first architect to make an impression on Singapore was the Irishman **George Coleman**. He was employed first by Raffles as a town planning consultant in Batavia (now Jakarta), but in 1826 moved to Singapore to take up the position of Town Surveyor. The beautiful little Armenian Church (see page), Caldwell House and Maxwell House (now Parliament House) were all built to his specifications. His own fine villa was sadly demolished in 1969 to make way for the *Peninsula Hotel*, but the road retains his name. Coleman skilfully adapted the Palladian style of architecture to suit the tropical climate - Doric columns, high ceilings, open floor plans and wide verandahs to provide relief from the heat. In addition to his building programme, Coleman oversaw the draining of the marshes and created the network of roads which is still evident today.

Following Coleman's death in 1844, **John Thomson** became Town Surveyor. He continued where Coleman had left off, embracing many of his ideas and in particular the tropical Palladian style. As Singapore became more affluent through the 1830s and 1840s many of the flimsy constructions that had been flung together in the early years of the settlement made way for more permanent brick buildings. St Andrew's Cathedral, and the Cathedral of the Good Shepherd both went up at this time, as did the Thian Hock Keng Temple and the Hajjah Fatimah Mosque.

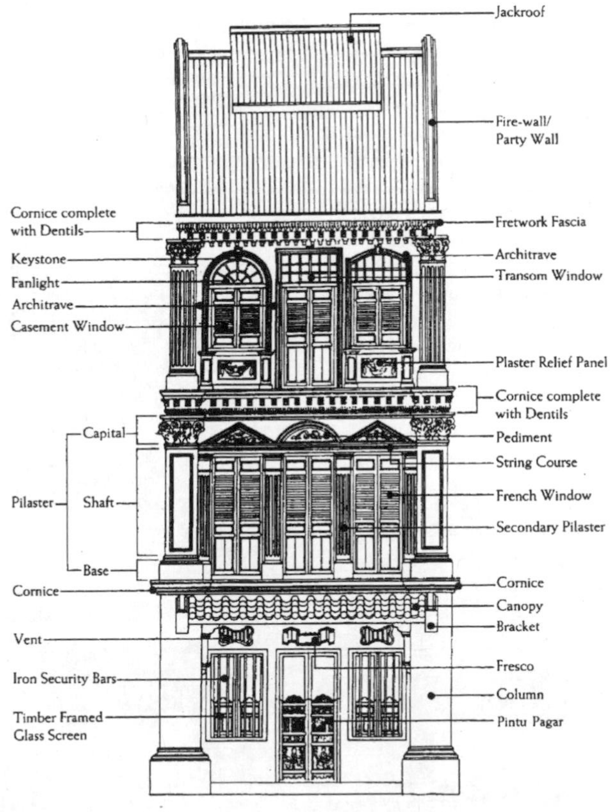

The shophouse: architectural features
(with kind permission of UAR)

Traditional house styles

The shophouse

The shophouse is the definitive Singaporean building. It was originally designed as a business premises with living quarters on the upper floors. The distinctive covered passageway - known as the Five-foot Way - was Raffles' innovation, and was created to provide a continuous covered pathway, offering shelter from the rain.

Chinatown, Little India and Arab Street all have their idiosyncratic shophouse styles, with the Arab Street buildings being the most flamboyant. The Chinatown styles are described and illustrated below and the Indian varieties in a box describing a walking tour of Little India on page 106. Although there are important differences between these various shophouse styles, the adoption of classical elements on the façades remained consistent, additional ornamentation becoming very popular later on. Until the arrival of modern building techniques, the width of the shophouse was determined by the length of felled timber available. Shophouses were painted in pastel shades, reminiscent of the colours of the finely stitched kebayas, worn by Straits Chinese women or Nonyas (see page 186).

The Chinese shophouse

The Urban Redevelopment Authority have identified five different shophouse styles: Early; First Transitional; Late; Second Transitional; and Art Deco. The **Early** style were built between 1840 and 1900 and are very simple in design with two storeys, simple Doric columns and very little ornamentation. The **First Transitional** is less stolid in appearance and in many cases boasts a third storey. In addition, there is a little more ornamentation, with the use of vents and some Chinese petal designs. However the most significant difference between the Early shophouse and the First Transitional is that the latter is significantly taller and therefore more vertically elongated. The **Late** shophouse, examples of which were built between 1900 and 1940, is much more fussy in appearance with three windows to each shopfront (instead of two). This reduces the wall space but made for cooler houses with better ventilation. Columns in Late shophouses are Corinthian rather than Doric and ornamental plaster "swags" decorate any remaining wallspace. Ceramic tiles were also used on the columns. The **Second Transitional** style dates from the late 1930s. The look is more austere, and although it retains the three window openings much of the ornamentation is lost. Perhaps this was a reaction to the flamboyant

Early shophouse (Nos 7-13 Erskine Road)

Late shophouse (No 21 Bukit Pasoh Road)

exuberance of the Late shophouse style or, perhaps, architects were starting to be influenced **Art Deco**. The style also dates from the 1930s and buildings in this style continued to be built into the1960s. Geometric elements were employed and many of these buildings had plaques dating them, which makes identification that much simpler.

The Peranakan house

The houses of the Peranakan or Straits Chinese (Babas, see page 186) were distinct from those of the Chinese. A traditional Peranakan house was long and thin. The first room on entering was the reception hall, where guests were received and the household shrine was kept. Traditionally the room was decked out with heavy blackwood chairs and tables set around the walls. Walking deeper into the house the next room was the ancestral hall, a private place where only close family and friends could enter. The ancestral shrine was housed here. As a family rather than a formal room, the mixture of furniture might well have been eclectic - a clutter of tables, chairs, photographs, portraits and mirrors. Beyond the airwell, there was a living room, where the family could relax and sit and create their distinctive embroidery pieces. Again, the furniture would have been varied with, for example, planters' chairs, Art Deco furniture and Chinese blackwood cabinets. At the back of the house was the kitchen (or *perot rumah* - the stomach of the house) and beyond the kitchen, the bridal chamber, the focal point of the 12-day wedding celebrations. The bridal chamber housed elaborately carved 'red and gold' namwood furniture.

The bungalow

Apart from the plethora of shophouses, there are a few remaining examples of one- and (later) two-storey bungalows. The word is derived from the Bengali word *bangla* or *bangala*. Bungalows were built by the British in Singapore and Malaya from the 1830s. The early versions were one storey affairs, raised off the ground on brick piers or timber posts to encourage the circulation of air. In general these bungalows were arranged on a symmetrical plan, with a front portico (*anjung*) and verandah (*serambi gantung*), high ceilings, a kitchen to the rear (the *kapor* or *dapor*), and servants' quarters separated from the main body of the house. Access to the house was by two external staircases.

Second Transitional shophouse (No 10 Stanley Street)

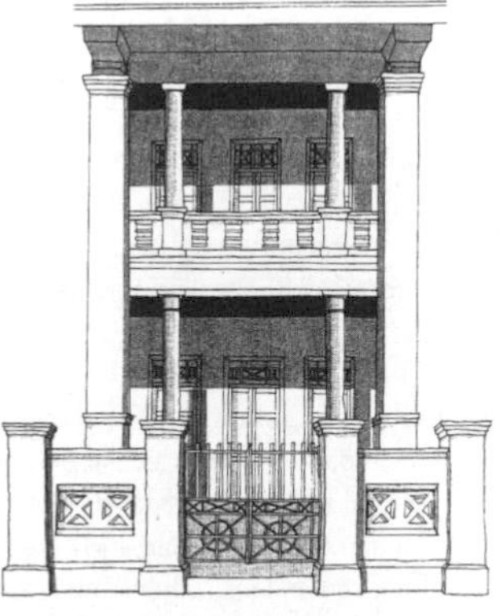

Art Deco shophouse (No 30 Bukit Pasoh Road)

The URA identifies five styles of bungalow corresponding (roughly) with five periods of construction. The simple **Early Bungalow** had its heyday during the 1860s and it shows clear links with British protoypes, though with various tropical adaptations including a verandah and timber or brick supporting piers. The **Victorian Bungalow** emerged in the 1870s. These were more solidly built, incorporating load-bearing brick walls, and were also usually considerably larger. Decorative flourishes became more pronounced with turrets, ornamental columns, iron work and fussy plasterwork. The beginning of the 20th century saw the emergence of the so-called **Black & White Bungalow**, named after the black exposed half timbers. This type of bungalow excluded all ornamentation and reverted to the use of a verandah encircling the house. The **Art Deco Bungalow** emerged in the late 1920s. This style saw the use of concrete, with classical motifs. The layout of the house changed during this period. With a greater emphasis on family living, the kitchen and the servants' quarters were brought into the main house. Both this and the final **Early Modern** style, which appeared in the 1950s, were strongly horizontal in design, sometimes with flat roofs and curved corners. Examples of these distinctive bungalow styles, combining European Classical, Chinese and Malay elements, can be seen behind Orchard Road and on River Valley Road.

Chinese temples

The Chinese temple form is based on that of a traditional Chinese house or palace and is a grouping of pavilions around open courtyards - this method of constructing Chinese temples has changed little over the centuries. Chinese builders are also bound by the strict principles of Yin and Yang, and the complicated nuances of Chinese geomancy or *feng shui*. To do otherwise is to court catastrophe (see below for further information on *feng shui*).

The entrance to a Chinese temple, or pagoda, is usually guarded by a step - designed to trip up evil spirits - a pair of guardian lions, one male and one female (the latter identifiable by the cub under her paw), and ferocious guardian-warriors painted on to the doors. The visitor or worshipper then enters a series of rooms and enclosed courtyards. The main shrine room will contain images of the Buddha (the historic Buddha), various Bodhisattvas (future Buddhas), as well as an array of figures from Chinese history and mythology (for mention of some of the more common see page 194). There will often be large sand-filled urns where joss sticks can be burned for good luck and sometimes side-shrines where images of minor gods and spirits - often local - are displayed. Many of the figures are contained within glass cases. Perhaps the most striking aspect of Chinese temples are the magnificently adorned roofs with their multitudes of figures moulded from clay and fired with rich glazes. Inside a Chinese temple there is often little of the hushed holiness of Theravada Buddhist temples or Christian churches and it is not unusual to find a janitor wearing shorts and a vest, puffing away on a cigarette while he plays cards with his cronies. Visitors need not take off their shoes as they do in a Hindu or Theravada Buddhist temple, and decorum of dress, so essential in a mosque, is also unnecessary. Outside the temple buildings there may be a large courtyard, also often walled, where ovens burn luck money and other offerings from the faithful.

Feng shui

A critical consideration in the alignment of Chinese temples is *feng shui*. Even in modern Singapore and in secular buildings, *feng shui* plays an important role in architectural design. This extends from the orientation of buildings right down to the arrangement of furniture and other aspects of interior design. *Feng* means 'wind' and *shui* means 'water'. Chinese superstition dictates that the 'dragon' must be able to breathe life into any building and that doors, walls and furniture must be aligned according to the principles of geomancy to prevent good spirits, wealth and harmony flowing out. There must be running water nearby too. If a building in

Singapore does not meet the *feng shui* criteria it is extremely rare for a Chinese to live there. All the big hotels and office blocks are designed with *feng shui* in mind; expensive alterations are made to buildings that do not have the required qualities. New buildings are also opened on auspicious days. The classic case of this was the towering OUB Centre in Raffles Place. Its construction was completed in 1986, but its official opening was delayed until 8 August 1988 (8-8-88), which translated into quadruple good luck.

Promotion of the arts

As part of its effort to transform Singapore into Southeast Asia's Centre for the Arts, the government announced a plan at the end of 1994 to invest US$300 million in a new arts centre. Construction is now well under way and the 'Esplanade: theatres on the Bay' project is scheduled for completion in 2001 (see page). This is unlikely to mean that the City State will become a centre for avant-garde art - the emphasis is more likely to be on mainstream artistic endeavour. Nonetheless, Singapore is not an artistic wilderness and some literature is daring and faintly subversive. For example, in September 1994 Philip Jeyaretnam published *Abraham's promise*, an excellent novel about a teacher whose life is ruined when he falls foul of the ruling party. It is hard to believe that the fact that Philip Jeyaretnam's father is Joshua Jeyaretnam, better known as the opposition politician JBJ who was bankrupted by former prime minister Lee Kuan Yew and publicly disgraced, is a coincidence. The book, though, has been published by a Singaporean publisher (Times Books), and it has been favourably reviewed - even by the *Straits Times*, which the novel caricatures critically.

Culture

People

"Probably at no other place in the world are so many different nationalities represented as at Singapore, where one hears a babel of tongues, although Malay is the lingua franca, and rubs shoulders 'with all sorts and conditions of men' - with opulent Chinese Towkays in grey felt hat, nankeen jacket, and capacious trousers; Straits-born Babas as proud as Lucifer; easy-going Malays in picturesque sarong and baju; stately Sikhs from the garrison; lanky Bengalis; ubiquitous Jews in old-time gabardine; exorbitant Chetties with closely-shaven heads and muslin-swathed limbs; Arabs in long coat and fez; Tamil street labourers in turban and loin cloth of lurid hue; Kling hawkers scantily clad; Chinese coolies and itinerant vendors of food; Javanese, Achinese, Sinhalese, and a host of others - in fact, the kaleidoscopic procession is one of almost endless variety."

Wright (1908) *Information for tourists.*

Population

Singapore's population
Chinese 77%
Malays 14%
Indians 7%
Others 2%

When Stamford Raffles first set foot on Singapore in 1819, the island had a population of about 150 - mostly pirates and fishermen. By the time of the first census, 5 years later, the population was 10,683 and growing fast. It included 3,317 Chinese, 4,850 'Malays', 756 Indians (Muslim, Hindu and Sikh), 74 Europeans, 15 Arabs and 16 Americans; there were also Javanese, Bugis, Minangkabau, Filipinos and Terengganu and Kelantan Malays. The Bugis comprised one fifth of the population in the 1820s, but they gradually merged with the Malay and Javanese communities. By 1827, due to massive immigration (see page 187), half the population was Chinese; by 1860 this had risen to 65 percent. At the turn of the 19th century, Singapore was the most polyglot city in Asia.

The island now has a population of 3 million of whom 77 percent are of Chinese extraction, 14 percent are Malay, seven percent Indian, and the remaining two percent belong to other races, including Eurasian. It also has one of the highest population densities in the world, with over 4,600 people per square kilometres. Because most people live in tower blocks, about 61 percent of the population lives on just 17 percent of the land area. Around 30 percent of Singaporeans are under 20 years of age, and another 37 percent are aged between 20 and 40.

Singaporeans

The government has worked hard to stop Singaporeans thinking of themselves as reChinese, Malays or Indians; it wants them to think of themselves as Singaporeans. The republic's 'ambassador-at-large', Professor Tommy Koh (who also heads the government think-tank) wrote in 1991: "The primordial pull of race dominates ... group identity, but for most Singaporeans, especially the younger Singaporeans, their racial identity is weaker than their group identity as Singaporeans. The fact that this has been achieved in 25 years is a remarkable example of nation-building." As Prime Minister Goh Chok Tong once pointed out, in the space of 25 years, Singaporeans were British subjects, Japanese subjects, Malaysians and are now Singaporeans.

Singapore likes to take Switzerland as its model, because Switzerland has a Swiss identity that supersedes the separate German, French and Italian ethnic and cultural influences. The difference is that Switzerland has been a confederation for 700

Population policies and designer genes

At the same time as encouraging Singaporeans to 'go for three' children to prop up the declining fertility rates, former Prime Minister Lee Kuan Yew also instigated the selective 'breeding for brilliance' campaign. This sought to mobilize the latent talent in Singapore's limited gene-pool. He promoted procreation among the more prosperous and better-educated members of Singapore society. In 1983 he warned that if something was not done: "Levels of competence will decline, our economy will falter, the administration will suffer and society will decline." These were ominous portents of the future but Lee's genetic engineering policy was very unpopular and prompted mocking disbelief abroad. Once, when regaling Britain's Princess Royal on the virtues of eugenics, she reportedly retorted: "Very interesting Prime Minister, but I can tell you, it doesn't work with horses".

The policy was officially shelved in 1985, but this did not stop Lee continuing to propound it. Lee himself got a double first at Cambridge (with a distinction) and his wife got a first; together they have produced highly intelligent offspring. He remains concerned that highly educated women are not having superior babies because of Singapore men's apparent 'immature' preference for younger, less-well educated girls. He said that Singapore's female graduates face "the stark option of marrying downwards, marrying foreigners or staying unmarried". Notions of love, even of affection, don't seem to enter Lee's breeding equation. He tells the story of a young, educated woman who came up to him and said: "'But Prime Minister, if a man wants to marry me for my genes, I don't want to marry him.' And I thought to myself, 'What a silly ass of a girl.'"

Singapore's drive to reverse its declining birth rate has had its amusing moments. Senior government ministers regularly attend baby shows and talk of procreation as if it were an industry. Meanwhile, the local press has continued to sing the joys of parenthood and the Social Development Unit – the government funded computer match-making agency – is forever dreaming up new schemes for getting people (particularly bright people) together. The head of the SDU – better known as 'Chief Cupid' – organizes discos, barbecues, computer courses and harbour cruises in the SDU 'love boat'. The SDU – which wags have dubbed Single, Desperate and Ugly – has 13,000 clients.

In 1991, 1,643 pairs of college graduates married, up from 704 pairs in 1984. More than half of male graduates now marry fellow graduates, compared with 38 per cent ten years ago. One of the hottest-selling books in 1993 was the Ministry of Community Development's Preparing for Marriage. Later, a Chinese-language edition rolled off the presses, offering tips on how to woo in the vernacular. The government is behind the matrimonial rush in more ways than one. Women have to be 35 or over to qualify for their own Housing Development Board flats. Marriage therefore offers a means of escaping parental homes.

More worrying than the SDU's efforts to get educated couples to marry and procreate was the Sterilization Cash Incentive Scheme launched in 1984, but now abandoned. Under this scheme, couples where neither the husband or wife had finished secondary school, could claim S$5,000 towards an HDB apartment if the woman agreed to be sterilized.

As if to underscore his residual angst over his breeding hang-ups, Lee raised the whole subject again in May 1994 during a tour of Australia. He said in Sydney that he regretted ever giving Singaporean women equal educational and employment status way back in 1960. He said the price for having a generation of highly qualified, confident female graduates, was that men won't marry them. It was a stinging condemnation of the Asian male who, said Lee, "does not like to have a wife who is seen to be equal at work and who may be earning as much if not more than he does. He is not wearing the pants. That is an enormous loss of face." Apoplectic Singaporean women graduates bombarded The Straits Times *with letters, saying Singapore ought to be proud of this achievement.*

years. Critics of the Singapore government have voiced concern over the 'Sinification' of Singapore and fear that in the long term, resentment in minority communities could turn Singapore into a Sri Lanka instead. The spectre of ethnic unrest, however, is far from being a reality. Today, Singaporeans are affluent and their prosperity has largely distracted them from ethnic prejudices. Even the Malays (see below) are, on average, better off in Singapore than they are in Malaysia, and the Indians have no doubts. Goh Chok Tong said in 1991: "So long as the economy is growing, there is plenty for everybody, I don't think people will fight over small things. But if the pie is shrinking, that will be the real test of whether we are cohesive, solid or whether we are fragile".

Chinese Historian Mary Turnbull writes that "as a largely Chinese city state in an alien region [Singapore] could not afford to build up a cultural Sino-nationalism. Its salvation lay in a secular, multi-racial statehood, encouraging communities to take pride in their cultural roots and language but conforming to a common national character." The government's efforts at forging this national character have been professionally stage-managed. On National Day every year crowds of cheer-leaders repeatedly sing 'One people, one nation, one Singapore' as if trying to convince themselves that they do have a national identity. But as the older first-generation immigrants have died off, the proportion of Singapore-born Singaporeans has risen, which has helped towards building a sense of nationhood. More than 80 percent of the population is now Singapore-born. Today, national pride is not in question: Singaporeans rarely tire of boasting to visitors that they have the best airline in the world, the best airport in the world, the busiest port in the world and one of the fastest growing economies in the world.

Baba Chinese Although it is common to read that Singapore is a (largely) Chinese city state, the Chinese population is not homogeneous in its origins. The four main dialect groups to set sail from China and settle in Singapore were the Hokkiens, Teochews, Cantonese and Hakkas. But before them came the so-called Straits Chinese or Peranakan Cina - popularly known as the Babas. The Peranakan Chinese are Singapore's - and Malaysia's - most distinctive group and were labelled "Straits Chinese" because of their association with the Straits settlements of Singapore, Melaka and Penang. Today, however, *Baba* is largely used with reference to the Singapore and Melaka populations. Tan Chee-Beng in *Chinese Peranakan heritage in Malaysia and Singapore* (1993) sums up the Peranakan identity in these words:

> *"The image of Baba is really one of both acculturation and cultural persistence, best symbolized by speaking Malay and practising or taking pride in Chinese customs such as 'old-fashioned' Chinese weddings. Thus the Baba identity is really an indigenized Chinese identity. The Baba experience is one of both being indigenous and being Chinese at the same time."*

When Peranakans began to be known as such is not known. Baba came into common useage during the 19th century and it is thought that Peranakan was already a well-established label at that time. *Baba* does not seem to be of Chinese origin but is probably derived from Arabic, or perhaps Turkish, roots. To begin with, Baba was used to refer to all local-born foreigners in Malaya, whether they were ethnic Chinese, Indians or Europeans. However before long it became solely associated with the Straits Chinese - and particularly, male Straits-born Chinese. Women were known as Nyonyas.

The cliquey Peranakan upper-class assimilated easily into British colonial society, following the formation of the Straits Settlements in 1826. The billiard-playing, brandy-swilling Babas, in their Mandarin dresses, conical hats, pigtails and thick-soled

Chinese immigration: Singapore's life-blood

Today, Singaporeans attach great social prestige to claims to be third or fourth generation Singaporeans. Immigrants flooded into Singapore from virtually the day it was founded and within months the local Malay Orang Laut population were outnumbered. The first junk arrived from Xiamen (Amoy) in February 1821. By 1827 the Chinese had become the biggest community on the island and by the turn of the century, they made up three-quarters of the population. The first Chinese immigrants came from the neighbouring Straits Settlement of Melaka. But most came from the south Chinese provinces of Guangdong, Fujian and later Hainan; the different dialect groups included Fukien, Cantonese, Teochew, Hakka and Hainanese. The Chinese were concentrated in trade and merchandising and agriculture (vegetable farming and pepper and gambier cultivation). They also worked as coolies.

Most immigrants were young men and a big prostitution industry sprang up to service them. As late as 1911 there were more than 240 men to every 100 women. Despite China's Ch'ing government outlawing emigration, they continued to arrive, driven by overpopulation and civil war. The new immigrants were known as sinkheh. *Most were illiterate and penniless; for their first year, while paying off the cost of their passage, they received no wages. Immigrant groups from different countries settled in particular districts, and were administered by local community leaders, or kapitans. But in the Chinese community, real power was vested in the secret societies.*

The wealthiest of the Chinese immigrant communities were the Straits-born Chinese (the Peranakans – see page 186), many of whom came to Singapore from Melaka, where their extraordinary Chinese-Malay culture had taken root in the 15th century. Most spurned Chinese-vernacular education for English-language schooling, and many went on to university in Britain. They were set apart from the sinkheh immigrants by their prosperity. Although they were among the first to arrive in Singapore, they only accounted for about a tenth of the population by the turn of the century. But they continued to make money in the tin, timber and rubber trades and were unabashedly ostentacious with their wealth.

By the early 1900s the transitory nature of Singapore's population was beginning to change as immigrants married, settled and raised families. This encouraged the immigration of more women. Immigration peaked in 1927 when 360,000 Chinese landed in Singapore. Three years later the government began to impose restrictions following the onset of the Great Depression. In 1933 the Aliens Ordnance imposed a monthly quota for male immigrants, which was aimed at balancing the skewed sex ratio. Politically, Chinese immigrants were more attuned to what was happening in China. In the mid-1920s a local legislative councillor, Tan Cheng Lock, began to call for elected representation for the Straits-born population on the governing council. Its local members were nominated by the governor. The first local nominee had been an immigrant Chinese merchant called Hoo Ah Kay (but nicknamed Whampoa, after his birthplace) who was appointed in 1869. Despite Tan's efforts to raise their political consciousness, the immigrant communities remained more interested in trade than politics until after World War Two.

shoes successfully penetrated the commercial sector and entered public office. Many became professionals: lawyers, doctors and teachers, although they were barred from entering government above the clerical level. "Strange to say," wrote Vaughan, "that although the Babas adhere so loyally to the customs of their progenitors they despise the real Chinamen and are exclusive fellows indeed; [there is] nothing they rejoice in more than being British subjects ... They have social clubs of their own to which they will admit no native of China." In Penang they were dubbed 'the Queen's Chinese'. Over the years they evolved their own Malay patois, and, in the 19th century, English was also thrown into their linguistic cocktail. They even devised a secret form of slang by speaking Baba Malay backwards.

The Peranakans of Singapore saw their futures being intimately associated with the British. They learnt the English language, established close links with the colonial administration system and colonial businesses, and even their newspapers were written in English rather than Chinese. Although they chose not to mix with immigrant Chinese, they retained a strong interest in events in China. The Straits Settlements provided a refuge for exiled reformers from the motherland – most notably Dr Sun Yat-sen, who lived in both Singapore and Penang in the early 1900s and became the first president of the Republic of China in 1911.

With the massive infusion of new Chinese blood from the mainland beginning at the end of the 19th century there emerged a two-tier Chinese community. The Peranakans were concentrated in the commercial and professional sectors, and the 'pure' Chinese in the manual sectors. But as the 20th century progressed so the influence of the Peranakans declined. Competition from non-Baba Chinese became stronger as their businesses expanded and as sheer weight of numbers began to tell. The Straits Chinese British Association (SCBA) was eclipsed in Malaysia by the Malaysian Chinese Association (MCA) as a political force and the Peranakans found themselves marginalised. As this occurred so the Babas found themselves the object, increasingly, of derision by non-Baba Chinese. They were regarded as having 'sold out' their Chinese roots and had become ridiculous in the process.

Today Peranakan culture is disappearing. Few Baba Chinese identify themselves as Baba; only in the Malaysian city of Melaka - and to some extent in Singapore - does the Baba cultural tradition remain strong. But although Peranakan culture is gradually disappearing, it has left an imprint on mainstream Malay culture. For example the custom among Peranakan women of wearing the *sarong* and *kebaya* has become subsumed within Malay tradition and has, in the process, become inter-ethnic. Baba cuisine has also been incorporated to some extent within Malay/Chinese cuisine.

The Peranakans may be the most colourful piece in Singapore's Chinese mosaic, but the vast majority arrived from China rather later, as penniless immigrants. They left China because of poverty, over-population and religious persecution. In the early mid-19th century, these newly arrived immigrants came under the jurisdiction of secret societies and *kongsis* - or clan associations (see box on page 105).

Secret societies made their money from gambling, prostitution, opium and the payment of protection fees. It has been estimated that 95 percent of prostitutes worked with the protection of secret societies. 'Donations' would be given by gang members while 'subscriptions' would be paid by non-members who happened to work in an area controlled by a particular secret society. Each would have its own turf and this would be defended to the hilt.

The first secret society in Singapore is thought to have been the Ghee Hin *Kongsi* and its origins can be traced to the Hung society in China. The Hung society was more of a political organization (they hoped to throw out the Manchus and restore the Ming Dynasty to power) than a criminal gang and the Ghee Hin *Kongsi* was, at least to begin with, just a mutual aid society to support new arrivals in a foreign land. It was also open to all dialect groups. It was only later that different dialect groups began to break away, the Hakkas in 1822 (Hai San) and the Hokkiens in 1830 (Ghee Hok). In 1879 secret society membership totalled about 40,000.

Malays The Malays in modern Singapore are considered a downtrodden minority, despite the government's stated efforts to build a multi-racial society. While Malay is still the country's official language, the Malays themselves have been subsumed by the dominant Chinese culture and they complain of feeling alienated in their own

Singapore's secret societies (c.1860)

Name	*Supposed strength*	*Dialect group*	*Meeting hall*
hee Hin	*15,000*	*Hokkien*	*Rochor Rd*
hen Chen Kow	*1,000*	*Teochew & Kheh*	*New Bridge Rd/ North Bridge Rd*
hee Hok	*800*	*Teochew*	*Carpenter St*
aisan	*6,000*	*Hokkien & Teochew*	*Cross St*
en Bing	*500*	*Hokken*	*South Bridge Rd*
hee Leong	*500*	*Hokkien*	*Upper Hokkien St*
ock Bing	*600*	*Hokkien & Hainanese*	*Upper Nankin St*
ng Bang	*400*	*Hokkien*	*Teluk Ayer Rd*
ee Sin	*1,500*	*Teochew*	*Java Rd*
ee Kee	*1,500*	*Teochew & Kheh*	*Beach Rd*
ee Soon	*1,500*	*Hokkien & Hainanese*	*Kampong Bencoolen*
hee Hin	*2,500*	*Hainanese*	*Honkong Rd*
hoo Koon	*3,500*	*Teochew*	*New Bridge Rd*
hee Hin	*4,000*	*Macao*	*Rochor Rd*

Source: Blythe (1969) The impact of Chinese secret societies in Malaya.

country. Malays have not taken to living in tower blocks - they are kampung people by nature - and within Singaporean society, they are regarded as under-achievers, particularly in business and finance, where the Chinese reign supreme. This becomes most obvious when an embarrassing fuss is made of Malays who succeed in the academic world or as professionals. Today Singapore's Malay community has a poorer academic record in school, a higher drug addiction rate and less economic muscle than any other community. Malay (and Indian) community leaders have criticized the government's 'Speak Mandarin' campaign as racially divisive.

Ironically, however, the roots of Malay nationalism, that led eventually to calls for independence from the British, were first planted in Singapore. In 1926 the *Kesatuan Melayu Singapura* (KMS), or Singapore Malay Union, was founded by the 'father of Malay journalism' Mohammad Eunos bin Abdullah. He was Singapore's first Malay legislative councillor and magistrate, having been educated at the élite English-language Raffles Institution. The KMS set up branches in the peninsula and was the forerunner of the United Malays National Organization (UMNO) which has been at the helm of the Malaysian government since independence.

Indians

Of Singapore's population, 7.3 percent, or some 220,000 (1996) are Indian. In 1824 when the first census was undertaken Indians comprised the same percentage of the populations (although their numbers were just 10,683) and Indians have always played an important role in Singapore's economy and society. When Raffles stepped ashore in 1819 he did so with 120 Indian sepoys and several Indian clerks in tow. An Indian trader also accompanied Raffles. To begin with Indian immigrants arrived under their own initiative from Penang, or directly from Sri Lanka or India. They took up jobs in the civil service, but also played roles as traders, teachers and engineers. Within 4 years of its establishment Singapore became a penal colony and several hundred Indian convicts arrived and laboured on public works projects. Many more, mostly from South India, came under the system of indentured labouring. This was banned in 1910 after widespread criticism of its abuses. From 1910 until the early 1950s, when controls on immigration were introduced, there was a continuing flow of

Kiasu and Kiasuism

From the early 1990s Singaporeans began to talk about the trait of kiasu *and* kiasuism*. The word comes from the Hokkien, the most widely spoken Chinese dialect, and means 'fear of losing out' or 'scared to lose'. In* Singapore state of the art *it is defined as a "pathological fear of losing even the most minute of advantages". As the cartoon character Mr Kiasu explains "Better grab first, later no more". This philosophy of life can be seen in action in buffets across the city. Plates are piled high with food, far too much to eat, yet the fear of missing something, of not having as much as the next person, drives the average Singaporean to defy gravity as they build their edifices of victuals.*

Mr Kiasu is not just scared of missing out. He is also brash, obnoxious and rude. Yet the cartoons are required reading in Singapore and the cartoon books – the first was titled Everything also I want *– repeatedly top the bestseller lists. Mr Kiasu is a commercial success. Companies use him to promote their products. McDonald's designed a kiasuburger – where the chicken pattie was larger than the bun (and even had extra sesame seeds): 1.2 million were sold in eight weeks.*

Even the government has embraced Mr Kiasu in road safety and other public service campaigns – while at the same time urging people not to over-load their buffet plates. David Chan argues, though, that kiasu means more than just a fear of missing out. It is also equals conformity; the herd instinct where if the person next door is rushing out to buy some electronic gadget then it must be good and must be bought, preferably several times. In the No[...] the Singapore song book *(see page 205) there is a song titled* Oh my kiasu, *sung to the tune of* Oh my Clementine. *It runs:*

Mr Kiasu, Kiasu King,
Scared to lose out, always must win;
Number One in everything!
Grab first; don't talk,
Always jump queue,
Help yourself to sample things.
Look for discounts, free is better,
Never mind what they all think!
Must not give face,
Winner takes all,
Hamtam [Singlish for pulverize]
everyone you know.
Take but don't give, hide the best things;
Get there first or else don't go!
Always quit while you are ahead.
Pushing helps to set the pace.
I want! Give me! First in all things!
That's the way to win the race!

migrants from the subcontinent. Today something like 80 percent of Singapore's Indian population are South Indian in origin.

Singapore, unlike all the other countries of the region, was an 'artificial' creation. There was no great kingdom, no indigenous civilization, no tradition on which the colonial power could build. As the anthropologist KW Kwok has put it, Singapore "was born into modernity". The cultures that made up the entrepôt initially looked over their shoulders to China, India or Britain for cultural inspiration. Gradually their children learned other languages and, arguably, a new Singaporean emerged from the formerly plural society. This is reflected in the government's emphasis on the 'four Ms' - multiracialism, multilingualism, multiculturalism and (clumsily) multireligiosity. The communities that make up the Republic are allowed to maintain their identity and distinctiveness, and each is equal to the next. But, individual identity is allied with the discipline of national interest.

New Singaporeans

Most accounts of Singapore maintain the 'ethnic melting pot' angle to the country's population. However, there is also a sense in which a 'new' Singaporean is emerging, one who is a product of the years since independence and who has been moulded into a distinctive personality. Philip Jeyaretnam, one of Singapore's most talented young novelists and author of *Abraham's promise* (1994), argues:

> *"... the true subject in Singapore is fear: of being thought different, of our true selves, of our neighbours, of those in power ... This fear has found its natural ally in materialism. The accumulation of goods has been both a bribe for political conformity, as well as the only approved outlet for expression."*

s a visitor, it is comparatively easy to see Jeyaretnam's views being played out on he streets, in the shopping plazas, and in the restaurants of the city. In the region, ingaporeans are often considered pushy and rude. Never a place to eschew a uzzword to support some public programme or other, the latest cry from the top s that Singaporeans should learn to be more 'gracious'. Graciousness, presumably, s meant to counteract the supposed Singapore trait of *kiasu* (see box).

eligion

Singapore's religious makeup

Buddhists 31.9%
Taoists 22.0%
Muslims 14.9%
Christians 12.9%
(Catholic 4.1%)
(Other 8.8%)
Hindus 3.3%
Other religions 0.5%
No faith 14.5%

ingapore can be viewed as a religious society to the extent that over 85.5 percent of the population aged 10 and over profess adherence to a faith. The majority of these follow one - or a combination of more than one - of the so-called Chinese eligions. Although the bulk of Singapore's Chinese population can be grouped under the loose heading 'Chinese religion', other religions have had a significant mpact. Of these, Islam has made the shallowest inroads among the Chinese although the Malay population as well as a significant proportion of Indians are Muslim) probably because it is hard for the polytheistic Chinese to embrace a trictly monotheistic religion, especially one with dietary prohibitions against the eating and drinking of pork and alcohol. Most important has been the influence of Christianity which has gained many converts, especially among the better educated. Evangelical and charismatic Christianity are particularly strong in ingapore.

hinese religions

Over half of Singapore's population follow what is usually termed 'Chinese religion'. This is an amalgam of Mahayana Buddhism, Taoism, and some Confucianism, all easoned with spirituality, mysticism and animism. But this is not to say that every Chinese worships these religions in equal amounts and there is considerable variation in practise, reflecting the influence of other religions and growing ecularization, not to mention the different traditions of the regions of China.

Buddhism

Buddhism was founded by Siddhartha Gautama who probably lived in Nepal between 563 and 483BC. He achieved enlightenment and the word *buddha* means fully enlightened one", or "one who has woken up". In the West, Siddhartha Gautama is usually referred to as The Buddha, i.e. the historic Buddha (but not just Buddha); more common in Southeast Asia is the title Sakyamuni, or Sage of the Sakyas (referring to his tribal origins).

Over the centuries, the life of the Buddha has become part legend, and the Jataka ales which recount his various lives are colourful and convoluted. But, central to any Buddhist's belief, is the fact that he was born under a *sal* tree, that he achieved enlightenment under a *bodhi* tree in the Bodh Gaya Gardens, that he preached the

First Sermon at Sarnath, and that he died at Kusinagara (all in India or Nepal).

The Buddha was born at Lumbini in present-day Nepal, as Queen Maya was on her way to her parents' home. She had had a very auspicious dream of being impregnated by an elephant, whereupon a sage prophesied that Siddhartha would become either a great king or a great spiritual leader. His father, keener on the first than the second of these options, brought him up in all the princely skills - at which Siddhartha excelled - and ensured that he only saw beautiful things.

Despite his father's efforts, Siddhartha saw four things - a helpless old man, a very sick man, a corpse being carried by lamenting relatives and an ascetic, calm and serene as he begged for food. The young prince renounced his princely origins and left home to study under a series of spiritual teachers. He finally discovered the path to enlightenment at the Bodh Gaya Gardens in India. He then proclaimed his thoughts to a small group of disciples at Sarnath, near Benares, and continued to preach and attract followers until he died at the age of 81, at Kusinagara.

In the First Sermon at the deer park in Sarnath, the Buddha preached the Four Truths, which are still considered the root of Buddhist belief. These are the 'Noble Truths': suffering exists; there is a cause of suffering; suffering can be ended; and to end suffering it is necessary to follow the 'Noble Eightfold Path' - namely, right speech, livelihood, action, effort, mindfulness, concentration, opinion and intention.

Soon after the Buddha began preaching, the Sangha monastic order was established. As the monkhood evolved in India, two things happened: it changed from being an ethical code of conduct into a religion; and it fragmented into two main sects - Mahayana and Theravada Buddhism. Nonetheless, the central tenets of the religion are common to both: the Four Noble Truths, the Noble Eightfold Path, the Law of Dependent Origination, the Law of Karma, and nirvana. In addition, the principles of non-violence and tolerance are also embraced by both. In essence, the differences between the two are of emphasis and interpretation. Theravada Buddhism is strictly based on the original Pali Canon, while the Mahayana tradition relies on later Sanskrit texts. Mahayana Buddhism also allows a broader and more varied interpretation of the doctrine. The Theravada tradition is more 'intellectual' and self-obsessed, with an emphasis upon the attaining of wisdom and insight for oneself whereas Mahayana Buddhism stresses devotion and compassion towards others.

Confucianism Although Confucianism is not really a formal religion, the teachings of the Chinese sage and philosopher Confucius (551-479 BC) form a central element in the amalgum that constitutes 'Chinese religion'. In essence, Confucianism stresses the importance of family and lineage, and the worship of ancestors. In Imperial China, men and women in positions of authority were required to provide role-models for the 'ignorant', while the state, epitomized in the emperor, was likewise required to set an example and to provide conditions of stability and fairness for his people. Crucially, children had to observe filial piety. This set of norms, which were drawn from the experience of the human encounter at the practical level, was enshrined in the Forty-seven Rules for Teaching and Changing first issued in 1663. A key element of Confucianist thought is the Three Bonds: the loyalty of ministers to the emperor, the obedience of children to their parents, and the submission of wives to their husbands. Added to these are mutual reciprocity among friends, and benevolence towards strangers.

Taoism Taoism is based on the works of the Chinese philosophers Lao Tzu (circa 6th-5th century BC) and Chuang Tzu (4th century BC). Like Confucianism, it is not a formal religion. Taoism and Confucianism are two sides of the same coin: the Taoist side is poetry and spirituality; the Confucianist side, social ethics and the order of the world.

The Asian way

Before the Asian crisis there were Asian values - or, sometimes, the Asian way. This was rooted in the idea that 'Asia is different'. Sometimes scholars and analysts would go so far as to intimate, like the international relations scholar James Teng, that "Western values appear to be set on a collision course with Asian traditions". For much of the 1990s, Asia enjoyed apparently miraculous economic growth while experiencing low levels of crime and other forms of 'social malaise'. While the experience of the West was quite the reverse. Commentators began to wonder whether Asia and the Asians had got it right. Was the West decadent and rotten to its very core?

Asian values – often thought to be Confucianist – are seen to embody such things as respect for elders and the law, hardwork, and recognition that the needs of society may transcend those of the individual. Nowhere has the Asian values thesis been more enthusiastically promoted than in Singapore. "A Confucianist view of order between subject and ruler", Senior Minister Lee Kuan Yew explains, "helps in the rapid transformation of society ... in other words, you fit yourself into society – the exact opposite of the American rights of the individual". These values are reflected in rapid economic growth, low crime rates, stability and rising prosperity. Unfortunately, or perhaps fortunately, this view of Asia, and of the Asian success story, is hugely simplistic.

First, Asia is so diverse that to talk about a single set of Asian values is nonsense. Even 'Confucianism' as currently presented bears little relation to the sage's The Analects *written in the 5th century BC. When Asian politicians try to summarize what Asian values are all about they risk descending into pronouncements of such crassness as to be almost embarrassing. There is a tendency to characterize 'Asia' as Singapore – an undoubtedly peaceful and prosperous place – and the West as the south Bronx. (Asian commentator Ian Buruma writes of Singapore as a "huge tropical boarding school", easy to police by the "nanny" state.) The reality is that the murder rate in Thailand is higher than in the US, countries like China, Hong Kong and Japan face organized crime syndicates that are far more influential than many which operate in Europe, and corruption is endemic in some countries. Ian Buruma argues that in some of Asia's authoritarian states murder, theft, torture and larceny are institutionalized: rather than individuals doing these things to other individuals, the state does it to those members of its population who resist.*

Although this does not mean that the Asian experience should be rejected out of hand as fraudulent, it goes to show that all is not roses in the Asian garden. Many Westerners would find life in Singapore constricting. As Buruma wrote, referring to the caning of American 18-year-old Michael Fay in Singapore in 1994 for vandalism, "the firm smack of discipline always sounds sweeter when it lands on someone else's bum".

Despite the claim that Asia is different, some Asian politicians are actively trying to prevent westernization occurring. At the end of May 1994, the Singapore parliament debated the Maintenance of Parents Bill which would allow parents to sue their children if they did not support them financially in retirement. As the Straits Times *put it in an editorial supporting the Bill, there is a danger that the younger generation "will grow up self-absorbed, middle-class and very likely, westernized in reflex. In that milieu, financial support for parents as a time-honoured tradition would whither". There are many other signs that Asia is not impervious to the social trends evident in the West: divorce, crime, drug addiction and so on are all on the rise, just as incomes, level of education and life expectancy are too. The Asian economic crisis has also landed a heavy punch on the Asian values thesis. For the Asian way was founded, at least in part, on the ability of Asia to achieve economic success. Now that the economic rug has been pulled out from under the Asian Way it is harder to offer it as such an attractive alternative. Nonetheless, the government of Singapore may have taken some comfort from a survey of 700 Singaporean schoolchildren which revealed that they viewed the most important values to be, in order, filial piety, honesty, responsibility, and self-control.*

Of all the world's religions Taoism is perhaps the hardest to pin down. It has no formal code, no teachings, and no creed. It is a cosmic religion. The inscrutability of it all is summed up in the writings of the Chinese poet Po Chu-i:

"'Those who speak know nothing,
Those who know keep silence.'
These words, as I am told,
Were spoken by Lao Tzu.
But if we are to believe that Lao Tzu
Was himself one who knew,
How comes it that he wrote a book
Of five thousand words?"

Yin-yang Central to Taoist belief is a world view based upon yin and yang, two primordial forces on which the creation and functioning of the world are based. The yin-yang is not specifically Taoist or Confucianist, but predates both and is associated with the first recorded Chinese ruler, Fu-hsi (2852-2738 BC). The well-known yin-yang symbol symbolizes the balance and equality between the great dualistic forces in the universe: dark and light, negative and positive, male and female. In *Taoism: the way of the mystic*, J.C. Cooper explains the symbolism of the black and white dots: "There is a point, or embryo, of black in the white and white in the black. This...is essential to the symbolism since there is no being which does not contain within itself the germ of its opposite. There is no male wholly without feminine characteristics and no female without its masculine attributes." Thus the dualism of the yin-yang is not absolute, but permeable.

To maintain balance and harmony in life it is necessary that a proper balance be maintained between yin (female) and yang (male). This is believed to be true both at the scale of the world and the nation, and also for an individual - for the human body is the world in microcosm. The root cause of illness is imbalance between the forces of yin and yang. Even foods have characters: 'hot' foods are yang, 'cold', yin. Implicit in this is the belief that there is a natural law underpinning all of life, a law upon which harmony ultimately rests. Taoism attempts to maintain this balance, and thereby harmony. In this way, Taoism is a force promoting inertia, maintaining the status quo. Traditional relationships between fathers and sons, between siblings, within villages, and between the rulers and the ruled, are all rationalized in terms of maintaining balance and harmony.

Chinese folk religions and mythology Chinese popular folk religion is based on the premise that the spirits of the dead who throng the heavens in countless numbers are controlled and governed by a judicial bureaucracy that mirrors the earthly bureaucracy of Imperial China. Multiple gaudy images of these officials - usually denoted 'gods' by most Westerners - are found in Chinese temples. Historically they may have been folk heroes, figures from Chinese mythology or history, or even emperors. They are imbued with divine powers and wisdom and these powers can be harnessed to bring good fortune, cure illnesses, or ward off evil. However, the gods are also sufficiently 'human' to become upset or annoyed by events and they therefore need to be assiduously cultivated and their egos continuously massaged. The 'gods' reflect life in Imperial China in another sense: a commoner couldn't possibly deal face-to-face with a real emperor and the same is true of haughty celestial emperors. This is where the cosmic officials come in: they act as go-betweens, conveying the wishes of earthly worshippers to the emperors.

Emperor gods There are two groups of emperor gods worshipped in Chinese temples. First, there are the figures from Chinese mythology. These include the Three Mythical Sage Emperors, Fu Xi (the Emperor of Heaven), Shen Nong (the Emperor of Earth) and

Huang Di (the Emperor of Humanity). Fu Xi is said to have ruled China between 2953 and 2838 BC and brought order to a chaotic world. He was effectively the foundation emperor of China, socializing the people of the kingdom. Shen Nong took over from Fu Xi in 2838 BC and reigned for an improbable 140 years until 2698 BC. Shen Nong's reputation lies in his agricultural abilities and he is regarded as the patron god of farmers. For the record, Shen Nong is also the patron god of herbalists, potters, restauranteurs and dung dealers. Fu Xi and Shen Nong are usually depicted as clean-shaven Oriental cavemen, crouching down on rocks with unkempt hair (or bald) and dressed in skirts of leaves. They sometimes have a scar running down the middle of their heads and often two protrusions as if horns are about to burst through their skulls.

Huang Di is also known as the Yellow Emperor and he gained the throne after Shen Nong's death in 2698 BC. He reigned for a comparatively modest 101 years - until 2597 BC. He is also reputed to have imbibed the elixir of everlasting life after the vital essence of no less than 1,200 women had been distilled into a peculiarly effective high proof drug. This gave him the time to create a whole host of useful inventions from the compass to the wheeled-vehicle. Fortunately for China's womanhood he died before the country had been completely depopulated of females. Huang Di is usually represented wearing rich, gilded clothes, usually with a flat-topped crown, and a beaded veil hanging down over his eyes.

Fu, Shen and Huang were succeeded by a second group of rulers known as the Three Emperors from the Dawn of History - Shun, Yao and Yu. The first two are men of myth and legend but Yu is probably a historic figure, the first emperor of the Xia Dynasty, coming to the throne in 2202 BC and ruling for just 8 years. In Chinese temples they are usually grouped together as the Three Rulers. Of the three, Yu is the most important and he is usually depicted bearded, sitting on a throne, and holding two stone tablets, one in each arm, looking rather like an Oriental Moses.

In addition to these emperors from Chinese mythology, temples also contain images of dynastic emperors from Chinese history. These are many and varied and date from the dawn of Chinese history through to the 20th century. Although Mao Zedong and Chiang Kai-shek have not been deified they are 'worshipped' in mainland China and Taiwan respectively. The importance of these emperors is that they can bestow gifts or good fortune on supplicants.

The forebears of the majority of Chinese in Singapore (and Malaysia) came from southern China, particularly Fukien and Guangdong provinces, and the brand of religion practised in Singapore shows clear links with this region of China. One of the most characteristic aspects of Chinese religion in Singapore is the custom of *chih poeh* - divination using bamboo or wooden spatulas. It is thought that this custom originated during the Han or T'ang dynasties when coins were used instead of sticks.

Islam

Islam is practised by virtually all Malays as well as many Indians - in total, Muslims comprise 15 percent of Singapore's population. Singaporean Muslims are under the authority of the Majlis Ugama Islam Singapura (MUIS), the Islamic Religious Council of Singapore, which advises the government on all matters Islamic.

Living by the Prophet: the practice of Islam

Islam is an Arabic word meaning 'submission to God'. As Muslims often point out, it is not just a religion but a total way of life. The main Islamic scripture is the Koran or Quran, the name being taken from the Arabic *al-qur'an* or 'the recitation'. Most scholars are agreed that the Koran was partially written by the Prophet Mohammad. In addition to the Koran there are the hadiths, from the Arabic word *hadith* meaning 'story', which tell of the Prophet's life and works. These represent the second most important body of scriptures.

The practice of Islam is based upon five central tenets, known as the Pillars of Islam: Shahada (profession of faith), Salat (worship), Zakat (charity), saum (fasting) and Haj (pilgrimage). The mosque is the centre of religious activity. The two most important mosque officials are the *imam* or leader and the *khatib* or preacher - who delivers the Friday sermon.

The Shahada is the confession, and lies at the core of any Muslim's faith. It involves reciting, sincerely, two statements: "There is no god, but God", and "Mohammad is the Messenger [Prophet] of God". A Muslim will do this at every Salat. This is the daily prayer ritual which is performed five times a day, at sunrise, midday, mid-afternoon, sunset and at night. There is also the important Friday noon worship. The Salat is performed by a Muslim bowing and then prostrating himself in the direction of Mecca. The faithful are called to worship by a mosque official. Beforehand, a worshipper must wash to ensure ritual purity. The Friday midday service is performed in the mosque and includes a sermon given by the khatib.

A third essential element of Islam is Zakat - charity or alms-giving. A Muslim is supposed to give up his 'surplus' and through time this took on the form of a tax levied according to the wealth of the family.

The fourth pillar of Islam is saum or fasting. The daytime month-long fast of Ramadan is a time of contemplation, worship and piety - the Islamic equivalent of Lent. Muslims are expected to read one-thirtieth of the Koran each night. Muslims who are ill or on a journey have dispensation from fasting, but otherwise they are only permitted to eat during the night until "so much of the dawn appears that a white thread can be distinguished from a black one".

The Haj or Pilgrimmage to the holy city of Mecca in Saudi Arabia is required of all Muslims once in their lifetime if they can afford - and are physically able - to make the journey. It is restricted to a certain time of the year, beginning on the eighth day of the Muslim month of Dhu-l-Hijja. Men who have been on the Haj are given the title Haji, and women hajjah.

The Koran also advises on a number of other practices and customs. In particular there are prohibitions on usury, the eating of pork, the taking of alcohol, and gambling. The use of the veil is becoming de rigeur in Brunei and increasingly in Malaysia. The Koran says nothing about the need for women to veil, although it does stress the necessity of women dressing modestly.

Islam in Singapore

Mohamad Shah's son, Rajah Kasim, was the first ruler to adopt the title 'Sultan', and he became Sultan Muzaffar; all subsequent rulers have continued to preserve and uphold the Islamic faith. The Portuguese and Dutch colonialists, while making a few local converts to Christianity, were more interested in trade than proselytizing.

On Friday, the Muslim day of prayer, Muslims congregate at mosques in their 'Friday best'. The 'lunch hour' starts at 1130 and runs through to about 1430 to allow Muslims to attend the mosque. Men traditionally wear songkoks - black velvet hats - to the mosque and often wear their best sarung (sometimes songket) over their trousers. Those who have performed the Haj pilgrimage to Mecca wear a white skullcap.

Christianity

Christians account for nearly 13 percent of the population, about 60 percent of whom are Protestants and Protestant 'fundamentalism' is Singapore's fastest growing religion. Christian missionaries arrived in Singapore within a year of Raffles founding the city.

Following the government's allegations in 1988 that the Roman Catholic church had been infiltrated by Marxists, the government introduced the Maintenance of Religious Harmony Act, which totally barred the mixing of politics and religion. It also introduced very strict rules regarding inter-religious proselytization. Evangelical Christians, for example, were banned - on pain of imprisonment - from any sort of missionary work in the Muslim community, which had been outraged by Christians handing out tracts and leaflets on Christianity. The bill also banned the teaching of any religion in schools. The government is acutely aware of the need to remain a secular state and is extremely wary of anything it perceives as 'fundamentalist' and as a threat to ethnic harmony.

Hinduism, Sikhism and Judaism

Hindus make up just over three percent of the population and the most important Hindu shrine is the Sri Mariamman Temple in South Bridge Road, which was built in 1827 (see page 108). There are some 20 other principal Hindu temples on the island. There are also eight Sikh *Gurdwara* (temples) and two Jewish synagogues.

Language

There are four official languages in Singapore: Malay, English, Chinese and Tamil. Malay is still officially the national language. English is the language of administration and business. This means there are very few Singaporeans who do not speak it - although Singaporean English (commonly known as 'Singlish') is virtually a dialect in itself (see page 37). Since 1979, the government has enthusiastically promoted the use of Mandarin - probably in the hope that Singaporeans who are bilingual in Mandarin and English will provide a bridge between the West and the world's greatest emerging market, China. Mandarin is increasingly being used instead of Chinese dialects. Although minority communities might regard the 'Speak Mandarin' campaign as evidence of Chinese cultural dominance, it is not uncommon to find even Tamil children in Singapore who are fluent in Mandarin. Today 46 percent of the population is literate in two or more languages. The main Chinese dialects still spoken in Singapore include Hokkien, Teochew, Cantonese, Hakka, Hainanese and Foochow. About 80 percent of Singapore's Indians are Tamil, but other Indian languages are spoken, including Punjabi, Malayalam, Telegu, Hindi and Bengali.

Dance, drama and music

The Ministry for Information and the Arts was created in 1990; it was immediately dubbed 'the ministry of fun' and is presided over by a senior cabinet minister. The intention is to make Singapore into a cultural and entertainment hub and no expense has been spared in bringing art exhibitions and top stage acts - theatre, dance and music - to the republic as well as promoting the arts within Singapore.

The Singapore Symphony Orchestra gives regular performances - including many free open-air shows in the Botanic Gardens - and the National Theatre Trust promotes cultural dance performances and local theatre as well as inviting international dance and theatre groups to Singapore.

Traditional Chinese street operas (*wayang*) mostly take place during the seventh lunar month, following the Festival of the Hungry Ghosts (see page 88). Wayangs are regularly staged on makeshift wooden platforms which are erected in vacant lots all over the city. To the sound of clashing cymbals and drums, the wayang actors - adorned in ornate costumes and with faces painted - act out the roles of gods, goddesses, heroes, heroines, sages and villains from Chinese folklore. Many professional wayang troupes are freelancers who come from Malaysia and Hong Kong to perform.

Modern Singapore

Politics

> *"If you like good, you've got to oppose bad. If you want honesty, you fight and kill corruption. If you want men with principles, you must destroy men without principles. There are no half-way houses". Former Prime Minister Lee Kuan Yew in the* International Herald Tribune.

In 1965, the newly independent Republic of Singapore committed itself to non-Communist, multi-racial, democratic socialist government and secured Malaysian cooperation in trade and defence. The new government faced what most observers considered impossible: forging a viable economy in a densely populated micro-state with no natural resources. At first, Singapore hoped for re-admission to the Malaysian Federation, but as Lee surprised everyone by presiding over one of the fastest-growing economies in the world, the republic soon realized that striking out alone was the best approach. Within a few years, independent Singapore was being hailed as an 'economic miracle'. Nonetheless, the government had to work hard to forge a sense of nationhood (see page 186). Because most Singaporeans were still more interested in wealth creation than in politics, the government became increasingly paternalistic, declaring that it knew what was best for the people, and because most people agreed, few raised any objections.

Singapore's foreign policy has been built around regional cooperation. It was a founder member in 1967 of the Association of Southeast Asian Nations (ASEAN) and has also been a leading light in the wider Asia-Pacific Economic Cooperation (APEC) grouping. Friendly international relations are considered of paramount importance for a state which relies so heavily on foreign trade and which, in terms of size and population, is a minnow among giants. Although Singapore continued to trade with the former Communist states of Eastern Europe and the Soviet Union throughout the period of the Cold War, Lee had a great fear and loathing of Communism. At home, 'Communists' became bogeymen; 'hard-core' subversives were imprisoned without trial, under emergency legislation enshrined in the Internal Security Act, a legacy of the British colonial administration.

Singapore's political stability since independence, which has helped attract foreign investors to the island, has been tempered by the government's tendency to stifle criticism. The media are state-owned and are so pro-government that they have become self-censoring. Foreign publications are summarily banned or their circulation restricted if they are deemed to be meddling in (i.e. critical of) Singapore's internal affairs. Probably because Lee Kuan Yew and the People's Action Party (PAP) have been so successful at bringing about the economic miracle, no credible political opposition has emerged. Politicians who have stood out against Lee's - and since 1990 Goh Chok Tong's - benevolent but autocratic style of government, have been effectively silenced as the government sets about undermining their credibility in the eyes of the electorate. A senior Western diplomat characterized Lee Kuan Yew as a 'traditional Chinese despot' to the journalist Stan Sesser, but did so in the positive sense. "He ranks with the greatest Chinese emperors", the diplomat said, but unlike those emperors wants to ensure his legacy survives him. Significantly, there have never been pictures of Lee plastered on government office walls. For 13 years, between 1968 and 1981, the PAP held every single seat in parliament. The London-based Economist Intelligence Unit says: "Opposition to the ruling party and its ideals of strength through economic achievement is welcomed in theory but not in practice. Those who criticise the government are, in such a small community, both visible and vulnerable." In 1990 the Committee on International Human Rights of the New York City Bar Association published a report on Singapore. It was highly condemnatory:

> *"What emerges from this review is a government that has been willing to decimate the rule of law for the benefit of its political interests ... Lawyers have been cowed to passivity, judges are kept on a short leash, and the law has been manipulated so that gaping holes exist in the system on restraints on government action toward the individual. Singapore is not a country in which individual rights have significant meaning".*
>
> (Quoted in Sesser, 1994:36)

The PAP: losing its way?

Through the late 1980s and into the 1990s the PAP did lose support, however, although it has always maintained a large majority in Parliament. In the 1984 election there was a 13 percent swing against the PAP, and support declined further in the elections of 1988 and 1991. The general election in October 1991 - which was meant to provide an endorsement for Goh's 'more caring' brand of government - saw the election of four opposition candidates to parliament, up from just one in 1988.

Perhaps another sign that the PAP was in danger of losing its way came with the country's first presidential election of August 1993, which was billed as a PAP stitch-up. Virtually all observers predicted that the result would be a foregone conclusion. In the event, the favoured candidate, former deputy prime minister Ong Teng Cheong (Lee Kuan Yew, despite much speculation, decided not to stand) did win, but he managed to attract less than 60 percent of the vote, against more than 40 percent won by his virtually unknown challenger, a former government accountant, Chua Kim Yeoh. Chua even adopted the novel electoral strategy of admitting that his opponent was a better man than he. As he did not actively campaign, analysts attributed his sudden popularity not to genuine support but to a protest against the PAP which had barred two opposition candidates from standing. One of them, J.B. Jeyaretnam - better known simply as JBJ - said the result was a 'clear rebuff' to the PAP. Singapore's most recent general election was held at the beginning of 1997 and some commentators were predicting a further erosion of PAP support as the republic's increasingly sophisticated electorate bristled at the restrictions placed upon them. This, though, is not what happened and Goh Chok Tong and the PAP won a huge - and surprising in terms of its scale - victory (see below).

Lee's succession

As Lee Kuan Yew came to be regarded as one of the region's 'elder statesmen', questions were raised over his succession. The PAP's old guard gradually made way for young blood, but Lee clung on until November 1990. Three months after Singapore's extravagant 25th anniversary, he finally handed over to his first deputy prime minister Goh Chok Tong. Lee, though, remained chairman of the PAP, and became 'senior minister without portfolio' in Goh's cabinet.

Harry Lee Kuan Yew – the father of modern Singapore

British political scientist Michael Leifer once described Lee Kuan Yew – better known as 'Harry' or 'LKY' – as "a political superman of his time, albeit in charge of a metropolis". The father of modern Singapore, who finally stepped down after 31 years as Prime Minister in 1990, believed he knew what was best for his country. Partly because of the Confucian ethic of respect for one's elders, and partly because his policies worked wonders, Singaporeans, by and large, assigned their fate to Harry Lee's better judgement. To western observers, Lee was variously cast as a miracle-worker, a classic benevolent dictator, and, in some quarters, as a tyrant.

However, by his own hand, Lee turned tiny Singapore into a by-word for excellence, efficiency and high-achievement. During his three decades in power, Lee built Singapore into a powerful economy, but his authoritarian style also turned Singaporeans – western commentators often say – into timid citizens. In 1991 London's Financial Times *wrote that Lee's laudable achievements had been "at the cost of creating an antiseptic and dull society". The* Economist *put it more succinctly, saying that "Lee ran Singapore like a well-managed nursery". He has been compared with a master-watchmaker who built the perfect timepiece, but could not resist the temptation of constantly taking it apart again and rebuilding it, to see if it could be improved.*

Harry Lee Kuan Yew was born on 16 September 1923. While his family was of Hakka Chinese origin, his parents were Straits-born Peranakan Chinese who had lived in the Straits Settlements for several generations. At home he grew up speaking English, Malay and Cantonese. He was the eldest son and was accorded all the privileges of a male first-born. In 1936 he attended the prestigious Raffles Institution. Even as a schoolboy, Lee was known for his aggressive streak and his domineering personality, according to his unauthorized biographer, James Minchin. In No man is an island *Minchin writes: "Since coming to office, Lee has tended to indulge his instinct to bully and demolish ... Within this dominant characteristic of aggression we may trace elements of rage, fear and self-aggrandisement".*

Although Singapore has been run as a meritocracy since independence, Goh is widely assumed to be a seat-warmer for Lee Kuan Yew's eldest son, Brigadier-General Lee Hsien Loong, better known locally as 'BG Lee' or 'The Rising Son'. BG Lee, like his father, got a first at Cambridge, returned to Singapore, joined the army as a platoon commander and within eight years was a Brigadier-General in charge of the Joint Operations Planning Directorate. During that period he obtained a Masters degree at Harvard and then in 1984, at the age of 32, was elected to parliament. The following year he became a cabinet minister and is now Deputy Prime Minister and head of the Monetary Authority of Singapore. But the seemingly inexorable rise of BG Lee was dashed by the announcement in May 1993 that Lee junior had made a recovery from cancer. In November 1992 he had been diagnosed as having a lymphoma. In a newspaper interview, his father said: "Singapore needs the best it can get. If Singapore can get a man who has never had cancer and who is better than [Lee Hsien] Loong, then that man is the answer. But if it can't, take the best man that is available." Significantly, Prime Minister Goh Chok Tong said the younger Lee remained his choice as a successor. In 1997 Lee junior was given a clean bill of health, compared with Goh, BG Lee can seem cold and stiff. His popular torch is virtually non-existent and, as a result, he doesn't receive a warm reception from the man and woman on the street. But then again, Lee Senior wasn't exactly a people's premier.

When Lee senior stepped down at the end of 1990, a new era began; it became known as 'The Next Lap' and the government-sponsored book of that title outlines

In World War Two Lee worked as a functionary for the Japanese occupying forces, but by the end of it he had become determined that Singapore should never again be ruled by foreigners. After the war he went to London (which he hated), and soon abandoned an economics degree at the London School of Economics. He was then accepted by Cambridge University to study law where he graduated in 1949 with first class honours. On returning to Singapore he set up a law firm with his wife but resigned as a partner when he became Prime Minister in 1959. Lee proved to be a shrewd political operator – characterizing himself as an 'Anglified Chinaman' – and quickly became known for his traits of honesty, efficiency, firmness and intolerance.

Lee was also known for his disciplined, austere lifestyle; he exercises regularly; he watches his diet carefully; and steers clear of anyone with a cold. One of Lee's most telling speeches, which gives some insight into his personal philosophy was given in 1973. He said: "The greatest satisfaction in life comes from achievement. To achieve is to be happy. Singaporeans must be imbued with this spirit. We must never get into the vicious cycle of expecting more and more for less and less ... Solid satisfaction comes out of achievement ... It generates inner or spiritual strength, a strength which grows out of an inner discipline."

Despite stepping down as Prime Minister in 1990, Lee retains the post of Senior Minister in Prime Minister Goh Chok Tong's cabinet. He is now Southeast Asia's best-known elder statesman. In the run-up to his 'retirement', Lee pushed through a controversial constitutional amendment allowing for Singapore's future presidents to be elected, rather than appointed. The next presidential election will be in 1999 when Lee will be 75. Whether he decides to run or not, few doubt that he will remain a forceful presence. In his 1988 National Day speech, the old puppet master gave his most definitive statement on his future intentions. "Even from my sickbed, even if you are going to lower me into the grave and I feel that something is wrong, I'll get up". Singaporeans joked that with his new threat of resurrection, the old visionary had begun to cast himself in the messianic mould.

the general directions of national development over the next 25 years. Goh promised to usher in a more open, 'people-oriented', consensus-style of government. Among his first acts was the creation of a new ministry for the arts and to underscore his faith in Singapore's maturity, he permitted the showing of blue movies, which proved very popular (see page 55). The rationale behind the new openness was to create a more cultured and less restrictive environment aimed at dissuading Singapore's brightest and best from emigrating due to boredom and concern about the country's authoritarian government. Goh's government heralded a more relaxed atmosphere; he made moves towards encouraging a freer press (particularly in regard to foreign publications), released long-term political prisoners and allowed ageing exiles to return home. But this evidence of a relaxation in government attitudes should not be regarded as a shift to Western-style liberalism (see page 204). Indeed, analysts have perceived a slight hardening of attitude as Goh's premiership has worn on. The way in which the PAP won the most recent election confirmed, for some, the willingness of the government to play hard ball to win the game.

The 1997 elections

Singapore's most recent elections were held in January 1997. The ruling PAP under Goh Chok Tong took 65 percent of the vote, up from 59 percent in 1991, and won 81 out of 83 parliamentary seats. Opposition MPs won just two seats, down from four. Prime Minister Goh, reasonably enough, took this as a massive endorsement of his style of government. He also interpreted it to mean a rejection of Western-style

Singapore's General Elections (1955-1997)

Date	*Winning party*	*% of the vote*
Apr 1955	*Labour Front*	*27%*
May 1959	*PAP*	*53%*
Sep 1963	*PAP*	*46%*
Apr 1968	*PAP*	*84%*
Sep 1972	*PAP*	*69%*
Dec 1976	*PAP*	*72%*
Dec 1980	*PAP*	*76%*
Dec 1984	*PAP*	*63%*
Sep 1988	*PAP*	*62%*
Aug 1991	*PAP*	*59%*
Jan 1997	*PAP*	*65%*

***NB** The elections between 1955 and 1963 inclusive were for the Legislative Assembly; elections for Parliament commenced with the 1968 general elections.*

liberal democracy.

Critics, of course, read the tea leaves in a slightly different way. They noted that Goh had made it clear that those constituencies which voted for opposition politicians would find their Housing Development Board blocks last on the list for upgrading under the government's S$20 billion renovation programme. They might also forgo other infrastructural improvements. With their hands firmly on their wallets, people voted for the PAP. This was classic pork barrel politics, a long and noble tradition in many Western countries. But it was not just a case of economic arm-twisting, as some publications in the West have tried to portray it. The divided opposition scarcely put together a convincing programme of policies and in a sense they did not offer the electorate a reasonable alternative to voting for the PAP.

Although it was never in any doubt that the PAP would win the election (opposition candidates did not run in more than half of the constituencies making overall victory impossible), those standing against the PAP nonetheless found themselves under sustained attack. Tang Liang Hong was portrayed as a 'Chinese chauvinist' and then found himself the subject of a slew of law suits - 11 in all - when he accused several PAP leaders of defaming him and, allegedly, lying. Shortly after the election, Mr Tang fled to Malaysia.

The PAP's massive majority in Parliament - holding nearly 98 percent of seats - vastly exaggerates the true measure of the government's support. This is because, like the British system on which it is based, the first-past-the-post system greatly favours popular parties. After all, although the majority of the population did vote for the PAP around one in three voters did not. Their voices are scarcely represented in Parliament.

Libel The lack of an effective opposition is also reinforced by the government's use of libel suits as a deterrant. The August 1997 libel case which pitted veteran opposition politician JB Jayaretnam, or 'JBJ', against the current Prime Minister, Goh Chok Tong, former Prime Minister Lee Kuan Yew, and nine other PAP leaders illustrates this nicely. The 11 ministers sued JBJ for announcing at an election rally in January 1997 that another opposition candidate, Tang Liang Hong, had filed police reports against certain PAP leaders alleging "lying and criminal conspiracy". This, they argued, amounted to defamation by innuendo. George Carman QC represented JBJ. He adopted a tough approach to the case, treating government ministers to withering and aggressive questioning. To Prime Minister Goh he stated "You pay lip service only to the full rights of democracy". "You say you believe in the principles of freedom of speech and freedom of the courts, but there comes a time when you adapt them for your own purposes to stay in power and stifle opposition." He also accused Goh of being "economical with the truth". The judge delivered his decision on the case at the end of September 1997. He found for the Prime Minister, awarding him S$20,000 damages. In July 1998 the court of appeal increased this to S$100,000. He also ruled that JBJ should pay 60 percent of the plaintiff's costs. JBJ claimed that he could not pay the fine and has no assets. If he is declared bankrupt he will be automatically barred from sitting as a MP. The decision vindicated Goh in the sense that he 'won', but the damages were only a fraction of

Criticism, libel and punishment

Scarcely a year goes by without Singapore's government trying to set down the limits of public debate. The trial of an American academic, Christopher Lingle, formerly a member of staff at the National University of Singapore, is an example of Singapore's attempt to deal firmly with those who cross the line.

In October 1994, Dr Lingle wrote an article for the International Herald Tribune in which he suggested that governments in some Asian countries use a "compliant judiciary to bankrupt opposition politicians". Although Singapore was not specifically named the Singapore government filed a contempt-of-court action, and former prime minister Lee Kuan Yew, a civil libel action. In December the International Herald Tribune backed down, offering an unreserved apology. Nonetheless, the contempt case was heard and the government won in January 1995. As the government has sued and made bankrupt 11 opposition politicians between 1971 and 1993 there could be little doubt that the piece referred to Singapore, even if not by name.

Tang Liang Hong, who stood as a Worker's Party candidate in the January 1997 general elections, faced no less than 11 defamation suits from various senior figures in the PAP. His crime was to have reportedly accused them of lying when they charged that he was a 'Chinese chauvinist'. Tang fled Singapore for Malaysia soon after the election, but his wife who stayed behind had her passport confiscated. Tang believed that Goh Chok Tong and Lee Kuan Yew wanted to 'bury him politically and financially'. (See page 202 for an account of the JBJ libel suit that resulted from Tang's accusations.)

It seems clear that the Singapore government will continue to pursue and attempt to punish anyone who crosses the line that they have metaphorically drawn in the sand. That Singapore is serious about such things is reflected in the number of international publications that have had their circulations restricted by the Singapore government due to some slur or perceived inaccurate report: Time Magazine, the Asian Wall Street Journal, The Economist, Asiaweek and the Far Eastern Economic Review. The government insists on a 'Right of Reply' and the alacrity with which the permanent secretary of the Ministry of Information and the Arts and other government functionaries send missives to various publications means that scarcely a week seems to go by without some defence, explanation or invective appearing in the international press. At the beginning of May 1995 a reader of The Economist had a letter published in the journal asking: "Why ... must you continue to subject the whole world to the ceaseless barrage of banal blather from the Singapore High Commission [in London]? ... If you caved in to every government as demanding and petty as Singapore's, the letters section would no doubt dwarf the rest of the magazine." Singapore's leaders have responded to their critics offering the challenge of a public debate. William Safire, a virulent American critic of the government, has said he will take up the challenge, but only on neutral ground: Switzerland.

those sought by the Prime Minister. Goh also found himself paying a portion of his legal costs. The case was widely covered in the media in the West. The *Economist* argued on 4 October 1997:

> *"... they [the PAP] might be wise to kick their litigious habit. It risks ridicule: would not the People's Action Party be better named the Libel Action Party, it will be asked? It is certainly unbecoming for a mighty government to break butterflies on the wheel, especially when there is such a strong correlation between might and right: no Singaporean leader has ever lost a libel action. Above all, it is foolish, because by stifling criticism Mr Goh & Co risk stifling useful debate and, in time, confidence and even investment."*

Salary games: the highest (legally) paid: politician in the world?

At the beginning of 1995 it was announced by Singapore's government that its top politicians would receive a hefty pay rise. Even before the salary rises Singapore's prime minister was receiving a pay cheque four times larger than the president of the United States, and seven times larger than that of Britain's prime minister at the time. With the 1995 salary hikes the differentials widened to seven and over 10 times. (Although Britain's Prime Minister received a large pay rise in Summer 1996.) Mr Goh's salary is a whopping S$1.5mn. In many democracies, it might be expected that this would lead to a public outcry over politicians feathering their own nests. In the debate in Singapore's parliament, the rise was justified in two ways. First, it was argued that good salaries are the only way to keep corruption at bay – such a feature of neighbouring countries. Second, that growing differentials between public and private sector pay was making it increasingly difficult to attract and then keep good people in place. As ever, the logic and the mechanics are, apparently, faultless. Ministers' salaries are pegged to the top four earners in six professions and then discounted by a third.

However, the government's own 'feed-back unit' reported deep voter dissatisfaction with the rises and the opposition leader Chiam See Tong quoted former US president Jack Kennedy when he remarked "Ask not what your country can do for you, but what you can do for your country". Prime Minister Goh and Senior Minister Lee Kuan Yew shrugged off the barbs, the latter asking, true to form, whether ordinary people were in a position to judge such things. Perhaps as a sop to public concerns, Prime Minister Goh said that he would forego his own increase for 5 years – leaving him with a comparatively measly S$1.1mn to scrape by on.

A kinder and more sensitive Singapore?

Coinciding with the introduction of Singapore's long-promised and more relaxed style of government, a cartoon book appeared on bookshelves in late 1990 entitled *Hello Chok Tong, Goodbye Kuan Yew*. The new cabinet was portrayed as a football team with former Prime Minister Lee Kuan Yew as the goal-keeper, shouting things like "Just try it!". The cartoonist was reported as saying that Singapore's 'glasnost', a result of Goh's 'kinder, gentler Singapore', allowed him to publish a book that a few years previously might have been beyond the pale. The former Prime Minister's son Lee Hsien Loong, was portrayed as the would-be striker on the team's right wing. The script reads: "Fans and opponents alike are watching carefully how quickly he matures in an attacking role ... Tends to over-react under pressure. Would do a lot better if he relaxed".

There have been signs that Singapore is easing up a bit politically, although following the republic's political tradition, Goh has been tough on anyone vaguely construed as a political enemy or perceived as a possible threat. Lee had assured the electorate that his successor would be 'no softie'. Goh has done his best to prove himself, saying he could be 'a little deaf' to people in opposition constituencies.

At the end of 1994, there was a fascinating exchange in Singapore's *Sunday Times*. In an article entitled the *Great affective divide* author Catherine Lim (see Suggested reading, page 59) criticized Prime Minister Goh for reneging on his commitment to a 'kinder, gentler' style of government. The Prime Minister's Office responded in true style, blasting off a reply stating that "A gentler, more open political style does not mean allowing crudity and obscenity to pass off as avant-garde theatre, or ignoring political criticism which masquerades as political expression." There are limits to the politically possible even in a more open Singapore. Allowing Ms Lim to write and have published an article is one thing; to expect a sympathetic and measured response is another. Prime Minister Goh welcomes "well-meaning people who put forth their views in a very well-meaning vay", but anything presumed to be snide or mocking would be dealt a "very, very ard blow from the government in return". In the bars and taxis of the Republic eople are a lot more critical than the rather colourless local media might lead one o believe. One joke doing the rounds shows the ability of Singaporeans to laugh at hemselves:

An American remarks to a Somali, a Ukrainian and a Singaporean that food seems to cost a lot of money in the city state, and asks their opinion of this state of affairs. The Somali replies, "What's food?" The Ukrainian demands, "What's money?" And the Singaporean quietly asks, "What's an opinion?"

Subversion, Singapore-style

iterary satire also now has a place of Singapore's bookshelves. In 1988 the sychological Defence Division (sounds Brave New World-esque, lah!) of the Ainistry of Communications and Information published a book called *Sing ingapore*. The largely inane songs in this official publication were to be taught in chools and transmitted on television and radio. As Dr Yeo Ning Hong of the Ainistry explained in the introduction: "Singing the songs [in this book] will bring ingaporeans together, to share our feelings one with another. It will bring back hared memories of good times and hard times, of times which remind us of who ve are, where we came from, what we did, and where we are going." *We are ingapore* gives a flavour of the lyrics:This is my country

This is my flag
This is my future
This is my life
This is my family
These are my friends
We are Singapore Singaporeans
Singapore our homeland
It's here that we belong

few years later, however, the *Not the Singapore song book* appeared to cock a aradonic snook at the original by borrowing some of the tunes and putting them o new lyrics. It represents popular resistance Singapore-style. *Count! Mummies of ingapore* pokes fun at Singapore's family planning policy:

We have the ova in our bodies,
We can conceive,
We can conceive.
We have a role for Singapore,
We must receive,
We must receive.

hen there is the *SDU March*, sung to the tune of *Colonel Bogey*:

Hey girl!
Why aren't you married yet!
You girl!
A man's not hard to get!
Now's the time for you to choose
your mate!
Don't delay! Do not procrastinate!

)ther subversive songs include *Babies keep formin' in my bed* (sung to *Raindrops eep falling on my head*), *Three Cees* (condominium, credit card and car), *Gold card lues*, and *Oh my kiasu* (sung to *Oh my darling Clementine*). As Lily Kong explains, ingapore's political culture does not permit overt expressions of dissent, so ingaporeans have to find alternative avenues for opposition. The *Not the Singapore song book* is just one of many forms of covert popular resistance.

To people from countries with long histories and a well-established sense of nationhood *Sing Singapore* may seem rather crass. But Singapore's leaders have always been worried that a country which did not exist half a century ago could be just as quickly and easily snuffed out. Senior Minister Lee, for example, has remarked: "There is no second chance for us". This is why the country's leaders got so agitated recently when a survey showed that only six out of 50 young Singaporeans knew that their country had once been part of the Malaysian Federation. This is why the National Heritage Board is so enthusiastically conserving historic sites and why Singapore's history is taking such a prominent place in exhibitions.

Singapore and the Internet

The conflict between control and freedom is being played out in microcosm in the debate over what to do about the Internet. Singapore, as government blandishments like to emphasize, is a place at the cutting edge of computer technology and the forefront of the information revolution. There is much talk of creating an 'intelligent island' where nine out of 10 homes are plugged into the Internet. In late 1996 there were twice as many Internet accounts held by Singaporeans (about 150,000, and rising fast) than by individuals in the People's Republic of China with a population 400 times larger. Yet by surfing the Net, Singapore's growing number of cybernauts not only show the world how deft the city state is at reinventing itself as technology advances; they can also read things about their own government and society that are taboo at home. So the government is faced with something of a dilemma: the Internet is the future/the Internet is destabilizing and corrosive.

They are responding in a number of ways. First, the Singapore government is trying to re-make the Internet in its own image by encouraging sanitized rebellion. There is, for example, a Board for On-line Graffiti where angry young men and women can scrawl faintly daring ditties without being hauled in front of the local magistrate. Second, they are hoping to encourage self-policing to keep the cyber-waves free of offensive material, whether that be of a sexual, religious or political nature. Third, Cyber Cafés are required to have 'Net Nannies' to maintain a 'Surf Watch' so anything deemed beyond the pale can be nipped in the bud at Cyber Birth. Moreover, net providers are held responsible for the content of the material that they channel while local political and religious groups have to register if they want to use the Net Waves.

The key question, of course, is whether the government can successfully keep something so anarchic under control. Sites in Singapore should be fairly easy to police; the ones based abroad, especially in the US, will be much harder to control. As Nicholas Negroponte, head of the Massachusetts Institute of Technology's Media Lab put it: "The Internet is a decentralized medium ... There is no head-end, hierarchy, or point of control. People who try to 'control' the Net don't realize this. They don't understand it is more like phone conversations than print publications." Anyone willing to pay the price of an international call to Hong Kong, for example, will be able to circumvent these controls.

Defence

Singapore spends more than US$2 billion a year on defence - over a third of government expenditure. It promotes the idea of 'total defence', meaning that everyone plays some role in protecting the country, economically and militarily. Regular emergency exercises are conducted involving the civilian population, which is designed to instill preparedness. This policy is probably influenced by memories of Singapore's inglorious surrender to the Japanese in February 1942 (see page 167). Men have to serve a compulsory 24-30 months in the Singapore Defence Forces, followed by annual 40-day training exercises for reservists, who undergo

ingapore traffic – no more for the road

ngapore has one of the highest ıtomobile densities in the world with 81 ırs per kilometre of roadway, against 43 Japan and 27 in the US. Yet its visionary rban planners have avoided the gridlock pical of most other capitals in the region. he country's first traffic control scheme as introduced way back in 1975. Between 975 and 1991 the speed of traffic in the entral district during rush hour almost oubled, to 36 kilometres per hour.

Part of this is to do with the CBD strictions, but more importantly, the overnment has ruled that the car opulation cannot grow any faster than he road network. Due to this policy, ngapore's cars are about the most xpensive in the world. There is a 45 ercent import tariff, a 150 percent egistration fee and an annual road tax nked to engine size. For an average-sized apanese car the tax is S$1,400. Even etrol costs substantially more than in eighbouring countries.

Because all this was still not deterring ingaporeans from buying cars, the overnment introduced a Certificate of ntitlement (CoE) in 1990, which ould-be car owners must obtain before hey purchase a car. These are sold hrough a complex auction system. Prices f cars vary each month depending on ow many people are bidding for them nd how much they bid. The government ets the cut-off price for each model ccording to the bids, and anyone below hat price does not get their car. In ebruary 1997 a certificate of Entitlement or a Mercedes E200 cost S$64,000, naking its total on the road price almost $250,000 (US$180,000). In addition, all new cars are now legally required to have catalytic converters fitted, which increases the price still further. And because Singapore does not want its roads clogged with old bangers, owners of cars which are more than 10 years old have to pay a road tax surcharge of 10 percent which rises to 50 percent on a car's 14th birthday.

The latest ploy is the installation of the world's first Electronic Road Pricing (ERP) system which came on stream in April 1998. Every car entering the central district has a sensor fitted into which a charged smart card is inserted. When a car passes beneath an overhead gantry a fee is deducted from the card. And should the card not be charged with sufficient funds then a picture is taken of the offending vehicle, and the owner fined. The cost of the whizz-bang electronics? S$197 million.

Has all this helped? In one sense, yes. Traffic moves more freely in the central district, even during rush hour. But critics highlight some unintended consequences. Some argue that because of the cost of driving into the city centre, people leave their cars on the outskirts, increasing congestion just outside the restricted zone. (The government disputes this, though.) Economists have also said that expensive inner city roads are now underused and are not being fully exploited. It also means that having invested roughly S$200,000 in a car with a government imposed shelf life, they drive it into the ground. The average car in Singapore is driven 20,000 kilometres each year - the same as the average car in the US. But the US is 15,200 times larger.

wice-yearly physical fitness tests until they are 40 years old. Being a predominantly hinese state in the middle of the Malay world, Singapore feels very vulnerable, and overnment ministers have expressed their fears of a 'Kuwait situation', despite ingapore's good relations with its Malaysian and Indonesian neighbours. The rmed forces are known to be trained by Israelis. Singapore is also the biggest arms nanufacturer in the region and is an entrepôt for the arms trade. The island is the enue for Southeast Asia's biggest airshow every February, which has become the egion's main show case for new civilian and military aircraft as well as other nilitary hardware. Ian Buruma, in his book *God's dust: a modern Asian journey* (1989), vrites of his fear in Singapore of simply being engulfed: "Singapore was an accident of history, like a bunny that popped out of the magician's hat by mistake. One sleight of hand and the bunny could vanish as swiftly as it appeared."

Singapore and its neighbours

Singapore is a member of the nine member Association of Southeast Asian Nation (ASEAN) and enjoys generally good relations with its neighbours. However, there have been times of friction, particularly during the mid-1960s when Singapore left the Malaysian Federation and had a diplomatic spat with President Sukarno of Indonesia. As a minute city state with a population less that two percent of Indonesia's, Singapore's leaders have always been acutely aware of the need to build and maintain good relations with its regional neighbours.

Even so, Singapore has not always managed to avoid offending its larger neighbours. This particularly applies to Malaysia, a country with which it shares a common colonial history, but from which it is divided in so many other ways. Malaysia's majority are Malay and Muslim; Singapore's are Chinese. Malaysia has a national policy of positive discrimination in favour of ethnic Malays or *bumiputras*; Singapore is a meritocracy. Malaysia is still a developing country, albeit a so-styled economic 'miracle' (at least until the crisis which hit the country, along with much of the rest of Southeast Asia in 1997 - see Economy, below); Singapore has a standard of living amongst the highest in the world. This makes for a fierce competitiveness between the two countries which disguises a lingering bitterness that some commentators trace back to the ejection of Singapore from the Malaysian Federation in the mid-1960s. Malaysia is quick to take offence at anythir that smacks of Singaporean superiority.

In 1996 and 1997 relations between Malaysia and Singapore sunk to their lowes level for some years. In June 1996 Lee Kuan Yew offered the thought that Singapor could, conceivably, merge once more with Malaysia. Two months later Goh Chok Tong seemed to use this as a threat when he warned that if Singapore slipped up, "we will have no option but to ask Malaysia to take us back". The Malaysian government took this as a slight. In their view, the prime minister was threatening the electorate with the possibility that they might be absorbed into Malaysia. During 1997 bilateral relations got even worse. In March, Senior Minister Lee Kuan Yew put his foot in his mouth when he suggested that the Malaysian state of Joho Bahru was "notorious for shootings, muggings and car-jackings" (this was in relation to opposition politician Tang Liang Hong's decision to flee there from Singapore). The Malaysian press and some sections of the government reacted wit outrage. The Youth head of the ruling United Malays National Party (UMNO) accused Lee of being "senile and uncouth". Singapore's Senior Minister apologized 'unreservedly' but the damage, so to speak, had already been done. Singapore's *Straits Times* then compounded Lee's insensitivity by publishing an article listing recent crimes in Johor - which Malaysians saw as a crass attempt to justify his comments. Just as this spat had run its course, the Asian crisis created further tensions. Malaysia felt Singapore was not doing enough to help the poorly economy of its neighbour across the Strait of Johor. In September 1998 Malaysia closed its air space to the Singaporean air force. Then, just a few days later, Lee Kua Yew published the first volume of his memoirs - a characteristically blunt and uncompromising account, particularly with respect to Singapore's expulsion from the Malaysian Federation in 1965. Malaysia's Prime Minister Mahathir was, as it is said, not amused. In Singapore, internet newsgroups were full of calls to boycott Malaysian goods and in Malaysia, during the opening of the 1998 Commonwealth Games, the Singapore team was booed.

Singapore at the end of the millennium

Singapore's political system fits no neat category. It is both democratic and authoritarian. This has led some scholars to describe the city state as an illiberal democracy and they point to three key aspects of the political system to support their case. First, the fact that the state is highly interventionist - it is an 'in your face' state where the government is continually meddling in people's lives and affairs. They point to the fact that while a liberal democracy is seen to be effective when it leads to a change of government, in an illiberal democracy elections are used to legitimate the rule of an entrenched government. Second, in an illiberal democracy the judicial system lays down rules for its citizens, while in a liberal democracy one of its key roles is to test and interrogate the state. And third, in an illiberal democracy there is 'democracy without politics'. The ruling party remains dominant and all-encompassing. Potential opposition is directed into specialized interest groups which operate under the umbrella of, and not against, the state.

Whether the People's Action Party will be able to continue to dominate Singapore's political landscape, as it has done throughout the period since independence, is a key question. There are certainly challenges which the PAP will have to confront. To begin with, social differentiation is making it harder for the PAP to please almost all the people almost all of the time. People's interests are diverging as Singapore's affluence grows. Second, there is the question of whether the PAP, in creating a 'thinking society' necessary for economic success, it is not also creating a society which will be more politically creative and combative. Third, and related, there is the question of whether the population will continue to accept such a low level of public debate. As Martin Perry, Lily Kong and Brenda Yeoh write in their book *Singapore: a developmental city state* (1997), the media in Singapore amounts to "little more than an annoucement service for the government". It is tempting to characterize Singapore as a totalitarian state. It is not. It may be authoritarian, but it is not totalitarian.

Economy

Singapore is a developed country - or so everyone from *The Economist* to Prime Minister Goh Chok Tong thought at the beginning of 1996. Although the nuances of whether Singapore can be defined as 'developed' or not may keep academics and journalists tapping away at their word processors, for most visitors the proof of the pudding, so to speak, is in the eating. With a per capita income of US$26,730 in 1995, higher than that of Britain (US$18,700) and France (US$24,990) - glistening tower blocks, a state-of-the-art transportation system and much else besides, it is hard to come away from the island state thinking that it could in any way be placed in the same bracket as other 'developing' countries. Singapore is affluent - and this alone should be counted an enormous achievement. The fact that Western politicians should come to Singapore in order to learn from the island state, rather than lecture to it - as Britain's Prime Minister Tony Blair did at the beginning of 1996 - is evidence that the place has come an awfully long way since independence which, it is all too easy to forget, was little more than 30 years ago.

It is when raw income statistics are converted into 'standard of living' estimates that Singapore slips down the world income league. In 1997 the London based National Institute of Economic and Social Research placed Singapore 16th in the world in terms of GDP per person (this, though, was based on 1992 data). When this was converted into GDP per hour worked the republic slipped to 21st, and when the figures were adjusted once more to arrive at a 'quality of life' index (notoriously slippery) Singapore dropped to 24th - the bottom of the table.

The roots of growth

How has Singapore achieved one of the most remarkable transformations in human history? To begin with, it has certain natural advantages: its strategic location and an excellent harbour. It could also be argued that the fact it is a small city state, with no poor rural hinterland to service and support, has helped. The island owes an undoubted debt to its founding father, Stamford Raffles and to former Prime Minister Lee Kuan Yew. Raffles allowed unrestricted immigration and free trade, declaring Singapore a free port. In this respect, Singapore was the first place to adopt 18th century Scottish economist and philosopher Adam Smith's principle of *laissez-faire*. This policy was enshrined as the *modus operandi* of Singapore's flourishing merchant community and was the most important factor influencing the commercial growth of Raffles' trading centre. It quickly eclipsed the other, more venerable, Straits Settlement of Georgetown (Penang, Malaysia) and for more than a century-and-a-half, Singapore boomed as a regional trans-shipment centre.

For his part, Lee Kuan Yew gave Singapore political stability unrivalled in the region, making the island republic a magnet for multinational investment. His pragmatic and far-sighted government ploughed the profits of the booming economy into the island's physical and social infrastructure. It also concentrated on building Singapore up as a financial centre. Following independence, Singapore maintained its *laissez-faire* image only when it came to international trade; in every other sector of the economy the government has been interventionist. For Singapore's vitality is based as much on government intervention as it is on the mysterious workings of the market. As some scholars have termed it, Singapore (along with places like South Korea) is a 'developmental state'. Perhaps most importantly, Lee and Goh have given just about every Singaporean a stake in the country's continued success.

The government set up strategic public sector firms to direct and catalyse rapid industrialization and a 1997 report by the US Embassy estimated that 60 percent of GDP is generated by the government or government-linked businesses. The Republic's remarkable development represents a challenge to Western free-market recipes for success. The government plays a dominant role in planning the island's development. For example: it subsidizes public housing, health and education; manipulates wages through the National Wages Council; controls trades unions by means of the National Trades Unions Congress; and owns large chunks of land. For potential foreign investors, the government has created a honey pot state with an enviable combination of an open trading economy and social stability. Bi-lingualism and vocational training focussing on the skills required by targeted industries has also helped to make Singapore the chosen location for many foreign companies. Singapore's public housing policies are now legendary. New high-rise towns have sprung up around the island and the government demolished village after village, moving people into tower blocks. Something like nine-tenths of the population live in Housing Development Board flats, of which three-quarters are now owner-occupied (see page 177). Singaporeans are encouraged to use their compulsory savings in the Central Provident Fund (CPF) to purchase their flats from the government. The government has been careful to keep these blocks racially mixed: if, for example, you are a Chinese and want to move out, you cannot sell to another Chinese.

From poverty to affluence

When Singapore became an independent country in 1965 it had a per capita income of US$700 a year and virtually no natural resources. To compound the problem, the British military withdrew from their bases in Singapore in 1971; they had contributed a fifth of Singapore's GDP and employed nearly a fifth of the labour force. Within 12 years of independence, however, per capita income had risen to US$2,500 and by the early 1980s Singapore had the third highest per capita income in Asia after Japan and Brunei. In 1995, the World Bank estimated that Singapore had a per capita income of nearly US$27,000 - considerably higher than Britain's, the former colonial power. It is now, in terms of personal wealth, one of the richest nations in the world: the World Bank places it 8th. Britain lies 18th. Singapore is also rated the least-risky Asian country for foreign investment after Japan (attracting almost S$7 billion in 1995); it came second after the US in the 1998 World Competitiveness Index produced by the Institute of Management Development in Lausanne, Switzerland and which is based on no fewer than 223 criteria; and overall has been judged the world's second best economic performer.

Singapore's economy has expanded by an average of nine percent a year since independence in 1965. In 1995 the growth rate was 8.8 percent, in 1996 6.2 percent, and in 1997 a healthy 7.8 percent. The likely figure for 1998 is a source of considerable dispute. As is often the case, economists in the private sector are rather more pessimistic, offering figures of between one percent and three percent - abysmal by Singapore's standards. There is even the possibility that Singapore might go into recession in 1999.

Notwithstanding the uncertainties connected with the Asian crisis (see below), it is hard not to conclude that government policies have been instrumental in forging this litany of success. The only periods of slow growth were during the early 1970s when Singapore was badly hit by the world recession associated with the first oil price hike, in the mid-1980s when a contraction in a number of the Republic's key export sectors caused the economy to shrink by 1.7 percent, and the current difficulties connected with the economic crisis in neighbouring Asian countries. Singapore has no external debt and a healthy balance of trade surplus. In 1988 the United States removed Singapore from its list of preferential developing country trading partners, which was the first official sign that Singapore had ascended - in the eyes of the industrialized West - to the status of a Newly Industrialized Economy (NIE), along with the other 'Tiger Economies' of Hong Kong, Taiwan and South Korea.

Making a miracle

In 1965, when the government was still reeling at separation from Malaysia, the top priority was job creation and basic industrialization. During the 1970s, when more sophisticated industries set up, the government focused on diversifying the economy and upgrading skills. Export promotion, aimed at finding new markets, coupled with the intensive campaign to attract foreign investment, meant that Singapore became less and less dependent on entrepôt trade. The services sector was expanded to build up financial services and the tourism industry. Great emphasis was placed on mechanizing and increasing productivity. By the end of the 1970s, Singapore's scarcity of labour was beginning to bite and the government began to switch from labour-intensive industries to capital-intensive and hi-tech industries, including aerospace, biotechnology, information technology and petrochemicals. This was called, rather grandiosely, the Second Industrial Revolution. Instead of assembling radios for example, production line workers began making disk drives - of which Singapore is currently the world's largest producer. Corporations were given tax incentives to facilitate their use of Singapore as a regional headquarters and international purchasing centre. Within Singapore the buzzword was 'excellence'.

The recession which hit Singapore in 1985 and 1986 came as a shock to a country which had experienced fast and furious growth for two decades. But it allowed for a stock-taking exercise and the government carefully drew up a recovery strategy. The recipe for recovery - cooked up by a specially created committee headed by Lee Kuan Yew's son Lee Hsien Loong - was to reverse the policy of pushing up wage rates ahead of inflation (which had been used as a means to force companies to upgrade), lower employers' costs, liberalize the economy, and de-emphasize manufacturing in favour of services.

By 1987 economic growth was nearly 10 percent again and the following year it topped 11 percent. The efforts put into promoting Singapore as the financial hub of Asia quickly bore fruit; by the early 1990s, the financial services industry was growing by more than 20 percent a year. Then, in 1990 the Gulf Crisis erupted and the US suffered an economic downturn. To the delight of the Singapore government however, its economy - although dented - did not slide into recession. *The Economist Intelligence Unit* noted that " ... this demonstrated that the Singaporean economy had finally come of age and was no longer vulnerable, in the classic newly industrialized country manner, to sharp slowdowns in world trade".

While Singapore might have withstood the global slow down of the 1990s, it couldn't shake-off the Asian contagion (see below). 1998 saw the slowest rate of economic growth since the mid-1980s.

Sausage makers and paper tigers

Foreign investors have continued to flock to Singapore because of its unrivalled infrastructure and international communications links. This is despite the fact that Singapore is no longer a cheap place to locate. Land is expensive and so is labour: employers have to contribute 20 percent of workers' salaries to the Central Provident Fund as well as paying a skills development tax. (The CPF is a compulsory savings scheme with some S$80 billion [US$49 billion] under management - explaining why the country has the highest savings rate in the world.) But while the costs of locating in Singapore have continued to rise markedly, there has not been a corresponding rise in productivity, which has made analysts question how long the investors will keep coming.

This observation that so-called Total Factor Productivity (economic expansion after account has been made of labour force growth and that associated with investments in labour and capital) in Singapore has not grown caused the American economist Paul Krugman to argue in 1994 that Singapore's success was built on 'perspiration rather than inspiration'. Between 1966 and 1990 the economically active proportion of the labour force expanded from 27 percent to 51 percent. It is this sheer expansion in the numbers of people in work which explains Singapore's success, leading Krugman to suggest that when Singapore's labour force stops growing - as it will do fairly soon given low fertility rates - then so too will the economy. In 1995 *The Economist* framed the same argument rather more prosaically in terms of the "Myth of the sausage-makers": "If you invest in more sausage machines and employ more sausage-makers, of course you will make more sausages. Where's the miracle? Growth will slow down when you run out of extra sausage-makers" (1995: 71). Krugman's paper caused considerable consternation in Singapore - and other economists retorted that Krugman had been cavalier in his assessment of TFP - which, as a residual, is notoriously hard to estimate.

Although Krugman's paper elicited the greatest response his views are really a development of Japanese economist Yoshihara Kunio's observation that Southeast Asia is characterized by what he termed 'technologyless industrialization'. Singapore has no great entrepreneurs and no great inventors. It is, he argues, merely a production centre for multinational firms - albeit a highly efficient one. He coined the term 'ersatz capitalism' to explain growth in Singapore and the other growth economies of Southeast Asia.

In 1997 there were an estimated 4,000 multinationals operating in Singapore and these account for more than three-quarters of total investment in manufacturing. The failure of Singapore's domestic industry to takeoff is bothering the government and there has been much debate in the newspapers about why a country with educational levels apparently higher than Britain's spawns so few entrepreneurs and inventers. (The number of patents lodged by Singaporeans is miniscule compared with those lodged by Western countries, even accounting for differences in population. There is virtually no world-class research being undertaken, save for one or two exceptions like medicine and some facets of economics.) The Ministry of Education's own research has revealed that Singapore's graduates are competent when it comes to standard problems, but when a task requires creativity, they lag behind. The head of research at a local bank explained to the *Far Eastern Economic Review* in 1996: "If you give [Singapore workers] a handbook, they'll follow the procedures meticulously. But you tell them about a problem and ask them to think of an alternative solution, and they can't do it." These types of criticisms seem to have hit home. In early 1998 Education Minister Teo Chee Hean announced that he was going to cut the school curricula by up to a third to give children more time for 'creative thinking'. Rote learning, the memorizing of facts for the sake of facts, and the examination tread mill were, he said, all to go in the interests of students' well being and creativity. In May 1998 the *Straits Times* published a survey which revealed that 68 percent of students aged 15 or above found life very or quite stressful. But critics like the author Catherine Lim reject such efforts as 'managed creativity'. While there are, assuredly, many thinkers in Singapore, most of them do their thinking very quietly indeed. And for students, examination success remains uppermost. "This", as Koh Tai Ann, dean of the National Institute of Education told Ben Dolven of the *Far Eastern Economic Review*, "is a nation of test takers".

Not only does it seem that Singapore has still to make the leap from being a mere production base to becoming a leader in manufacturing but the government also worries that over-dependence on potentially footloose foreign companies has created an environment of dependency and vulnerability. There is nothing stopping these companies simply upping sticks and shifting to other locations should conditions require it. As James Clad wrote a few years ago, foreign companies seem to view Singapore more as a parking lot than a country. The government is trying to change this state of affairs by - characteristically - intervening. In 1996 Prime Minister Goh announced the creation of a 'thinking skills programme' while the Economic Development Board (EDB) established an 'innovation development scheme'. As Chow Tat Kong, the director of the EDB's Industrial Development Division put it, the scheme is designed to 'kick-start the whole process of innovation'. Singapore is to become an 'intelligent island' with a telecommunications infrastructure which is second to none and where everyone is computer literate. Already Singapore is one the world's most competitive economies. The 1998 World Competitiveness Yearbook placed it second in terms of overall competitiveness, behind the US.

What Singapore lacks is any entrepreneurs. This is partly, one imagines, the result of an over-programmed education system which does not produce risk takers and innovative thinkers. It is also linked to the dominant role of the government. Singapore's brightest students tend to enter public service, not the private sector. Jeffrey Goh, one of the republic's few entrepreneurs, wryly told Ben Dolven of the *Far Eastern Economic Review* that "the Singapore government has been very effective in eradicating entrepreneurs". Even more worrying, perhaps, he added that "All the things that make Singapore so successful today will make it unsuccessful in the 21st century".

Singapore and the Asian contagion

In mid-1997 the economic optimism that had characterized Southeast Asia since the late 1980s was shaken by a financial crisis that began in Thailand, and spread to Indonesia, Malaysia and the Philippines. The Thai baht, Philippine peso, Indonesian rupiah and Malaysian ringgit were all effectively devalued as their pegs to the US$ were shattered by heavy selling. The IMF stepped in with a US$15 billion rescue package for Thailand, and then over US$40 billion for Indonesia. In Malaysia, Prime Minister Mahathir ran a characteristically uncompromising campaign against currency speculators labelling them 'morons', 'anachists' and 'rogues'. In Thailand the economic crisis forced a peaceful change of government at the end of 1997 and in 1998 Indonesia's President Suharto was ejected after over 30 years in power.

Looking north across the Straits of Johor to Malaysia, or south to Indonesia, Singapore would seem to have weathered the Asian economic crisis relatively well. Indonesia, Malaysia and Thailand experienced hefty negative 'growth' in 1998 (-15 percent, -6 percent and -8 percent respectively), resulting from a welter of bankruptcies as apparently solid companies went to the wall. Singapore's economy was expected to shrink by a comparatively modest two percent. This is dire given the country's history of rapid growth but considering Singapore's dependence on trade with other countries in the region and its own small domestic market, one would have expected an even more severe effect. In early 1998 Seagate Technology, Singapore's second largest private employer and a massive maker of disk drives, sacked ten percent of its workforce. Unemployment more than doubled from 1.8 percent in 1997 to 4.5 percent in the third quarter of 1998 as redundancies spread. Singapore's workers are finding their salaries cut and bonuses slashed and more expensive restaurants are half full. But the great majority of people are still in work and while the Singapore dollar slumped some 15 percent against the US$, it didn't crash like the ringgit, baht and rupiah. This means that visitors to Singapore from other countries in the region have found the island prohibitively expensive to visit. The dire economic circumstances in Indonesia also led to a surge of illegal immigrants crossing the Straits of Melaka and the marine police in Singapore stepped up their patrols to intercept those foolhardy enough not to be put off by the prospect of four to six strokes of the rotan (cane), six months' imprisonment, and repatriation. In March 1998, 117 'illegals' were sentenced with the prosecution asking for stiff deterrent penalties to be imposed, remarking that "We are, literally, a nation beseiged".

So how has Singapore managed to weather the economic storm or at least catch 'flu' rather than pneumonia? Partly it is because Singapore's export markets beyond Asia have remained buoyant. Perhaps more importantly, the republic is an island of fiscal rectitude when compared with the crony capitalism of Indonesia and the patronage politics of Malaysia. Singapore's business environment and public administration is regarded as one of the cleanest in the world. Transparency International's 1998 Corruption Perceptions Index placed Singapore as the World's seventh least corrupt country (Denmark was top dog). Lee Kuan Yew remarked during the height of the crisis that "relationships among businessmen, ministers and civil servants must not degenerate into cronyism where favours are given for return favours". Singapore is well managed and squeaky clean and these two reasons, more than any other, explain why the Republic should emerge from the crisis battered but not beaten.

Labour squeeze

With no mineral wealth, oil or timber, people are Singapore's only true resource and, despite the government's efforts (see page 185, people are in short supply. The government says tight labour supply will continue to limit Singapore's economic growth, and that rising labour costs will curb its exports. Manufacturers report difficulty in recruiting production workers and there is a continuing exodus of professionals. A poll published in August 1997 revealed that 37 percent of adults had contemplated, or were contemplating emigrating. Because of Singapore's race to industrialize, demand for labour has always exceeded supply. It has traditionally got around this by importing labour from Malaysia, Indonesia, Thailand and the Philippines. There is virtually no unemployment in Singapore - even with the problems created by the Asian crisis unemployment only rose in 1998 to four percent - and because the labour market is so tight, skilled white collar workers have been able to demand higher and higher salaries. Labour costs rose in 1995 by 7.1 percent - far ahead of inflation. The government plans to raise the mandatory retirement age to help fill the labour gap, to introduce more labour-saving technology and allow an even greater influx of migrant workers.

In early 1993 the head of the International Manpower Policy section of the Economic Development Board (EDB) announced that Singapore would be attempting to recruit researchers and scientists from the former Soviet Union in an effort to bolster its high-tech industries. In 1995 the EDB arranged recruitment drives to Britain, the US, India and Australia. They have placed advertisements in newspapers in Madras and Moscow and have set up a web site for prospective migrants. For the interested or inquisitive, log onto: http://www.singapore-careers.com.

Foreign workers

Today nearly one in four of the republic's workforce is a non-Singaporean. In 1992 it was one in eight. In total there are 450,000 foreign workers legally employed in the country, cleaning streets and public conveniences, watering the verges, labouring on construction sites (in 1997, 72 construction workers died on site, the great majority from falls or impalement), and washing, ironing and cleaning for Singapore's increasingly affluent national population. While white-collar workers in the financial sector can command huge salaries, blue collar labourers are paid about S$400 a month and maids, mostly from the Philippines, just S$300. While there are quota restrictions ('dependency ceilings') on the number of foreign workers allowed into each sector of the economy, the government is alarmed that foreigners now represent nearly half the workforce in certain sectors. One economist predicted in 1997 that by 2010, 44 percent of Singapore's workforce will be foreign. The maths is comparatively simple: with each year's growth of seven percent the economy requires an extra 100,000 workers but only 50,000 Singaporeans join the workforce.

The drive to increase labour efficiency has been a major policy thrust in recent years. Industrial robots have helped trim the workforce in many manufacturing plants. Manufacturers who are unable to automate their operations have gone to cheaper locations in nearby Indonesia or Malaysia, which have both benefited from the overspill. Prime Minister Goh Chok Tong, appears to have found a solution of sorts in his 'Growth Triangle', which comprises Singapore, Johor (the southernmost state on the Malaysian peninsula) and Pulau Batam (the northernmost island in Indonesia's Riau Archipelago).

Growth triangle

The Growth Triangle is seen as a strategy that can exploit the economic complementarities that exist between Singapore, Malaysia and Indonesia. Singapore has technical excellence, marketing muscle, an excellent communications and financial infrastructure, good skills, and represents an excellent base for firms. Johor and Riau have cheap land and labour and less stringent environmental regulations and planning controls. Put the two together, some analysts believe, and you get yet more of the economic miracle. Over recent years, scores of transnational investors have stampeded across the causeway to Johor, and investment in Batam is picking up. Singapore benefits enormously from its new-found hinterland and unskilled foreign workers can be kept conveniently at arm's length so that they do not upset the flavour of the city-state's racial cocktail. Further afield, Singapore has been investing in Vietnam, India and China. Economically speaking, Singapore is a comfortable 10-15 years ahead of its neighbours and intends to stay ahead. The Economic Development Board is training people with a vengeance and has labelled them 'thinking workers'. Policy makers believe that once they are in place, no labour crisis will ever be insurmountable.

At the other end of the labour market, in the professional, white-collar sector, there have been problems too. The government has become particularly concerned about 'the emigration problem' in which thousands of highly skilled Singaporeans have been choosing to live and work abroad. Many are Malays and Indians, who claim their long-term opportunities are limited in Singapore. Emigration peaked in 1988 when nearly 5,000 families left Singapore, and this came as a double blow to a government already facing a serious labour shortage. To stem the 'brain drain' an aggressive overseas recruitment campaign was launched for white-collar workers and this was matched by the liberalization of immigration regulations for foreign professionals. In an effort to ensure that there is a continued supply of skilled labour, Singapore offered tens of thousands skilled Hong Kong workers and their dependants permanent residence status in 1989. By 1995 about 40,000 applicants had been approved although only a fraction of this number - 6,500 - have actually moved to the city state. The Singapore government hoped to cash in on fears arising from the colony's reversion to Chinese rule in 1997. Singapore was secretly banking on poaching Hong Kong's brainiest emigrés before they went to Canada or Australia. The government has been careful, however, to assure Singapore's other ethnic communities that should this distort the current racial mix, it will permit the immigration of Malays and Indians to maintain the balance.

Singapore and its competitors

"We are like someone being chased by tigers with a cliff in front. The tigers are closing in fast but the cliff is difficult to scale. The tigers are the dynamic economies like Thailand, Malaysia, Indonesia and China. The cliff is the formidable challenge posed by the developed countries" (Prime Minister Goh Chok Tong, 1992).

Singapore has always been worried about its future as a small and vulnerable Chinese city state surrounded by larger and more populous countries with a Malay/Muslim cultural heritage. Now that Malaysia - not to mention places like Thailand, Indonesia and China - is challenging Singapore economically the issue of the sustainability of Singapore's economic miracle has taken on even greater resonance. Kuala Lumpur's new airport is aiming to take business away from Changi while the upgrading of Port Klang is already eating into the dominance of Singapore's ports. In 1997 Malaysia's Prime Minister Mahathir Mohamad unveiled an ambitious programme to create a multi-media corridor south of KL and even Indonesia has plans to expand air and port facilities in the Riau islands of Batam and Bintan. Taken together, and combined with Singapore's high labour costs, it is not hard to see why the republic's leaders constantly urge Singaporeans to strive to maintain their competitive edge. As Senior Minister Lee once remarked, "There is no second chance for us".

The contest between Singapore and Hong Kong, Asia's two super-successful island states, has intensified in recent years. At the end of 1995 the Singapore government ran a series of advertisements on Hong Kong television reminding viewers what a green, clean, safe and prosperous place the republic was. The subliminal message seemed to be: come while you can. But although to the outside world Hong Kong and Singapore may appear to be virtual Siamese twins - they came second and first respectively in the World Economic Forum's 1997 competitiveness league - on the ground the differences are palpable. For a start, Hong Kong is populated largely by people from Guangdong (Canton), while Singapore's Chinese are mostly Hokkien. Perhaps even more significantly, Hong Kongers relish the racey and slightly anarchic atmosphere of their territory. By comparison, Singapore appears dull, constraining and authoritarian. This is probably why so many Hong Kong residents who decided to secure another passport before the hand-over at the end of June 1997 opted for places like Canada and Australia: hardly Asian - although both have large Asian populations - but in terms of life style probably more like Hong Kong than Singapore. Singapore has also been careful not to offend China. To have plucked all the best people from the colony before it was handed over would not have gone down too well in Beijing. For this reason, the hard sell was disguised.

Foreign Workers in Singapore

Total: 450,000
Indonesia: 100,000
Philippines: 60,000
Thailand: 60,000
China: 46,000

While Hong Kong Chinese may not relish the idea of relocating to Singapore, many multinationals show less reticence. A survey conducted among 6,000 Asian executives at the end of 1996 revealed that three-quarters believed Singapore to be a better regional base than Hong Kong. Compaq, Levi Strauss and Reuters all shifted their Asian headquarters from Hong Kong to Singapore ahead of 1997. What is significant though is that the obvious reason - the handover of the colony to China - was not always the key factor. Quality of life (low crime rate, clean streets, green environment) and efficient infrastructure (public transport, telecommunications), seemed to play as great a role in the decision. Not that the game is only going Singapore's way. Hong Kong still has a much larger and more sophisticated financial sector and it also has an incomparable entrée into China.

While Singapore has achieved considerable success enticing foreign multinationals to invest in the republic, Singaporean companies have also been busy investing overseas in an effort to escape high labour costs at home. By the end of 1994 Singapore's cumulative foreign investment totalled nearly US$40 billion. In 1995 the republic was Thailand and Myanmar's (Burma's) second largest investor, lay in third place in Russia, fourth in Vietnam, fifth in China and sixth in Indonesia.

Tourism

Tourism is now one of Singapore's most important industries; over 7 million visitors entered the country in 1996 - well over twice the island's population - staying an average of 3.3 days. Between them, they spent US$551 each or around US$4 billion a year and tourism contributes about 16 percent of Singapore's foreign exchange earnings. More than a quarter of visitors come from neighbouring ASEAN countries, and another third from the rest of Asia. Nearly a million Japanese visit Singapore every year, about half a million Australasians, 300,000 Britons and just over a quarter of a million Americans.

Why do so many people come to Singapore? It is hard to believe that it is for 'exoticism'. Singapore may be 'in the East', but it is hardly 'of the East' - despite what the Singapore Tourist Board might lead one to believe before arrival. Guide books have been extolling the virtues of Singapore as the cultural and geographic crossroads of the world almost since the genre was invented. In *Information for tourists* published in 1908, Wright wrote that:

> *"a curious combination of Orientalism and Occidentalism is to be observed on every side. From the midst of tawdry-looking native shops rise modern European establishments of commanding appearance; hand-drawn rickshaws and lumbering ox-waggons move side by side with electric tramcars, swift automobiles, and smart equipages; and the free and unfettered native goes on his way regardless of the conventionalities which are so strictly observed by the European. East and West meet, and the old is fast giving way to the new but there is, nevertheless a broad line of demarcation between them."*

But the reality is that, compared with all its neighbours, modern Singapore is distinctly lacking as an exemplar of the Exotic East. Many people arrive merely as a stop-over en route elsewhere, taking advantage of the Republic's strategic location and excellent airport. Others, however, visit to revel in the city's reputation (now partly undeserved) as a 'shopper's paradise'; more come with the knowledge that the hotels are excellent and you can drink the water and cross the road without too many worries; the food is an undoubted plus; and there are also large numbers of businesspeople who visit for conferences or on incentive breaks. Perhaps it is simply that the Singapore Tourist Board, like the rest of the economy, is doing an excellent job.

It is significant that the STB has recently changed its campaign slogan from 'Surprising Singapore' to the rather more verbose 'New Asia-Singapore: so easy to enjoy, so hard to forget'. Presumably on the basis that Singapore is more like the rest of the developed world than it is different from it, the STB found it hard to promote the island on the grounds that it was 'surprising'. Instead, the marketing rationale is that it is 'easy'. Everyone speaks English, public transportation is painless, it is safe and clean ... and so on. There is also a great deal to do in Singapore and the 'attractions' (most are modern and man-made) are well run and some are world class. Perhaps the most revealing aspect of Singapore's tourism industry is that expatriates in other Southeast Asian countries visit Singapore for their R&R. In other words, this is where people resident in Asia come to escape from Asia.

It is perhaps appropriate to end this briefing with a comment from an interview with Lee Kuan Yew held in September 1998. The theme is a familiar one: of struggle in a Darwinian world where Singapore's competitors will give no quarter:

> *We have no oil, no gas, no gold, no diamonds, no copper underground ... Nobody is going to lend us money ... If we get careless, we will just be wiped out, finished." Lee Kuan Yew, interviewed in the Far Eastern Economic Review, 24.9.98.*

Footnotes

Footnotes

Singapore food glossary

Chinese and local food

Bak chang local rice dumpling filled with savoury or sweet meat and wrapped in leaves

Bak choy Chinese cabbage

Bak kut the local pork rib soup, with garlic and Chinese five spice

Belachan fermented prawn paste

Bird's nest edible nest of the swiftlet, made from glutinous secretions of their salivary glands

Char kway teow broad rice noodles fried with sweet sauce and additions of cockels, Chinese sausage, bean sprouts or fish cake

Char siew Chinese sweet barbecued pork slices

Chendol a dessert: a cone of ice shavings topped with coloured syrups, brown syrup, coconut milk, red beans, attap seeds and jelly

Cheng ting a Chinese dessert of a bowl of syrup with herbal jelly, barley and dates

Chicken rice rice boiled in chicken stock and ginger, served with steamed chicken slices

Chilli padi an extremely hot variety of chilli

Choi sum Chinese vegetable served steamed with oyster sauce

Claypot rice rice cooked in a clay casserole with pieces of chicken, Chinese mushroom, Chinese sausage and soy sauce

Congee Chinese porridge

Dian sin/dim sum Chinese sweet and savoury dumplings served at breakfast and lunch

Dow see Chinese fermented salted black beans

Fish sauce known as *nampla* in Thai, a brown sauce made from salted dried fish, used as a salt seasoning

Garoupa white fish popular in Asia

Gula malacca coarse palm sugar sold in lumps, from the sap of the Palmyra palm

Hainanese chicken rice chicken served with spring onions and ginger dressing, soup and rice boiled in chicken stock or coconut milk

Hoisin sauce Chinese thick seasoning with a sweet-spicy flavour

Hokkien mee yellow noodles fried with sliced meat, squid, prawns and garnished with strips of fried egg

Kang kong a Chinese vegetable - water convolvulus

Kway teow broad rice noodles

Laksa spicy coconut soup of thin white noodles garnished with bean sprouts, quail's eggs, prawns, shredded chicken and dried bean curd

Lor mee a dish of noodles served with slices of meat, eggs and a dash of vinegar in a dark brown sauce

Rojak salad of cucumber, pineapple, turnip, fried beancurd tossed in a prawn paste with peanuts, tamarind and a sugary sauce.

Tau hui a dessert made from a by-produt of soya bean, served with syrup

Teh tarek tea made with evaporated milk

Yu char kway deep-fried Chinese breadsticks

Indian

Aloo gobi potato and cauliflower dish

Bhindi okra or lady's fingers

Biryani North Indian dish of basmati rice and meat, seafood and vegetables

Brinjal aubergine or eggplant

Dhal pureed lentils

Dhosas large crispy pancakes served with potatoes, onions and spices

Gulab jumun fried milk balls in syrup

Idli steamed rice cake

Keema spicy minced meat

Kofta minced meat or vegetable ball

Korma mild curry with a yoghurt sauce

Lassi yoghurt based drink

Murgh chicken

Murtabak roti (bread) which has been filled with pieces of mutton, chicken or vegetables

Pakora vegetable fritter

Pilau rice fried in ghee and mixed with nuts, then cooked in stock

Pudina mint sauce

Raita side dish of cucumber, yoghurt and mint

Rogan josh spicy lamb curry with yoghurt

Roti prata flat round pancake-like bread

Saag spinach

Sambar fiery mixture of vegetables, lentils and split peas

Tandoori style of cooking: meat is marinated in spicy yoghurt and then baked in a clay oven

Tikka small pieces of meat or fish served off the bone, marinated in yoghurt and baked

Vindaloo very hot curry

Malay/Indonesian

Assam sour

Ayam chicken

Babi pork

Daging meat

Es avocado chilled avocado shake

Es delima dessert of water chestnut in sago and coconut milk

Gado-gado cold dish of bean sprouts, potatoes, long beans, tempeh, bean curd, rice cakes and prawn crackers, topped with a spicy peanut sauce

Garam salt

Gula sugar

Ice kachang similar to *chendol* (see Chinese food) but with evaporated milk instead of coconut milk

Ikan fish

Ikan bakar grilled fish

Kambing mutton

Kepala ikan fish head, usually in a curry or grilled

Kerupak prawn crackers

Ketupat cold, compressed rice

Kueh cakes

Lemang glutinous rice in bamboo

Limau lime

Lontong rice cakes in a spicy coconut-milk topped with grated coconut and sometimes bean curd and egg

Makan food

Manis sweet

Mee noodles

Mee rebus yellow noodles served in a thick sweet sauce made from sweet potatoes. Garnished with sliced hard-boiled eggs and green chillies

Mee siam white thin noodles in a sweet and sour gravy made with tamarind

Nasi biryani saffron rice flavoured with spices and garnished with cashew nuts, almonds and raisins

Nasi lemak rice boiled in coconut milk

Rijsttafel Indonesian meal consisting of a selection of rice dishes, to which are added small pieces of meat, fish, fruit and pickles

Roti canai pancakes served with lentils and curry

Roti john baguette filled with sardine/egg mixture

Roti kosong plain pancake

Sambal spicy paste of pounded chillis, onion and tamarind

Satay pieces of chicken, beef or mutton skewered onto sticks and grilled

Sayur vegetables

Sayur masak lemak deep fried marinated prawns

sejuk crab

Soto ayam chicken soup

Sotong squid

Tahu beancurd

Telur egg

Tempeh preserved deep fried soya bean

Udang prawn

Thai

Gai haw bai toey fried chicken in pandanus leaves

Gai tom kla chicken and coconut soup

Kaeng jud soup

Kaeng paad curry

Kaeng phet kai hot chicken curry

Kai tom kha lemon grass chicken soup with coconut milk

Khao rice

Larb minced chicken or pork flavoured with spices, herbs and lime

Mi krob crisp thin noodles with shrimp, egg and sweet and sour sauce

Pak krasan a cabbage-like vegetable

Phrik chillies

Pla thot sam rot fried garoupa with sweet and sour sauce

Poo paad gari curried crab

Tom kam kung hot and sour spiced seafood soup

Yam salad

Shorts

Special interest pieces on and about Singapore

Index

Maps

Where to find Footprint

Footprint Handbooks are available in most good bookshops. A small selectic useful addresses follows:

Footprint Handbooks
6 Riverside Court
Lower Bristol Road
Bath BA2 3DZ
T 01225 469141
F 01225 469461
E Mail handbooks@
footprint.cix.co.uk

Argentina
Distal
Corrientes 913
1043 Buenos Aires
T 01 326 1006
F 01 322 0114

Australia
Peribo Pty
58 Beaumont Road
Mt Kuring-Gai
NSW 2080
T (02) 9457 0011
F (02) 9457 0022

Austria
Freytag-Berndt Artaria
Kohlmarkt 9
A-1010 Wien
T 01 533 2094
F 01 533 8685

Belgium
Craenen BVBA
Mechelsesteenweg 633
B-3020 Herent
T 016 23 90 90
F 016 23 97 11

Bolivia
Los Amigos del Libro
Avenida Heroinas e 0311
Casilla 450
Cochabamba
T 02 425 1140
F 02 411 5128

Brazil
Siciliano
Av Raimundo Pereira de
Magalhaes 3305
Cep 05145-200
São Paulo SP
T 011 839 5500
F 011 832 8616

Canada
Ulysses Travel Publications
4176 rue Saint-Denis
Montréal
Québec H2W 2M5
T (514) 843 9882
F (514) 843 9448

Caribbean
Kingston Publishers
10, LOJ Industrial Complex
7 Norman Road
Kingston CSO
Jamaica
T 001876 928 8898
F 001876 928 5719

Denmark
Kilroy Travel
Skindergade 28
DK-1159 Copenhagen K
T 33 11 00 44
F 33 32 32 69

Nordisk Korthandel
Studiestraede 26-30 B
DK-1455 Copenhagen K
T 33 13 26 38
F 33 91 26 38

Ecuador
Libri Mundi
PO Box 3029
Juan Leon Mera 851
Quito
T 02 234791
F 02 504209

Finland
Akateeminen Kirjakauppa
Keskuskatu 1
FIN-00100 Helsinki
T 09 12141
F 09 121 4441

Suomalainen
Kirjakauppa
Koivuvaarankuja 2
01640 Vantaa 64
F 08 52 78 88

France
L'Astrolabe
46 rue de Provence
F-75009 Paris 9e
T 1 42 85 42 95
F 1 45 75 92 51

VILO Diffusion
25 rue Ginoux
F-75015 Paris
T 01 45 77 08 05
F 01 45 79 97 15

Germany
GeoCenter ILH
Schockenriedstrasse 44
D-70565 Stuttgart
T 0711 781 94610
F 0711 781 94654

Brettschneider
Feldkirchnerstrasse 2
D-85551 Heimstetten
T 089 990 20330
F 089 990 20331

Geobuch Gmbh
Rosental 6
D-80331 München
T 089 265030
F 089 263713

Gleumes
Hohenstaufenring 47-51
D-50674 Köln
T 0221 215650

Globetrotter Ausrustungen
Wiesendamm 1
D-22305 Hamburg
F 040 679 66183

Dr Götze
Bleichenbrücke 9
D-2000 Hamburg 1
T 040 3031 1009-0

Hugendubel Buchhandlung
Nymphenburgerstrasse 25
D-80335 München
T 089 238 9412
F 089 550 1853

Kiepert Buchhandlung
Hardenbergstrasse 4-5
D-10623 Berlin 12
T 030 311880

Greece
GC Eleftheroudakis
17 Panepistemiou
Athens 105 64
T 01 331 4180-83
F 01 323 9821

India
Roli Books
M-75 GK II Market
New Delhi 110048
T (011) 646 0886
F (011) 646 7185

Israel
Geographical Tours
8 Tverya Street
Tel Aviv 63144
T 03 528 4113
F 03 629 9905

Italy
Libreria del Viaggiatore
Via del Pelegrino 78
I-00186 Rome
T/F 06 688 01048

Librimport
Via Biondelli 9
I-20141 Milano
T 02 8950 1422
F 02 8950 2811

Netherlands
Nilsson & Lamm bv
Postbus 195
Pampuslaan 212
N-1380 AD Weesp
T 0294 494949
F 0294 494455

Norway
Schibsteds Forlag A/S
Akersgata 32 - 5th Floor
Postboks 1178 Sentrum
N-0107 Oslo
T 22 86 30 00
F 22 42 54 92

Tanum
PO Box 1177 Sentrum
N-0107 Oslo 1
T 22 41 11 00
F 22 33 32 75

Pakistan
Pak-American Commercial
Zaib-un Nisa Street
Saddar
PO Box 7359
Karachi
T 21 566 0419
F 21 568 3611

South Africa
Faradawn CC
PO Box 1903
Saxonwold 2132
T 011 885 1787
F 011 885 1829

South America
Humphrys Roberts
Associates
Caixa Postal 801-0
Ag.Jardim da Gloria
06700-970 Cotia SP
Brazil
T 011 492 4496
F 011 492 6896

Southeast Asia
APA Publications
38 Joo Koon Road
Singapore 628990
T 865 1600
F 861 6438

Spain
Altaïr, Balmes 69
08007 Barcelona
T 93 3233062
F 93 4512559

Bookworld España
Pje Las Palmeras 25
29670 San Pedro
Alcántara, Málaga
T 95 278 6366
F 95 278 6452

Libros de Viaje
c/Serrano no 41
28001 Madrid
T 01 91 577 9899
F 01 91 577 5756

Sweden
Hedengrens Bokhandel
PO Box 5509
S-11485 Stockholm
T 8 6115132

Kart Centrum
Vasagatan 16
S-11120 Stockholm
T 8 111699

Lantmateriet Kartbutiken
Kungsgatan 74
S-11122 Stockholm

Switzerland
Artou, 8 rue de Rive
CH-1204 Geneva
T 022 311 4544
F 022 781 3456

Office du Livre OLF SA
ZI 3, Corminboeuf
CH-1701 Fribourg
T 026 467 5111
F 026 467 5466

Schweizer Buchzentrum
Postfach
CH-4601 Olten
T 062 209 2525
F 062 209 2627

Travel Bookshop
Rindermarkt 20
Postfach 216
CH-8001 Zürich
T 01 252 3883
F 01 252 3832

USA
NTC/ Contemporary
4255 West Touhy Avenue
Lincolnwood
Illinois 60646-1975
T (847) 679 5500
F (847) 679 2494

Will you help us?

We try as hard as we can to make each Footprint Handbook as up-to-date and accurate as possible but, of course, things always change. Many people write to us - with corrections, new information, or simply comments.

If you want to let us know about an experience or adventure - hair-raising or mundane, good or bad, exciting or boring or simply something rather special - we would be delighted to hear from you. Please give us as precise information as possible, quoting the edition number (you'll find it on the front cover) and page number of the Handbook you are using.

Your help will be greatly appreciated, especially by other travellers. In return we will send you details about our special guidebook offer.

Complete listing

Latin America
Argentina Handbook
1 900949 10 5 £11.99

Bolivia Handbook
1 900949 09 1 £11.99

Brazil Handbook
0 900751 84 3 £12.99

Caribbean Islands Handbook 1999
1 900949 23 7 £14.99

Chile Handbook
0 900751 85 1 £10.99

Colombia Handbook
1 900949 11 3 £10.99

Cuba Handbook
1 900949 12 1 £10.99

Ecuador & Galápagos Handbook
1 900949 29 6 £11.99

Mexico & Central America Handbook 1999
1 900949 22 9 £16.99

Peru Handbook
1 900949 31 8 £11.99

South American Handbook 1999
1 900949 21 0 £22.99

Venezuela Handbook
1 900949 13 X £10.99

Africa
East Africa Handbook 1999
1 900949 25 3 £14.99

Morocco Handbook
1 900949 35 0 £11.99

Namibia Handbook
1 900949 30 X £10.99

South Africa Handbook 1999
1 900949 26 1 £14.99

Tunisia Handbook
1 900949 34 2 £10.99

Zimbabwe Handbook
0 900751 93 2 £11.99

Asia
Cambodia Handbook
0 900751 96 7 £9.99

Goa Handbook
1 900949 17 2 £9.99

India Handbook 1999
1 900949 24 5 £16.99

Indonesia Handbook
1 900949 15 6 £14.99

Laos Handbook
0 900751 89 4 £9.99

Malaysia & Singapore Handbook
1 900949 16 4 £12.99

Myanmar (Burma) Handbook
0 900751 87 8 £9.99

Nepal Handbook
1 900949 00 8 £11.99

Pakistan Handbook
1 900949 37 7 £12.99

Singapore Handbook
1 900949 19 9 £9.99

Sri Lanka Handbook
1 900949 18 0 £11.99

Thailand Handbook
1 900949 32 6 £12.99

Tibet Handbook
1 900949 33 4 £12.99

Vietnam Handbook
1 900949 36 9 £10.99

Middle East
Egypt Handbook
1 900949 20 2 £12.99

Israel Handbook
1 900949 01 6 £12.99

Jordan, Syria & Lebanon Handbook
1 900949 14 8 £12.99

Europe
Andalucía Handbook
1 900949 27 X £9.99

Wexas
Traveller's Handbook
0 905802 08 X £14.99

Traveller's Healthbook
0 905802 09 8 £9.99

What the papers say

"I carried the South American Handbook in my bag from Cape Horn to Cartagena and consulted it every night for two and a half months. And I wouldn't do that for anything else except my hip flask."

Michael Palin

"Of all the main guidebook series this is genuinely the only one we have never received a complaint about."

The Bookseller

"All in all, the Footprint Handbook series is the best thing that has happened to travel guidebooks in years. They are different and take you off the beaten track away from all the others clutching the competitors' guidebooks."

The Business Times, Singapore

"Footprint's India Handbook told me everything from the history of the region to where to get the best curry."

Jennie Bond, BBC Correspondent

"Footprint Handbooks, the best of the best!"

Le Monde, Paris

Acknowledgements

Many people have been extremely helpful during the preparation of this edition. We are grateful to everyone who put pen to paper (or fingers to keyboard) to send us comments on their travels. However, in particular we would like to thank the following people who gave their time and support: Colin Lauw of the Urban Redevelopment Authority; Goh Kersing, Hayley Wood, Jocelyn Ng and Terence Wong all at the Singapore Tourist Board; Lim Sun Sun from the National Heritage Board; Tan Boon Hui, Assistant Curator at the Asian Civilisations Museum; Jo Tan at the Four Seasons Hotel; Janet Tao at Conrad Centennial Hotel; Elizabeth Chin at the Merchant Court; and Patricia Davis at the Hyatt Regency Singapore.